Henry Lazarus

The English Revolution of the 20th Century

A Prospective History

Henry Lazarus

The English Revolution of the 20th Century
A Prospective History

ISBN/EAN: 9783337236366

Printed in Europe, USA, Canada, Australia, Japan

Cover: Foto ©ninafisch / pixelio.de

More available books at **www.hansebooks.com**

THE ENGLISH REVOLUTION OF THE TWENTIETH CENTURY

A Prospective History

WITH AN INTRODUCTION AND EDITED BY

HENRY LAZARUS
AUTHOR OF "LANDLORDISM"

SECOND EDITION

WITH A NEW PREFACE

LONDON
F. L. BALLIN
5, AGAR STREET STRAND, W.C
1897

PREFACE TO THE SECOND EDITION.

When the poet Burns wrote those oft-quoted lines:—
"O wad some power the giftie gie us,
To see oursels as others see us!"
how lightly he must have conceived them, and how idle would be the experience based upon the consummation of his desire. Is there any mortal who has a more frequent opportunity of seeing himself as others see him than an author? Especially an author who treads on corns political, social, and parochial, with an utter disregard for anything except the truth, as he is able to see it. I purpose in the following pages to regale my readers with a slight review of reviewers. They will see how protean is my personality: from heaven-born genius to hopeless imbecile, with all the delicate grades between, have I not been declared to be? One gentle critic opens to me the Gates of Parnassus, the next hurls me ignominiously into Hanwell. Some critics aver that they have been refreshed as with a draught direct from the life-spring of Pieria; others declare they have wallowed in a mud-fountain whose turbidity they require the slang dictionary to describe.

But let not the humblest of authors complain of the vagaries of critics. Where he can learn from them he is grateful; where they are spiteful he has sympathy for them; where they are malicious he pities them; where they lack judgment. . . .

Where they lack judgment! Shall a small author be discouraged if he is misunderstood, when the greatest of all authors is not only misunderstood but decried and abused?

Eighteen-hundred-and-ninety-five was the centenary of Thomas Carlyle. Froude closed his biography of the great sage with words that have already passed from prophecy into partial realisation—for the house of Carlyle is no longer the home of cats, but has been saved to an appreciative nation by a small body of earnest and loving disciples; and already pilgrims visit the shrine whence Carlyle sent forth his fearless teachings to the world. These are Froude's words:—

"In future years, in future centuries, strangers will come from distant lands—from America, from Australia, from New Zealand, from every isle or continent where the English language is spoken—to see the house where Carlyle was born, to see the green turf under which his dust is lying. Scotland will have raised a monument over his grave; but no monument is needed for one who has made a practical memorial for himself in the hearts of all to whom truth is the dearest of possessions."

I have no doubt whatever of the justice and wisdom of that prophecy. I believe that Thomas Carlyle is among the greatest teachers, if not the greatest teacher, that Providence has vouchsafed to mankind.

Upon the occasion of the hundredth anniversary of this great thinker appeared the following appreciation by a modern critic; not spoken in a lunatic asylum; not in the purlieus of mud-gutter journalism—but given to the world as the deliberate opinion of the *Times* in a commemorative leading article:—

"Now that the turbid elements of his writings have settled, the sediment of truth deposited by them proves to be small. . . . To the youth of these days he has little to offer." . . .

To the youth of these days he has little to offer! To the youth fed with fifty thousand copies of silly sexual novels, Swinburne froth-poems, Clodd-creations, Evolution-gospels, etc. But let the *Times'* critic continue:—

"The last places where the clever youth of to-day would seek for the instruction which he most desiderates are the extinct volcanoes of Mr. Carlyle."

Of "Mr." Carlyle! Observe that, Mr. Reader, and try to appraise the soul of the critic, and of the *Times'* editor who could print it. The great Goethe was a contemporary of Carlyle. Think of "Mr. Goethe," "Mr. Beethoven," "Mr. Tennyson."

This diminutive-souled critic continues:—"He (Carlyle) had come to repeat his familiar formula and incantations with mechanical iteration, much like the revolutions of the rotary praying machine which moved his frequent mirth. . . . . He had learned and unlearned nothing since he wrote *Heroes and Hero Worship*, he had not even kept up his knowledge of what he once knew well."

Those words were written of the man who, since the time mentioned, had given to the world such a work as *The History of Frederick the Great*, in the preparation of which he had visited Germany, and studied books and battle-fields, the mere enumeration of which would form a volume. And as if the infamous "criticism" already quoted were not enough, the inspired leader writer proceeds to prophecy, listen to him, Reader:

WE (observe the lofty, magnificent WE), "We can conjecture what is the judgment of these days, and *what is likely to be that of times to come*, as to Carlyle's" (the Mr. dropped here as not befitting the true prophet) "place in literature." Then, after duly denouncing the mud-products of Ibsen, Neitzsche, Problem-plays, and "The antics of the fishers for novelties in muddy waters," the article dares to add that "some of these gentry could claim to be his (Carlyle's) offspring . . . . Neitzsche for example, so far as there is sanity in his rhapsodies they do little more than carry out what Carlyle used to say." . . .

I venture to call this the blasphemy of criticism. But why dare I, the very humblest of the disciples of the great master, presume to refer to him and his vile critic in this place? Reader, it is because that if the greatest, and wisest, and bravest, and most self-sacrificing of men can thus be appraised, shall it not teach patience to the smallest, though earnest, author when the abuse of criticism chances to fall upon him? The ignorant and obscure leader-writer, hopelessly asinine, hidden beneath the editorial lion-skin "WE," spurting his foul ink at the titanic Sage, is indeed the very Anarchy of criticism, "for is not anarchy," Carlyle asks, "the rule of what is Baser over what is Nobler, the one life's misery worth complaining of, in fact the abomination of abominations?"

Was there ever a time, or has it always been so, when anarchy in the matter of criticism reigned more supreme than it does now? I do not at all mean the abuse of good and earnest work, *that* has rarely varied; what I particularly refer to is the oily, sugary approval of the unending cartloads of washy sentimentalism which the press turns out with quite "mechanical iteration." In fact there is no more instructive lesson for an intelligent mind than to compare the columns of sleek approval which the *Times* pours forth upon periodical sensational novelism, with its appreciation of the greatest genius of literature which has been quoted in the preceding page.

The aspiration then of the poet Burns having been granted to me, and I having seen myself (at least literarily) as others see me, it will do a reviewer or two no harm if he see himself, or they see themselves as an author sees them. There is the *Saturday Review*, for example, under the editorship of Mr. Walter Herries Pollock, assuring me that :
"It is impossible to read a single chapter of THE REVOLUTION OF THE TWENTIETH CENTURY without crediting the author with a passion for reforming the world that is both deep and sincere;" and the same review concludes by saying that "The great revolutionary broom has, we think, swept wisely not less than well." Those are not unpleasant opinions to a humble author, nor are they one whit the less to be appreciated—rather the more—because the reviewer expresses his dissent from and condemnation of perhaps two-thirds of the work. But, lo and behold, some months after the review appeared from which I have just quoted, the *Saturday Review* changed editors, and the unionist, Mr. Walter Herries Pollock, gave way to a gentleman of social democratic fame, Mr. Frank Harris. Poor Mr. Harris—evidently unaware that the *Saturday Review* had already seen depth, sincerity, and wisdom in the reforms advocated in THE REVOLUTION OF THE TWENTIETH CENTURY—seems to have become perfectly rabid with the book because, probably, in spite of his revolutionary doctrines, the author saw through and exposed the futility of so-called social democracy. Accordingly the new-edited *Saturday Review* falls like a cartload of editorial bricks upon Carlyle Democritus, whom his predecessor had approved. Editor Frank Harris determines that there is no wisdom, only "the most concentrated twaddle it has ever been our (Harrisonian) misfortune to come across." It is not wise, it is not well; it is mere "stuff," mere "absurdity," and the perturbed critic proceeds to exhaust his ink-pot in abuse, all most welcome to an unrepentant author. But the *Saturday Review's* conclusion is really curious. The

author has dared in his book to expose some of the fraudulent company promoters in high places. Whereupon the critic weeps forth and sighs : " We suppose the publisher, however, has taken his lawyer's advice on the contents of the book. . . ."

The anxiety of social-democracy for the good name and fame of the wholesale fraudulent company promoter is too affecting, and in this stage of the book the merciful author will not induce his reader to tears. But it is indeed worth noting how readily, in the delicate organisation of modern civilisation, the millionaire scoundrel finds friends, whilst the poor gutter thief, often driven to crime through misery, finds social (and other) democracy silent. Only the other day a train-thief, practising his three-card trick for sundry pence, received his due reward, upon detection, within the precincts of one of Her Majesty's gaols. About the same time a huge city thief does the three-card trick for £385,000 sterling, his victims, not a few solitary country louts, but a holocaust of poor widows, half-starved clerks, and such silly bait. Will it be believed that the millionaire's fraud was scarcely noticed by the leading papers outside the mere law-report, and not at all by Her Majesty's Government? The shilling scoundrel is prosecuted, is put in prison ; the lying swindler of £385,000 sterling is let go scot-free! Perhaps not quite scot-free, for one of the victims brought an action against the millionaire for fraudulent misrepresentation, in having induced him to pay two or three pounds for shares not worth as many shillings, and gained his case. And it may be, and I devoutly hope that it has been, that sundry of the poor widows and clerks referred to—those of them who may have chanced to hear of the case—have called upon that wholesale thief and made him disgorge some at least of his pelf. But the fact remains that the public prosecutor who seizes upon the shilling three-card-trick man, is totally blind to the £300,000 trickster.

Did space only permit, and were the victim worthy of the trouble, I would treat the reader to some interesting letters which ensued upon the Harrisonian reviews, but, perhaps, enough for the present.

There was another reviewer, a reformer this one, though some of his friends opine that he has a bee in his bonnet —I have even heard say a whole bee-hive. And this reviewer accorded me the honour of fourteen closely printed columns, plus a whole page illustration by his special artist. I hope the reviewer in question will not think me ungrateful for the considerable prominence he gave my book if I only quote one line from his introductory criticism. He spoke namely of a "preposterous misconception of facts." I was interested to discover what could be the "preposterous misconception." For if there is one merit THE REVOLUTION OF THE TWENTIETH CENTURY dare lay claim to, it is a rigid adherence to accuracy of treatment in substance and in detail.

Although in parts, fact and fiction may seem curiously interblended, he who runs may read that the fiction is but the frame to the picture, and it is as impossible to confound the one with the other as it would be to confound the work of the cabinet-maker with the oils and colours of the painter. I applied to my reviewer for information. Then it appeared that in certain denunciations of quacks and quackeries this good editor was gibbeted as a believer and advertiser of, one of the hollowest quackeries that this century of quacks has perhaps produced. I had dared to denounce the description of coloured water as a "cure for cancer," and alas, also to denounce the folly of the able editor who had backed up the vendor of the worthless compound. "No other preposterousness?" I humbly enquired. "There is not one statement of fact in that book, Mr. Editor, for which I cannot give you chapter and verse." The worthy editor hesitated, cleared his throat, he could not, and did not, name any other "preposterous misconception."

Anxious as I am to amend any untrue thing, or any misconception whatever—preposterous or not preposterous—I cannot do it, for the simple reason that I am not cognisant of any, and with the exception of the one quoted, which I must emphatically confirm, and not withdraw, I cannot call to mind any other "misconception of facts" anywhere referred to by any one of my manifold reviewers.

A word might be said here upon the origin of the book. A bookseller's reader has printed that "I know Slumland as no other living Englishman knows it." That may or may not be an accurate description of my knowledge of poorland. Here is perhaps a more accurate description:—

That I have penetrated so deeply into what is called Slumland, and come to know with such reasonable accuracy the modes of life of its dwellers; have also been compelled to observe how this so-called Slumland, instead of diminishing, is increasing, and how the misery of its inhabitants is becoming intensified, that it occurred to me that someone should undertake the task of enlightening those who live in palace-land as to what are really the conditions of the submerged millions and—what is infinitely more important—what will inevitably be the result (what in all places and in all ages has ever been the result) if the present condition of things is allowed to go on and increase, as it is going on and is increasing.

Indeed I wrote the work in spite of myself. In a manner I was constrained to write it, constrained namely by a mind ripe with the experience of years of toil among the scenes that are described, and of study into the causes which have helped to bring them about, and by a heart sore for the woe and misery it had witnessed.

Does not the reader think that he who puts forward a solution of the gravest problems which confront us to-day, is entitled to a little attention and consideration?

Not merely because he puts forward these solutions, but because so many of his critics, even some of the unfriendliest, have admitted their feasibility and their practicalness. I shall venture therefore in this place, in a rather long footnote, in very small type, and with such modesty as I can command, to append some "opinions of the press." They are boiled down, from over one-hundred closely printed columns of reviews. The reader may glance at them, or pass them by.*

Publisher's Note to the First Edition.

"In this volume the author has described the hydra, called Modern Civilisation, in terms so precise, has attacked party governments with such a wealth of sarcasm and illustration, that the total effect of his work is most startling. Like others, the author comes forward with his Utopia, and of the ingenuity of this invention there can be no question. It is probably the most carefully thought out revolution and instauration yet planned."

The Daily Chronicle.

"We were prepared to welcome any work by this author, whose exposure of the wrongs wrought by 'Landlordism' earned for him a tribute from *Punch* and a recognition from all social reformers. There is throughout the volume the noblest feeling of sympathy with suffering mankind, very keen flashes of insight, and very useful practical suggestions as to a better way of managing social affairs."

The Pall Mall Gazette.

"The author has quite sound views about trade, fair and free; India, Mr. Gladstone's policy, the two Houses of Parliament, Radicalism, the Navy, and some other matters"

I assure him that *The* REVOLUTION OF THE TWENTIETH CENTURY may be really described as a fervent endeavour to prevent *a* revolution of the twentieth century.

Birmingham Daily Gazette.

"The author is an earnest man, endowed with a Carlylean insight, a brilliant imagination and a vigorous style. His comments upon nineteenth century company promoting are bold and interesting; but the peculiarities of nineteenth century libel law forbid quotation."

The Standard.

"The book is marked by a keen appreciation of some, at least, of the perils of modern civilisation. The hero, the champion of the oppressed, is not merely to ride the storm of the coming terror, but, by his wisdom no less than his valour, to usher in a golden age of justice and contentment."

The Whitehall Review.

"The author is a powerful writer of the Carlyle school, and not a few passages in the work are eloquent and picturesque. In fact, as a literary effort, pure and simple, the book deserves the highest commendation, and should establish the author's reputation as a brilliant and incisive writer."

The Methodist Recorder.

"This really remarkable book is an attack upon the social, moral and political evils of the present day delivered from the standpoint of a right-minded Imperial Englishman, with an impetuosity and directness which cannot but command admiration. We must confess that an attractive and seemingly possible era is opened. The final picture is full of bright colour, abounding in life and health. It is altogether a book to make one's pulse and heart beat quicker. The author finds a solution for every ill, and never pulls a tottering fabric down without erecting something stronger and more beautiful in its place."

Black and White.

"We are bound to express admiration for the author's powers in tackling a mighty problem. There is that in the book which every man would do well to read and ponder."

Review of Reviews.

"The reader will find in the book much matter for reflection. Of the painstaking effort which the author has made to think out the ways and means by which a better social system might be established amongst us, there can be no doubt."

The World.

"This work sets forth with force and reason a great deal of truth concerning the social facts too rarely discerned of the multitude, and too little considered by the authoritative few. The book is interesting, and has a great deal in it that is wise and suggestive."

Publisher's Circular.

"We do not remember any forecast more important looking than this book. The problems discussed are so important, and the manner in which they are dealt with is so bold and thorough, that the work should claim readers among all persons who are interested in the solution of the many problems that beset us in the civilisation of to-day."

Morning Leader.

"The riddle of the Sphinx: Nations have perished in trying to answer it, and nations have perished in hoping to shirk it. The author sees a solution to the English riddle in sweeping reforms. His book is eloquent of social sorrow and struggle. The value of such a work consists in the forcible manner in which an outworn social system is made to appear ridiculous and wicked. With plenitude of scorn, wealth of fact, amplitude of quotation from poet and philosopher, this remarkable volume drives home the injustice of existing social and industrial relations."

Liverpool Courier.

"There is a refreshing novelty in a scheme which is definite but not limited to any one specific, and these characteristics belong to the ENGLISH REVOLUTION OF THE TWENTIETH CENTURY. The author goes into the question of State finance with sufficient elaborateness to show how—with reduced taxation—the revolutionized nation would command a larger revenue, rid itself of the incubus of a national debt, and establish a national reserve fund in its place."

Among the questions dealt with, and for which simple solutions are put forward are :—
The Land Question.
The Irish Question.

The Christian Commonwealth.

"The work shows much originality, a passionate love of the people, and a large grasp of things of the future. No one can read it without being made to think. The writer has many visions that can and will be made practicable.'

The Scotsman.

"These reforms are all worked out in detail. The most remarkable feature in the book is the small amount of reliance which the author puts in State interference. He shows a zeal which is much to his credit, to deal with abuses on an individualistic basis one by one, instead of flying to some heroic remedy, such as State socialism."

The Chamber of Commerce Journal.
(The Official Organ of the London Chamber of Commerce.)

"The bitterest critic of the wholesale revolutionary doctrines this work preaches, will derive pleasure from its perusal. There is much to interest business men and leaders of industry. The work is as full of facts and opinions as an egg is full of meat."

The New Weekly.

"The author has a genuine insight into the real conditions under which society in this country exists."

Rochester Standard.

"The practical reforms contained in these pages are indeed a valuable contribution to democratic literature. Everybody who reads the book will be offended at something in it. This is pardonable in these uninteresting days, when books without any qualities whatever, neither satisfactory nor annoying, flood the market. Those who cannot purchase the book should secure its adoption by the nearest free library. The whole of the book is eminently readable and unquestionably sincere."

The National Observer.

"This volume is very enjoyable. It contains telling truths which deserve the earnest consideration of the statesman and the philanthropist. With marvellous skill the author has exposed many Jubilee abuses.'

The Auckland Star.

"The author depicts a state of society as corrupt and effete as that of Rome preceding the disruption of the Empire. He attacks the Church as being undermined by luxury, scepticism, and selfishness, the aristocracy as sunk in extravagance, and an industrial system which grinds the face of the poor and dependent."

Liverpool Post.

"The man who failed to sympathise with the social misery which this book depicts could hardly be a subject for envy."

The Enquirer.

"This Prospective History differs from all others we have seen. It is a serious, scathing and fearless attack upon the social, political and national evils that abound in our midst, and an attempt to offer a way out of them. It has the merit of appearing in a serious guise, a style which would entitle it to range with the most earnest books of history or of philosophy on our shelves. The book is most remarkably up to date."

Bradford Observer.

"The author has much to say that is well worth pondering; he indicates with great good sense the shape which much needed reforms should take. He gives the reader abundant matter for thinking, and he has much to say about party jobbery, inane judicial decisions, the sufferings of the poor, the method of dealing with the land and the unemployed, the reform of the Church, the Law, National education, and a host of other subjects.'

The Control (to eventual extinction) of Public-house (or liquor) Traffic.
Abolition of the Slums.
The Status of Women.
Education.
Deliverance of what, for want of a better classification, are called the submerged classes, estimated by various students and historians (and they will be found carefully investigated in their proper places in the book) at from two to four millions.
Free Law and Justice.
Church Reform.
Simple Wording of Acts of Parliament.
Settlement of Agricultural Labourers on the Land.
The Abolition of the National Debt and its substitution by a National Reserve.
The Abolition of Casual Labour.
A Simple Franchise with Equal Numerical Representation, and
National, instead of *Party* Political Organisation.

The Westminster Gazette.
"A very able criticism and commentary on the existing state of society."

The Methodist Times.
"Here is Utopianism mingled with shrewd, sound sense. There are a great many very valuable suggestions as to social reform and social reconstruction. The reforms advocated in relation to Land, Taxation, Pauperism, Crime, Vice, the Law, the Army, the Navy, the Church, Woman, Education, and Parliament, are mainly wise, and present a capital programme for to-day. There is also a great deal of valuable material casting light on the existing conditions of society. It is a book full of use and suggestion to all interested in social evils and social reconstruction."

The Nottingham Guardian.
"This is a remarkable book, one so great as to narrowly have missed being a gigantic failure. There can be no doubt about the pains the author has been at to work out the means by which a better state of things is to be brought about. The chapter dealing with the decline of British trade is one of the most suggestive accounts a political economist could read. The author has displayed an ability in marshalling his ideas which is worthy of the highest praise. Some of the scenes are described with a realism that absorbs the reader's interest."

The Investor's Review.
"This book is one which should be read by all who are interested in social problems. contains much that is suggestive and instructive. It shows industry, enthusiasm, sympathy, and the gift of vigorous expression. Its richness of oratory and unfettered freedom of fancy make it an eminently readable book."

Westminster Review.
"THE ENGLISH REVOLUTION OF THE TWENTIETH CENTURY is a remarkable book. We respect the author's sincerity and admire his enthusiastic philanthropy."

As evidence of the necessity for the two last reforms, it may be interesting to quote the following analysis of six hundred members of the existing Parliament. The reason that only six hundred members are enumerated is for facility of comparison with the numbers which would be necessary were there proportional representation—say in round numbers, one representative for every fifteen thousand electors, that number allowing nine millions of male electors on a manhood-suffrage, restricted only by an education qualification, and the elimination of any person who has suffered a criminal conviction :—

Dividing the present representation broadly into two classes, we have :—

Landlords, Land-owners and Mine-owners	155
Liquor and Lawyer Representatives -	124
Representatives from the Peerage -	96
Cabinet ex-officials - - -	12
No occupation - - -	20
	407
Manufacturers, Ship-owners, Literary and Professional men, Merchants and Commercial men, altogether, only - -	71
Labour members - - -	11
Army, Navy, and Civil Service - -	33
	115
Irish and other members not easy to specify and not included in the above total - - - -	78
Total	600

And now let any reader who is concerned in the well-being of this nation consider the work that is laid before him in the following pages, naught extenuating, but also naught setting down in malice.

HENRY LAZARUS.

38, TAVISTOCK SQUARE,
    October, 1897.

"RAISE THE VEIL BOLDLY!"

"FACE THE LIGHT!"

"GO THOU FORTH, BEARING PRECIOUS SEED'

—Ruskin.

Be fearless, O people, and ye shall be feared! Tremble, O people, and ye shall be despised!

Aim at perfection, and though it is not in man's power to attain the mysterious fruit, all that is achieved on that path is a flower of perfection.

CARLYLE DEMOCRITUS.

The people have judgment when it is not misled by orators.

When the well-being of a nation is at stake, individual considerations cease to exist.

NAPOLEON.

The despair of a nation is the sword of Damocles, which outraged Justice poises over the heads of worthless Governments

Napoleon said that in Revolutions there were two sorts of people, those who made them and those who profited by them. Be you, my people, as the wise merchants, who make their businesses and who profit of them also.

CARLYLE DEMOCRITUS.

Ye of the fluent phrasemen make your king,
Therefore your steps have wandered from the path.

DANTE.

I esteem those to be the best teachers which teach the common people most plainly and simply, without subtlety, screwed words, or enlargements. . . . The Pope's power was above all Kings' and Emperors', which I opposed with my little book, and, by God's assistance, overthrew it.

Unfaithfulness is also stealing;
Thieving is the most common trade in the world;
Great thieves go Scot-free, as the Pope and his crew.

LUTHER.

Lord Lauderdale.—Why do you, as a private man, meddle with politics?
James Harrington.—My lord, there is not any public person, nor any magistrate, that has written on politics, worth a button. All they that have been excellent in this way have been private men, my lord, as myself.

JAMES HARRINGTON,
Author of "Oceana," under examination at The Tower, 1661.

"History is a free emporium, where poetry, divinity, politics, physics, peaceably meet and furnish themselves; and Sentimentalist, Utilitarian, Sceptic, and Theologian, with one voice advise us—examine history, for it is philosophy teaching by experience."   CARLYLE.

"The purport of Nature betrays itself in the use we make of these signal narrations of history. I am ashamed to see what a shallow village tale our so-called history is; an old chronology of selfishness and pride. Every history should be written in a wisdom which divines the range of our affinities, and looks at facts as symbols. . . I see that men of God have from time to time walked among men, and made their mission felt in the heart and soul of the commonest reader.

Every Reform was once a private opinion.
Every Revolution was first a thought in one man's mind."
EMERSON.

"If history can tell us little of the past, and nothing of the future, why waste our time over so barren a study? History is a voice for ever sounding across the centuries the laws of right and wrong; RIGHT, the sacrifice of self to good; WRONG, the sacrifice of good to self. . . . For cruelty and oppression the price has to be paid at last; not always by the chief offenders, but paid by some one. Justice and Truth alone endure and live. Injustice and falsehood may be long lived, but Domesday comes at last to them in French Revolutions and other terrible ways."   FROUDE.

"We are sometimes told that the accumulation of materials has made the writing of edifying history impossible. The tendency to think one fact as good as another, the inability to find significance in the teaching of history tempt men to wish that uninstructive, ponderous accuracy were replaced by lucidity. . . . But the minutest scholarship is compatible with philosophic insight, and it is possible to pass from an acute, critical examination of authorities, to a lucid statement of economical or political problems."
The Times (Article on Mommsen).

"Think of all the vice and ignorance and disease, of all the sordid abject misery, of all the lawless passions that are festering within our great towns. Consider how grave and how numerous are the dangers that threaten our prosperity, from within and without."   LECKY.

DEDICATION.

"THERE is Genius, with its pale face, and worn dress, and torn friendships, and bleeding heart. . . . Strong only in struggling; counting all loss gain but truth and the love of God. . . . And there is Respectability, with its sweet smiling home, and loving friends, and happy family. . . . Choose, O man, at the parting of the ways! Choose. You may have one; both you cannot have. . . . Yet, if you do choose the first, choose it with all your heart. You will need it all to bear what will be laid upon you: No wistful lookings back upon the pleasant land which you are leaving—no playing with life. You have chosen the heart of things, not the surface; and it is no child's play. . . . The moments of insight are short, the hours of despondency are long. . . . The absolute worth of goodness is seen as distinct from power. Through all history we find the bitter fact that mankind can only be persuaded to accept the best gifts which Heaven sends them in persecuting and destroying those who are charged to be their bearers. . . . A thousand patriots go to the scaffold amidst the execrations of mankind. Out of those thousands, perhaps, after-generations remember one."—FROUDE.

CONTENTS.

―――o―――

PART I.—DESTRUCTIVE.
BOOK I.—REVOLUTION ESTABLISHING ITSELF.

CHAP.		PAGE
	PROEM	1
I.	UNLEARNT LESSONS. A NEW VISTA OF HISTORY	17
II.	JUBILEE PERIOD, YEAR 1887; PERIOD: 1880-1894	22
III.	AFTERWARDS. THE NEW REVOLUTIONISTS	27
IV.	THEIR CHIEF, CARLYLE DEMOCRITUS	32
V.	THE WAR-DOGS OF TERENCE GREY	36
VI.	HOUNDING DESPAIR INTO DESPERATION	40
VII.	ORGANISATION	44
VIII.	THE DAY OF REVOLUTION, 14TH FEBRUARY 19—	48
IX.	THE REVOLUTIONARY PATROLS	57
X.	THE GREAT REQUISITION	62
XI.	PARLIAMENT BY PARTY AND OBSTRUCTION ENDS	66
XII.	INTERVIEW BETWEEN CARLYLE DEMOCRITUS AND THE KING	69

BOOK II.—REVOLUTION ESTABLISHED.

I.	THE REVOLUTIONARY COUNCIL	79
II.	INTERCALARY—JUBILEE UTOPIA, OR "EVERYWHERE"	83
III.	JUSTICE RETRIBUTIVE!	88

PART II.—CONSTRUCTIVE.

BOOK I.—REVOLUTION JUSTIFIES ITSELF AND SOLVES THE SOCIAL PROBLEM.

CHAP.		PAGE
I.	CARLYLE DEMOCRITUS'S MANIFESTO TO THE ENGLISH PEOPLE	95
II.	THE LAND QUESTION ANSWERED	108
III.	THE LAND AND THE NEW PROPRIETORS	124
IV.	FINANCE—REVENUE	132
V.	EXPENDITURE (National Debt transformed into National Reserve.)	145
VI.	THE CONSECRATION OF THE GREAT REQUISITION—1. THE QUIETUS OF PAUPER IMMIGRATION	151
VII.	2. WORK FOR THE WEAKEST AND THE WORST	156
VIII.	3. WASTE HANDS ARE WEDDED TO WASTE LANDS	165

BOOK II.—LABOUR.

I.	SLUMLAND REGENERATED	175
II.	STATE EMPLOYMENT AND NEW AVENUES OF LABOUR	188
III.	MASTER LABOURERS	202
IV.	"TOOLS AND THE MAN"	234
V.	TOILERS OF THE DEEP	267

BOOK III.—NATIONAL.

I.	THE PAN-ANGLICAN UNION	287
II.	THE ARMY AND THE NAVY	304
III.	THE CHURCH : PASTORS OF CHRIST. PANTHEON PURIFIED	323
IV.	WOMAN	338
V.	EDUCATION	359
VI.	LAW	366

PART III.—APOTHEOSIS.

BOOK I.—PARLIAMENT AGAIN.

CHAP.		PAGE
I. THE NEW ELECTORATE	. . . .	417
II. THE SIX HUNDRED OF GREAT BRITAIN	. . .	427
III. THE FIVE HUNDRED OF GREATER BRITAIN	. .	434

BOOK II.—CONCLUSION.

I. THE REVOLUTIONISTS DISARM	. . . .	441
II. CARLYLE DEMOCRITUS LAYS ASIDE THE THORN-CROWN	.	445
III. EUTHANASIA	.	451

Note.—THROUGHOUT THIS HISTORY THE TIME IS DIVIDED INTO TWO PERIODS—THE PRE-REVOLUTIONARY, OR "JUBILEE PERIOD," 1880 TO 1894: AND THE PERIOD OF REVOLUTION 19— AND ONWARDS.

A scornful person asked the General Iphicrates who he was, as he seemed neither heavy-armed soldier, nor bowman, nor targeteer. And the General answered, "I am he who leads and makes useful all these. . . . ." Wisdom is neither gold, nor silver, nor fame; neither health, nor wealth, nor beauty, nor strength. Wisdom is that which can use all those well.

PLUTARCH.

PROEM.

THE HISTORY OF A MANUSCRIPT.

LATE one night, in the piercing winter of a recent year, I was driving homeward in the creakiest of old cabs, whose poor worn-out horse stumbled and slipped at every step of the glassy, frozen road, till finally, and in spite of plentiful rough coaxing from the snow-covered driver, down it fell, and there was no possibility of raising it again. The shaft had broken in the fall, and a large splinter had torn the wretched animal's side, whence trickled slowly the little blood of life the beast possessed.

The accident occurred in one of the narrowest of those poverty stricken lanes off Seven Dials, but the inclemency of the weather and the lateness of the hour tempted not one soul to view the catastrophe.

"It's my own horse, sir, him is; I come out this evening at six o'clock; I've took one fare beside yerself, and they're expecting me to bring 'em enough to pay our rent and—and feed the little ones. Ah, sir, there be too many on us at this, as at all trades. God knows what's a-coming to 'em all! Dan, my lad, if ye live they'll tremble afore ye yet."

What this latter ejaculation could mean I had little opportunity just then of inquiring, or of guessing. The poor old Jehu looked the picture of despair; a rough, weather-beaten, massive son of toil, there shone through his heavy-browed eyes a tenderness of heart which no breeding can produce, but which much so-called breeding oftentimes destroys. He evidently lived near the locality of the accident, for he proceeded to leave the cab and its fallen horse, even forgetting to ask me for the fare. Mechanically I followed him, and we soon entered together by a miserable enough damp and broken staircase, or, rather, inclined ladder with a side-rail to it, a tiny room which smelt of stable and human breathing, so close that, for many minutes, respiration was painful labour to me. On a small couch at one end of the room—if a box some eleven feet by ten may be called a room—slept three children, the eldest apparently about ten years old, the youngest about five. For furniture, besides this couch, there were three well-worn, but not broken, wooden chairs, and a small strong table; at this was seated a youth, or perhaps man (it was difficult to judge his age by the faint light of the shaded lamp, whose feeble rays were concentrated on a pile of paper which the student was eagerly covering with pen and ink). He rose briskly as we entered, anxiously and affectionately embraced my companion, and said, "Dad, what's amiss? We can't go much lower—"

"Dan'el, my boy," was the reply, "it's all up. Luck's agin me; it's the Work'us, Dan, the Work'us."

Here Daniel looked at me with so keen and searching a scrutiny that I felt as if he read into my very soul, and, for a moment, an unaccountable sense of awe completely overcame me. The scratching of his pen, as he completed the writing that we had interrupted, roused me from the strangest emotion that the presence of a human being had ever invoked in me. "Who is this, uncle?" asked the youth, as he quickly, but without flurry, tied up his papers and put aside his pen. "He does not seem like one who would add to our or any one's misery."

"Not he," said the cabby; "it ain't him as is to blame; he's a kind soul, or he hadn't a' come here."

"God bless you, sir, if you're good to him," said Daniel to me, "for a better man, and more worthy of sympathy, there is not in Britain. What is it, uncle, tell me?"

"The nag's fell dead, lad, and I ain't took but two bob all night, but you must come and help me in with the cab; p'r'aps the gentleman 'll lend a hand too."

On the way back to the cab, where we found two policemen inspecting the ruins, Daniel became communicative. I listened fascinated. The man's evident breeding and culture, found under such conditions, fairly astonished me. He did not appear more than twenty-four years old, if so much. His physiognomy was of a type so far removed from the man he called "Dad," that the two seemed of quite impossible relationship, or even connection. This Daniel was tall and remarkably well proportioned. His face was pale, but strangely beautiful, and capable of intense expression. Crisp golden hair clustered round a brow as earnest and inspired as that of an ancient prophet. His dress was of the plainest and humblest but was carried with a grace which the finest cloth could not impart.

The friendly police gave help, and we soon wheeled the cab back to the stable. Once again in the little parlour, where now the wife was also come from the adjoining bedroom, I commenced by asking Martins what his position really was.

Martins :—" Well, yer see, sir, it's just this ; I've been at this 'ere bizness for over thirty year. I've done my best to save and put a little by for rainy days, but sickness soon swallows up savings, even though yer *do* belong to Societies, but what's worse than illness is, the trade itself is sick—too many on us, sir. Many a day I've had to come home after fourteen and fifteen hours on the box without enough to pay the horse's keep, let alone pay the rent and feed these mouths here ; and the missis, bless her, eats little enough, God knows !" and Martins sank down with bent head to hide the salt tears which all his trying could not restrain. His poor old wife stood comforting him.

Daniel :—" Sir, let me say a word to you. I know you will not misinterpret me. If sympathy is the first essential of insight, as the greatest and truest writer of our day, or any day, has said, then I know you, and can dare to speak. Listen, sir. This man, poor as he is, is of that pattern which God intended man should be, strong of body, tender of heart, loving to her and to these little things, as he is to all that's weak, and to me I cannot say what he has been. Like many, many thousands of others all around us, he has worked and toiled to gain an honest living. Day by day the possibility has grown less and less, until now, after thirty years of toil, during which period he has paid in taxes to the State far more in proportion to his income than does the proudest lord of entailed estate, there remain to him but three alternatives—Either to break the great God's law and end his life ; to starve and see his wife and children starve ; or to enter with them the Workhouse, be separated from them and the good woman who has loved him and shared his toil, and there break stones or pick oakum like a common felon."

I :—" Cannot *you* help them? You seem to possess no common ability, such powers surely would find good market."

Daniel:—"Sir, I have tried until bootless trial has nearly maddened me. I have offered to serve for nothing to prove my value, but a thousand clerks are ready to rush into every single vacancy. I clean the old man's cab, tend the stable, and do the little that I can to help, but another work is mine as well——"

Martins:—"Ay, he'll not tell all. You listen to me, young master. This here lad is my brother's son. The brother and me was better bred than the looks of me might warrant. But I never could do school-learning, even if I'd had the opportunity, which I hadn't; and when our father died, I being eight year old and the brother twelve, though father had been keeping our mother and us in fine ways, and like a lord, no one knew how he managed it. He used to go to Races, I've heard mother say, so most likely as how he wasn't much better than he should be. But, to cut a long matter short, he was throwed from his horse one day and killed, and when things was looked into, the balance was only debts. The fine house was all sold up, and mother found herself with just the things she stood in, and a few pounds and some jewelry to support herself and boys. That didn't last long. She used to make a little by working things for shops, and she managed to feed us this way, and by begging a little help from some as knewed her in better days. But when I was twelve and Tom was sixteen, she died, wore out. Tom was just old enough when the father died to see what it was, and feel what it was, to be the fine gentleman. So mother never could get him to take to poor work of any sort. But me, young as I was, she used to put to help at stabling work; and I stuck to it, until by saving and saving I got to be a driver, and at last bought my own cab. Tom, meanwhile, went off to America, and there he seems to have led a wildish sort of life, and got this son. Determined that his boy should not know what sort of life he led, he sent him over to England as soon as he was old enough, and paid into a bank a lot o' money, more than a thousand pounds, I think, to give the boy ten years' education at a college down at Oxford—he'll tell you the name. Three years after doing that he died; but the boy was kept at the school from his tenth to his twentieth year, and now you know how he got his learning. He got a tutorship down there for a time, but getting to write about subjects which frightened the people—Socialistic they called 'em—they drove him out of employ, and he got from bad to worse, as many a skolard afore him 'a done; and then he remembered that his father had spoken about a brother he had left in London. So up he comes to London, gets the Salvation Army papers to advertise after me; some one showed me the advertisement almost the first time it was in the paper, and that's how Dan and me come together. That's near five year ago. I was saving a bit then, and Dan made a little by writing for clubs sometimes. When things began to darken, the boy got wild at the misery and wretchedness he saw day by day surrounding us in this big district. He couldn't 'elp it, bless yer! His soul seems to have been made of a sort of tinder which any sorrow or misery quick kindles to a blaze, and last year, when them rows were taking place with the unemployed, Dan got up a meeting at the old Straw Barn down yonder. There was a crowd of folk got together, and when they heerd him they were nigh a worshipping of him. At that there moment, sir, I seemed to know how a revolution grows and makes a beginning. Among the lot as was met in that old barn all warent o' the best, but there wasn't one but would have followed him then and there to the Devil himself if Dan had a-lifted his hand. Since that day the roughest on 'em don't pass him without a touching of their heads as if he was a lord, and there ain't no jealousy about it neither, although the girls do show a good deal too much liking for him——" Dan was getting more and more uncomfortable during the progress of Martins' enplanation, and he here interrupted the recital.

Daniel:—"The long and short of it is simply this; I knew that those Trafalgar Square meetings were simply useless, and could do harm and never good. The object of our meeting was to dissuade true workers from any display that was without real force. Real power, I showed them, could only be possible if the *bona fide* workmen out of employment would organise themselves under a trusted leader, accept one and all a definite and absolute programme; that if they would truly emancipate themselves and their fellows from the terrible bondage of no-work, there was but one way to its attainment, and that way, the united determination of the vast nation of workers that Labour, its solemn rights and privileges, should be recognised by their Parliament, neither before nor after, but co-equally with the rights of the wealthy classes, called the rights of property. But let me not detain you, sir, with any wearisome iteration of my words. I knew beforehand, and too well, the awful nature of the agitator who alone in the end can combine the masses. His names are Misery and Starvation. That terrible uniter of those who despair is fast pressing forward his dread authority, so that when the true leader comes he will find the sluggish circulation of the masses already raised to fever heat. It is a slow arterial system which governs the actions of the working classes of any people, and, before it can be finally aroused, an infinite waste of misery and suffering must combine, and indeed already there are outward signs enough that the giant pulse beats more quickly than any wise political physician would calmly contemplate. But where, sir, in the body politic, is wise discernment discoverable? Modern statesmen view with apathy a dangerously wasteful pauper immigration, side by side with choked labour markets, overcrowded workhouses, deaths and suicides caused by starvation and no-work, the neglected and filthy condition of labourers' dwellings; whilst, on the other hand, wealth and luxury are pandered to, and remain the sole centre of power and influence. I see but one issue to such a state of things. And even as you came in this night has my pen traced the last word of a prophecy which shall surely come to pass if England awaken not quickly to the misery of her long-suffering and patient workers."

The passion and enthusiasm with which these words were uttered I must despair of picturing. The physical beauty of the speaker, his sinewy strength, the fervour of his language, his magnificent earnestness, thrilled me as though a messenger of warning from the Eternal Judge had appeared before me. *Had* appeared?—yes, for before I could regain control of my senses the man was gone. In my hand he had left a roll of manuscript. Full of emotion more strange than ever before had moved me, I opened the sheet, with a feeling of mixed curiosity and superstition, and on the first page read the words:—

"THE ENGLISH REVOLUTION OF THE TWENTIETH CENTURY:
A PROSPECTIVE HISTORY."

I should have turned the pages to read more, but a sob from

Martins roused me. He held a letter in his hand outstretched and open, inviting me to read:—

"GENEROUS PROTECTOR, GOOD OLD UNCLE,

"To-night I must leave you; no longer is it given me to doubt the work which Fate ordains me in this world, which may bring to any man connected with me anguish and misfortune. I am called away, but in years to come you may hear again of me as the saviour, or the victim of my people. Like the Divinity whom we both adore, perhaps the saviour and the victim both.

"The trouble that has weighed on you so long will vanish from this night. I have seen your helper; a career of humble brightness and success lies now before you. Good-bye, father, good-bye, truest and dearest friend. I have kissed the sleeping children, whom, with you, I commend to the Great Protector of us all. DANIEL MARTINS."

"Poor prophet, Dan, my boy," sighed old Martins, "your letter should have been writ afore the nag fell dead; Mary, tell the gentleman to read that letter to you."

"Better than that, Martins," I said, "your nephew commences his prophecy so well that I am burning with impatience to read his manuscript. Cheer up, good fellow. This purse will provide a new horse for you, and rent and necessities for a time to come, and on the first of every month be assured of further help until independence and prosperity shall render you above requiring it."

Martins started up, tall with astonishment and gratitude, and eager to express his heartfelt gladness; but I disappeared almost as suddenly as Daniel had, hugging the manuscript, which I now lay before the world.

. . . .

In justice to the sturdy courage and independence of the old cabman, let me add that before many months[*] were over he

---

[*] The delay in publishing Martins' manuscript has been due to the fragmentary nature of his papers. Many of them were in great disorder, and had evidently been penned in the midst of the scenes which they describe. Time has also been required to verify the numerous references to current events, which, with few exceptions, have been satisfactorily traced, and to which the numbers in the margin of the text refer. These references will probably

secured a clean and wholesome cottage for his wife and children, owned three cabs, and several horses, and insisted upon repaying me in instalments the money he had received.

---

form the subject of a key to this volume. It is hoped that the completeness of the index will make amends for the occasional divergence of the subject-matter from the title of the respective chapters, to have altered which might have marred the harmony of the work.   H. L.

THE MANUSCRIPT.

PENDENTE LITE.

"Paupertas fugitur, totoque arcessitur orbe."—*Lucan.*

—o—

LETTER FROM DANIEL MARTINS TO HIM WHO SHALL BE INTRUSTED WITH THIS MANUSCRIPT.

"UNKNOWN ONE, who shall help me to pour forth my heart upon the world—

"Bear with me, be patient with me. I have lived amidst the horrors which I describe. I have known the agonies of slow starvation and not complained, of the deepest sorrows of mortal man, and communed only with my God. I have seen the darling ones, more sweet than life to me, fall day by day before the awful spectre of Want; little children pining for food, strong men sunk in despair. I have watched innocent child life as the bodies waned and the eyes grew large—large till they could see the reaper whose name is Death. Then have I seen the parents die—self-murdered—unable to bear sorrow more. Oh, you who shall come when my work is done, to bear it to the world of men, tell them not to look at the form of the words, but only at the meaning of them, for I am like St. Paul, of whom it has been said: 'He had not a mind adapted to the composition of books. He had not the patience that is required for writing; he was incapable of system.' All that, and more, is true of me. And I have not written a book. Not a book, but a prophecy. Things cannot last as they are, cannot, must not, shall not. I tell you, O unknown one, the things that I have written shall come to pass. From the top, by a fearless and brave reform, or from the nethermost by horrid revolution, beside which even that of France shall pale. Give my work to the world in some way, but give it that I may be still, whilst the world bethinks itself of its abandoned duties, and the universal necessity for Reform. If they have hardened their hearts and can no more hear, then, by the Eternal Name, let them beware. For the spirit which God has raised in me, and in those who follow me, cannot die. DANIEL MARTINS."

Need the editor add much to that letter? Martins might have continued his passage from Renan, which runs: "With his marvellous fervour of soul, Paul has yet a singular poverty of expression. A phrase besets him, he recurs to it at every turn. It was not sterility; it was complete indifference to the requirements of a correct style." So it seems to me to be with the book of Martins. It is not, therefore, as a work of literature that I have laboured to give some sort of order to the remarkable papers he gave into my hands, but as a glowing work of insight into the evils which are sapping our country to its very foundations, and their remedy which, though not absolutely unknown to certain inquirers (for there is nothing new under the sun), has never before been presented so luminously. Martins' pen has torn the nettle from the earth to its last root and fibre, and left it dying in the sight of men. But it has not stopped there. It has filled up the vacant weed-hole with new loam, and planted in it rich seed-corn. Is there enough national life in England to insist that the seed-corn shall be let grow in the new rich soil, or has the national spirit fallen so low, that it will permit the thistle of abuse to be re-planted and let flourish, in the way of thistles, until . . . ? Until . . . But I am no more able than Martins to write books. Let me then invoke the greatest English master of history of our time, him who sows his pages with a wisdom as rare as his eloquence, who is amongst the few who know how to breathe into the dry bones of vanished ages the spirit of life, and to draw from the buried past the lesson for the living present. Writing of Rome, once as great as the Empire we are day by day dissipating in wantonness of Party strife, insincerities, and corruptions—of Rome, at the period of her decline, the historian Froude says: "The age of Cato, Pompey, Cicero, and Cæsar, stands before us with vividness, with transparent clearness, the more distinctly because it was an age in so many ways the counterpart of our own, the blossoming period of the old civilization, when the intellect was trained to the highest point which it could reach. It was an age of material progress and material civilization; an age of civil liberty and intellectual culture;

an age of salons, and of dinner-parties, of Senatorial majorities and electoral corruption. The highest offices of State were open, in theory, to the meanest citizen; they were confined, in fact, to those who had the longest purses, or the most ready use of the tongue on popular platforms. Distinction of birth had been exchanged for distinction of wealth. . . .

"*The free cultivators were disappearing from the soil. The whole country was being absorbed into vast estates, held by a few favoured families and cultivated by slaves, while the old agricultural population was driven off the land, and was crowded into towns.* The rich were extravagant. The occupation of the higher classes was to obtain money without labour and to spend it in idle enjoyment. *Patriotism meant the ascendency of Party.* Religion, once the foundation of the laws and rule of personal conduct, had subsided into opinion. The educated in their hearts disbelieved it. Temples were still built with increasing splendour. But of general belief that life had any serious meaning, there was none remaining beyond the circle of the silent, patient, ignorant multitude. The whole spiritual atmosphere was saturated with cant—cant moral, cant political, cant religious, which flowed on in an increasing volume of insincere and unreal speech. Unless there be a revival in some shape or other, the forces which control the forms in which human beings adjust themselves will make an end again, as they made an end before, of what are called free institutions. Popular forms of government are possible only when duty is of more importance than pleasure, and Justice than material expediency. Rome had grown ripe for judgment."

Let the reader not flatter himself that the Romans had slaves and the English none. Slavery is but a name. Get you behind the *name,* and see into the *fact.* And I tell you that the poorest Roman slave was not so poor as the downtrodden English slave. If there be one reader so ignorant of the things that are passing every day around him as to dream that slavery is dead, here, in free England, let that reader stand for an hour on a freezing winter's day outside a soup kitchen, Or let him go at any time, after nightfall,* down to a free England slum. After that double experience, if he be a truth-loving man, with a fear of God in his heart (with any other mortal I have nought to do; let us go

---

* Pages 84-87.

each our paths in peace and generous pity)—if, after the true and earnest soul has emerged from slum land and soup-kitchen land he should tell me there are no British slaves, then may he be sure there were no Roman slaves, for both were human chattels, bought and sold for coin, the only possible difference being that the Roman slave had always a price—the British too often none.

These were the characteristics of falling Rome :—
1. Parliament majorities and electoral corruption.
2. Political career open to all in theory; but, in fact, open only to money, never mind how acquired; or to speech, never mind how insincere.
3. Patriotism meant the ascendency of party.
4. Religion degenerated into Cant.
5. The people driven off their land and forced into the over-crowded towns.
6. An age of dinner-parties and of material progress.

Progress ! Progress to Heaven ? Or towards night and eternal hell blackness? Reader, you are living in the midst of a Rome as corrupt and as surely falling as that ancient one. Do not treat this history lightly, for it is full of abundant meaning. The author was poor, unknown, despised; so was once a greater, an All-Divine Author.

You need this history most who have thought how fair this English world is. Renan, a wise, though too rhetorical man, has truly said that it is a "common error of society people to think that the world which they see is the entire world. The society man, with his frivolous sneers, passes continually, without knowing it, the man who is going to create the Future." Pass not in that fashion, in your minds, Daniel Martins, Terence Grey, nor Carlyle Democritus. They are not men it is wise or safe to pass. One word more, and I am done : Do not judge this history by a page, a chapter, or by any *part* of it, but only after a perusal of the whole.   H. L.

THE ENGLISH REVOLUTION OF THE TWENTIETH CENTURY.

ADVERTISEMENT.

COUNTRYMEN,

There are things in this book which will cause you to open wide your eyes. There are those amongst you, a fractional, microscopical percentage, to whom such an ocular operation is not unusual; the light of Wisdom will not startle you; you, the seers—neither optimists nor pessimists. To you, my brothers, greeting! To the exceeding multitude I say: Be not dismayed at the novel light, but be admonished. Ye are as those who rise up late, as against the few who waken with the dawn.

Attend all men:

This Book is the WRITING ON THE WALL! Remember, that a hundred years ago there was not one who actually foresaw the Revolution of the French; but to-day there has come one who here foresees the pending Revolution of the English.

VELUTI IN SPECULUM!

D. M.

PART I.
DESTRUCTIVE.

Book I.
REVOLUTION ESTABLISHING ITSELF.

"Behold, I set before you this day a blessing and a curse."—DEUT. xi. 26

CHAPTER I.

UNLEARNED LESSONS. A NEW VISTA OF HISTORY.

History is the encyclopædia of nations, in whose mighty volumes man may discern the penalties and the rewards of human conduct. What are a few of the universal chapters in history's world-pages which are not meaningless? Let us examine one or two, inquiring inwardly first: Is mankind as the grass-blades which grow overnight, and which perish in a day? Are nations like unto the frog in the fable, swelling themselves with vanity until they burst; and if so, why?

Four thousand years ago a certain Nimrod set up the foundation of a mighty nation, and Assur about that time was founding another empire scarcely less great. Where are Babylon and Assyria now? And the Hebrew people were becoming a nationality about that time. We scarcely know where ancient Tyre existed, so completely has her greatness disappeared, yet was she a God-fearing nation once, and so were mysterious Egypt and all-powerful Rome. There is one keynote to all their greatness; there is one keynote to all their littleness. Great empires were founded by the courage and high-mindedness of the early builders; but the nations grew in strength upon one great food alone; something more than courage, fearlessness, and strength, do we require to explain national greatness. These qualities are the stem, the branch, the leaf, whereof godliness is the root and life-giving sap. Examine well, examine with your hearts and with your understandings, and you shall find, never mind how various the forms with which the nations have clothed their lore, religiousness—reliance upon their God, or gods—was the foundation of their greatness. Not mock-reliance, never that. The mock-reliance, the mock-worship, the mock-godliness, conveniently classed as cant, or hypocrisy, are so abundant with us to-day that

B

we need but to look around lightly to discover the poison which sapped the life-blood of all those nations, and which is fast sapping our own. History records this one short, simple ethic to mankind: Justice, truth, sincerity, God-fearingness—and nations grow to greatness, power and wisdom. Injustice, lying, make-believe, mammonism — and nations bleed to exhaustion, decay, and disappear.

Most people learn from their histories that which interests, pleases, or flatters them. They seem studiously to avoid those chapters and pages which, could they but see aright, contain the vital matter, whose teachings duly observed will lead to a nation's future greatness — and the neglect of which will as surely lead to ultimate ruin. If there is one lesson beyond all others which every history sets forth in letters as of blood and fire, that lesson is to be found in its chapters on popular discontent, revolution, and final decadence. There is one study which is, or which should be, the principal pabulum of a statesman, viz. the cause which has led up to those red turbulences; how they might have been avoided; and how the nation which he has sworn to serve may be safely guided far away from similar rocks of injustice and neglect.

French history shows us the frightful penalties inflicted upon king, legislators, and nobles, who believed that self-indulgence, luxury, wanton neglect of all the sweltering wretchedness surrounding them, might fitly usurp the virtues which had raised their nation—and every other nation which has achieved greatness —into power. Regard for the oppressed and weak? Care for the wretched? Food for the hungry? Were not the starving, penurious people, reduced to skin and bone, a very gift from the gods to supply, at nominal wage, their tyrants' wants? Were not their very weakness and exhaustion a guarantee against revolt? For how could worn-out, starving people resist steel swords and grape-shot? And so the rich continued to indulge in luxuries, weltered in fine ambrosial feedings, ignored—where they did not mock—the foodless bodies dragging their miseries in slums provided for them. But kings and courtiers need for ever new gold to pay the cost of all their splendour, and who can better furnish it than these unresisting—unable to resist—down-trodden ones? Yet more and more oppression; yet more and more determination of the flesh-pots not to yield of their store; yet more and more reversal of the law which God had spun His world upon. One law only now prevails, one Psalm of psalms—to *gold* all glory and all worship. Misery, suffering, starvation, hide ye in your beggars' dens, so that we see none of it, and can swear before Eternal Heaven, "Rottenness, starvation, filth, and degradation are NOT EXCEPTIONAL!" Nor *were* they exceptional, had they not become the order of the day? Exceptional! By the Lord of Truth, there rot and starve no more to-day than there starved and rotted yesterday; do not our Blue-Books prove it? 1,976,417 souls starving yesterday, and 1,976,415 souls starving to-day! Do not we *see* less? Do we not cramp the bone and skin things close in their slum-courts and alleys so that we often see them not at all? . . . But yet they *were* seen, those hollow-cheeked, foodless, mortals; He who made them saw them; He who to some is known as the Awful God, the long-suffering and merciful, who visits the sins of the fathers upon "the third and fourth generations" of them that hate Him, and despise His commandments . . . GOD saw their misery, and the wrath of outraged heaven fell upon accursed France: no longer alleys, courts, and slums hived starving souls in compressed filth and want—no longer flaunted wealth and luxury. POVERTY, poverty got himself crowned king; fed himself to bursting; hacked, in bloody wantonness of long-stayed vengeance, the well-fed courtly ones, their sires, and sons, and tender women. "Mercy? Mercy, ye ask? Did ye give mercy to *our* suffering babes and women? The mercy that ye gave to us, that mercy will we give to you." . . . Open that French history page, O statesmen who disregard the cry of misery—open the page and read, and be forewarned—or be fore-doomed.

(1)

History, then, if we look into the sybil-pages aright, has all the lesson of life to teach us. History hitherto has contented itself with a record of the past. History has one hitherto undiscovered power; she can record the story of the future!

These pages shall open up to the English people the history of their immediate future. . . .

Hast thou travelled upon the boundless ocean and seen how the careful pilot, with distance-destroying glass, has anxiously regarded upon the vague horizon the tiny speck, the herald of storm, invisible to ordinary sight? Hast thou not wondered wherefore, in the midst of brightness and of calm, silent and ominous orders spread around; the ship is quietly but determinedly bared of flapping sails, is left a tied and bandaged thing in midocean? But soon have golden lights darkened and lowered into grim forbidding clouds; harsh winds commence to moan around the creaking ropes; soon heaves the worried sea and breaks over the helpless barque; and a fierce, angry tempest threatens ruin—ruin, death, destruction—but for the mariner's timely care!

Reader, it is the time-destroying glass of Wisdom that I have applied to history, and she unfolds to me in solemn prescience the storm sign in the volume of my country's records! Give heed, O mariners, and trim the vessel. Bind up the rotten places with new wood . . . . Give heed to the rotten planks which are drinking in the treacherous waters! . . . . Wait not till the storm be upon you, O captains and helmsmen. Read!

JUBILEE DOGGEREL.

(Anno Jubili, 1887.)

" How much longer will it last, we wonder?

"England was decked from end to end
  With flags and banners gay,
  A thousand bonfires pierced the night,
  Bright lamps lit every way;
  And in our ' England of the Free '
  We kept a Royal Jubilee !
  The crowd was amiable and loyal,
  Its streets were gay and bright. . . .
  But through the loyal, agreeable throng
  A whisper ran—' How long, how long ? '
  Not heard by all. Faintly by some
  Whose loyal heads were bowed ;
  But 'twas as thunder in the ears
  Of some among the crowd—
  Some who abhor the pageantry
  Of this unmeaning Jubilee,
  Some who remember that of old,
  When came the Jubilee,
  The people got their land again,
  And every slave went free.
  What use to decorate your streets
  With flag, and fool, and wreath,
  And hide with gilding all the mass
  Of misery beneath?
  This Jubilee of empty fools
  And loyal prigs and boors. . . .
  The genial gaping imbeciles
  Who shout and cheer and sing
  Might really make sane men despair
  Of doing anything.
  What can a people hope to be
  Who drivel at a Jubilee ?
  Yet every one's not quite asleep,
  And some are wide awake :
  'Tis these make History—not the dolts
  Who shout for shouting's sake—
  'Tis these who see the mass of wrong,
  And mutter low, ' How long, how long ?' "

CHAPTER II.

JUBILEE PERIOD—1880-1894.

THE STATE OF ENGLAND PRIOR TO THE YEAR 1900.

I. JUBILEE PERIOD.

"But consider, while work itself is so scarce . . . . in strange contrast the Jubilee ceremonies, for in general the aspect of Paris presents these two features—Jubilee ceremonials, and scarcity of victual."

CARLYLE.

NEARLY a generation has passed away since the time of the Victorian Jubilee. The spirit of that time having been a very garrulous one, has left behind it a keen impress of blatancy. Happily for the future historian, curious sycophants had worked hard at indices upon the subject. The word "Jubilee" (compiles one exultant sycophant) was printed by the leading newspapers of the day 3,765,293 times within a period of eleven days preceding and succeeding the day of Jubilee. The eulogies to the Sovereign (estimates another sycophant) in the columns of the said journals occupied a space, measured end on, exceeding thirteen miles, five furlongs, and seventeen yards. The abuse heaped by the *Blackswhite* (the name of the Radical leading newspaper) upon the *Whitesblack* (the name of the Tory leading newspaper) during that period and down to the conclusion of the sitting of the Jubilee Parliament and its successors, exhausted the blackest fluid of the three largest ink-manufactories in Britain. But all this is as nothing beside the Parliamentary braying which, growing
(2) apace for a time past, was culminating towards that Jubilee period. Philologists had, to their own satisfaction, proved, by internal evidence as well as by scientific research, that "parler" and "mentir" were the original roots from which the word Parliament had grown. Members, with few exceptions, lost little time in profiting by the flood of rhetoric which such an extension of mean-

ing admitted in their assembly. Truth, earnestness, courage, were qualities which the Jubilee and succeeding Parliaments looked down upon with contempt. Lying, subterfuge, circumlocution, verbiage, were indeed recommendations for a Jubilee statesman. The Prince of Liars, once thought to be the title in ordinary of the Devil, had long since been usurped by the party-leader—Sorrypebble. What he swore to-day he foreswore to-morrow, and the mob, called by Sorrypebble the "Nation" or "Civilized World," —always as discerning, as noble, as discriminating that day in Britain as when such a mob, two thousand years ago in Palestine, chose Barabbas and rejected Jesus,—chose this rhetoric word-machine for Earth-God, and well he served them. (3) (4)

As most of the Jubilee statesmen were cast upon a similar model—verbose, more or less circumlocutory (six-syllable word for lying), the people had little to choose between soft-sawder A or soft-sawder B.

There were at those times some six hundred and seventy "representatives of the people," and historians of the time pay tribute to King David's prophetic lore—had he not said that verily "all men are liars."

Doubtless there were true and fearless men to be found amongst the herd of party-seeking creatures and time-servers rampant in those Parliaments, but one finds not easily their individuality. They stood as much chance of remaining pure in such an atmosphere as a lily dropped in a vat of tar.

The Jubilee noblemen stand next for appreciation—they were a remarkable crew. Many descendants of the most ancient families had publicly sold their ancestors' pictures and libraries to pay for their profligacies; more had figured in law courts or turf scandals, but they were not the worst. The Peerage was constantly increasing and degenerating by new creations from the most venal of the commoners. Of these new creations there were, for instance, the Marquis of Bung—his merit, three millions made out of beer; the Earl of Loanes—merit, money, and only money; the Duke of Sopps—merit, one million made out of beer, and two millions out of selling to the public the dregs of his brewery;* Lord Dreck—merit, constant voting with his party against every scruple of conscience for many years. From the last cause of

---

* Page 434.

creation the House of Lords was becoming so populous that it had been proposed to transfer its sittings to the Albert Hall. Among the hundreds of modern creations may be found a thin percentage of England's bravest soldiers and workers, but they form only an exceptional few. The vast majority were mere political time-servers and place-hunters; or Mammonites grown rich, —never mind how. "There is no merit but servility to party, except successful worship of the material God who rules all parties —Mammon." So much for Jubilee peers. Of Jubilee bishops and minor doctors of the Church, the system being corrupt, the nominees lacked not taint. Christ had ruled that His priests should be poor, humble, and pious men. Mammon ruled: they should be rich, self-assertive, and blatant men; so with park and castle, carriages, and ten, or fifteen thousand pounds a year, these over-paid and over-fed pomposities looked down upon the humble starvelings, who, as rectors or curates in London slums, or country villages, shared misery and starvation* with their wretched flocks.

(5) Of Jubilee Charities there was no lack. Did a little black girl starve in Timbuctoo, a legion of fashionable fools assailed the papers and the post with letters begging collections. Two black men killed by English soldiers in South Africa caused Ministers in Parliament strings of questions, full of rotten sympathy and quack tenderness, whilst the massacre of a whole company of British
(6) soldiers passed unheeded. An eastern Musselman or a western Jew was sought as convert and as prize for heaven at any cost.
(7) Missions to here, missions to there, missions to everywhere, except
(8) to the narrow slum where the white man starved, and the children,
(9) foodless, pined; millions to convert the savage, who hails his brother savage as a fellow-man to live or to die with him. Missions to far Cathay to convert an inconvertible people to the blessedness of drink, to the saintliness of cant; whilst one-tenth part of the sums, defrayed upon the poor gutter savages, had reared poor starving Christian children to honesty and worth,
(10) instead of letting them descend through misery and crime unto the gallows.

Ah! It was a Jubilee—the Jubilee of CANT.

And the Devil, looking forth from hell that day, chuckled mightily.

---

* Pages 84-7, 324.

II. JUBILEE AND PENALTY.

But Nature has silent laws which circumscribe the growth-power of everything; the laws are mighty and eternal; they work slowly, even with a terrible, mysterious, and awful slowness sometimes; and her time-limit to abuses works slowest of them all. Slowly does Nature cover the neglected field with weeds and rankness—she long awaits the thrifty husbandman. Before such dank vegetation grows as to unfit the field for human labour, Ages pass. Her final wildness, as of moorland or of jungle-growth, at last defies the husbandman, and only submits to fire and axe. Yet the jungle knows its limits; its brambles grow not into trees, nor its grasses into shrubs; and its trees send not their roots to hell for sustenance, nor do their branches flaunt the heavens in defiance. Nature has set laws, mysterious but discernible, in the soul of man. Man's wisdom, like the trees, may stretch forth proudly, sucking the richness of earth and air, yet can his powers not reach beyond the limit of that which is good for him to know. Science and metaphysics, dream their votaries, will pass the limit; but, like elder-trees in the growth, their stems are hollow, their seeming strength but vanity. And with Man as with Nature, where the husbandman abandons and neglects his field, a jungle also sprouts with time—slowly yet surely, and is not curable but by axe and fire.

When the fields grow no more corn and pasture, but are left to weeds and thorns for game and deer; when the human soul forgets the truth, and cultivates the false, is it not time to inquire the penalty? (11)

Shall the jungle grow till, through the clouds, it suck the ocean dry? Shall lies expand and thicken until God's laws are made invisible to man? There *are* eternal laws, and men must learn them. If men ignore them, there is penalty!

When a bishop, the religion gone out of him, representative of a tenet which he believes not, draws from the realm a princely pay, lives in a palace, his work pretence, while the true priest starves on a beggar's mite for noble work, which wears out heart and hope, there will be penalty!

When the worthless descendant of the worthless son of a former worthless king, be-titled duke, or lord, or earl, sucks from a nation's wealth huge pay for a lying office which need not exist, for work that was never done,* whilst the money which pays him is drawn from the funds of toiling and hard-worked men, their lot often to starve in hard times, there will be penalty!

When a duke, or an earl, or a lord, or other son of Mammon, extorts in rent from lands which the people make rich, which their toil has gone to enhance; when that wealth is drawn from the Nation to profit that single one, to feed his ease and luxury, and to work no good in the world, whilst a million toilers starve and find neither work nor bread, there will be penalty.

When five hundred lordly peers, your bishops amongst the crowd, and six hundred representative legislators, but pother, and bluster, and rant, guile ignorant folk with lies, and seek but their own sole weal; when the lot of them hunt but for place and power, only full of their own concern, heed not their people, bow only to vulgar wealth, make laws which ignore the most helpless, tie up yet tighter and stronger all wealth in gold and in land to an idle and thriftless few, whilst the million sweating toilers struggle and starve, filling the land with woe, there will be penalty!

. . . .

(12) Yearly the Parliament publishes a thin and ominous record like a leaf from a battle field. It tells of the men and the women, even children swell the score, who have died in the streets, on dust-heaps, in barns, of STARVATION. Think, O ye lords, not one or two, but scores. In London alone twice a score. And where by Government computation forty souls have thus wasted to death, know ye the numbers dying like this of whom the Government gives not a record? And know ye the thousands who for every one of these die a death which is more terrible still, a slower (13) and crueller lingering with wives and children lingering too?

In the richest centre of this large city, in its grandest and broadest square, at that Jubilee time were sleeping in mid-winter, on stones, cast down in despair, men and women and children (14) foodless, and none to care.

In winter, year after year, beseechings and prayers abound, "Give us work, O ye governors, Work. Let us feed our young (15) ones and live." But ever the same cowardly answer, the lying (16) promise which statesmen invent: "We'll consider, consider." Season and session pass on, verbiage, debates, and mere barren cant. Seasons and sessions roll on, and the Lords and Commons for ever pile up a mass of insensate 'laws' binding, protecting, the rich man's wealth, and ignoring the millions who starve.

* Page 309.

CHAPTER III.

THE NEW REVOLUTIONISTS.

"To see so many millions of hands that would be industrious all idle and starving: oh, if I were legislator of France for one day, I would make these great lords skip again!"—ARTHUR YOUNG. *At the Time of the French Revolution. Quoted by Carlyle.*

THE Parliament afforded no help. They held this argument: "Yearly the people starve; the misery is wide, is deep; but has not this *always* been? Come, Griffin, and bring thy figures. Prove to this ravenous crew that if five million and seventy souls lie low in workless misery, last year five million and seventy-one were even in similar plight—distress is NOT EXCEPTIONAL. 'Twas the same the year before!" (17)

Giddy and mazed, as if drunk with woe, the hapless throngs increase, hidden in slums of filth and mire, in misery running deep. No help, despair, will no one come, is God no longer Lord?

Slowly grow the weeds and the jungle when man refuses to till, but sure and strong and deadly abandoned but long enough; and wild and poisonous life is breeding where flowers had grown before. Sleep on, ye besotted governors, sunk deep in your search after place. Riches and power are strong—Liberals, Tories, Radicals, a sorry sickening crew, reviling and cursing each other, and the Irish befouling all three. "Tax wealth as wealth?" said ministers. "Reduce large holdings in land? Set workless men to till Colonial fields now idle? Australia, wide as Europe, crying aloud for labour, labour starving here crying aloud for work? What is all that to us? We make prisons, gallows, and workhouses; hide sorrow and misery there!" There were those who believed that the land had been stolen from them—the people—that wealth had been robbed from their toil. Hearken to the voices of these as they preach in dark alleys and barns. But before we enter one of these weird halls of wretchedness, let us speak of the men whom we shall meet in them. (18)

(19)
(20) The Victorian era had produced many remarkable men. It had given birth to one or two who for godliness of purpose, depth of genius, self-sacrificing sincerity, soul's devotion to the divinity within them and to humanity beyond, may in future ages perhaps be equalled, but in all time be never excelled. In their literature they had had their Christ in Carlyle; war had given them Gordon; and the social problem had called forth a sort of Luther-Bunyan in action—William Booth.

(21) It is with the third we have to deal. Cæsar commanded not an army more adoring him than William Booth. Each was a soldier's general, each has left posterity his commentaries. There let comparison end. For Cæsar Booth towers as high above the other Cæsar as any valiant saviour of men above their slayer—both being in soul and purpose equal.

"When a mere child, the degradation and helpless misery of the poor workers of my native town, wandering gaunt and hunger stricken, crowding the workhouse, toiling like galley-slaves for bare subsistence, kindled my heart," says Booth in his Commentaries.

That infinite sympathy grew with the child's growth, strengthened with his manhood's strength. His whole life was a labour to undo the evils of soulless state-craft. It was not given him to see the apotheosis of his sublime ideal. But it was given him to see the completion of an organisation second to none that the world has ever seen: "Thousands are ready at my call and under my direction to labour to the very utmost of their strength for the salvation of others without the hope of earthly reward. Of the practical common-sense, the resource, the readiness of every form of usefulness of my officers and soldiers, the world has no conception. Still less is the world capable of understanding the height and depth of their self-sacrificing devotion to God and to the Poor." Those were his officers. He thus describes his army: "They (the soldiers) are recruited from the poorest of the poor. It is a religious body. Its condition of service is implicit and unquestioning obedience. The Salvation soldier is taught to obey as is the soldier on the field of battle."

And the Battle is the Battle of Life—the battle against Misery, Starvation, and Disease. Cromwell had one thousand Ironsides, Booth had a hundred thousand. In Booth's lifetime his officers numbered over ten thousand, spread throughout Great

Britain and her Colonies and the world. Of the numbers of the rank and file some idea may be gathered from the fact that a collection raised by them in one week from amongst themselves —the poorest of the poor—produced over £20,000.

An enumeration, made two years before the outbreak of the Revolution, gave 25,000 officers, 200,000 regulars, and 5,000,000 rank and file. This classification had been unknown in General Booth's time; it had been introduced by one Carlyle Democritus, of whom presently.

After the death of General Booth and the resignation of his successor, a vastly different spirit to that originally prevailing had become diffused throughout his army. Its discipline was more perfect and more absolute than ever; its obedience more "implicit and unquestioning," even, than in the brightest days of its first great General's authority. Day by day, and year by year, the heart-throb of this God-fearing soldiery grew louder and more devoted. And day by day, and year by year, the misery and the wretchedness they were slaving to allay waxed and increased in spite of them. Until one officer commenced to question of another, Is there no readier method than the bootless one of prayer and importunity to bring wealth and poverty to a juster knowledge of each other? There was one particular officer who suggested a solution, and with it every member of the staff became illumined and identified, until each one deemed himself the originator of it. He who was its author had come amongst them, as was common in the Salvation Army, under a name assumed. He called himself Carlyle Democritus.

There was a certain Democritus, contemporary with Confucius; he flourished some five hundred years before Christ. He had been a great traveller, had reduced himself to poverty in search of wisdom. His disregard for mere wealth, his close application to study, and his contempt for the vanities of mankind, had raised him many enemies, and they sought (says an old tradition) to lock him up for a madman, and a Court physician was ordered to examine the philosopher. The task fell to the great Hippocrates, and *his* verdict was that the courtiers were insane, but not Democritus. Similarly was our wise and gentle Harrington (the author of "Oceana") treated by that beast-king, Charles II., and for similar reasons, also provoking from the philosopher a similar reply (after foul and cruel imprisonment), "They are mad who think me so." The new Democritus had also travelled, and infinitely wider than the ancient one, he had devoted all his energy since College days to that and to study. After returning home, he had (22) bought himself a seat in Parliament. This is quite accurate. True, the system was not called "Bribery and Corruption," but it *was* that nevertheless, only much more complicated than the older method. The accounts of Democritus lie all before me as I write, and show in detail the expenditure entailed upon him by his candidature. Here are some of the items:—

Paid to the Local Election Committee towards general expenses, £850. Six hundred and seventy-three donations and subscriptions to Charities, Hospitals, Bazaars, Concerts-in-aid-of-, Cricket Clubs, Workmen's Clubs, Smoking Concerts, and other deserving institutions of the borough and county, £2850. Cost of "Registration Expenses," borne by the candidate for three years, £780. Return of Election expenses required by law to be made to the returning officer, £350. Balance of Election expenses not included in the said return, but too well known to every ordinary election victim, to larger or lesser extent, £790. To agent and other "voluntary" and "honorary" (23) workers, at sufficient interval from the Election, £500. Carlyle Democritus had sighed for the older days of *acknowledged* bribery and corruption, for he reckoned he could have given £2 a head to every one of his constituents, and been less mulcted than upon the existing system. For, to add to his bleeding, the other side appealed against his return—ineffectually, it is true—but still the law sucked two big thousands out of his pocket, not to mention an action which he was compelled to bring against his opponent (since he was not permitted the privilege of horse-whipping him) (24) for having published an abominable libel against him, and which case he also "won," and saw his traducer condemned in a heavy fine and costs, but which nevertheless left him out of pocket several additional thousands. To nothing of that did his family object, for that was the established order of things, but, unfortunately for their peace, it was precisely on that account that Democritus, after a few years' intimate acquaintance with politics and politicians, threw up the "safe seat" which was now his own. Worse still, he threw up his palaces in town, and his castles in the country; threw up his name inherited from kings, and vowed to work out the people's salvation, or perish in the attempt. Therefore was it that he became subjected by his family to an ordeal like that which his namesake had had to suffer, and with a similar result. He had sacrificed a great insignia, had determined to devote the revenues of a huge inheritance to the outcasts of his people, instead of squandering them on Piccadilly heroines, or ballet or music-hall celebrities. A ducal peer had shot himself for want of sources to invest the last half million of his accumulations. That was pardonable. But who could forgive the investment of a patrimony in a vast attempt to solve the Social Problem? (25)

Professor Huxley was a great man in those days, and not a Peer, nor even a politician, but a really learned Professor. Even he decided, to his own and the great TIMES's satisfaction, that the methods of the mercy-loving, self-sacrificing, and devoted William Booth, and his scheme of aid for the utterly destitute and despairing, was comparable to the thrice-damned hideousness of an Ignatius Loyala, arch-author of the Jesuitries of the Spanish Inquisition—beastliest fiend-mortal who ever desecrated this God's earth. The master-stroke of the worthy Professor (which he quite cooed over) was his definition of the Salvation Army as "Corybantic Christianity." He did not doubt that that classical illustration would as effectually confound the entire forces of General Booth as Fielding's application of "Isosceles Triangle," obfusticated the mythical Irish lady. The learned Professor had probably forgotten that the Corybantes, as well as affecting the wild musical and other methods common to the Salvationists, were accredited with the education of Jupiter himself. But let us give the Professor credit, for that he did add in that same criticism these penetrating words: "It is not to be doubted that unless the irremediable misery is effectually dealt with, the hordes of vice and pauperism will destroy modern civilisation." The great "Thunderer" of those days printed in large type that veritable prophecy, of which this history is about to record the fulfilment. (26)

In spite of all discouragement, Carlyle Democritus joined the Salvationists—nor could any doctor be got to pronounce him other than "eccentric." There was no Hippocrates, in the Jubilee time, great and candid enough to call the noble family mad.

CHAPTER IV.

CARLYLE DEMOCRITUS.

Amongst the many strange letters which reached the Salvation Army headquarters towards the year 19..., a general council was one day summoned to consider a communication of peculiar importance. After reciting the causes which had led the writer to desire to cast in his lot with the great General and his officers, the letter went on to say: ". . . I ask, then, to be accepted as a probationer for two years, during which time you permit me unrestrained intercourse with the officers and men of your establishments in all parts of the world, especially in the colonies and dependencies of our Empire. Should my purpose change after the two years, I undertake to preserve inviolate whatever information during that time I may have gathered, and to hand over to the General, for the use and furtherance of the Salvation Army, the sum of £100,000 absolutely, and this sum shall be deposited with the bankers of the Army on the day of signature of our deed. On the other hand, should my present purpose be sustained after my two years' experience, I purpose to devote my entire inheritance to the service of the Army upon conditions mutually to be agreed."

It was decided to invite the author of the missive to attend a Council meeting, at which the General, Secundus Booth, presided. The interview lasted for some hours, and resulted in the adoption of the candidate, but the General declined any pecuniary deposit or undertaking whatsoever. The words of the brave master may well be transmitted to posterity : " Brother," he said—" for brother you are now become—we cannot permit that you bring to your task any other pledge than that which all our brethren here have brought—a heart, a mind, a will, undivided—and devoted before the all-merciful God to the salvation of our suffering people. If after two years, or less or more than two years, you still can love the work and our cause, we will love and welcome you. If, however, it shall be that your purpose change, from any cause not now foreseen, all that we ask is that you part from us in peace and goodwill, leaving us your sympathy, or, if that may not be, your silence. . . . Brother Carlyle Democritus, from to-day we admit you to our fullest confidence ; we are one and all convinced of your devotion, your enthusiasm, and your sincerity." . . . The organ in the great hall, at a sign from the General, gave forth the inaugural chant, and the formal installation of the neophyte followed.*

. . . .

The purpose of Democritus and of the Salvation Army being the reverse of that pursued by the Catholic Church, of advertising noble converts to her fold when she gets them, and not unfrequently when she gets them not, no one was made acquainted that Colonel, the Marquis of Dære, had retired from His Majesty's army, had gone abroad, and had returned as Carlyle Democritus— later to be elected General-in-Chief of the Salvation Army.

It is not the province of this history to follow Democritus in his wanderings at home and abroad amongst outcast humanity, nor to follow him step by step in his masterful conversion of the Salvationist into a stern and well-drilled soldier ; how he instituted, side by side with the slum drill of these self-sacrificing troops, physical drill also; how he disseminated his troops in every district throughout the Empire ; how he enlisted in his devoted ranks every poor enthusiast in the country ; how he sent his best and staunchest men as recruits into the army, navy, and police, until there was not a regiment in all Britain, nor a vessel on the seas, whose men in numbers bore not beneath the scarlet and the blue the fiery cross of the Salvationist tattooed upon their breasts. The old and noisy demonstrations of the Salvationists had given place to gentler and more winning methods. They carefully eschewed all conflicts with those who disagreed with their aggressiveness. Street processions, except in districts where they entirely prevailed, were altogether discontinued. They still continued, and more widely than before, the "conversion" of the submerged, but less obtrusively, and therefore more effectually.

. . . .

---

* See Archives of the Revolutionary Army, published by Order in Council after the Restoration.

When the new organisation of Democritus was complete; when, throughout the length and breadth of the Empire, the cross of the Salvationist glowed on every bosom of the General's multitudinous followers, then, upon a given day, early in the year 19—, the order was promulgated to gradually spread forth the doctrine of the League of the Social Revolution. Very slowly, at first, was the warm mystery allowed to spread; from the General-in-Chief to the Generals of Divisions, thence to the Colonels, Majors, Captains, and Lieutenants; then, with ever deeper caution, to the more trusted of the Regulars, and downward to the rank and file. To these last was committed but sufficient to arouse in them a vague but real hope, and their task was to draw others to them in sympathy from outside their actual ranks.

February the 14th, 19—, was the day fixed for raising the standard of revolt. Meanwhile various committees were formed throughout the country, who received verbal instruction from the Central Committee. Only Generals of Divisions received written orders, and these in code, which each had committed to memory, and of which no written record has ever been discovered.

A new element had been introduced into the Salvationist Army—a sort of lay preachers, quite distinct from the spiritual teachers. They were drawn entirely from amongst those who had actually suffered the pangs of privation and starvation. For this purpose Carlyle Democritus had recruiting officers in all directions: a would-be suicide, a repentant gallows mite, a sinner in despair, the wretched anywhere who showed one spark of feeling and humanity, were his choice recruits. Many a desperate father, bewailing his starved wife or child, was saved from self-destruction by a word from Democritus. "Brother," he would say, as some poor wretch was brought before him, and left alone with him, "touch my hand, and with it my heart. I suffer together with you. Your grief is my grief; come to me; help me to save others from this death-life which insensate governors have brought on you and them. Let the pure soul of your lost one at rest in heaven shed light upon your efforts, until, thy duty done, God calls thee, and me also, to share His eternal peace." There was no lack of such stricken ones. Too awful an abundance of them filled the avenues of poverty on all sides. These preachers of revolt, or, to use their own words, "of a new salvation"—for the actual purpose was not divulged until the vast train was ready to be fired—wore not the Salvationist uniform. Their only distinguishing mark was a scarlet cross, worn on the left shoulder of the coat, bearing the words underneath, "For God and the People." It was not from any spirit of economy, but only of policy, that this branch of the Salvation workers continued externally to appear, as inwardly they were, of and with their audiences. Carlyle Democritus himself lived in the Salvation Army Shelters, not only because he despised all luxury, but he had vowed—and had registered his vow in a manifesto to his army—that until he had rendered possible to every worker in Great Britain "labour, food, and home," and established that as his countrymen's undying right, he would live the life of the suffering masses around him. This marvellous devotion not only brought him into the heart of hearts of his ever-increasing followers, but his habit of constantly changing from Shelter to Shelter familiarised his person to them all, and helped to inculcate in them something of his own exalted patience, forbearance, and courage. He could not stay the ragged worshippers from falling on their knees in unconscious adoration as he entered their dismal halls; but he knelt also, and his mighty voice, rich in reverence, love, and sympathy, rang out in the solemn stillness of the night—"To every one of us, O God, according as we serve and love each other." This simple, eloquent prayer, uttered in the intense emotion first evoked by the men's grand devotion to him, pealed at last throughout the hearts of millions, like a giant diapason, and ended by making them a mighty company of God-devoted men. He rose in the morning before the men were astir, for he was always at Headquarters before dawn.

It was by the ceaseless devotion, perfection of organisation, genius, and inspiration of such a man, that the loyal, brave, well-disciplined forces, military and civil, of the State became gradually but surely permeated with a leaven of revolt so thorough that, at the application of the touch-word on that memorable 14th of February, the gigantic machinery of the State became reversed as facilely as a floating warship to the "Port," or "Starboard" of her commander.

CHAPTER V.

THE WAR-DOGS OF TERENCE GREY.

THERE was also under the command of Carlyle Democritus a band of men trained by one of those fierce spirits which times of revolution never fail to produce. As from the ranks of this band issued the most ardent organisers of the starving multitudes, it will be well to briefly sketch the career of their chief. The "war-dogs" of Terence Grey were a set of men rendered wild and exasperate by suffering and sorrow, physical or moral, or both. Grey had collected them round him, and imbued them with his own devil-spirit, compound of savage despair and uncompromising self-sacrifice. No man was admitted to his League unless he subscribed to a vow of unhesitating obedience to the chief and his officers. The object of the League was briefly declared to be :—

    1. Abolition of Money-Government.
    2. Establishment of Merit-Government.
    3. Relentless justice upon those who had fostered and defended the oppression of the poor.
    4. Deliverance of the submerged people.

The band of war-dogs, as they called themselves (not without meaning, as will shortly appear), would have brought about a revolution had there not been a Carlyle Democritus; but it would have been a wild revolution of mere revenge, a second Reign of Terror, leaving the social problems which had called it into being only purged of one form of abuse, in more or less hideous fashion, but open to no wisdom of subsequent remedy. Happily, the leader of this fierce contingent fell under the magic influence of Carlyle Democritus, and instead of wasting its great energies in mere butcheries, the wise general caused its men to be gradually dispersed through the ranks of his own more disciplined forces. The leader of this band was one named Terence Grey, who in earlier years looked more like a dreamy poet than a soldier; had more the appearance of a suffering Christ than of a son of Mars. Yet the once bright painter of word and other pictures—for he could use pen and brush with equal skill—had become the fiercest and bravest lieutenant of the Revolutionary Army, and was always held accountable, he and his troops, for the terrible scenes which took place at a later date outside the slum prisons.* Grey had been a quiet, peace-loving student in his earlier life, with a strange notion that things were not as they ought to be, and whatever he wrote or painted was tinged with a half-savage melancholy which brought him more fear than admiration. He was of high family, and enjoyed an independent income, which he spent for the most part, after supplying his wants in books, paint, and brushes, in the courts and alleys of Slumland, amongst the poor little wasted children, over-abundant there. He was a familiar figure in half the slums of London; he was an altogether undiscerning and mischievous philanthropist. He filled the slum children's stomachs with cakes and sweets, and taught them an appetite for more, which neither he nor any other had power to satisfy. He would go down an alley just able to walk for his burden of pennies, and would come back with his pockets turned inside out, that being the only signal upon which the children would permit him to retreat. None of these little ones ever went to church; churchmen seldom came to them, so the little things readily got to believe that he *was* the Christ, whose picture he somewhat resembled; their mothers told them that it was so, and that was why he loved little children. One day it happened that a simple, frail, by no means beautiful maiden met him home-going from such a journey. "Oh, Mr Grey," said she, "is that you? After so many years, do you remember me?" Grey remembered having casually met the little lady, and with an abundance of pity in his weak heart for the troubled look in the face before him, and the poor appearance of her garments, he felt — ashamed — his empty pockets, and dared not inquire how it fared with her. He saw with pain that there was cruel poverty here as well as in his slum-regions. They met frequently, until nearer intimacy prompted him to try, in a gentle, delicate, helpful way, to lighten her distress. But no urgings of friendship could gain him permission to afford

---

* Page 90.

such help. He admired what he thought was her pride, had neither wisdom nor experience enough to know that it was only design. The maid soon began to worship him in a more earnest way than that of the little slum children.

"Take me altogether, Terence; then you shall help me as your heart would wish." Now Grey felt pity, which his poetry might liken to love, but which he knew was far enough from that passion; he felt an unaccountable distrust in her presence, for which his sensitive heart rebuked him directly he was alone; then he would write to her forthwith some exquisite letter of contrition, which she mistook for evidence of her power, although the maiden was neither simple nor innocent. So for long months letters of that sort were exchanged, interspersed with occasional interviews. And this went on until a day arrived when they told him there was trial and poverty in the home of the maid, and he sent generous help, in a manner more generous still. But the simple, confiding maiden, full of adoring words and lip-worship, would have the poet and not the poem, and she wrote him coyly that she was used to poverty, which had ever been allied to her, and she only wished she was as near to him. After two years of silly struggle, she refusing any other way to help, Grey went to the maiden, as other Adams have done. Time passed, and fame came to Terence Grey. He had painted a great picture of his slum children—a wide group of little suffering souls cramped in their cruel mud-courts, and in the background, in death-struggle, the gaunt figures of Crime and Death grappled with each other to clutch them. He called his picture "The Babes in the Wood—The Modern Version." The Academy hung the picture on the line, and all London echoed the name of Terence Grey. One morning, shortly after his fame, a strange lawyer came to his studio, sent by the simple maid, to demand "Money, Marriage, or Lawsuit." A third had come on the scene, a poet or non-poet.

When Grey was sought for on the morrow, he was not found, but this bit of a letter instead: "I only had money to give the woman from the first, but she would not have it without me; now she wants the money, and *not* me. Give it her. One crime shall not make two. Nature wants a devil, not a man, to cope with the evils of the slum world; and I am become that devil."

And the simple maid went with the other man.

Down into the thickest of the poverty-stricken districts went Grey, in grim humour changing his name to Black. He had left himself just enough to live upon, but as his influence over the dangerous people he worked with grew, he shared his little with them, and, their numbers increasing, at last their chief store of food became a strange one. They found they could maintain health and strength on dog-biscuits, and from this, their chief article of diet, they got to call themselves in irony, "War-Dogs." When Carlyle Democritus first met Leader Black, as his men called him, he had some ten thousand of these war-dogs in train. They joined their forces to the Salvation troops, and Terence Grey became one of the Chief Staff Officers to the General.

From the ranks of these determined men went forth the principal preachers of the Revolution. They left no court or alley unvisited. One of their methods was to collect together the most horrible examples of slum misery and degradation. On their platforms were to be found no "eloquent honourable gentlemen," but more forcible eloquent products of the result of government by "honourable and right honourable gentlemen"—frozen women and men, emaciated and half-naked children, corpses of any who had died from want. No Hell-scene of Poet Dante surpassed in grim horror the awful reality of one of their "Hunger Meetings," as they called them, or "Parliaments of Despair." Let us now enter one of their poor meeting-houses, or rather barns, and listen to one of their Parliaments of Despair.

CHAPTER VI.

HOUNDING DESPAIR INTO DESPERATION.

"HUNGER HALL" is a filthy, bare, dismantled barn of considerable dimensions. It is night. The dismal place is faintly lighted at one end, where is a sort of platform, upon which are ranged appalling attenuations of human figures, circled round a tall, gaunt, famished-looking man, who is addressing with wild enthusiasm some thousands of still wilder, hungrier looking men and women. We must try and hear what this speaker says. This is one of those meetings which preceded for some time the outbreak of the Revolution. They had been held in all the large towns of England, Scotland, and Ireland, and were continued to within a day preceding the outbreak. This particular meeting is one of the last held by the organisers of the Revolutionary League, a full report of which may be found in the Revolution journals of those times, where also appear detailed accounts of similar meetings held in most of the important labour centres. The ghastly figures which surrounded the speaker had not been difficult to gather together. Although the number of meetings, at which similar incitements to popular frenzy were employed, needed many thousands of such victims to starvation and privation, there was no lack of them; there was indeed only too fearful and abundant a supply. Ever since Jubilee Year, scores upon scores of such were to be found in every alley of Slumland. The speaker is one of the minor officers of the Revolutionists. It is evident he has been one of the unemployed. His haggard cheeks bespeak not over-fedness; nor the tattered garments any amplitude of wardrobe. In strange contrast to his rags, and almost ominous, is a scarlet cross on the left shoulder of his coat. A sombre air of silence pervades the eager, listening multitude; the speaker has worked them into a dangerous pitch of excitement, but it shows itself less in open shouts and gesticulations, than in occasional half-suppressed galvanic hisses and groans, sometimes rising into a shriek of hate, as if a hell-gate had opened suddenly, and howled forth shouts of defiance —as one after another of the wretched victims of starvation is held up to the audience, with short and meaningful introduction. He has just drawn a ragged shawl from a woman scarcely able to stand for weakness and exhaustion; at her feet are barefoot children, nearly naked, shivering with cold and hunger. "Look, O my brothers, this is a woman, made in the likeness of God, and this is her man, and these five her children ; this shawl is her only covering, threadbare and filthy enough. Look, see the sunken eye, and the breast but skin ; see the babe not feeding, it's dead. . . . Look again, it's five months born and three hours dead, the mother a-dying, starved ; and these seven have shared a rotten crust in three-and-twenty hours. Brothers, they are the representatives of thirteen rookeries, of one hundred and twenty rooms (tenements they call them, friends), the homes of seven hundred as wretched and starving as these, owned by a Peer! Howl, my brothers, ay, (29) howl; but nay, quiet ; dawn comes, for soon will the blackness be complete.—But wait ; this one here is Dorothy, the fair-haired little maid of old Jenks. . . . him as was working for forty years, and was turned off with the December lot, eleven hundred of them, from the Government Yards in the winter months to starve. (30) Jenks cut his throat, for he couldn't see his wife starve, nor the girl. The mother lies there, dead of want, and this one's a-going fast. Look at her, brothers, look at her ; she's had a basin o' soup since yesterday morn. . . . These three boys won't last long. We found them huddling their dead mother for warmth, unfed for twenty hours. Who said pity? Down with him—Revenge! Revenge, O my brothers, Revenge ! But look here. We took this thing from a Bishop's carriage. Look, it's a girl. Never mind her tears ; see her fine silks and the soft white clothes. That's a Vicar of Christ's young child, that is. He's one of yer rulers, he is. . . . Lead her safely out, and take her to the Christly Palace of Humility, you, Jim, over at Lambeth there; her time ain't come just yet. . . . You glance once more, my brothers, at these. This is a frozen corpse—frozen to death in one of Webster's garrets. It's a woman of seventy-three. Her clothes are two sacks, deftly sewn. She was working for threepence a day to feed herself and son. This is the son ; broke his arm some three weeks ago stacking bricks. He's thirty, and weighs six stone. . . .

Brothers, this is a meeting of which, all over the country, at this very day and hour, many are being held. This picture of weltering misery here upon these boards is a type of the want and the woe which is crushing the souls of millions of our people. We've tried, and we've tried, and we've tried to make those Lords of Westminster legislate for our rights—but we'll leave the jawing to them. Our time has come to WORK! Hold up your hand, each man, who wills to die short and quick, as lief as this lingering "— and a thousand fists shot wild and grim through the air.

"Soldiers of the New Revolution, meet here to-morrow. Women, who have no fear to die for the Cause, give sign by lifted hand. Good! To-morrow also be here, the head uncovered, the hair in a knot at the top; you who have babes are to stand first." And, dragging their miseries slowly away, the crowd disappeared in the night. Although the last of these meetings were summoned and held in great privacy, the earlier ones had been public enough. But what were such scenes to a Government—a Government just back from its partridge-shootings? There is a strange hardening of the head and heart of the Government. It *would* not, until it *could* not, see. It remained as blind to all these warnings as before it had been deaf to appeal.

But there was passing one man through these scenes like a giant spirit of hope. Fierce and morose to all others, the crowd yielded meekly to him. The "worthless," the "abandoned," bowed to him and blessed him as he passed; rotting, starving, wretched all of them, but veneration yet possible to them, gratitude, love. Strong men touched him in reverence; the coarsest were quiet when he came. No ordinary Salvationist he. The tall, strong figure of him was familiar, not only to the denizens of London slums and hunger meetings, but throughout the length and breadth of the three kingdoms he was known and venerated by the fiercest and most dangerous of the exasperated people. Attired in a plain, black military-looking suit, and cap which bore the Salvation Army badge, but which he only wore when visiting amongst the people, the Chief of the Salvation Army, like the great general he proved to be, left no detail of his vast organisation unvisited. His face and form were known to every stricken wretch throughout the land. The sinewy strength of the man, his fervid eloquence, his still more eloquent silence, his undying devotion to the struggling masses, linked all men to him with a fierce, indissoluble bond. He was their giant spirit of hope, where before had been only despair. Throughout the millions whom his Salvation soldiers had infused with his and their own never-failing sympathy, and whom his great pattern swayed, there was never one who would ask in vain a brother Salvationist to share his crust with him. The women and children simply worshipped him. The roughest jail-bird had no evil word for him.

In form and feature he appeared a very messenger of love and sympathy to them all. Though still young, the pale, earnest brow was already furrowed by care and by sorrow. As he spoke some gentle word of hope or sympathy to the suffering wretches with whom his daily labours brought him in contact, his countenance would unbend with more than a woman's tenderness. His large, dark, hazel eyes were deep and silent as Truth's well, and, when the black, draping lashes were upraised, they shone fierce and piercing as a flaming judgment sword. The full lips seemed to press each other into constrained silence, but withal bespoke an eloquence as lofty as their intense compression presaged a supernal power of will. Habitually his expression was that of some dread herald of a *dies iræ*. The people knew him as General Carlyle; he had taught them so to worship the name of England's Sage, that in the end they fixed upon him the name which to them conveyed all earthly honour and glory. He had been installed General-in-Chief of the Salvation Army as Carlyle Democritus, and as Carlyle Democritus he continued to be known throughout the country. At first an endeavour had been made to conceal his origin, but it was impossible to disguise his extraordinary personality, nor was it with less worship that the people finally learned that one of England's greatest noblemen had yielded up rank, place, and wealth, and devoted himself and his inheritance to an organisation which to him embodied the noblest attempt the world had ever seen to combat neglect and misery as universal as they were criminal. When he was elected General-in-Chief there went up a shout of *real* jubilee, far different from that fabricated one of "Eighty-Seven."

CHAPTER VII.

ORGANISATION.

WE have glanced at the lay element which the new General had introduced into the Salvation Army organisation. This had not superseded the religious element; he too deeply realised and valued the intensity of the craving of the human soul for spiritual as well as material succour. The two great ministrations of humanity worked side by side, hand in hand, and heart to heart. The authorities did not take alarm at his deep and wide-spreading influence. These and other signs and wonders fell on blind, unheeding Governors. Nor had the sense of security in any way left the upper classes. There had been riotous outbreaks in the streets for years past, but they had been easily suppressed, and (31) these were never countenanced by the Salvation Army. On the contrary, Carlyle Democritus's entire policy was one of silent, patient working, preparation, organisation. His was not the restless, asinine simmer of the shallow demagogue or frothy agitator. But like the profound travail of the ocean depths, of the seismic-gathering; like the silent, unseen concentrating of the pregnant hurricane, inaudible before its mighty burst—so he gathered and concentrated the giant forces of the angry multitude, until the time should be ripe for the overwhelming mass to assert its storm-power. There had been murmuring heard amongst the troops, including even the picked regiments of the Guards. Indeed, disaffection in the Army had gone beyond mere murmuring, and incipient mutiny had displayed itself abroad as well as (32) at home. But the heart and ear of man are more intimately attuned than the thoughtless are aware, and when the heart minds not the moan of misery, its hardness quickly deadens the infinitely less sensitive tympanum; so stolid statesmen were content to exert all their cunningest ingenuity to invent excuses as mendacious as they were fallacious. "For to him that hath shall be given and to him that hath not shall be taken away even that which he seemeth to have," and thus to the merciful come (although the coming be delayed) love, affection, loyalty and devotion; and to the merciless, distrust, abhorrence, hatred, and revolt. No official or non-official believed, or even imagined, that the periodic winter gatherings of clamorous, starving hordes, displaying their rags and wasted forms in hungry groups wherever a soup-kitchen doled out merciful, but almost useless charity, or at meetings in Trafalgar Square and other thoroughfares, meant anything serious to the established order of things. Indeed, was not the established order of things declared by Sorrypebble's greatest law-minister to be that "the most dire distress and poverty, side by side with the great accumulation of wealth, was a universal law"? Whether (33) of God, Devil, or Sorrypebble that " UNIVERSAL LAW," the record sayeth not.

A few thoughtful people may have considered that perhaps an extra policeman was not an altogether wanton luxury, and it was not uncommon in some great households to find a constable, generally in plain clothes, amongst the inside or outside staff. (34)

The trained bands of Carlyle Democritus worked noiselessly. Scarcely had the thousands of his patrols been even noticed, though for months, towards the end of 19—, they had patrolled in and about the squares and streets of the wealthier quarters of the metropolis and the great provincial cities, as also the towns and villages. Not a house but was watched. The method was ingenious and complete; five men were told off to every hundred houses, the five taking duty on various watches. After six months of patrolling, these patrols were to the full acquainted with the order and way of the houses and their inhabitants in their respective beats. They kept a record of the number of persons in each house, of its general protection, and of the social position and condition of the owners; these records were carefully entered in cipher in the books of the Central Committee, so that there was scarcely a house in Kensington, St. James, or other of the fashionable or unfashionable parishes whose condition in every necessary particular the General of the Revolutionary League could not at a moment discover. With funds the Committee were amply endowed, yet such was the widespread wretchedness that in no case would the most difficult or arduous duty have been stopped for want of workers or supplies.

There was scarcely a soldier in the Army whose relation, near or distant, helped not to fill the ranks of the unemployed, in some form or other.* In one regiment, two years before the Revolution, only three men had not signed the pledge which bound a man to protect, if need be at the risk of his own life, the person of a brother member of the League. This had proved the easiest part of the League's organisation. Scarcely two years had passed since the first devoted member of Carlyle Democritus's revolutionary recruits had joined the 113th Regiment, and there was not a regiment, no matter where stationed, but had amongst its men at least ten members of the Revolutionary League, whose duty it had been to gain the soldiers over to the cause of their stricken comrades. If any soldier in a regiment did not readily respond to the overtures of a Leaguer, no efforts were made to bring him over; but his name was recorded as an enemy, to be left alone until the time of uprising should arrive. The method then was (unless in the meanwhile the constantly increasing numbers of his comrades in active sympathy with the League had enlisted his adhesion), that the night before the final promulgation of revolt by the Central Committee, the non-subscriber was informed of the leading facts of the organisation, confronted with his comrades who had joined the League, and it seldom happened but that he eagerly espoused the general Cause. Where any signs of weakness or irresolution appeared, no word of persuasion or opposition was used. But the order was secretly given: "A waverer—death by bayonet at bugle call to-morrow." In nearly every such case some friendly comrade of the waverer apprised him of his impending fate, and invariably turned refusal or lukewarmness into energy of assent. Thus it came that on the night before the great upheaval—of the 90,000 non-commissioned officers and men serving at home, not thirty stood condemned, and only a few hundred appeared on the Committee list as "doubtful." Towards the 100,000 men serving abroad the same tactics had been pursued, the terms alone being different—it being provided that any regiment ordered home after the fatal day must refuse, any man disobeying the Revolutionary

---

* Page 304.

order to be at once struck down. Amongst the police a somewhat similar method had been employed, but with less success, owing to the greater difficulty of gaining entry to the force. Of the 50,000 police in the metropolis, the League could reckon upon two-thirds, enough to prevent any serious opposition by the rest; and nearly all had, in self-defence, gone over to the League when the final moment had arrived.

CHAPTER VIII.

THE DAY OF REVOLUTION, 14TH FEBRUARY 19--.

THUS organised and prepared, the General-in-chief held his last council of war on the eve prior to the great upheaval of the 14th of February. The final orders had been transmitted to all parts of the world, and, in every case, had been acknowledged and confirmed. To the smallest detail the organisation was everywhere complete. For the first time since the inauguration of the new organisation, armed Revolutionists were massed in the enormous barracks at Headquarters. Three thousand picked men, armed with revolver and dirk, uniformed in deep black, whereon shone the Salvation Cross with ominous lustre, slept, ready to march with the dawn.

The arming of the Salvation fighting men had been the most anxious care of Carlyle Democritus. He knew that revolution was no affair of rose-water, but he was determined no single drop of blood should flow wantonly. Throughout his enormous forces only the most tried and trustworthy were armed, and their discipline was as subtle as their steel. Where any doubt of a corps existed, the commanding officers only entrusted the chosen amongst them, whom they placed in the front ranks, with fire-arms. The rest were armed with sword or dirk. And as each weapon was given out to the men on that devoted day, this printed exhortation accompanied it :—

"Revolutionist! remember thy oath of service! 'For God and for the People!' to bring about His divine justice in the world, and to protect His suffering children, these arms are entrusted to thy keeping. My brother, use them worthily, or use them not at all. CARLYLE DEMOCRITUS, General."

The morning of the 14th of February broke amidst gathering fog and rock-hard frost. Towards five o'clock the Barracks at

Knightsbridge, till that moment quiet, cold, and almost isolated, began gradually to be the scene of a noiseless and weird assemblage. In ones and twos, never in larger groups than five, men might be seen tiding in from the streets which faced one side of the building, or across the Park which faced the other. The police on the beat, and the soldiers keeping guard (where they were not already members of the League), at first unmindful, then surprised, at the numbers and strange appearance of the men, whom at first they thought were labourers trudging to their early work, had little time for wonderment;—before staff or musket could be even thought of, a dozen fierce determined hands had overpowered and bound each sentinel and policeman.

Three shrill notes from a fife pierced the cold, gloomy air, and, like magic, the throng, till now in appearance almost purposeless, stood close and serried as the lines of an army. The uniforms, apart from those of the front battalions in each regiment, were rags in every sadness of distress; uniformity was only observable in the head-covering of each man, namely, the Revolutionist cap with scarlet cross, and on the right breast of each man's coat where a similar symbol appeared. The leaders of each company bore the scarlet cross with bars of gold braid, according to their rank, on each shoulder. The call which brought the Revolutionists into line was answered from the barracks by the immediate opening of gates and doors. A company of the men entered, a portion of whom were soon busy serving out swords, bayonets, and guns to the unarmed portion of the Revolutionists; but not without some bloodshed was this effected. No soldiers of the Army, but several officers of the garrison, opposed the rebels and were slain.

About an hour elapsed before the men marched off, ten deep, in silence the more profound because the broken and wretched boots, worn by too many of them, made but slight tramp upon the snow-covered roadways. Sufficient men were left to guard the barracks; the rest proceeded at sharp pace towards Trafalgar Square, so recently the nightly harbour of hundreds of homeless and starving wretches. For the first time a loud and frightful howl of welcome rent the quiet air—from more than ten thousand attenuated men and women, who crowded in upon the steady ranks of the ragged battalions from all sides of the Square and adjacent streets. At this moment arrived a troop of horsemen led by a tall commanding figure, whose appearance was the signal for another outburst of

(14)

enthusiasm, but which was quickly stayed by the upraised hand of the horseman. He is the man whom we caught sight of, for an instant, passing through the meeting at Hunger Hall. With a loud penetrating voice he commands "Silence!" and all is still: "Remember the watchword is 'Organisation,' 'Discipline.' Men and women, Revolutionists, let us prove ourselves deserving of emancipation, and we will win it. Think that upon the earnest courage, the devoted obedience, of each one of you, depends success." By prearranged instructions the crowds take up positions, ten deep, in rear of the armed battalions, who from their steadiness of discipline and formation give evidence of the perfection of their training. The women—of whom there were many thousands—formed in close bodies in front and rear of the procession. This was Carlyle Democritus's final effort to stay unnecessary bloodshed. He knew that British soldiers would not slay women, many of them their very mothers and sisters. His men were prepared to die, but before he would give loose to Civil War he had determined upon a nobler ordeal. Only if that had failed, should the dread alternative of murderous strife ensue. A trumpet sounds in the darkness of the February morning, and all down the vast line huge banners of red unfurl, displaying ominously in large black letters: "The day of His wrath has come." Once more the trumpet cries aloud, and the thousands upon thousands of starving wretches who yesterday had craved for bread and work: "Make us an army of labour," and were ignored and left to starve, are now the Army of Despair, the Army of No-Work, the frightful army of Destruction and Revenge. The time had come when those who had let the poor and wretched starve and suffer, must at their hands expect a similar doom. It is only the difference of the class which is to suffer. Ponder a little on this, O reader.

Whilst the great centre of revolt pursued its course towards Buckingham Palace, thither were also wending vast divisions which had carried out precisely similar tactics throughout the military depôts of the Metropolis. And although in every instance absolute mastery and success attended the Revolutionists, alarm had spread in many quarters, and messages flew over the wires to Whitehall, and were received by the Revolution officers commanding there (for the place had been already gained):—"Twenty thousand armed men marching towards St. James's, declaring themselves Army of Revolution. The troops here have declared for them, and murdered or imprisoned their officers."

Towards nine o'clock, as the weak winter sun struggled faintly to pierce the fog which had thickened over the entire metropolis, eager watchers at the Palace could see, steadily advancing across the Park, and up each avenue, dense masses of men, whose numbers had been swelled by contingents from all quarters of the vast city. The front ranks marched in steady and unwavering phalanx, small reflected flashes of light now and then glancing from sword and bayonet. Arrived half up the avenue, the procession stopped; confronting them, in magnificence of military array, sit, fixed upon their steeds, two thousand of the King's Royal Guards. But the ministers and their officers had forgotten that under scarlet cloth, and under the burnished steel, were hearts of flesh and blood. Their General advances close up to the lines of the women; at a signal, these open their ranks and let the General approach to within five rows of the rebel leader and his staff, who, with loud, clear voice, speaks: "Men, fanatics, I call upon you, in the name of His Majesty the King, to disperse. If you do not turn, and go quietly to your homes before my horse shall carry me to my men, the order stands, and the cavalry shall charge upon you." But the only sign or sound in reply is the rebel leader's call to "march." Slowly the living mass again starts forward. With loud command the Guards are bid to "charge." But louder and clearer is heard the stentorian voice of one amongst the foremost of them, who, rising in his stirrups, thus speaks: "Men, fellow soldiers, we have sworn to do our duty to our country, to bleed in its defence, to guard its sacred borders from the foe. But these before us are NOT our foes, nor the Nation's; they are our flesh and bone; our mothers are there, our children, our brothers, and our sons. Not these our foes, not these nigh-starved and stricken ones. Foes are they to the Nation; the panderers at Westminster, those Commoners and Lords who, in their souls foresworn, have abandoned their high duties and driven a long-suffering and laborious people to despair and to revolt—*with* these and *for* these we will live and die." A shout of sympathy and approval rewards the speaker, when, with uplifted sword and sudden charge, the General rushes to lay low this utterer of sedition, thinking by fierce and bloody stroke to quench incipient revolt. But, scarcely has his horse approached the line of red and steel, before it and its rider fall pierced by a hundred wounds. Dismayed and conscious of the hopelessness of their cause, the lesser officers endeavour to urge on the stubborn troops, but in vain. At this moment the Revolutionary leader, surrounded by his staff, their scarlet banner waving as they advance, approaches the Palace gates. A blare of trumpets at a given signal, transmit an order to the assembled multitude, whereupon the unarmed throngs open up their ranks, and ten thousand armed Revolutionists, their scarlet banners, bearing the Salvation cross in black, looming through the lifting fog, march within ten paces of the Palace gates, which upon challenge the sentinels at once throw open. A halt is sounded; two companies advance through the ample gates, in their midst the Revolutionary chief surrounded by his staff. As they move, a gentle wind curls up the fog-mist, and reveals the unending multitudes assembled. The red winter sun, as with lambent flame, touched the pale leader's face. His devoted followers saw in the sudden light the halo of a saint; and with a shout that rent the skies, went up the Revolution watchword, "For God and for the people!" A visible emotion shook the strongest there. The heart of a mighty nation had cried aloud. Awful was the silence which followed the gently uplifted General's hand, that well-known signal of united humility, sympathy, and command so familiar to them all. With stentorian voice he addresses the Guards: "Soldiers, brothers of these wasted multitudes, the time of words is past, the time of action has arrived. Patiently and bravely, even as yourselves in time of war, upon the devastating battle-field, have these poor people borne the slaughterer—a thousand-fold more terrible than he of war—the stealthy, cruel smiter by famine and disease. Workless, they have prayed for work; foodless, they have craved for food; but only scoffing and neglect have their governors meted out to them. Brothers of the sword, protectors under God of justice against injustice, we swear fidelity to you, as you have sworn to us; we are one; your protection ours, our protection yours. Officers, only this—the people will work their own deliverance without furtherance from you, but also without hindrance. Your position, your duties, remain unchanged, except that your Parliament, your master, for a time has altered. Life and honour await you whilst true to your regiments and your office; immediate death at the slightest attempt to evade the one or the other. Lead back your men to barracks." Stunned by the suddenness of these events, awed by the immensity of the leader's power, as if mechanically, the order is sullenly given, but with alacrity obeyed.

As the breast-plated soldiers pass through the dense masses of the people who, at the order of their officers, make passage for them, men greet them loudly, mothers hold their children up to them, maidens offer warmer cheer. It is a strange procession, a tender battle-field. Even the officers are warmed to sympathy.

The telling of the first act of the Revolution has taken longer than its performing. Leaving one company in possession of the Palace, the Salvation troops march northward to complete their Army's hold of the Metropolis, and to render help to such of their other divisions as might require it. Meanwhile the tens of thousands who filled the Park are divided by their officers into extended double columns, and soon a strange procession arrives and winds slowly between each pair of lines—huge carts laden with bread, and vans with milk bring provisions for such as may not find it at their homes. Hungered as many of the wretched people were, not one man left his place until the provision train was stopped, and then quickly and with military precision the rations were dealt out.

Whilst the heavy-armed regulars were engaged in taking possession of all the barracks, armouries, and magazines of the Metropolis (similar tactics, it is to be remembered, prevailing throughout the three kingdoms), lighter armed troops in small or larger companies, as might be necessary, took possession of all the armourers' shops and every bakery throughout London. Every public-house was closed, and a strong guard posted to keep it so. Alarm was quickly allayed by the admirable precautions which had been taken everywhere by the leaders. A printed notice was handed to the owner of every place affected :—

"IN THE NAME OF GOD AND THE PEOPLE!

"KNOW ALL MEN

"That on the morning of this, the 14th day of February 19—, the Government of Great Britain has fallen from the hands of party-mongers, place-hunters, and self-seekers. The Nation has risen in mass against a base and lying Ministry, and has deposed them. The King and the Constitution, purged from abuse, will be preserved.

"The rights of every true and honest citizen are sacred to the new Government, and shall be held inviolate. The immediate necessities of a long neglected portion of the Nation have rendered it imperatively necessary that the business and premises of ——— ———, baker (or in the case of gunsmiths the word "armourer" appeared) shall be temporarily attached; but his general business will not be interfered with, after the pressing necessities of an exceptional period have been satisfied. Full compensation and payment will be made to him for the present requisition of his stores and services, and assistance will be given to him to prevent disturbance to his ordinary customers.—In the name of the Revolutionary forces of the United Kingdom,

"CARLYLE DEMOCRITUS, General-in-Chief."

The publicans received a briefer notice. Underneath the usual Revolutionist heading it ran: "That inasmuch as the masses have arisen in their might to save Great Britain from destruction by a base and party-ridden Government, and because the public safety requires that temptation to strong drink shall not beset weak and ignorant men, this public-house is hereby closed till further order. Any attempt to disregard this notice, or to give, or sell, liquor from this establishment, will be met by the summary execution of the offender."

In all the barracks throughout the kingdom, and on all vessels abroad and at home, official notices of the rising were proclaimed. The sailors and soldiers throughout the length and breadth of the Empire, being parties to the rising, facilitated synchronous and ubiquitous action. From all parts telegrams since an early hour besieged the Home and Foreign Offices, but these departments were already in the hands of the Revolutionists, as were the persons of the Ministers who filled them; and messages were dispatched to all parts confirming the rising, describing its success, and commanding the various regiments, and men-of-war, to remain at their stations. Officers of the fleet and of the army, from highest to lowest, were apprised that the outbreak was general, that in no case would any appointment be interfered with, but that any attempt to leave his post would subject the holder to instant arrest wherever and whenever he might be found. In many vessels of the fleet strange scenes followed the posting up of the Revolutionary notices. The account forwarded by the Special Correspondent of the *Newtimes* from Egypt, dated 14th of February 19—, and appearing in the next day's issue of that paper, may be transcribed :—

"Shortly before twelve o'clock this morning the English colony here was thrown into amazement and horror by the arrival of telegrams to the effect that a revolution had broken out in London and the provinces, and that the entire city, the Government and the Governors, were in the hands of the rebels. It is quite impossible to convey, in the space of a telegram, any idea of the dismay and consternation the news evoked. Messages after messages were delivered thick and fast, all in the same tone, some more or less wild, but all confirming the central statement, 'The people have risen against the Government.' At the Embassy all that I can learn is that Lord Wiltshire is ordered to continue at his post and to confirm all officials, military, naval, and civil, in theirs. Terrible anxiety is evinced by the ladies of the Embassy for the safety of their friends at home, yet no one dares to leave.

"On board the *Great Commander*, anchored off Besika Bay, blood was spilt, but on board the other vessels of the Fleet stationed here, beyond sharing the general consternation, no serious mishap has occurred. Full particulars of the *Commander* outbreak are not yet to hand; but it appears that Admiral Oxley, who, it may be mentioned, is very unpopular with his men, on rising early this morning, saw the revolutionary placard, a red sheet about one foot square, printed in black letters, stuck up on his looking-glass, and after reading it imagined that some of his men had placed it there as a daring hint at his known aristocratic tendencies. Enraged at the act, he rushed half-dressed on deck, and ordered the quartermaster to pipe all hands on deck. Holding the red paper in his hand, he inquired what man dared to place it in his cabin. At this moment, other of the officers informed him that they had all received similar intimation, and that already the consul's boat had come off to announce the receipt of ominous news by wire from home, confirming the words of the printed notices. But Captain Oxley still determined that the man who had dared to fix the notice in his cabin should answer for the breach of discipline, but detection proved impossible. It was evident that all the sailors were aware of, and in full sympathy with the rising; for, when, later in the day, Oxley determined, against the pressing advice of his officers, to disregard the red authority and make for English waters, not one man would help to heave the anchor. 'Mutiny!' thundered Oxley, 'by God, we *will* go, in spite of them,' and he approached the steam-winch. Thereupon, one of the quartermasters, with due salute, displaying the red notice, warned him to desist. Losing self-control, and towering with rage, Oxley proceeded to strike the man with his sword, but he had scarcely half drawn the blade when the men in a body rushed upon him with cutlasses drawn, and Oxley fell. We hear that at the country stations the military have everywhere received similar notices and instructions, so that doubt of some grave national uprising is no longer possible."

Meanwhile tragic scenes were occurring in the homes of ministers in London, most of whom were in town in readiness for the Session which was to have opened on the morrow. But this must form the subject of another chapter.

CHAPTER IX.

THE REVOLUTIONARY PATROLS.

PERHAPS the most extraordinary feature in all the wide-spreading network of organisation was the marvellous system of patrolry which the revolutionary leaders had established, the method of which has been described in a previous chapter. On the memorable Sunday morning of the 14th of February, 19—, at eight o'clock, there was not one street or square of any importance throughout London (and exactly the same tactics were pursuing throughout the country, never mind how small the village or how large the city) but was policed in this new and ominous manner :—At each corner of a street was stationed an armed patrol in black uniform bearing on each shoulder the red Revolutionist cross. Every such one was a commander of a small staff of ten men, who in their turn patrolled contiguous streets and remained within whistle-call of the leader. This system answered so thoroughly its designer's intentions that, in all the vast city, but few of the numerous prisoners, whose persons were "wanted" by the Central Committee, had been able to evade apprehension. Nor was the system, overwhelmingly sudden and complete as it was (perhaps for that very reason stunning resistance), productive of any general panic or particular fright. Every house had posted upon its door the red placard apprising the Establishment of the Revolution, and warning peaceful inhabitants against venturing into the streets. In the case where an inhabitant of any house was required to appear before the Council, notice followed that his person would be awaited by the guard outside his house thirty minutes after the service of the notice ; but failing to deliver himself up at the expiration of that period, his house would be entered, himself be taken by force if discovered, or failing that, every inhabitant of his household would be seized as hostage. In few cases was there bloodshed. That Sabbath day saw the close of many a modern's "greatness." But also it was the natal day of a greatness of far more value to the world than the old which it was superseding.

Before the church bells had sounded half-past eight, the door of many a proscribed house had opened, and the owner, half-incredulous, half-dazed, asked, as he placed himself in the hands of the watch, what might be the meaning of the warrant? Of the few cases of resistance which occurred, the following excerpt from the *Newtimes* of the 15th and 16th of February will convey some notion:—

"RESISTANCE TO THE PATROLS AT GOVERNOR STREET.

"The patrols told off at Lord Davidxhume's residence having rightly surmised that the Minister would not be likely to yield himself without resistance, were in force sufficient for any emergency. Sergeant Dickson with five patrols stationed himself at the main entrance, twenty men as a reserve were drawn up alongside the high wall which runs about fifty feet in front of the garden of the house. All the men were armed with revolvers and small swords. Fifty additional men, armed with rifles, were in reserve at lower parts of the street. At nine o'clock exactly Dickson struck the door three times with the butt end of his musket. The usual flunkey opened the door. 'Better doff that humbuggery before to-morrow!' said one of the men to him. 'To-day we want Lord Davidxhume.' 'My lord is away from home,' the man answered. 'That's a lie,' thundered Dickson, as he fired his revolver at the man, and as a signal to his followers. The second door in the passage was locked and barricaded, but could not long resist the patrols, who, with shot and blows, quickly brought down door and barricade. 'Follow me,' called Dickson, and the party made through the breach. They came upon a frightened serving-maid, who nervously endeavoured to persuade them of her people's absence. 'Woman,' said Dickson, 'we know your masters are here. Our men have watched you far too closely for such weak yarns to avail. You have fifteen souls here of the Minister's family and friends. They've defied our order; they'll pay the price of it.' Posting four men with loaded muskets to guard the door, they entered a large room to the right of the hall. 'Now then,' said Dickson to the woman, 'we give you one minute, sixty seconds, to send your fifteen swells into this room; if they are not here sharp to the second, my men will search, and they will find them; and, mind you, fifteen of them altogether. With me to rule my fellows, your masters will meet with protection of a sort, but, hark ye, I'm not responsible for one man's action if hide-and-seek's your game.' The last argument seemed decisive, for the sixty seconds had not elapsed when through the open door appeared the form of Davidxhume pale with excitement and emotion. On a sign from Dickson six men seized the Minister and secured his wrists. Anticipating resistance, Dickson called out to him, 'Sir, resistance is hopeless, and can only subject you to indignity.' At this moment the rest of the household filed into the room—the women, emblems of fear and horror; the men only prevented from savage resistance by the imploring voices and entreaties of the women, and the evident hopelessness of such a course."—But let us not descend through details of misery and horror which avail not the action of this history. Lovely women employed their influence in vain upon an outraged people, one of whom spoke truly enough when he said to the beautiful daughter of one of the accused, on her knees before him imploringly, "It's too late for all that now, lady. Had ye spoken to him," pointing to the Minister, "in that angel way, whilst we were all a-starving, our women and children dying for a little help, he might have heard ye perhaps, though he never would the likes of us; it's too late now."

Before noon all the ministers were secured. Some had been taken at their country houses, and were now on their way to London closely guarded. Where any proscribed citizen was abroad his entire family were seized as hostages till his return.

Not only political ministers engaged the energies of the patrols; spiritual ministers were seized in their palaces, and many members of both Parliaments filled the jails. Of the Lords, the whole of the twenty-seven bishops were taken, both the archbishops, seventeen dukes, eighteen marquises, and between two and three hundred assorted peers. Not to be lightly passed over is the remarkable fact that in no instance was a peer arrested merely on the grounds of his nominal nobility. Amongst the seizures were all members of Commissions who had been parties to "granting" hundreds of thousands of the public money in commuting pensions for sinecures held by noblemen and other gentry, and who were, in the end, made responsible to the public funds for all those amounts, which had to be made good from their personal estates. Of modern creations all those who owed their rise to so-called political merit, money privilege, fortunes made out of beer, and kindred recommendations were seized, and the prisons were crowded with beer-dukes, mammon-lords, and political time-servers.

The patrols also had promptly seized upon the persons of all officials who had been jerked into lucrative posts by mere favour. When their time of trial came, their sentences proved as mild as they were just—dismissal from their posts, except in such instances (which proved very few) where they in any way justified themselves and were found fit for them.

The Banks next engaged attention. The managers were early apprised of the rising, and ample assurance of protection was given to them; military guards were posted at every bank in the metropolis, over the Sunday, and until the opening of the bank on the following day. All the managers were warned against meeting any drafts issued by any member whose name appeared on a list which was appended to each notice, and which contained the names not only of those who were imprisoned, but also of all those large landowners whose cases had yet to be decided by the Revolutionary Courts. In this way the Revolutionary committee had protected the nation against any sudden withdrawal of capital or evasion of a justice which they had determined should be retributive. The bankers were further cautioned against meeting any exceptional demand for funds from any quarter, and the notice concluded with these words: "Whereas the fullest protection will be afforded to those who respect these commands (and in no way will ordinary commercial business be interfered with), any departure from them will have to be answered before the Tribunal of the Revolution."

Meanwhile, another and very different duty had been carried out by another section of the patrollers. Ingress and egress to all the workhouses in the kingdom had been made free. Mothers were allowed to have their children, husbands were no longer divided from their wives, rations were increased, and the organisation of the places quickly assimilated to that of barracks. Wherever there was spare room in them, and other quarters were not available, the poor and the rebel troops were there housed and fed.

The streets were almost deserted. The utmost silence prevailed everywhere, excepting in the one or two instances, earlier in the day, where resistance had been offered to the patrols, and also in the immediate neighbourhood of the workhouses and barracks, where enthusiastic scenes of excitement prevailed. Yet there was no drunkenness (all the public-houses being forcibly closed), or riot of any kind. The whole of the vast city was wrapped in a profound and wonderful peace. Order was everywhere; the patrols alone broke the monotony of the deserted streets. Although Sunday, the churches remained deserted. London seemed a City of Sleep.

CHAPTER X.

THE GREAT REQUISITION.

Outrage of any sort was rigorously provided against, and wherever it attempted to show itself was instantly, and with the utmost vigour, suppressed.

The Revolution, whose history these pages are unfolding, had been silently preparing through many years. Although the whole nation had, in the end, responded to it, still could it not have succeeded without provoking hideous civil war, had it not been for the genius of the great Commander who controlled and directed it. That grave problem which faces every general—adequately to provision his forces—seemed in the case of an army, for the most part recruited from the ranks of the nearly starving, an almost insuperable problem. True, that want of funds has never stayed internecine or other strife, and starvation has gone side by side with wholesale bloodshed in every Revolution. But Carlyle Democritus had not arisen to increase the misery of the poor; he had determined to better their lot from the very hour of Revolution, as well as after its successful establishment. The problem before him was to provide food and shelter for the gaunt, famished army, which on that memorable 14th of February was to take the field throughout Great Britain. We have seen how the rations for the first few days were furnished, and whence obtained. But unless the bakers and the general providers received their just remuneration, neither their bread nor their services could be long commanded. We shall see with what master-stroke Carlyle Democritus solved the problem of feeding the hungry, without exhausting the food supplies, or touching the necessities of the well-fed, or even of the over-fed, and without pecuniary levying whatsoever. We have seen how the patrols had everywhere established their control. On the morning of Sunday, the 14th of February 19—, their energies had been concentrated upon seizing, and duly possessing themselves of the persons of political, social, or other offenders. At noon of the Sunday they were again at their posts, but engaged in a duty other than man-hunting. The officer in command of each patrol (increased in strength by detachments from the armed forces now released by the fall of the Government, and the surrender of all the military depôts) now led his band to the wealthy quarters of the towns, cities, and palaces of the country. At every house they visited, the officer presented this brief printed order:—

"In the Name of God and the People!

"Whereas women, children, and strong men are starving and require bread. Your own stores will not be touched to help feed them, nor your household goods, nor your money, nor anything whatsoever that is useful to you, or your household,—all these will receive the protection of the State and of the new Government, and of this, their patrol. But, that which is absolutely useless to you and to yours, that which lies idle and serves no mortal, beast, or thing, that which is but a relic of barbarism, wantonness, and waste—*that* you are hereby required to instantly produce and deliver to —— —— the officer in command of the —— Division, of the —— Corps, of the Revolutionist Patrols. This order refers to every article of jewelry in this establishment, of what nature soever it may be, excepting only watches and watch-chains, articles of personal use (buttons, studs, links, etc.), or memorial tokens bearing an engraved record. Any attempt to resist this order, or to refuse compliance therewith, and your house will at once be given up to indiscriminate search.—By Order of the Revolutionary Army,

"Carlyle Democritus, General-in-Chief."

If ever there was a merciful and wise requisition, this was one. No one was one whit the worse off after the levy than he was before it. The receipt given by the patrols, combined with the fact that they left the empty jewel cases in every instance with the former owners, soon completely comforted them. The receipt was as follows:—"The —— Division of the —— Corps of the Revolutionary Patrols hereby acknowledge the surrender, to the purposes of the State, of sundry articles of barbaric ornament, in gold and gems, to be converted into food for the starving, and to furthering the welfare of the hitherto neglected and oppressed. We think too well of the quondam owners of such trifles to believe it necessary to express to them any other sentiment than extreme congratulation that a noble purpose has been found for things hitherto but inert uselessness." The Crown Jewels were not excepted. All fell in the great requisition. Some of the "great families" were found to have possessed millions tied up in this quintessence of barbaric vanity and folly, millions thus idly wasting whilst women and children were dying for want of bread. In many instances these heirlooms filled huge coffers at the banks, whence—early on the following Monday morning—they were one and all abstracted.

It may be well imagined that had such a deluge of precious gems been suddenly let loose "on the market," they would have become extrinsically as useless as they intrinsically were. But, like all Carlyle Democritus's plans, wise measures had been taken against such a possible disaster. Agents for the disposal of the precious things had been appointed long beforehand at all the Courts and fashionable centres of Europe, Asia, and America, so that before the world had even learned of the great Requisition, black, brown, and white barbarians had taken up, greedily and readily, by cash purchase, the entire stock. Within a few weeks of the levy, the Bank of England held to the credit of the Revolutionary Government no less a sum in hard gold, notes, high-class foreign bank remittances, or telegraphic transfers, six hundred millions sterling, which vast treasure did not include a further four hundred tons of gold trinkets, plate, and utensils, to be cast into the melting-pot for mintage. Supplies for food and pressing social reforms were thus provided without any one suffering privation in the slightest way. Now came the not less pressing problem of housing the shivering multitudes hitherto homeless, or overcrowded in filthy slum-boxes. Here, again, the problem was as triumphantly solved as the first, and also without touching the necessities of any one. The country was full of palaces and mansions standing idle and empty. It was quite a common thing for a wholesale number of Peers to possess from six to a dozen of such. All empty and unfurnished houses in convenient thoroughfares were temporarily requisitioned from their owners. And wherever a Peer or person owned more than one palace, all his others were requisitioned and quickly converted by gangs of labourers, who had long been held in readiness for the task, into warm quarters for the poorest families most in need of them. All works of art were carefully packed and stored away. A perfect army of labour was set to work all over the country to effect these alterations; and as each palace or mansion was completed, the people were housed in them under proper management and supervision. The most thorough-going measures were taken to ensure order, cleanliness, and discipline everywhere. Any breach of duty, or abuse of the generous shelter provided, subjected the offender to immediate punishment and removal. Thus, then, were the two initial problems completely settled, viz. the temporary feeding and housing of the suffering people until, by the establishment of labour laws, the settlement of the people upon the land, the formation of Colonies at home and abroad, and other remedies, they should be definitely and permanently provided for.

CHAPTER XI.

PARLIAMENT BY PARTY AND OBSTRUCTION ENDS.

FOR authority as to the proceedings in Parliament, which met for the first time after the autumn prorogation, on the 15th of February 19—, we rely for the most part on the publications and despatches of the Revolutionary leaders and of the *Revolutionary Journal*. Few of the daily papers afford much information, as none of their representatives were allowed in the House on that day. A curious evidence of the temper of the people may be noticed here. The Revolutionary patrols had taken steps to protect the offices of the great representative papers from attack, but no attempt was made against any of them, except the *Daily Guide to the Gin Shop*. On the other hand, the self-styled "People's Papers" were furiously set on by their supposed admirers, and it became evident, when too late, that the wrong offices had been protected. Mud-gutter Radicalism, and its grovelling placards pandering to mere ignorance and vulgarity, had been seen through, and put an end to, in the most summary fashion. Such an evidence of intelligent discrimination on the part of the mob folk caused Revolutionary thinkers no little astonishment. All the offices that had escaped the fury of the people were strongly patrolled, in their own behalf, as well as in that of the public. No paper was allowed to be issued until it had passed the officer in command. All the editors were warned against issuing exaggerated, alarming, or mendacious accounts of Sunday's occurrences. No truthful or unvarnished report was in the slightest manner interfered with, but any attempt at "Blackswhite's" views, or "Whitesblack's"* commentaries, subjected the paper to suppression for that day. Outside the Houses of Parliament nothing indicated any coming struggle. The police

---

* Page 22.

were on duty as usual, but many of the men were changed. Any attempt at crowd gathering was quickly frustrated, and members (such as remained at large after the previous day's arrests) who were in town, to their considerable surprise, and perhaps increased apprehension, found their ingress as free as upon any former occasion. Inside the House a slight increase of police officers and many new faces might have been perceptible.

With less rhetoric and circumlocution than he had employed since the day of his first election, an Honourable gentleman rose to address the scanty House. Of Right Honourable gentlemen there were none. But we need not here add to the myriad reports of printed loquacity which had filled all newspapers and Hansard-volumes for years past: "What is to be done, and how shall we do it?" was the burden of the Honourable gentleman's mournful would-be-defiant address. Before he had occupied the attention of the House many minutes, there entered in hot haste a member, who interrupted the speaker, to apprise them that their venerable House was surrounded by upwards of twenty thousand armed men; that already two thousand of them filled all corridors and internal avenues of the House; that he was bearer of a message from the Leader of the Rebels, one calling himself General Carlyle Democritus, who demanded to be heard at the Bar of the House. Honourable gentlemen might decide whether they would hear him by force or by favour. Hon. gentlemen hastily decided that Carlyle Democritus should be admitted and allowed to speak at the Bar of the House. Whilst yet the House was recording its assent, the General entered, with a dignity undisturbed by the majesty of the traditions or the unrealities of the august assembly. Some members rose to protest against the entry of seven of the General's staff officers, who accompanied him; and especially against the intrusion of the armed followers who filled all the galleries of the House.

"Citizens," thundered the voice of the General, "stay this vain and purposeless jargoning. Facts are before you and on all sides of you. The time of empty protest has gone. I speak in the name of the millions till this moment *un*represented, and whose representative you discover in me. To you this people have appealed for years, indeed for generations past, and you would not hear them, nor shall they appeal again; THEY NOW COMMAND! You have been deaf to their sufferings, you have been blind to their despair. Your Ministers and others of your House are in the custody of the people, and by the people they will be judged. Of the righteous cause God will be the Arbiter, as He is our Guide, and as He has *not* been yours. You have elected to waste the energy of a great nation; it will be our task to restore it. You have elected to ignore the wretched and fallen of your people, whom it was your sacred duty to protect. Tens of thousands of their women you have compelled to starvation and to sin, their children to death or to neglect; to their strong men who lie in helpless idleness, you have offered only death or despair.

And now we have arisen, in the name of Truth and Mercy, to give them life, and to render hope possible for them. Let those now here and who value their life depart in peace from hence. This assembly, its pledges forsworn, its duties betrayed, has forfeited the trust of God and of men. In the name of the people I bid you GO!" A member rose, would yet be heard, would— "Clear the house, men!" was the General's loud response, and with background of bayonets, members filed sharply from the chamber. As each Hon. gentleman passed the precincts of the chamber, a paper was handed to him. It warned him to keep quiet, that the day of stump-oratory was past; that for any attempt at public meeting he would have to answer before the Tribunal of the Revolution.

A similar quietus closed the career of those who remained of the *other* august assembly.

CHAPTER XII

INTERVIEW BETWEEN CARLYLE DEMOCRITUS AND THE KING.

THE following extract from the archives of this remarkable period, bearing upon the relations which the Revolution had brought about between the Monarch and the new Republicanism, will not only explain the constitutional side of the question, as between the Revolutionists and the King, but will throw light upon various collateral issues connected with this history. Accompanying a formal command from the King to Carlyle Democritus to present himself in person before His Majesty, was a letter written by the King's hand, part of which may be transcribed :—

"St James's Palace,
"February 22nd, 19—.

"To THE GENERAL CARLYLE DEMOCRITUS.

"MY DEAR GENERAL,

"If to an ordinary Commander controlling a vast and victorious army compliance with such a Royal summons as I am issuing might appear fraught with any degree of danger, the prescience with which you have ordered things, including the Revolutionist patrols who guard my person, require not any assurance from me to you that your coming and your going will be, by me and mine, safeguarded. Eight eventful days have passed since, from one end to the other of our mighty Empire, you have established a dominating influence such as the world has never known before. As the Constitutional Ruler of Great Britain addressing its rarest citizen, I add my earnest request to the mere formal command, that you will not delay to arrange an audience."

The day following the receipt of the Royal autograph, Carlyle Democritus was closeted with the King. Here are the stenographers' notes of the interview, the original whereof may be found deposited in the Historical Manuscripts Department of the British Museum :—

"The King, having been apprised of the approach of Carlyle Democritus attended by his bodyguard, awaited him in his private parlour attended only by two of his secretaries, one of whom, strangely enough, bore the Revolutionist cross of the highest order on the right shoulder of his military uniform. As Carlyle Democritus entered the Royal presence, accompanied only by one of his aides-de-camp, the King rose with that urbanity and air of cordial welcome which was the very atmosphere of His Majesty, and which had in no slight degree helped to earn for him his popularity. The General entered the Royal presence with a rare grace and dignity; he seemed a personification of human beneficence and intellectuality in its purest and noblest form. In him the spirit had levied a heavy toll on flesh, and his worn, attenuated form seemed to hold but lightly his towering spirit to the earth. His Majesty, though well advanced in years, enjoyed a large and right substantial presence. In form and feature he was even more rubicund and jovial than the broadest picture we possess of Henry VIII. Nor did the few remaining snow-white locks of the King in any way detract from his general air of Royal merriness.

"The attendants having retired to some distance from their chiefs, the King and Democritus seated themselves, and this dialogue ensued :—

"*The King.*—General, whilst unable to make any comment upon the extraordinary events which have resulted in this present interview, I would commence by giving you an Englishman's as well as a Sovereign's thanks for the steps you have taken, from the outset, to spare me and mine from molestation or alarm. I have not to assure you that no consideration of personal fear could enter here; but, as husband and father, your loyal letter assuring us of the devotion of your troops and of yourself, and of their protection to the Royal House, which you and they have since fulfilled, move me to express my sincere and heartfelt gratitude. I am naturally anxious to learn from your own lips the course you contemplate to pursue as regards ourselves and the nation we represent.

"*Carlyle Democritus.*—Your Majesty, we recognise the remarkable manner with which you have filled the difficult and thorny seat of a constitutional throne; which has been almost made to totter by the servility, time-servingness, and self-seeking of political cowardice. There can scarcely be a sane man in Great Britain but who must realise the immense advantage a nation enjoys provided with a perpetual Presidency, unattended by the ever-recurring basenesses which characterise the selection of so many of the temporary presidents. For, in actuality, there never has been a Republic more ideally exact than England's; and though we call our President 'King of Britain and Emperor of India,' he has never swerved one hair's breadth from the people's will.

"*King.*—Do you contemplate to perpetuate the present occupation?

"*C. D.*—God forbid, Your Majesty. We shall with utmost dispatch, consistent with wisdom, complete the pressing measures of reform which have called us into being. We shall establish them so that the people may know them and get to appreciate them. We shall then submit to the country these new reforms and the charter of a new constitution for them to confirm, or alter, or amend. But we will not renew the folly of the old Revolutionists; we will not call together a set of men utterly out of touch and sympathy with the people who most need protection. We shall only invoke a General Election after the most far-reaching alteration of the Franchise.

"*King.*—Whilst I fully recognise how effectually you have evoked the enthusiasm of what really may be called the masses, actually the millions, have you not ostracised the middle and upper classes irrevocably, and indeed exasperated them by that universal requisition? That, I must confess, was an ordeal to us all; the Queen will never forgive you the loss of her pearls; she has shed tears upon that loss which, could they be hardened, would have replaced her own pearls and all the Kingdom's. We get a sort of fondness for these toys, General. I have regretted that centre-stud of mine more than, as a man or King, I ought, perhaps, to own. Indeed, when your patrols presented that terrible order, I was for defying it; and, indeed, many of my courtiers urged me to, excepting that one, General, who drew me aside and taught me, as by a lightning touch, how masterly and how widespread was your power and influence. My bravest, wisest, and most intimate friend, when other arguments failed, lifted his lapel and showed to my astonished eyes the Revolutionist cross. 'Sire,' he said, 'the best of all your servitors bear also this red cross; the whole army are pledged to the protection of you and yours; attempt not resistance to this edict. I would not give a straw for the life of man, woman, or child, in all this palace if you let loose these dangerous fanatics. They have seen starvation and profoundest misery sucking the life-blood of their most beloved. If they had to cast the wretched gewgaws to the wasteful ocean-depths they would have them, but they require them to feed the hungry with; and it were safer to face a famished lion than these dangerous hungry multitudes in revolt.' I saw the hopelessness of resistance, and your patrols left us not a single precious stone. See, General, my hands are bare. They refused me even an inscribed signet ring, and when I pointed to the order excepting memorial things, they returned the ring to me, but first withdrew the diamond.

"One of the courtiers refused to swear that he had yielded up whatever jewels he possessed. The man was obdurate, and boasted that he would defy the order; they took him, strong as he was, and twirled him to a lamp-post, pinning upon him a label—so my people told me later—'The body of one who preferred to see his fellow-men starve sooner than yield up his useless gems to get them food.' And there they left him hanging for three days, under a numerous guard.

"*C. D.*—They did well, O King. If it be as you fear, and any considerable portion of the 'classes' deeply resent our requisition, they are an emptier and more barbarous folk than the lowest. But I fancy theirs is only a very transient sorrow, which will not leave a lasting pang. They have only to put on coloured glass, if the idle toys indeed delight them, or why not tinsel and spangles? If this Revolution has only cleared the land of that one idiot-vanity, I would count the success beyond all praise; but when I reflect that those useless toys have helped to furnish food and warmth to famished millions, then, O King, I have no words to record my delight. And rosy children well fed and merry, who before knew only filth, misery, and starvation, are sweeter pearls for a good woman, and a Royal Queen, to contemplate than those grey drops from an oyster-shell.

"*King.*—Did you clear the jewellers' shops as well, General?

"*C. D.*—Oh, no, Your Majesty. For more reasons than one. The jewellers own their stock to get them trade. I hope, but cannot realise, that the clipped feathers of poor vanity will not grow again. And it would not be a wise general who destroyed the depôts which had furnished his supplies. I have discovered to future sufferers whom the laws neglect a harmless source of revenue. Let not future governors provoke their people to fall back upon such a remedy.

"*King.*—Then I have only to inquire how you purpose to deal with the Royal Allowance? Is any alteration contemplated?

"*C. D.*—We would rather increase than decrease the Royal Allowance, Your Majesty; for we are not blind to the fact that however large it may seem when compared, let us say, with an American President's £10,000, those who would correctly make the comparison must not leave out of account the wasted millions which International courtesy requires I should not detail. But we certainly must reform the method hitherto prevailing, Your Majesty. Those forsworn Ministers and Parliaments, who have squandered rich salaries upon millionaire peers and others who required them not, for filling sinecure offices around Royalty: all those we shall abolish. Nor shall we continue the old custom of dower or provision to princely foreigners in any form. Future sovereigns will enjoy a wiser and less sycophantic training than hitherto has been possible for England's princes; and we look forward to being able to inculcate in them the conviction that neither regal nor domestic happiness depends upon profusion of expenditure, nor shall we require of our future princes the severe labour inflicted on our early ones, of opening mixed assortments of bazaars, hospitals, almhouses, and asylums, or presiding at charity and other dinners. All that description of princely labour will cease, because most of those institutions will disappear when Justice takes the place of so-called charity. In that case the Royal occupation would be gone, were we not to provide another. And that we hope to do, Your Majesty. But to revert to the Royal Allowance. We intend to propose to Parliament that it make to the Royal House the liberal grant of £200,000 annually. This amount will comprehend and include every possible charge, and no further item will be considered. It will be left to Your Majesty to dispose of your revenue in the best and wisest manner, but neither yachts nor sinecure officers nor palaces (beyond one in the capital and one in the country, wherever Your Majesty may select) will come within the purview of Parliament. I do not think that Your Majesty will keep up the hundreds of useless drones hitherto besetting the Royal House. Some have computed that not far short of a thousand of this flunkey-breed, of one description or another, have fastened upon your Royal House like so many over-dressed vermin. All the details of Royal expenditure which have hitherto had to come before Parliament and the public do not tend to heighten the Royal dignity. The Cornwall and Lancaster Duchies fall under the reformed land laws, and will not any more pertain to the Royal revenues. It is for this reason I have urged upon my Council to recommend to Parliament the ample allowance named to Your Majesty. Since out of that large revenue the King will have to provide for all members of his family, it will be left to you and the Privy Council to determine what portion of the grant should remain in trust as provision for the children of the Royal House.

"*King.*—Do you propose no additional grant upon the marriage of a prince or princess?

"*C. D.*—Absolutely none, Your Majesty. The immense figure I have named, whilst I do not consider it beyond the limit of reason for a great and powerful nation to bestow upon its respected Chief, I do consider ample for every provision which a wise King and Father need have to make for his descendants.

"*King.*—General, I agree with you. I think the Grant not only sufficient, but thoroughly liberal. As to the number of my palaces, beyond the two, I shall be happy to be quit of them. They are of the burdens and not the delights of Royalty. As for your proposal to dispense with the silver-sticks, gold-sticks, Chamberlains; in fact, the whole nine hundred and seventy of them (that's about their number, General), why, I hail your Revolution if it had only brought that measure of relief to us. But I would fain know if we could not, in our Court, further the great reform you are establishing. Be frank, General; I feel that you cannot but desire change somewhere. It would afford me a great satisfaction to let my people know that we are not hide-bound by stale custom. We have always striven to bring our Royal House in line with the advancement and aspiration of the nation. Let me hear your proposition. I can see you have one.

"*C. D.*—There is one boon my Council would beseech of you. They would not willingly enforce it as a condition arising out of the new order of things. They have left it to me to respectfully lay before Your Majesty to consider (not in the old Parliamentary way, we hope, Your Majesty), and they contend that never did

Revolution require a gentler promise. It is, Sire, that you would pledge your Royal word that, so far as your fair Court is concerned, you would never in future countenance or approve the wearing of jewels by man or woman, in any form or shape. Your Majesty well understands we do not mean by jewelry those harmless, and almost necessary, articles used in apparel, made of plain gold, and already excepted in our original Requisition. But jangles, bangles, gems, and precious stones of any sort, we submit, should be absolutely eschewed as relics of a barbarous taste. We would not care to slight the Royal dignity by having to join such a condition to our now preparing code, nor will we if Your Majesty can see with us the wisdom of helping, by good example, to for ever stop this silly, idle, and most wasteful fashion. And this one other favour. It is a little thing, but one that leads to a greater end—I mean the fashion, unnecessary to a woman's modesty, and hitherto insisted upon at Court, of baring her bosom to the vulgar multitude. Custom can harden us to many things, Your Majesty, and one must needs visit and know the women of Eastern nations, whom the innocent and ignorant in this country deem beneath them, to realise even faintly the loathing and contempt which that disgusting European 'fashion' practised by our women arouses in any purely modest woman's mind. If the Royal House will promise us to discountenance those two things, we will, on our part, heighten our endeavours to preserve, further, and increase the love and loyalty of the people to the Throne.

"*King.*—Well, General, your first proposal I shall grant because the ground upon which you urge it is unanswerable. The habit *is* a barbarous one; I have thought it over, and must confess cannot defend it as in any way preferable to the custom of base savages who disport a similar taste—or want of taste—when they bedeck themselves with beads or such stupidities. As for the loathsome fashion practised of our women, you and I, General, if rumour is to be at all relied upon, are not accredited with a lack of appreciation of their beauty—whether the Venus be of Apelles, Praxiteles, Medici, or Middlesex—and pardon me if I say, in the words of some of my commercial friends, the 'latter preferred.' Yes, General, I think the perfect female form infinitely beautiful, whose 'variety's the very spice of life that gives it all its flavour'—or, I would say, the best part of it. But, General, I assure you that habit of exposing a sample, as it were, of their bodies is revolting to me, and in that matter I would apply, or perhaps misapply, 'aut Venus aut nullus'—either Venus of Medici, or of Middlesex; either wholly clothed or unclothed. The Court will henceforward, I promise you, on the word of a King, set its face rigorously against quarter or half-naked women.

"Shortly thereupon the interview terminated."

Book II.

REVOLUTION ESTABLISHED.

CHAPTER I.

THE REVOLUTIONARY COUNCIL.

A GENERAL revision of officers in the army was one of the first acts of the new Government. Many who, under the recent system, had risen from the ranks, and had cast in their lot with the men, were promoted to higher posts. Those who stood in any way related to the families of men arraigned by the Revolution were drafted to regiments on foreign service. All were required to swear adherence to the new governing powers, or resign their commands. On the staff of each regiment trusted men were stationed. Most of the non-commissioned officers were direct members of the Revolutionary League, and were promoted to higher grades in the service as soon as fit men could be found to fill their places. Thus Carlyle Democritus had at his command 60,000 tried soldiers, in addition to the vast body of Revolutionists variously armed, who were his most willing and enthusiastic followers. With these and the police, now entirely subject to the new system, his hold over the country was absolute and complete. With what abounding wisdom and righteousness his rule was fraught this history will in due time disclose. Never since the time of Cromwell had Britain stood so high, so venerated, and so feared amongst the nations of the earth as in the years following the memorable rising of an indignant and neglected people, against the vain pretence of a Government dreaming itself "constitutional." Party Government had been effete and dying for so long a period past, that the final removal of the rotting carcase of it —the soul, long extinct—proved no insuperable burden, once the right man found to do the work.

The nation was like a strong sapling, full of energy, sprouting straight from the roots of a decaying tree. Thus Jesus from corrupted Judaism; thus Luther from the rotten Catholicism;

thus Cromwell from the decay of patriotism; thus also, from an era of *Laissez faire*, Carlyle Democritus. But the sapling grows not to the tree over night; first must it learn to brave the summer's drought, and the winter's storm—grim foster nurses of all young life whose destiny is strength—through years of silence and of striving.

Not suddenly had Carlyle Democritus become the giant to upraise a nation from incipient decay, but by the Mencius-like abandonment of princely wealth and place to follow, unknown and unregarded, through toilsome years of contumely and anguish, the trials of wretchedness and misery, which sucked, vampire-like, the life-blood of millions of his people. Who was he who, in the midst of sleet and snow, far in a winter's night, stalked through a filthy slum, tapped at a poor pastor's door, and drawing a small book from his breast, asked: "Sir, is this a new Dante, picturing hell to us, or is it indeed a record of that which thine eyes have seen here upon God's earth, in the midst of a wealth vaster than all Rome ever dreamt of? Thou offerest to show thy reader thousands in this small spot, thousands of men and women, and of innocent children half starving, workless in this cruel winter, and no help, no help anywhere. Thou writest of such things as canst thou prove half true, hear my vow, before high Heaven: 'Heart and soul, my life, my fortune, my estate, all until now a useless and accursed vanity, I yield up wholly to this people. God in His wisdom, power, and mercy, hear me and strengthen my resolve to serve them, for only as I shall serve them shall He show mercy unto me.'"

Have you heard, O people, how late that night, like a Christ of love and mercy, a sorrowful man visited den after den of wretchedness and woe, leaving everywhere as he passed a ray of help and comfort? How, day after day, and night after night, souls (by their governors called the "abandoned," the "worthless") despairing, learned to hope? Not here can we search through a life in its forming. History inquires only of the man the complete soul, imaged of his Maker, or of the man, soul desecrated, defaced from the Master pattern.

One sits there, stern and forbidding, a tall, sinewy man, his wild, brown hair shading a face whose pale, oval features we scarce notice first, so drawn are we by the ocean depth and steelful strength of the look of him. The dark brown piercing eyes read you at a glance; you would not dare to argue with that man; there is a look in him which warns one that "facts are wanted here." You wonder if that mouth can open readily, so fixed set are the lips, yet did women and children see only love and sweetness there, and felt an abiding trust in him, and the lowliest swore that he was gentler than any woman.

His dress, which served more than to distinguish sex, bespoke a character as well as defined an office—a black, military uniform, with no tightness anywhere; the uniform seemed made for the man, not the man for the uniform; no weapon was outwardly visible; perhaps a revolver was there where three or four buttons at the breast were open. Some say that beneath the cloth is a close-knit shirt of steel, perhaps true, perhaps not true; he smiles when they ask him; replies shortly, "When my people want me no more, my heart is easily pierced; till then I've a stronger armour than of steel—soul the name of it, fearlessness of aught but God, and reliance in the love of my people." Of the influence which Carlyle Democritus obtained over his co-workers and subordinates, neither the historian can adequately describe, nor could the majority of his readers comprehend.

The people believed in him. Dost thou understand all the immensity of love and adoration contained in that word "Belief," my brother? The people had great cause to believe in him; he had not gained their suffrage by caucus or by rhetoric; he was entirely free of the fatuities of debate—spoke little, argued never. His orders were absolute, and were never challenged; his entire system was one of the most complete and exacting discipline, yet it pressed unjustly on no man.

In all his council there was one man whose hours of labour were without respite, whose energy never flagged, whose work was unceasing—that one was Carlyle Democritus.

Before bugle-call in the morning he was astir; no smallest cause of the humblest of his followers appealed to him in vain. There was no promise to "consider" any grievance; there was immediate and decisive judgment upon it. Let the oppressor beware!

And the officers were worthy of their General. Never were seen men more resolute. We see them late in the evening of one of the days following the memorable 14th of February in a large lofty room, close off the entrance of the Revolution Headquarters. Messengers arrive frequently with despatches. Besides Democritus and his coadjutors, a staff of writers are busy filing papers, writing orders, and receiving instructions from the leaders; it is a busy scene, the busiest of scenes. Of talk there is little; of method and of action let the succeeding chapters speak.

CHAPTER II.

(INTERCALARY)

JUBILEE UTOPIA, OR "EVERYWHERE."

"THE old order giveth way to the new." And there was not much of the old order, or disorder, which the Revolution left unreformed.

One order which was to disappear entirely was the order of the slums. But a portion of the slum order of things was, for a time, to be preserved for purposes to be explained later on. It is necessary, meanwhile, that the record of a Jubilee slum should be preserved. The present chapter will therefore transcribe from a certain slum history, written by a worthy minister of the Church of England, who lived in the slum he depicted—a somewhat condensed description of what may be called a Jubilee Utopia— except that instead of being nowhere, the Jubilee slum was to be found everywhere. The record may be prefaced by this remarkable (35) clause which one of the largest Jubilee Slum Companies required its tenants to accept as a condition of occupancy in their "National Model Dwellings, Limited": "No contract of letting shall be deemed to contain, or imply any condition, or undertaking on the part of the Company that the premises shall be fit for human occupation."

Given *that* "condition"—not a fancy condition, O reader, but an actual Jubilee condition—published to the world by "eminent Council" on behalf of the "National Model Dwellings Company, Limited," as a reason why a poor woman, who had been maimed by the neglect of the said Company, should not be compensated for her injuries, and you will perhaps be able to realize the swine- (36) conditions which Jubilee landlordism considered itself free to foist upon the poor generally. May it be hoped that those pious people who complacently believe that cleanliness, healthfulness, brightness, honesty, pureness of life, morality, frugality, and most other "alities," are impossible to be cultivated amongst the poorer classes, and that every opponent of that damnable doctrine is a dreamer, faddist, maddist, theorist, Utopiaist, anything-ist—except a philosophical or practical mortal—may it be hoped that they will not readily forget the "condition" upon which poor workers in Jubilee times had to accept their tenancies.

"Everywhere."

(86a) "The population of the Great Wild Street district amounts to some 6000 persons; it is mostly composed of costermongers, bricklayers' labourers, scavengers, scene-shifters, artisans out of work, women and girls who earn a poor living in all sorts of ways. This is how these people live:—The scavenger earns 18s. a week, has wife and seven children. They live in a miserable back room, for which they have to pay 6s. a week rent, subject to summary seizure of effects for arrears, and ejection even in mid-winter into the gutters. The rent paid, they have left 12s. a week for food, fuel, light, and clothing, or 1s. 4d. a week for each member of the family. Two of the children sleep in the same bed—generally a sack of filthy rag accumulations stuck on tubs or boards—as their parents; the rest lie in a heap on the floor—floor and walls dank with the neglect of years.

"There is a skilled artisan out of work—a teetotaller this one—with wife dying of consumption; they live with their children in a front room, which had been a shop. The whole family has to live and sleep in the same room as the sick mother, and when she at last died they had still to occupy the same room —the living and the dead. The rent of that wretched hole is 10s. or 10s. 6d. a week. The wretched artisan determines his wife shall want for nothing that he can provide for her. So all his property falls to the pawnbroker, even to the coat upon his back. Upstairs in the same house there is another room in which three families all live in community, day and night; they number twelve persons in all. And in the same street lives a woman of eighty years, lying in an attic—attic with large gap in the wall of it —and for many weeks during the most severe part of winter, there lay the old woman with the bitter winds playing about her head, and the rain and snow saturating the floor of her room." The clergyman who is describing all this must not interfere; the only result would be "to get the old woman and her daughter, and a widow living with her children downstairs, turned out into the street." And the stars are shining in the winter night, and in adjacent clubs there is much other shining . . . and God is above the vanity and the misery, and a Carlyle Democritus has arisen who will carry fire and sword through this upas jungle. . . . "About ten or eleven o'clock at night, outside our (minister's) house, barrel-organs begin to play, and continue playing till midnight. Around them are groups of young people indulging in the coarsest play and coarsest language; bands of little children dance to the mingled accompaniments of obscene songs and profane oaths. From the bars of the various public-houses emanate confused noise of men's voices brutalised by drink. The public-houses close at last, and the drunkards are turned out into the gutter, where their children are waiting for them, serving early apprenticeship to drunkenness and profligacy. Some of the less experienced or less hardened children take their parents by the hand, and say, 'Come home, father!' and 'Come home, mother!' But a daughter is struck down by many brutal blows in the face from her own mother. Home, indeed! they don't go home many of them; the men collect in groups, discuss 'politics' or 'religion,' which generally means wholesale denunciation of capital, property, authority, order, virtue, and of God. Suppose you had been dragged up from your birth in one of these dens, might you not have turned out even worse than many of those whom you now think so very bad?" It is the godly pastor who asks you this, English people, the pastor who knows and who records that even in all this Pandemonium of filth and degradation there was abundant human aspiration after a better life, could it only be possible—the God-breathed soul burns in many of those thousands —in *most* of them—" Is no Saviour there for us?" "Those who are too much intoxicated to discuss 'politics' and 'religion,' 'sing,' and the women and girls take chorus; the noise is as if the gates of Pandemonium were opened and the demon of darkness let loose upon the street; and the worst nights are Sunday and Saturday. On these nights, until three or four in the morning, there is continuous uproar"—the public-houses have well deluged their victims with beer- and spirit-Kings' productions. "Singing, chanting, howling, yelling, cursing, fighting; women's voices crying 'murder,' and the voices of little children screaming with terror, whilst their parents are desperately fighting with their boon companions, or with one another. In the morning I find the street door stained with blood!" The health of this real pastor and his wife fail at first in the stench and filth of Slumland. "But God strengthened us to stay and minister to these forsaken ones." And so good pastor and pastor-wife continued in Slumland, not in a £10,000 a year bishop's palace; and he writes the history of their poor flock for the behoof of us and of Utopia critics. He continues:—

"The majority of houses in this (Great Wild Street) district, if in thorough repair, would not be worth £50 a year, but in their present condition are not worth the rent of a good pigsty, yet are let out to about a dozen families, some of them numbering nine or ten individuals, some less. Let us take an average of five. This gives sixty human beings. Sixty, sometimes a hundred persons, are compelled to live in a house hardly large enough to afford proper accommodation to a seventh part of that number; and when thus driven to herd together like pigs—the accommodation actually afforded them is not equal to that which any respectable farmer would provide for his pigs—of what sort must we expect the majority of such persons to be? Godly, righteous, sober? Honest, loyal, pure? Suppose *you* had been dragged up from your birth in one of these miserable dens, might you not have turned out even worse than many of those whom you now think so very bad?"

Let us stop at this question, O pastor; for we must fain transcribe thy whole book of two hundred printed pages to give any adequate idea of only this one slum-Utopia to the readers of this history. Verily thou art a dearer pastor to us than the £10,000 or even £15,000 a year archbishop, intent upon Church house, which thy poor cobbler humbly inquires the meaning of, and which thou, with pious cant, O best of pastors! triest, quite vainly, to explain to poor benighted cobbler and rest of mankind.

Much of the preceding and yet more of kindred horrors did the Revolution cause to be printed as a sort of manifesto, and sent broadcast throughout the land. The conclusion of the famous "Slum Manifesto," as it got to be called, ran thus: "To such a pass have you been brought, O English workers, by party Government, with their fine-spun platform eloquences, electioneering dodgeries, charity subscriptions, political bun feasts! Will you

continue to have them, O English people, and *their* Utopias?"—
"Pandemonium-Utopias," says poor pastor—"or will you stand by
us who have vowed to wash away in blood, if need be, slums and
slum owners? Yes, O people, we are coming to your relief with
the armed humanity of Great Britain at our back, and woe to the
slum fiends, the slum abettors, the time-serving Parliament orators
who have tolerated them and the likes of them. When it is
darkest, approaches the dawn."

CHAPTER III.

JUSTICE RETRIBUTIVE.

"The Word of God came unto me, saying: Now, thou son of man, wilt thou judge, wilt thou judge the bloody city? yea, thou shalt show her all her abominations. Say then, Thou hast defiled thyself in thine idols that thou hast made. In the midst of thee they have dealt by oppression; in thee they have vexed the fatherless and the widow. Thou hast taken usury and increase, and thou hast greedily gained of thy neighbours by extortion, and hast forgotten Me, saith the Lord God. Behold, therefore, I have smitten Mine hand at thy dishonest gain which thou hast made. Can thine heart endure, or can thine hands be strong, in the days that I shall deal with thee? Ye are like wolves ravening the prey, to destroy souls, to get dishonest gain. Ye have used oppression and exercised robbery, and have vexed the poor and needy."—EZEKIEL.

FOR the present in no way were the established institutions of law interfered with; but side by side with the courts of the kingdom—which by judge and magistrate continued their dealings with the usual smaller criminalities—there came into existence "the Court of Judgment of the Revolution," presided over by Carlyle Democritus, whose power and wisdom equalled that of the ancient king who sat in judgment over the Hebrew people three thousand years ago, and whose judgments live to-day, and will for ever live unchoked by parchment, wigs, and mere verbosity.

The Court was a large and lofty octagonal hall; its ceilings and sides entirely covered by heavy drapings of black, upon which were written in characters blood-red these various texts: "Because ye have oppressed and forsaken the poor," "Whoso stoppeth his ears at the cry of the poor, he shall cry himself, but shall not be heard."

High over the entrance, underneath a symbol of the Divinity, "I call Heaven and earth to record this day against you, that I have set before you life and death, blessings and cursings."

The partial light of the room was led through coloured windows, so arranged as to fall directly upon the high raised canopy under which sat the stern, commanding form of the people's leader.

The first prisoner having been placed in the dock, a profound silence prevailed. Through the solemn stillness the deep voice of the accuser is heard, terrible in its earnestness : "Prisoner David xhume, you have been the first in all this land invested with a mighty power in the name of God, to justly guide and rule this English people, and you stand fatally and ignobly forsworn. Answer briefly, if you have answer, to the charges which lie against you, and against those who have worked with you.

"For thirty-seven years you have enjoyed the confidence of your country, have been intrusted with its care; you, self-imposed upon the people, not sought by them. You have seen, during that period, the wretchedness of the lower classes increase and multiply, until, by the records of your own officers, thousands of innocent men, women, and children have been decimated by misery and disease. During all that time the upper classes of your people have increased in wealth and luxury, yet you have, throughout your career, steadily ignored God's law, you have persistently neglected the poor who are in our midst, you have been one to feed upon their toil. To the thing of party, and to pretended reforms, you have prostituted your influence and that of your order, whilst gross injustice and neglect have been rife throughout the land.

"You have scattered broadcast the honours and rewards which this nation has long intrusted to your keeping, but they have been used by you to fatten your kindred upon, and to bribe the worthless, the vain, and mere political vampires. Retribution at last overtakes you. In addition to the sequestration of your property by the State, in the name of an outraged people, in the name of the God whose eternal laws you have ignored, you are judged. 'As you have done unto others, so shall others do unto you.'"

Rhetoric availed not here, and other answer there could be none. Prison vans in quick succession removed the condemned, and were busy with their loads until late into the night. One fate overtook them all—bishops, ministers, lords, and laymen; money lenders who had oppressed the people, owners of filthy slums who had bled the people; guinea-pig members of Parliament;

swindling or sinecure officials of all kinds; jobbing vestrymen, unjust licensing magistrates. The list was long, and the guilty numerous.

For weeks before the holding of the Retribution Court the filthiest slums in London had been the scene of a strange activity; blocks of thirty, and smaller allottings, were isolated, after having been cleared of their residents, these all being cleanly lodged and liberally fed in bright and healthy places, amongst them the palaces and mansions of the nobles and wealthy, whose property had been attached, and which had been converted into temporary lodgments for the people. Blocks in the slums were isolated by high and strongly built walls, guarded in all parts by strong bands of armed patrols. Into these dens of filth and disease, with their rotten floors, their dank walls, the roadways and pavements impregnated with loathsomeness of every kind; into these hells of stench and abomination which the wealthy had provided for the poor, the poor now incarcerated the wealthy.

Van after van set down their loads of men and women and children, for the judgments were not incomplete. "As ye have done unto others, so shall be done unto you," and the sentence of the condemned fell also upon his wife and child.

But not even this frightful Retribution could allay the wrath of the savage people. Those who had directly fed upon the misery of the slum denizens, the owners of the tenements, the millionaire nobles who owned and abetted them, those money lenders, pawn-brokers, and publicans who had fattened on all this filth and wretchedness, found no mercy. As each van set down its load, and one by one the name and sentence of the condemned was read out to each, the crime and the awful penalty, wherever the crime was "owning property in a slum and exacting exorbitant rents therefrom;" "keeping a public-house in a slum for the sale of vile and intoxicating liquors;" "lending money to the necessitous poor and exacting usurious terms;" "exacting the payment of iniquitous rents from the starving and suffering;" one frightful yell of triumph and revenge kindled again the hellish horrors of the place, and a thousand beings—no longer human—thrust and hacked the parasites of their misery to a hideous death; corpses, mangled beyond all recognition, strewed the narrow streets; such scenes, such demon work, that even the filthy slum seemed a heaven's refuge to the tender women whose terrible lot it was to witness these doings. On what an earth the stars looked down that night; within and without these horrible prisons, groans resounded on all sides; within of the living, without from those whose mangled forms still harboured life.

To have to live, thus bereft of hope, bereft of help, strong men despaired, wives prayed for death; yet for every one sentenced to imprisonment in those prison-slums there had lived and breathed a thousand; souls born of the Eternal God; sentient to pain, obeying co-equal laws. The penalty was complete in its infinite justness, wretchedness, and misery! And the crime? Had not that been great? Even until the cry of it had touched the mercy-seat!

Early the next morning they bring rough carts to remove the dead and give them burial; the horses wade through pools of gore, and stamp the bloody trail far on the frozen city roads; and further still, the awe-struck traveller traced the route by drips from the shaken bodies, unending, till the suburban burial-ground is reached.

A neglected, disused field was this; they dug a wide and ample pit, and filled it with the dead. In later days, a pyramid of stones was formed above it, and on a large, flat slab of granite these red words were inscribed, and may still be read:—

"Beneath this stone lie buried the remains of thirteen hundred and seventy victims who fell at the outbreak of the English Revolution. Less were they the victims of the people's fury than of their own accursed greed and Mammon-worship.

"Woe unto them that build by unrighteousness."

The sentence which fell upon the Bishops because they had also fostered slums and public-houses compelled them also to the (39) slums, there to fill the poorest places before held by their humblest pastors. Their entire properties and wealth were confiscated, and their office thenceforward abolished.

The sequestrations and confiscations of those already doomed by the Revolutionary Court reached scores of millions in land and property, all of which fell into the country's exchequer, and formed a special fund called "Retribution Money;" the interest of it alone sufficed to feed and house the entire mass of the poor until new labour laws and work could be established for them.

PART II.
CONSTRUCTIVE.

Book I.

REVOLUTION JUSTIFIES ITSELF AND SOLVES THE SOCIAL PROBLEM.

"And if, on due and honest thought over these things, it seems that the kind of existence to which men are now summoned by every plea of pity and claim of right, may, for some time at least, not be a luxurious one; consider whether, even supposing it guiltless, luxury would be desired by any of us, if we saw clearly at our sides the suffering which accompanies it in the world. Luxury at present can only be enjoyed by the ignorant; the cruellest man living could not sit at his feast unless he sat blindfolded. RAISE THE VEIL BOLDLY! FACE THE LIGHT! And if as yet the light of the eye can only be through tears, and the light of the body through sackcloth, go thou forth weeping bearing precious seed. . . . "—RUSKIN.

CHAPTER I.

CARLYLE DEMOCRITUS'S MANIFESTO TO THE ENGLISH PEOPLE

FEW are the revolutions that have seared and maimed the nations of the world from whose burnt ashes of putridity and corruption a new and glorious phœnix has arisen to bless the revolted people with wise, just, and equal government. And the reason is not far to seek. They have mostly been without direction. Generations of lies, injustices, foulness, and iniquity have festered and have suppurated till they finally have burst, in universal stench and Hell eruption. Sometimes a more or less able physician has been *afterwards* found to bleed the suffering nation yet a little, and patch, but scarcely heal, its gaping wounds.

Unfortunately it has occurred that the wise leader arrived too late. Revolutions have seldom been conducted until all leadership was futile, and when the spirit of devotion and obedience had been already slain, along with the evils which had exasperated them. Carlyle Democritus had betimes perceived this, and he adopted wise precautions against miscarriage. He organised reform *before*, instead of after, revolution.

Never, in times of revolution, did the suffering people know aught but that they fought to slay, revenge themselves upon, and exterminate the tyrants, bloodsuckers, and vampires who had fed upon them and outraged them, until human endurance had reached its term. Like the blind anarchists, rampant everywhere in that Jubilee period, created by the universal misery which they had hearts and entrails to witness and abhor, but lacked the knowledge how to overcome, they preached a mad destruction, but could not teach repair.

Not thus the wise Carlyle Democritus. He not only determined that his soldiers should utterly destroy the evil and spare the good, but he determined furthermore that every humble soul in Britain should *know* the evil and *see* the good. Therefore, and immediately upon the successful establishment of the English Revolution, he caused to be printed and circulated throughout the kingdom the order of things he was about to destroy because of their rottenness and abuse, and also the order of things he was about to establish in their place—the dictate of wisdom, justice, and divine right. Furthermore, in the form of a manifesto, he caused his programme of reform to be publicly read by an officer of the Revolutionary army in every church, town hall, and public assembly-room throughout the kingdom. Thus should the whole nation be imbued with a thorough knowledge of his measures, of their justice and of their wisdom, for he knew that *with* the people only could rest their final and assured success. Unless the whole nation understood and sympathised with his great reforms they could not attain stability. Remember, you who are reading this, that Carlyle Democritus saw God and truth in his every act. He was not a Sorrypebble, bewildering, misleading, and lying to the people; therefore when he wrote "The whole nation," he did not mean the most ignorant, debased, and disloyal fraction of the English people; nor did he mean the few thousands at the other extremity of the national scale, who had fed for generations upon the people, and out of their unending wretchedness had amassed besotten and useless wealth. The criminal outcasts of want, and the yet more criminal outcasts of wealth, he knew, would about equally counterbalance one another. He left their thousands quite uncounted. They might be one, or might be two hundred thousand, or more or less, but they were not, *either* of them, the English nation.

From his manifesto, and other edicts, we select the following:—

"Carlyle Democritus, in the name of the army of Revolution, to the people of Great Britain everywhere:—

"The time for mere speaking having passed away, and the time of action having supervened, the Council of the Revolutionary Forces hereby announce, as briefly as the importance of the matter will permit, the abuses which they found existing, and which they have risen to destroy, and the remedies they are about to substitute for them. These are the evils and abuses in their order:—(1) Parliament has not truly represented the nation; land-owners, lawyers, mere rich men, have been there in overwhelming prominence; but, except in individual instances, the labourer, the poor, the suffering, have had no real presence. One remedy will be the extension of the Suffrage to every adult man able independently to mark a ballot paper. Excepted will be criminals, and some few others who need not here be dealt with. The State will bear the entire cost of future elections, and stringent measures will be provided to ensure and to enforce the absolute independence of the elector and the candidate. (2) The land has been allowed by land-owning legislators to accumulate in the hands of a mere fraction of the people. It may be roughly put that there is one landowner out of every four thousand people, so that these four thousand English people have paid toll to that one. The largest of these landowners, directly or indirectly, practically stole their land in one manner or another from the Church and from the Nation. Only a few illustrations need here be cited. England's King Henry VIII. required an agent to go to France and gain French aid to favour one of his divorces. A certain William Paget successfully achieved that discreditable business. For 'reward,' the King, having sequestrated the Church lands wholesale, literally showered them upon Paget; more than twenty various manors in different counties, each manor comprising several parishes."

There was a page boy to the same King—one Richard Cecil—*his* first lift was from the Church lands of Stamford—the King quickly added other manors and parishes. The descendant of that young gentleman ruled England as Prime Minister towards Jubilee period. For one quite fractional portion of his numerous acres he demanded £50,000 from the people of London, *over and above the amount already assessed at an enormous figure*, because the people's toil had rendered a street improvement necessary upon land "owned" by that descendant. A third and last illustration— three hundred or three thousand might be given, but three will suffice—the frugal trader judges of his stock by sample:—Sutherland is a fair county, whose verdant pastures bore through long ages a brave and patient peasantry. Listen to the doom of that peasantry and their lands, brought about by a "noble lady," mother's mother to the jubilee owner, lord of nine palaces and castles. "Under their old Celtic tenures the men of Sutherland were the proprietors of the soil. The whole of Sutherland belonged

(40)

G

to the children of the soil. Never were those men of Sutherland conquered, never had any of them, then or afterwards, forfeited their ancient rights. Never had any lord the right to diminish by an acre the people's ownership." Great historians have proved this. Read your Stanhope, Sismondi, Burton—the cultivators, they who, after God, "made" the land; they, the brave cultivators, with righteous labour for their title, owned the land. Thus goes on Sismondi: "By cruel abuse of legal 'forms,' by unjust usurpation, modern lords expelled those peasants from their lands which they had tilled and occupied for ages." It was a peaceable, loyal, industrious, and religious people, and thus were they treated. Armed with cruel "legal forms," the Marchioness of Sutherland, grandmother to the Jubilee Sutherlands, took from those people their little farms, converted their 794,000 acres into a score and a half great sheep runs, each such sheep run bearing only one family. But how were the fifteen thousand peasants cleared—evicted? Listen, O English people. Those fifteen thousand men of Sutherland, each one of them a God-created soul, loved their land and clung to it, and would not *go*. So the tender lady "in due and legal form" did thus with them: The heather around their homes was set on fire—thus were the people's cattle starved. To save a few of them, the wretched peasants drove such as had not died to neighbouring markets to realize a little by their sale. In the absence of those peasants their cottages were pulled down over their wives' and children's heads, and set on fire. Fatigue and cold killed the poor people; women gave birth to children in open fields with the bare soil for couch; old men, women, and children, fever-stricken, were turned adrift indiscriminately. Contemplate a picture of one of the scenes by one who witnessed it, here on this God's earth, in this free and merry England—not in Spanish Inquisition days, not in Bloody Mary's times—but in this Jubilee century, in the years whilst fair Victoria was a child, training for the throne. Says the eye-witness: "I ascended a height at about eleven o'clock at night, and I counted two hundred and fifty blazing houses." In two parishes alone three hundred houses were thus fired by those noble landlords (or is it not rather land-devils?). Starvation set in amongst these people; wholesale and unending misery and wretchedness. "Their sufferings were incredible," says Hugh Miller. And this was the hotbed whereon in irredeemable wickedness an English noble grew

—to-day the "lord" of one million three thousand British acres—"acquired," says a brave historian, "by legal robbery, and taken possession of by high-handed cruelty, by wanton and inhuman crime, and violation of right and justice." Nor in later times had (41) the Sutherland brood in any way changed its merciless, murderous conduct towards its wretched tenantry. The Duke living in the year 1894, in imitation of his thrice-damned ancestors, who had turned out the old tenants from the crofting property of Loth in the county of Sutherland to starvation and torment, in order to convert their cereal lands into sheep-runs, tried to turn out some of the sheep farmers also, whose ancestors had been put in possession of those sheep-runs since the beginning of the century. The Sutherland duke applied to the Court to get possession of the whole property of those poor tenants, because they had *begun* to be in arrears with their rent. The Court examined the facts and *did not, this time*, help the Sutherland Duke to turn women and children out of their cottages into the fields, and then burn down their poor homes; but, instead, the Court wiped out forty-one per cent. of the arrears "due" to the money-grubbing, soulless Duke. (Duke means leader, you British people. What a Duke-leader for a free people to bow down before and pay rent to! Verily the slaves who tolerate such Duke-leaders deserve their chains.) Yes, the Court cancelled forty-one per cent. of the Loth croft-rents claimed by the "Duke," and reduced the remaining Loth croft-rents thirteen per cent. in addition. Women were not to be compelled to childbed on the frozen fields this time. Innocent children were not to be cast out to starvation in mid-winter. For this account of the Sutherland dukeries, or duperies, appeared in the *Times* of 1894. O ye men of Loth in Sutherland, and of all (42) Great Britain, shall a Carlyle Democritus call unto you in vain to stand by him whilst he rives the accursed chains wrought by Mammon Peers and Mammon Parliaments? But to continue the Sutherland records: "A large portion of this same family's Shropshire and Staffordshire estates consists of confiscated Church property." Enough — the majority of Irish, Scotch, and English landlords, or devils, owe their possessions to mere confiscations, robbery from the Church, and legal frauds, "sanctified" by a prostituted Parliament of freedom. One who has studied deeply this land villainy, examined and published the records of one hundred and twenty-two such nobles—the lords of some six million British acres, stolen from the people — assures us he sought not out the thieves, but faithfully continued his search into the records of noble houses whether they proved foul or fair. "Yet," says he, "of all those one hundred and twenty-two landed gentry, perhaps there are *one dozen* who have obtained their lands by commerce or professional pursuit."

(43)

(44) We have seen a little what were the methods of the Scotch evictions. Now glance briefly at those of poor Ireland:—

This is from the *Times*, not over-given to ungentleness for Irish landlordism, far otherwise:—"The evictions at Glenbeigh are still being carried out from day to day. The scenes of wretchedness, squalor, and misery which prevail among the tenants are most painful. Yesterday, after a tenant was evicted, it was represented to the agent that the tenant's child was dying, and its mother begged a shelter for it for the night, but the agent refused, and ordered the bailiffs to nail up the door. The poor woman cried bitterly, and laid the dying child in the pig-stye in the yard, and tried to procure straw for a bed *there*." Then the wild passion of an Irish Joan of Arc kindled in her, and seizing a spade, she rushed at the vile minions of the British "law," felled one of the law-things to earth,—and was seized by the main body of them and led off to "justice." . . . But the blood of the evicted was up, and they attacked the bailiff escort and rescued the maid, God be praised, and . . . Yes, reader, the evictors did not further tempt Revolution *that* time; the maid was left alone, and was not prosecuted. At Glenbeigh they turned the poor Irish out of their homes in the way you have just heard; then they burned down the little cottages. Not the sack of Troy, this, but the sack of poor Irish industry by absentee landlordism, British Jubilee Governments supplying law officers and bayonets. To a "question" in Jubilee Parliament, anno 1894, the Irish Secretary

(45) answered:—43,457 ejectment notices had been served on tenants under section 7 of the Irish Land Act of 1887. Poor Irish Jubilee Secretary had to carry out the "law"—the Jubilee Devil's law. What connection Jubilee LAW had with God's JUSTICE let no British man inquire, for to that there is but one answer—NONE. Reader, you will not confound the present historian amongst the cant-sympathisers of the moonlighting class,

or of the cant-priest, or cant-political class. Heaven forbid! But confound him also not with that yet more fatal class which for too long has endeavoured—and successfully enough—to persuade poor ignorant British folk that "evictions are the produce of agitators." The reverse is the truth. Agitators are the produce of evictions. Have you ever tried to "agitate" the peasant of a justly ordered state? Of a justly ordered *anything?* Try it, O son of man, thou wouldst find it easier to "agitate" the firmly rooted oak-tree. But place filth, fire, and faggot round your oak-tree, laden its every branch and twig with vermin, scratch off its bark year after year, and leave it naked before the winter winds. THEN thy agitation-process shall become possible; the root which held the goodly tree to the soil well killed; *then*, indeed, is agitation easy. But go *back*, not forward, to discover who and what killed the root. The agitator is the direct product of neglect, cruelty, and injustice. Scotch your producer, your infamous injustice, and your agitator will disappear like snow before summer sun. The Irish moonlighter is a coward and very devil's imp. Not so that Irish maiden in broad daylight felling the minion of British injustice. She is a heroine of womanhood to every breathing soul who hath heart and head to know true courage. As there is sunlight in the heavens, so is it sure that, given a nation of Irish spade-maidens, like that Joan-of-Glenbeigh heroine, and no evictions could any more be possible in Ireland. The day when Poverty shall say to Wealth, "My life is nothing, but justice my all—for that I will fight or die"—from that day is Poverty FREE. Free from injustice. Other freedom there need be none; for has not the wisest of men said, "Freedom means the right to be justly governed!" That, the only right of man. But was it not hopeless for poor Ireland—misery, want, starvation at home, and absentee landlords and liars abroad—and no race of Godly Joans of Glenbeigh, but only now and then an occasional one?

Here is a last bit from the *Times* newspaper of the year 1894, Jubilee Radical Government in full swing, intent upon universal anarchy:—"The people in the Isles of Arran are starving; they are in no way responsible for the distress that has come upon them. The summer parched up the light, sandy soil, which scarcely covers the limestone in Arran. As a consequence, the potato crop was an almost complete failure. Father M'Donald writes:—

'Even now a steamer is on her way from Galway bearing the agent and sheriff and a large force of police to evict these starving people, because they cannot pay rent for the land by which they lost seed and sweat and gained nothing but disappointment and misery.' He states that 'the Government had been applied to for assistance, and refused, and the poor people of the Isles are dying from starvation and exposure.' He sent the following message to the Government: 'As the result of our entreaties for relief, you have sent a force of police for evictions. Numbers of the starving poor of Arran are out among the bleak hills to-night.'" *

---

* This altogether brutal specimen of British Jubilee oppression, landlordism, or land-devilism, provoked a worthy member of Parliament, who actually left the House, crossed the Channel, and went to Irish Arran. Here is his report, duly published in the *Times* newspaper :—

"I have just visited Aranmore to see for myself the evicted tenants and the condition of the holdings and the people. I feel bound to say that the evictions seem unjustifiable. . . . In the case of the vast majority of the tenants the rent is charged : (1) For holdings created *entirely* by the people, who with enormous labour have spread layers of sand, decomposed seaweed, and mould scraped from the crevices over the bare flat limestone rocks ; and (2) For the precarious right of wading breast-deep in the sea to rake in the red seaweed which, when burned, becomes 'kelp.' In other words, the only thing the landlord has to dispose of on these islands is the use of the bare rock ; all the rest is contributed by the tenant. . . . Yet the rents will be found to be appreciably higher than for many districts on the mainland, where the landlord has something more than bare rocks to charge for. The natural result is that many, perhaps nearly all, the tenants are crippled with arrears. The drought of last year reduced the artificial soil—only six to nine inches deep, and with the rock peeping out at every few yards—to a dry powder, and the potatoes came to little or nothing. The seed potatoes had been eaten . . . the destitution is appalling. Many families are said to be subsisting on one meal a day, and that of Indian corn. . . . The priests are raising a small fund from other parts of Ireland to help them to get seed potatoes. . . . These people are rented on their own improvements. . . . It is not worth while to try to squeeze a pound or two out of them by the process of eviction. Here and there a few pounds may be got—not earned by nature or by industry, but levied on the charitable funds raised by the priests, or on the contributions of the Irish in America, and taking away the tiny remnant of saving with which a man might try to pull through—in any case, leaving the poor wretch more helpless than ever. I saw one old fellow of sixty-five, born on his holding of about twenty-eight acres, two-thirds of which he had made on the rocks by his own labour. He had paid over £16 last year, and has just saved himself from eviction by help from the priest

Good Father M'Donald, dost *thou* also feel in thy heart the noble rage, the fierce indignation, which thrilled the poet Tennyson when he denounced those vile "Hustings liars"?* Brave Father, they will not answer thee, those "Hustings liars," except with bayonets. And there followed the usual "questions" in Parliament, and the usual "answers," perhaps a little more tragic than many, for the Right Hon. Jubilee Minister admitted that, in the case of the starving peasants of Arran, who were being evicted to hopeless misery and wretchedness, by order of their absentee landlords and landladies, supported by British bayonets, that the said peasants had absolutely created the soil upon which they farmed; that originally "there was no natural soil on those Islands, but that the crops were grown on soil artificially created by the labour of the islanders out of sand, seaweed, and decayed ferns, placed in layers on the bare rock, and surrounded by walls to prevent it from being blown away; the soil of the islands was wholly the result of the labour of the tenants themselves." And now, when by the lack of rain the people were without food and no rent was possible, the land*lords*, ay, and the land*ladies*, were come to dispossess the poor peasants who, after God, had made that soil. To dispossess them, turn them, their women and their little children out into the blackness

(48)

---

and from a daughter, and even then is left with arrears from 1892 hanging like a millstone round his neck. . . . Some of the evicted families are huddled in utter misery—quite unimaginable till actually seen—with neighbours even more destitute. In one case were twelve persons in a hut smaller than a railway carriage. Such an island as Aranmore—and others are said to be in a much worse condition—is a grave economic problem." (Ay, most worthy Member of Parliament, grave indeed, graver than you, or the soulless ministers intent only on votes were aware.) "I would submit that the attempt at such a time as this to extort rents hard enough to scrape together (in the best of seasons) is merely to multiply the wretchedness and pauperism of these miserable people. . . . Would it not be better economy—would it not pay to be merciful? . . ."

"*Would it not pay to be merciful?*" No, O worthy Member of Parliament, mercy will never pay! Mercy will at first only sweetly *plead*, and when, no more to be heard, JUSTICE will come, outraged JUSTICE! Not meek any longer, but in fury of Divine wrath, as in Hell-fire of French Revolution, and will burn up the unutterable party fiends and all who have supported or tolerated them.

* Page 427.

of night and unending misery. Oh! Spirit of French Reign of Terror, who will not worship thee as a God, beside these devil-imps of a Jubilee England! Did inhumanity and injustice more horrible than those Irish evictions evoke thee? "The starving Frenchwomen gathering nettles, and the French nobility robbing them of each third nettle, and calling it rent!" But with these poor Irish peasants, because for a season there are no nettles even, shall the British land-devils turn them out into utter desolation. Slowly, slowly gathers the wrath of outraged heaven, but there is a limit to human infamy; there is a limit to infamous injustice:

"My Irish brothers and sisters, I am coming, I, Carlyle Democritus, with the armed humanity of Great Britain at my back, to HELP thee, no longer to *eject* thee from thy labour and from thy field.

"The receiver has ever been held worse than the thief, so were those titled and untitled landlords worse, if possible, than their Kings and Parliaments. The land of the people has been stolen from the people, and now the time has come when we will restore to the people their possessions. This is our remedy for the land abuse: The whole of the British soil, where it has not been acquired by honourable purchase or true service, will be forthwith sequestrated to the State. The law of entail and dual ownership will be absolutely abolished. No man shall have landlordship over any other man. Facility will be afforded to every man to acquire, upon just and reasonable terms, the perpetual leasehold of his own holding in town or country. Adequate compensation will be given in every case of *bona fide* acquisition. A Land Court, somewhat similarly constituted to the Jubilee Crofter Courts, will hear and decide all claims. Farms, and allotments for farm labourers, together with help at starting where required, will be afforded to agricultural settlers throughout the three kingdoms.

"3. The housing of the labouring classes has been a scandal for generations, largely due to the iniquitous land system and the more iniquitous land-owners (here followed the picture which will be found on page 84). Remedy:—Slum-land will be entirely demolished, and broad healthy streets and homes erected in their stead throughout the country.

"4. *Finance.*—The Revolutionary Funds are ample for all

requirements; and, were they not, they quickly should be made so, for we have determined that no just reform shall be delayed. The infinite cruelties of war have never stayed for want of money. The infinite mercies of right and justice shall not stay either for such consideration.

"5. *The Church.*—There will be wise reform here also. Hearken to the necessity of it. This is the history of a Jubilee Lord of Christ—one amongst many such. One Charles Manners Sutton (49) was (though the grandson of a peer) educated at the Blue-coat Charity School—a School founded for the maintenance and education of the poor. At an early age Court influence made young Sutton a bishop, and later on an archbishop. His fitness for the post may be gauged from the fact that in spite of the £100,000 (not bad that, whilst hard-working slum pastors were starving on sundry shillings a week) he had already received (prior to the (50) archiespiscopacy) from the Church Funds, he was overwhelmed in debt. History gives his income from the archbishopric at over £20,000 a year; some authorities put it at over £30,000 a year! Altogether, this one worthy received from the English Church Funds a sum far exceeding half a million pounds sterling; he saved towards the end of his life, and left to his sorrowing family the sum of £180,000. He had before his death used his influence to berth his family with the fattest livings he could touch. One of his sons-in-law filled four "livings."; We ought to say he *emptied* four livings, for he drew the monies from them, but did little else. Another of this gentleman's sons-in-law died a few years before the Jubilee Period, and the *Guardian*, the organ of the Church of (51) England, says that this holy man received from the Funds of the Church no less a sum than £168,680. Abuse can go no further. State and Church are alike corrupt. We will remedy them, and thus: All Church livings and property, from every source soever, will be made a common fund. Church palaces will not be longer tolerated, nor will Church public-houses, nor Church slums. The future (39) ministers of Christ and their sources of revenue shall accord a little with the Divine Master's teaching. No worthy pastors will be allowed to starve on a fifth-rate clerk's salary, nor will a bishop be allowed a palace and £15,000 a year. But there will be a rough average stipend of £400 a year for every worthy pastor, and we shall take measures to prevent there ever being any worthless ones. A Pastoral Conference will be established, in which every minister will be represented. And no livings will be any longer left in the gift of worthless gold- or title-owners. Many such persons, never mind what worthless society pests they had been,* enjoyed, at Jubilee Period, the privilege of purveying parsons of their own selection to a score of different parishes—but the sale, barter, or exchange of pastoral offices will be no longer tolerated.

(52)
(53)

"6. The scandals of the Pension List—infamous scandals—perpetrated by Parliament, whereby utterly worthless peers have been "compensated" for "relinquishing" mere sinecures with the hard-won money of the nation, in sums varying between £25,000 and £1,000,000, will not only be forthwith stopped, but measures will be taken, wherever possible, to make those guilty persons, who were parties to the squandering of the national resources, restore them to the National Exchequer. The Pension List in future will first provide for stricken labourers over sixty years of age laid low by hitherto prevailing merciless neglect. Other reforms can only here be glanced at. They will comprehend:—A scheme of Home Colonisation, and settlement of agriculturalists on the land, with inalienable right of perpetual leasehold. Reclamation of waste lands. A labour code establishing a maximum work day regulated for all trades. A minimum, or living wage, in spite of Jubilee assertions that the thing is ridiculous. The abolition of casual labour and the establishing of the permanency of the labour contract. State-assisted voluntary emigration. Immediate stoppage of pauper immigration. The establishment of a homestead law to protect the home, land, tools, and household effects of all workers. Control and considerable repression of the liquor traffic.

(54)

"On the completion of this Revolutionary Charter, a General Election will be held; and at the same time the whole of the reforms will be submitted to the electors by way of referendum, in order that the absolute will of the Nation may be pronounced upon them. Within one month of the meeting of the new Parliament, to be elected upon an entirely new franchise, the Revolutionary Army will lay down its arms, and will transfer the Government to the elected of the people.

"Let every wise citizen meanwhile preserve the peace, be assured

---

* Page 323.

of perfect freedom, and concern himself in the furtherance of his own affairs. Let the great English Nation be assured of this, that —of the forty millions of Britons in all our glorious Empire, thirty-nine and three-quarter millions will enjoy a nobler liberty by this too long delayed, but now most thorough restitution.—In the name of the Revolutionary Army,

"CARLYLE DEMOCRITUS,
General-in-Chief."

CHAPTER II.

THE GREAT LAND QUESTION—ANSWERED.

QUICKLY rages the fire that licks through dry and rotten structures in angry flames, until decay becomes destruction. Slowly rises the new building from the ruins of the old. Shall the new be constructed of the fire-singed planks, the burnt-up bricks, with the coagulated worthlessness for fundament? And shall a hollow sham and unreality, like the thing destroyed, peer—only new upon the surface—through chaos once again? Or shall the ruins of the lying Past be buried deep, deep enough for the rare convertive earth to change the foulness into fairness, the putridity into life-giving substance? And shall a God-fearing and wise architect design—no lying semblance of what was—but a firm and steadfast new building, time-defying, faith-invoking; a building uprearing to the Eternal Heavens, erected to shelter and protect God's people? Not a building to shelter some few of them in luxury, whilst the other many freeze and starve unsheltered. A temple shall the truthful architect make rise from the ruins, a temple complete in all its parts, a temple and haven of rest for all the Nation, built under the all-seeing Master's eye, established upon His Eternal Laws, which to ignore is Death, which to obey is Life for ever!

From the wreck of England's rottenness, which the Revolution had burnt up and destroyed, our history will now describe the structure which arose.

The sanctity and security of property in land, which the kings of the Middle Ages had rudely shaken, suffered a final and crushing blow when Carlyle Democritus's far-reaching edict pealed loud throughout all Britain :—" LANDLORDISM IS DEAD! THE LAND IS RESTORED TO THE PEOPLE! THROUGHOUT GREAT BRITAIN IS PEASANT-PROPRIETORSHIP HEREBY ESTABLISHED. Beyond the direct ownership, in perpetual lease, of his house, his garden, or his farm, or his place of business, by the immediate occupier, the State is henceforward the sole lord of the land."

Not more surely fell the whoring popes and cardinals before the fearless German monk than now the lords of land before Democritus. With one sword-thrust fell the great abuse, and in its fall there flowed into the English coffers such untold wealth as even an Aladdin had never contemplated, The present historian is not a lover of statistics, or rather of statisticians, *i.e.* those of the economical political sort, a class of people much in requisition by " Honourable gentlemen " and " Right honourable gentlemen " of the Jubilee period, one of whom had said, " Give me figures, and I'll prove anything." And indeed a political statistician *would* prove anything. He would prove that two millions a week of a Nation's income spent on poison-alcohol, besotting the brains of men, was a necessity and a benefit to the nation, and was "not exceptional," that it was an absolute necessity for providing revenue to the State. He would prove that millions of starving mortals was not an exceptional, but quite a normal condition of things, and he would prove it to you by piles of figures about " progress of the labouring classes, progress of the wealth accumulations," etc. He would prove to you that State-directed emigration was not a necessity. A necessity? Why, he would prove not only that emigration was not a necessity, but that it was altogether, absolutely (whether State-directed, or State-perverted, like Irish emigration)—henceforward, for ever, and eternally, IMPOSSIBLE!

(55)

Wherefore impossible, O English people, God-entrusted nation of many worlds; wherefore impossible? I cannot tell ye, for I have seen God's trust to ye in the Austral land—a fair and smiling Eden-Continent, wide as Europe but nigh unpeopled, except by a little brave and noble company of Saxon pioneers. In all that vast Australian group there are less folk than we can count in London city. . . . And because I have seen the rich prolific Southern Africa, with scope and space as wide, her swelling bosom everywhere proffering sustenance to her Saxon conquerers, another Almighty trust to this dear country, but also unpeopled except by a few fearless pioneers, part of a fertile continent infinitely wider than Europe and less peopled than a Yorkshire Riding. . . . And again because I know the prairie flowerlands of North America, mighty virgin soil inviting the sturdy husbandman: "Come to me,

O bridegroom of the spade, fecund and fruitful is my womb, and I will repay thy love and labour twice a hundredfold," a land less peopled than our Lancashire, yet again as wide as Europe. Other rich alluring countries intrusted by the All-Merciful to this brave England I have also seen. But enough, hearken to the Merlin-enchantment of a Party governed people. Europe consists of about three and three-quarter millions of square miles of territory, and has a population of some three hundred and forty-five millions, or say roughly, ninety people to every square mile. British America (Canada) consists of about three and a half millions of square miles, and has about five millions of inhabitants, or two inhabitants to every square mile. Two against the ninety of Europe. Australia has an area of over three million square miles, with a population of about four millions, or one man and a little boy to every square mile.

Upon those vast, rich, luxuriant, and scarce-peopled lands crying aloud for the brave husbandman, inviting idle populations to noble industry, the politico-economical statistician turns his back and with his blind eyes cast inward more hopelessly than an ostrich's embedded in desert sand, proclaims to party-ridden multitudes, "THE WORLD IS FULL!" "NO MORE ROOM FOR EMIGRATION!" I, the great statistician of the British Government say so, Oyez Oyez!

(56)

Good British people, were this other than a solemn, serious, even tragic history, you might well call in question the author's sanity, yet I speak to you but simple truth. Listen to the Oracle of England, and let all sheep tremble. The great *Times* newspaper was so convinced by the great Government Politico-Party Statistician, that it printed his actual words, and thus soothingly commented upon them in a leading article, for the wonder and instruction of gods and men :*—"Is Colonization fast reaching its limits, and is emigration as a remedy for the evils flowing from a redundant population almost exhausted? No ONE is more competent than MR GIFFEN [the Politico-Economical Statistician of British Government] to answer these questions, and he does so in the AFFIRMATIVE, with a degree of confidence and precision that will alarm *some* of us. It is sad to think that an outlet for poverty which has existed all these years of the world's history is coming to an end." *Very* sad. But is it not infinitely *more* sad

---

* The italics have been added by the Author.—ED.

that an able editor could swallow such statistical twaddle, descant upon it, utter downright idiotic reflection upon it; this, amongst other such, that "emigration was ever a serious evil!" Ye Heavens! Let us not go beyond that. Verily the great Government statistician and the able editor surpass each other. Let us be kind to *Times* and Giffen, and cap their brand new ethic with this gentle and older ethic, that "out of evil groweth good," for that may perhaps explain to bewildered mankind how the most good Australia, America, Canada, have grown out of the (Times-Giffen) evil—Emigration. (57)

A statistician is indeed a wonderful man; has he not, with loud approval of the same able editor, also "proved" that a wage to enable a man to live was not a necessity, was indeed and altogether utterly unreasonable? (54)

Oh, your politico-party-statistician would prove to you that Beelzebub was the God Almighty in disguise, and that his trappings were figures, figures, figures.

The present historian, therefore, loveth not the genus political statistician, yet he ventures to parenthetically instruct the unversed in land questions by means of a few faithful figures; he is anxious to bring home to the minds of his readers some slight conception of the abuses against which Carlyle Democritus's land laws waged ruthless war. "The earth is the Lord's, and the fulness thereof," had been interpreted by majority, Parliament, to mean, "The earth is the landlord's." And it required a Revolution, and Carlyle Democritus, to awaken the people to the fact that God in heaven was the Lord—His the earth, and His the fulness thereof —to be cultivated, that earth, in order that men might live upon it, and not merely kill upon it either grouse or partridges, hunt deer, foxes, and other playthings on it. Not that. (58)

"Wheat," says a high authority of those times, "may be regarded as characteristically the crop of England. Its area is steadily diminishing in England, and is even more rapid in Wales, Scotland, Ireland, and the small islands taken collectively. In England, in 1870, there were as many as 3,247,973 acres under wheat. In 1893 this number had fallen to 1,798,869 acres. Hence, in a period of less than twenty-five years, England has lost nearly half its acreage of wheat." In one year, 1893, 304,100 acres were withdrawn from the wheat crop of England alone, and

343,394 acres from the United Kingdom. Taking cereals altogether (wheat, barley, and oats), we find the area under cultivation to have fallen from 6,756,651 acres—the average of 1871-75—to 5,464,844 acres (area under cultivation in 1893), or 1,291,807 acres of cereal land thrown out of cultivation. That is for England alone. For the United Kingdom the figures are still more tragic, and show a total falling off (within the same period) of close upon two millions of acres. Not only has this land gone out of cereal cultivation, but much of it has gone out of cultivation altogether. "It is certain," says the same high authority, "that as many as thirteen English counties, in 1893, returned more than ten thousand acres each as practically gone out of cultivation into mere fallow land." Year after year the people were evicted from their native soil under circumstances of heart-rending cruelty. Men, women, and children cast out to starvation, and the rich land left fallow, to starvation also. Bear that shame-record of Jubilee Great Britain in your mind, reader, and with its record of infamous injustice, waste, and wickedness, hearken to these words, spoken sixteen hundred years before (quoted by Allison in his "Essay on the Fall of Rome"), against a precisely similar infamy which decadent Rome was inflicting upon *her* agricultural population:—

(59)
(60)
(61)

"The little proprietors of land are expelled from their estates by the ceaseless engrossing of wealth by the few ; everywhere the people are chased from their heritages ; they have no longer what they can call their own ; that which once sufficed for the maintenance of a city will now scarcely suffice for the pasturage of a single lord; the struggle of the poor against the oppression of the moneyed classes is ceaseless. 320,000 acres of the most fertile province of the Roman Empire have fallen into a state of nature." * Might those words not have been written of our Jubilee England, in place of corrupt and falling Rome, for is it not even so, and more so, with our increasing deer-forests and shooting-preserves? He who spoke those words to the Romans put these words into the mouth of struggling poverty: "O ye rich, beware ! For how great soever may be your possessions, when I am resolved to throw away my life, we are equal !" Since that warning was uttered, and *not* listened to, the Roman nation has disappeared.

"Shall a greater than the Roman Empire also rot away in

---

* Compare also page 281.

corruption and injustice, or will it listen while there is yet time?" Thus asked Carlyle Democritus, as he thundered forth to the people the burning words of the greatest sage whom the world has known for a thousand years—the words, namely, of Thomas Carlyle :—

"In no time since the beginning of society was the lot of the dumb millions of toilers so entirely unbearable as it is even in the days now passing over us. It is not to die, or even to die of hunger, that makes a man wretched; many men have died. All men must die. But it is to live miserable, we know not why; to work sore, and yet gain nothing; to be heart-worn, weary, yet isolated, unrelated, girt in with a cold universal *laisser-faire* [don't-care-a-damn-for-you]. It is to die slowly all your life long, imprisoned as if in the accursed thrall of the iron torture of want. This is, and remains for ever, intolerable to all men whom God has made." Intolerable to *men!* To *men* intolerable! To slaves, only, not intolerable. "Will you be men or slaves?" asked Carlyle Democritus. But we must revert to the land figures yet a little: The cultivable area of Great Britain at Jubilee period was about 65,000,000 acres; the cultivated portion of it about 50,000,000 acres. Of land lying fallow at that time, but ready of cultivation, such as unclaimed heath and moor, and arable mountain land, the area exceeded 1,000,000 acres. Of land capable of cultivation but not cultivated there were upwards of 14,000,000 acres.* Therefore the revolutionists saw fifteen million acres of land in Britain upon which pauper or waste labour, well organised, might be better employed than by being stived in no-work workhouses, eating its head off there in poor-rates and mere mockery of work. They also saw how the fifty millions of fine, rich, cultivated acres were allotted at the Jubilee period.

One duke "owned" one million three hundred and fifty thousand odd acres; twelve other people between them "owned" four and a half million acres; five hundred peers "owned"

---

* How moderate are these estimates may be seen from the following official authority: "Twenty-two millions of acres of productive land in Great Britain belonging to the estates of landlords and of the absentee and resident nobility are lying idle."—EXTRACT FROM THE REPORT OF THE UNITED STATES IMMIGRATION COMMISSION, 1892. Some authorities placed the cultivable area not cultivated at thirty millions of acres.

between them fifteen million acres, a little less than a quarter of Great Britain and Ireland. Two hundred other large owners were in the House of Commons. Briefly, then, at the Jubilee period, of the forty millions of people in Great Britain, some ten thousand "owned" between them over two-thirds of the entire British

(62) soil.

Try to realise what this "owning" meant, you English people. One duke, by "owning" a few acres of land in London, received, from quite a small nation of people there, in rents increasing year by year, by virtue of their increase and toil, millions of their wealth. The more the people laboured, and the more the people increased, the more the Jubilee landowner sucked from them their toilings, and called it rent. Such a duke could refuse to let any of them continue to live on the land where, perhaps for generations, they had been established. He was complete sovereign of the land and them, and the strange people submitted to him. One such duke grew so fabulously wealthy, whilst many of his shorn flock were starving, that from sheer despair to know how to invest a half million of his revenues, the poor man actually shot himself.

Well, peers of that sort and worse sort, sometimes even a better sort, but a mere handful of men, held fifteen and a half

(63) million British acres. In Scotland one man "owned" about two hundred square *miles* of land, from which he had cleared off the hard-working farmers, or crofters, so as to make of that small garden a shooting estate for himself—only two hundred square miles! And the only notice that the great Sorrypebbles' Radical Government—the self-styled people's party—took of the matter was to send soldiers and bayonets to force the old tenants, who bravely endeavoured to seize back their stolen farms, off the

(64) shooting lord's estate.

Yes; some forty millions of lethargic, party-ridden, rhetoric-blinded English people, under hereditary laws, paid at the Jubilee period annually a toll, called rent, of hundreds of millions sterling to a few thousands who "owned" their country; and furthermore, those blind forty millions paid nearly all their taxes as well. (See note, page 119.) And all that whilst many of those landowners were shooting partridges, hunting foxes, and storing up the honey which the toilers in slum and city were sweating and labouring for. Here is another, not party-politico-statistical fact, but a true historic fact: "The British Parliament between the years 1760 and 1845 sanctioned by Acts of Parliament the appropriation by private owners, utterly regardless of the interests of the public, of no less than five million acres of the people's land." This might be described as wealthy thieving in a constitutional manner. And let the reader not overlook the infamous wholesale jobbery of the Parliaments which sanctioned these acts, nor the fact that another million acres had been similarly appropriated since the years before-mentioned. The historian says: "There is only one portion of the British Islands in which there is sub-division of the soil, and that is the Channel Islands, and *there* prosperity is universal!" And he adds: "In proportion as estates grow large, so do the agricultural populations decrease." Yes, they *do* decrease. Every avenue of skilled and unskilled labour is glutted with starving peasants, harried off their natural fields of occupation by mercenary and relentless landowners. Thousands of men daily scramble and fight and tear each other at the various London Docks for the work which requires permanently but a part of their number. A million competing toilers in the grimy coal-mines grapple and strive there for a living wage, because fully half of them are superfluous hands driven by the ruthless talons of landlordism away from their native soil. All towns and town employments are choked by the starving country hinds, whilst the country lands are bare, except on the country roads, where the traveller meets the starving tramps, dragging their starvation and misery towards the towns and cities, there to fill the gaols and workhouses, or fester in misery in the slum gutters. All that is what a Carlyle Democritus has armed himself to battle against and overcome—"wholesale robberyism," or other "ism" notwithstanding. Indeed, there never will be wanting people to give hard names to any and every system which seeks to conquer and deal righteously with long-established abuses.

Was not Jesus, a rebel and a preacher of sedition, done to a cruel death? Was not Cromwell a regicide, his body hung in gallows-chains? The lawyer descendant of that man-God, Chancery solicitor, in George the Fourth's time, even found the name "a great disadvantage to him" in the lawyer-liar line, and he peremptorily forbade his son-in-law to continue it. Verily it is only the devils of the other world who can aspire to people's Godhood in this world.

And you yet shall see how Carlyle Democritus shall be gibbeted; Hell and Damnation too sweet a haven for him. Happily, Cromwells and Carlyle Democrituses court not but eschew the world's lip-praise. They know that the mass of the people is a deep and sentient but mostly silent multitude, which lacks not pulse- and heart-throb, only requiring the stethoscope of sympathy to discover it. Carlyle Democritus understood the giant circulation of the people in health and in disease; and he knew also that it is the essential nature of all parasites to resent disturbance from the body upon whose life-blood they are feeding. So he was prepared for an unending outcry. It must inevitably be so. Who shall hope to dislodge ten thousand wolves from millions of panting sheep, and not hear ravenous howling on all sides? The poor bleating of misery and suffering has ever been less audible, but in the end not always less meaningful.

Forty millions of exasperated people prepare to seize back the plunder which a few thousands amongst them have gradually stolen from the nation! Ay, there is the secret at once. The few who stole (or "acquired"), stole gradually, insidiously; the many strike at once, fiercely, suddenly, often savagely: claim back at one great judgment-stroke the pelf pirated by generations. But revolution is a purging fire; like the Parliament, "legalising wholesale robbery of the national land,"—Revolution legalises its restoration to the people, its rightful owners.

There was this tremendous difference between the revolutionary sequestrations and those of the Tudor, Stuart, and other kings: Carlyle Democritus remained the unenriched—indeed, the impoverished—amidst a fabulous wealth which his wisdom was day by day amassing for the nation and for the people. The kings sucked *their* wealth in to pay their petty wars or pettier minions. Democritus diverted the rich life-stream through every avenue of the toiling nation. The oppressed leaseholder learnt a newer freedom, a brighter love for the home which at moderate commutation was become his own.

These were the main points of the revolutionary far-reaching edict:—All ownership in land was restricted to the holding of such property as constituted the dwelling or trading place of a citizen; all beyond such individual possession fell forthwith into the national domains. The wording of leases and of all land transfers, and legal papers generally, was freed from the old fulsome verbiage.

The terms of all leases, freeholds, transfers, etc., were reduced to honest simplicity. The new code forbade the use of more than one sheet of paper six inches square to effect any land transfer; and the more thoroughly to cure an abuse which the lawyers of the Jubilee period had worked up to a fine art, the State issued printed forms, defining in plain, straightforward language the requisite terms and wording of a lease, etc., on the back whereof a map, in plain outline, had to define the exact boundaries of the land which was to be dealt with. The legal fraternity howled considerably; but not more than when, by a later edict, the drafting of Acts of Parliament was withdrawn from them for ever, and relegated instead to the Committees, Chambers of Commerce, or other Trade or Professional bodies directly acquainted with the requirements, necessities, and objects with which the particular Acts had to deal. By this means leases, land transfers, and Acts of Parliament became not only readable, but even understandable by men. Millions of tons of waste-paper were saved, and cart loads of legal verbiage were well obliterated. Under Carlyle Democritus plain English had its pristine and very noble meaning restored to it.

In agricultural properties, individual holdings were limited to fifty acres (except in the case of forest lands, which particular preservative laws dealt with). Private pleasure-grounds were limited to five acres; all beyond this became sequestrated or purchased by the State, and was, as we shall see, thrown open to peasant-proprietorship. The rents levied on farm properties were made approximate to a produce rent, commuted in money, and assessed according to the harvest returns. Thus in drought years, or years of failure of crop, there would be little rent to pay. The first principle of just Government must be that a man by honest labour be able to provide for himself and family. State rents and taxes may only touch *beyond* necessities, and not this side of them. How thorough, merciful, and just was that wise State principle for Scotch and other crofters, oppressed Irish tenants, and English agricultural labourers hitherto starved off their soil! "Irish Question," "Crofter Question," "Land Question," where are they, under the code of a Carlyle Democritus? For ever answered, and never to be heard of more.

Where house-property, in town or country, had been acquired by *bona-fide* purchase or service to the State, by either the present owner or his predecessor, the present owner received full compensation by terminable annuities, to be later on described. But estates held by peers and others, the gifts of kings, were confiscated to the State, the owner being allowed one residence and an annuity, according to the finding of the land court, extending through one, two, or three lives, as it might adjudge.

Towards public-house property a drastic course was adopted. As mere drinking-shops they were for ever abolished; but the method was tempered by a recognition of the fact that the Government had been as sinning as the publicans. In the case of private owners, reasonable compensation was given, but the Land Court dealt less liberally with the wholesale owners who had fostered what were known as tied-houses. Although the soul-destroying liquor traffic was instantly cut down, the best of the buildings, in reasonable number, and where the locality required them, were spared. But not as drinking-hells. They were converted into restaurants, where all manner of refreshments could be obtained, including unadulterated malt liquors and wholesome wines; but spirits were practically abolished by the high duties placed on them, and they ceased to be obtainable outside chemists' shops.

The State was now the sole landlord. It granted perpetual leaseholds to any British subject, or short leases, or annual rentals, if a tenant so preferred. But no longer were houses let at exorbitant rents, or upon arbitrary terms. A new and extensive administration was created for this work, which took the place of the former landowners and their agents, who had striven only how they could squeeze the last penny out of their long-suffering tenants. It was no longer possible for a noble duke or any other to raise a rent over a tenant (or evict him unconditionally) who had occupied his house, beautified it, and to whose family long occupation had rendered it sacred. Ended were those lords of the soil, whose relentless pressure and inconsideration of all save their pockets had long galled all thinking people, and raised loud complaints against a system which one would have thought that not men but only sheep could have so long endured; and which, indeed, could not have existed a month, had not a blind and party-mad generation submitted to any folly and falsity so long as grievances were glamoured over by the sickly rhodomontade of party squabbling and inanities, whilst real evils and abuses grew thick and multiplied, like flies upon a sun-scorched cess-pool. The State—that is, the people (in more real fashion than the old

French King deemed the State to be himself)—now owned the country; and for the State and for the people the country was administered, not only for a few thousand mammon-lords amongst them. Nearly every man now practically owned his house, and for the first time in History did the Englishman's boast that his home was his castle have real meaning in it. Not empty boast was it now, but actual fact. Those who at first had trembled at the advent of the revolution which carried fire and sword to hew down the upas-growth of cant, abuse, and make-believe, soon hailed it and its Leader as saviours of mankind; and when the people discovered that the new laws benefited the whole nation, and did not press unduly upon those few who had been let go free too long, they recognised in Carlyle Democritus a very messenger of salvation to them.

NOTE.

It has truly been stated in various parts of this history that the smaller tradesmen, householders, and tenement dwellers paid local and Imperial taxation out of all proportion to their incomes, and that whereas the wealthy classes paid in rates and taxes often but a mere fractional percentage of *their* net incomes to the State, that, on the other hand, the poorer their tenants, the more oppressive was the burden of their taxation. Let the reader take the following, by way of illustration :—

Dingee Street, of which at Jubilee time there were hundreds of specimens in all the districts, North, East, South, and West of London, consisted of one hundred houses. The property belonged to Sir Hardy Cheatem. The houses were all let to people of the respectable artisan, shop assistant, and milliner class, who occupied generally one floor, and sub-let the others. The "architecture" of the street was of the usual Jubilee type—a dismal brick wall some thousand feet long, in which were cut sundry square holes called windows, and sundry other larger square holes, near the street level, called doorways. They were eight-roomed houses, but as they were situated in a very congested and much-sought-after neighbourhood, they let readily for £75 a year, and it was rarely that a house was empty.

Amongst the tenants of one of the houses was an enterprising grocer's assistant. He proposed to the agent of Sir Hardy (Sir Hardy lived at Brighton, when he was not shooting tame partridges, or yachting, and had never seen any of his many Dingee Streets) to let him convert his front parlour into a grocer's shop, upon condition that if the alteration did not pay, the enterprising grocer was to restore the parlour. The agent consented. Enterprising grocer duly converted his parlour into a small shop, at what to him was considerable expense, and established a comfortable little business. After the first year his rent was raised £10, and as he continued to prosper by ingenuity and hard work, so did his landlord, and, after four years, our grocer had to pay a rent of £100 a year. His rates and taxes were raised in proportion by the local authorities, and the result of many years' hard work, strenuous endeavour, and unceasing devotion to his business, was in the end somewhat this :—

Rent to the Landlord . . .	£100
House rates and taxes . . .	34
Income-Tax on trade profits . .	3
Rent and Taxes .	£137

The *net* takings of the poor grocer (beyond the above-given rent and taxes) at the end of each year never exceeded £150, out of which he had to feed himself, his wife, and children, and educate the last. The present editor, who visited every house in Dingee Street, and was permitted a thorough investigation of the grocer's books, and of the other little tradesmen's also, whom he is about to refer to, discovered that after fifteen years' steady and honest trade the worthy grocer, by dint of rigid economy, had been able to put by, out of his earnings, an average of from £40 to £50 a year; it was less at first, but more later, when he was able to place his children in service. Next door to the grocer was a baker. He had been "permitted,"—at his own cost of course, and without the landlord or agent consulting the convenience of any of the tenants in the rest of the street—to convert his coal-cellars into a breadbakery, and his parlour into a baker's shop. The bakery, as may well be imagined, was the beastliest and filthiest hell-hole conceivable—but not worse than most of the other Jubilee bakeries, which were constructed in a precisely similar fashion—without ventilation of any sort worthy the name, and in which men, nearly

naked, stood streaming with perspiration, whilst they made the "bread" which was considered fit enough for English landlords' slaves. It is a disgusting admission, but a true one, that part of the salt and moisture, which helped to convert the flour into dough, was supplied from the dripping bodies of the wretched bakers, who were of necessity compelled to work in these dens. Well, our Dingee Street baker also had his rent raised from £75 to £100, but his risks were greater, and his customers fewer, than the grocer's, so that after a hard struggle for eleven years, during which he paid in annual rent to his landlord . . £100
To the State in rates and taxes 34

Rent and taxes £134

he failed, and the converted shop (which had exhausted all the poor man's savings of many years) and the cellar bakery became the property of the landlord. The baker's books show curiously how hard he had worked and economised. But, in spite of all his efforts, he had never been able to realise £15 in any one year over and above the bare cost of his living, clothing, and maintaining a small family. The baker's shop was quickly re-let, and another hard-working baker made and sold sweat-flavoured bread in place of the one who ended his days in the workhouse. There were altogether eight little shops in Dingee Street. A third was owned by a milk-seller. He paid the same rent, rates, and taxes as the two already described, and managed to put by about £30 a year, after paying living expenses, etc.

These three tradesmen, therefore, paid to the State in rates and taxes, local and imperial, in proportion to their actual *net* income— The grocer, £34 out of a net annual return of some £50, or about 70 per cent. of his net earnings in rates to the State. The baker paid *all* his small surplus to the State, and died a pauper. The milkman had a net surplus of £30 a year, after paying to the State £34, or more than the equivalent of his actual net earnings. And it was much the same with all the remaining Dingee Street tradesmen. As for the rest of the tenants of Dingee Street, their case was still worse. One example will explain them all :—John Roughem was a railway engineer, and earned forty-five shillings a week, or £117 a year. He paid to his landlord £75, to the State in rates and taxes £25. Although the accommodation of the houses utterly unfitted them for sub-division, they were all sub-let, as has already been stated. Roughem let his two floors at eight shillings a week each, and was thus able to pay his way and keep his family together. But the proportion of rates and taxes taken by the State from his net earnings exceeded 30 per cent., without making any allowance whatsoever for feeding and clothing himself and family.

Now let us contrast Sir Hardy Cheatem's balance-sheet:— Although Dingee Street consisted of only one hundred houses, it boasted two gaudy public-houses—one at each end—let at a very high rental. The street had altogether eight shops, and ninety dwelling-houses, and they produced altogether *net* to Sir Hardy Cheatem £8000 a year, thus:—

The two public-houses at £400 a year		£800
Eight shops at £100		800
Ninety dwellings at £75		6750
		£8350
Deduct annual salary to agent	£150	
"Repairs" to such of the houses as were not let on repairing agreement	200	
		350
Net rental		£8000

Sir Hardy Cheatem lived at Brighton, in a charming little house which he rented at £200 a year, and upon which he paid rates and taxes about £55 a year. Sir Hardy also paid an income-tax of sixpence in the pound on a return (not quite of £8000, but) of £5640, that being the net amount as returned to the Tax Commissioners by Sir H. Cheatem, after the most ingenious manipulation. Income-tax paid by Sir Hardy Cheatem, therefore, £141. Thus the total of all taxes paid by the noble baronet to the State out of his income of £8000 a year, which he did no work for, but which hundreds of tame slaves struggled to provide for him, was £196 a year, or less than two and a half per cent. of his actual income. Is it then clear to the reader how the Jubilee lower middle classes (and higher classes too, very often) were paying in rates and taxes, thirty, forty, and fifty per cent., and more, of their hard-earned net incomes, whilst those who did no work, but lived on the energy and life-blood of the workers, got off with a light two or three per cent.?

But there is a yet more instructive deduction to be made from the foregoing :—The total annual requirements of the State in the late Jubilee period were a hundred and sixty millions sterling, as is very clearly set out in the chapters on Finance. Divide that amount by the forty millions of inhabitants in the United Kingdom, and you have £4 as the contribution which was required of each person towards the Imperial and Local State service. Had the land rent in those times gone to its legitimate fount—the State—all of those oppressed Dingee Street tenants would have enjoyed the fruit of their hard toil, and could have saved at least £100 a year. True, the Sir Hardy Cheatems would have all had to work or go to the workhouse (as a great many of them later on had to go to the Penal Colonies*), but even breaking stones is worthier occupation for human-kind than shooting tame partridges, and sucking the life-blood from toiling and moiling humanity. And if it be ever necessary (which it is *not*) that any mortal should pass away his existence in a workhouse of no-work, it is better that one thousand should send one there than that the one should send the thousand. Jubilee Britain contained probably from twenty thousand to a hundred thousand Cheatems, about five millions of half-starving victims of the Cheatems, and thirty-four and nine-tenths millions of more or less subservient, toll-paying slaves to the Cheatems.

Verily the times called aloud for revolution. Not only wise thinkers foresaw an end to all this. The alert amongst the rich commenced also to see the end.

An American plutocrat, some twenty times millionaire, and therefore a tolerable authority on the subject of money-wealth, is thus quoted in the "Times":—"The worst profession I know (71) is to be a rich man's son, and I do not believe that the world will stand that profession much longer. I know something of matters and the way they are going in our own country; and now I have seen something of the old world, and I tell you candidly that I would not give twenty years' purchase to-day for any piece of property, I do not care what it is, in the civilised world." That is a notable prophecy; it was uttered in the Jubilee commemorative year, 1887; its fulfilment would require the year 1907. And the Revolution of Carlyle Democritus broke out in February 19—.

---

* Page 162.

CHAPTER III.

THE LAND AND THE NEW PROPRIETORS.

GROUSE-MOORS, pheasant-runs, fox-covers, knew their red lords no more. Where fifty miles of heath-land had exposed its nakedness before high heaven, human beings, formerly forced to idleness, starvation, and despair, now as busy husbandmen made the land teem with flowers, fruit, and corn. Labour colonies broke the stagnate earth, and brought forth food and fruit everywhere. Let us examine this transformation. Idle lands and idle men had become fruitful lands and busy men. Lands, formerly left bare in order that twenty thousand hounds might harrow them for fox, or stag, or hare—*their* day and their master's day being past—were now harrowed by careful labour in order that *men*, instead of foxes, might breed and prosper there. Records of these transactions were circulated in the slum-prisons, where the Governors and others, who tolerated and supported past abuses, were lingering in disenchantment; the conclusion of those notices was always: "Victims to abandoned duty, extreme as may be your misery, remember that for every one amongst you whom a terrible retribution has overtaken, for every one who suffers, there lived and suffered tens of thousands. Verily we give you bread, but even that you denied to those who filled the places which you now occupy."

On the 14th February 19—, when the signal was given for the rising of the people, there lay fallow in Great Britain upwards of twenty million acres of land. Before two years were passed that waste country had yielded to spade and plough, was supporting flocks and herds, or developing future woods and forests, and providing worthy work for hundreds of thousands of men, before that time wasting by disease and death in the ranks of fallen labour.

The Land Department which had been constituted consisted of

thirty of the most experienced agriculturalists in the kingdom, and nine members selected from the commercial class, the whole presided over by the Minister of Agriculture. The reason this Department was so numerous was because of the many committees it had to divide itself into, so vast was its work.

It must be well understood, from the outset, that fortune-making was never a consideration in any of the reforms of the revolution. The career of mere money-making was as open to all the world after the revolution as it was before. The model which Carlyle Democritus held steadily before his council and the nation was the provision of a healthful and manful means of loyal, steadfast life and labour, which should enable every man to fulfil the purpose of his creation—work, cultivation, usefulness. A man's labour should enable him to provide for himself, and those dependent on him, wholesome and adequate food, clothing, and shelter, together with due leisure for self-cultivation and relaxation ; and only in so far as that great principle is recognised, and adequately put into practice, does Government deserve the name of Government. By so much as any nation falls short of that great consummation, by so much is that nation steeped in barbarism ; and by so far as any nation rises above that consummation, by so far is that nation advanced in civilisation. Thus the highest ideal of National Government is that which compels *all* men to labour, in return for which labour they should find ample food, shelter, clothing, domestic comfort, and leisure for moral and material advancement. And the lowest order of National Government is that which divides its people into two classes, ever growing in opposition to one another, ever distrustful, and at warfare with each other; the one for ever piling up excessive and unnecessary provision, whilst the other falls day by day into ever lower degradation, misery, and wretchedness. Such a nation is like a garden, one half of which is poisoned by an ever-rising mountain of manure, whilst the other half is starved by a never-ceasing exhaustion which converts the primeval loam into desert sand and salt, as of Sodom. Death or deliverance from *such* a system of Government once and for ever !

This was the method of deliverance ! The new land code enacted, amongst other laws, that the entire agricultural lands of Great Britain (Ireland is everywhere included in this history under that proud title—there is no lying Sorrypebble now, God **be praised** !)

should be divided into plots of from one to one hundred acres, according to local demand, to the nature, or the purpose of the allotment, and these were made available, upon due terms and conditions, to the whole British people. It must be remembered, when mentioning so small a plot as one acre, that as well as providing land for agriculturalists and farmers, timber cultivators, cattle-breeders, etc., the one-acre allotments met the demand of an enormous class of factory, mining, and other labourers, as well as other folk, who cultivated them in their spare time, either for vegetable, fruit, or other purposes, or as ornamental gardens. Any of these small cultivators could avail themselves of the agricultural factories about to be described—provided the quality of their produce was up to the level of the factories' requirements. The larger cultivators were grouped together in farms round a common centre, after the manner so successfully achieved by Farmer Trieditt, as briefly described at page 158. Thus, one hundred families would be settled upon five hundred acres of land, each man owning, in perpetual lease, his five acres; the ablest farmer of the group would be elected by ballot of the hundred as working manager and director, the election renewable every year. Without descending into unnecessary detail, it may be explained that the object of this "Communal-", "Community-", or "Hundred-" System was to ensure capable and uniform management, and the adoption of a proper system of "rotation of crops." What is known as the "Five-Course," or "Four-Course" arrangement was left to the determination of each hundred, but the former was generally found to offer better advantages, and was the more generally adopted. The wisdom of this community of work need scarcely be demonstrated; it was Carlyle Democritus's "regimental system" of labour applied to agriculture. At any moment the labour of the Hundred—*plus* their family helpers—could be diverted to any point of the holding—*e.g.*, to save a hay crop in bad weather, when roots would not harm by delay. Threshing machines, ploughs, horses, field machinery could be thus held in common, which to any single five-acre farmer would have been impossible. The incapacity through illness of one or two owners would not mean ruin to them. But yet wiser regulations followed. What are known as "Creameries" were erected outside these community holdings, and served one or more such Hundred according to their size and situation, and thus ensured evenness and perfection of quality in the manufacturing of the farm produce. These Creameries, at first established by the State, were afterwards taken over by the Agricultural Guilds. They collected from the farms, and arranged the delivery to the various market towns of the eggs, milk, fruit, vegetables, and general produce, as well as made cheese, cream, etc., and arranged for their disposal. These Creameries were co-operative, and all profits arising from each such factory (over and above the market value of the produce paid to the growers) were divided into four parts, whereof one-fourth went to the labour employed, as a bonus over and above their regular wages ; one-fourth to a reserve fund, for the improvement and furtherance of the agricultural interests of the farms connected with the Creamery ; and the remaining two-fourths—in equal shares—to each farmer of the Hundreds which supplied and were served by it.

The State entered into occupation of the entire soil, but, as has been said, granted permanent leasehold or annual rental allotments, according to the desire of the tenant or cultivator. In every case the Local Assessment Committee determined the value of the land. Lands taken up as pleasure-gardens were assessed exactly as if they were used for agricultural or building purposes, according as they were situated in town or country. The time when a duke could live in a palace worth a quarter of a million, situated in a park of thousands of acres, and get it all assessed by a slave-ridden local authority at a few hundred pounds a year, was past. The (73) assessment bodies were now entirely composed of the local parish people, who were no longer dominated by peer, or landlord, or land-devil. Every provision existed for a just and popular valuation. Furthermore, there lay a power of appeal, by the tenant or the State, to the District or County Council, or, finally, the Lands Department.

The Parish Councils were empowered to provide seed, cattle, roots, farm implements, etc., to erect and equip cottages and farm buildings on any allotment, or to repair and improve those already existing. The cost of such work became a first charge upon the allotment, which could be spread over a long term of years. Every facility was given to the parish and district councils to raise loans for these purposes. For three years after the establishment of the Revolution, all allotments and farms were allowed free to those whose impecunious position required such assistance. The parish councils were responsible for the condition of all the buildings in their respective localities, as also for the degree of cultivation maintained. Neglect of the field or home was penal. And the district councils, and further, the county councils, moved by the Central Lands Department, formed a living check upon neglect or decay throughout the kingdom. Every parish council appointed its inspector or inspectors to exercise a wise but not inquisitorial supervision, and as these land inspectors were always chosen by, and from amongst, the most praiseworthy of the cultivators, England soon grew to be one vast garden. These were some of the conditions of settlement, and it will be observed how wisely Carlyle Democritus had bridged over those dangerous lacunæ which exist and breed destruction in nearly all other land systems, viz.: the power to sub-divide farms, or the yet more dangerous power to agglomerate them.* The title of the peasant was made inalienable. The land allotment could neither be mortgaged, sub-divided, nor increased. It could be sold, but only to an actual cultivator, who must be resident. The parish councils jealously guarded this privilege. Sub-letting was impossible. Landlordism, once slain, could not be allowed to insinuate its hydra head again. Therefore any breach of these laws—which were the very backbone of the charter—was made a crime, punishable by fine, imprisonment, and even forfeiture. Not only the land, but the farmer's tools and implements, the dwelling, furniture, clothes, and all chattels of the peasants, workmen, or farmers were protected against seizure by a homestead law of the most comprehensive nature. As for the rent assessment of a farm or allotment, this was based upon a produce rent, though payable in money. One tithe of the assessed produce formed the rent. If the tithe on any one farm or allotment exceeded in value the average assessment for the district, such excess returned to the owner, who could either retain it or use it for reducing the charge (if any) upon his holding. This provision formed an incentive to good cultivation and thrift.

---

*Agglomeration of land by marriage was effectually barred. The contracting parties could elect to live upon the allotment of either of them, the other remaining allotment reverted to the State, upon full compensation being paid to the party, or it could be transferred through the Lands Department to a new owner. Any attempt to evade this law rendered the estates of the contracting parties both liable to forfeiture.

Taxation bore lightly on the country generally, especially upon the land cultivator. It is impossible to give the entire land code established by the Revolution, but before closing this chapter a few more of its salient features may be indicated. As the lands were neither subdivisible nor agglomerable, provision had to be made in the event of an owner or lessee dying without heir. If no heir survived to claim the estate, it reverted to the possession of the Lands Department, but its full value (including improvements) in money was claimable by the next-of-kin of the deceased. Failing heirs or relations, the matter came under the ordinary law of intestate estates. Any owner desiring to dispose of his allotment could do so through the parish council only, who acted as local agent of the State Lands Department. The council, in the interests of the parish, as well as of the State, were moved to great care in the selection or acceptance of new tenants; but since the parish councils were entirely popularly elected bodies, no difficulty or friction occurred under this head.

Public-houses had been as severely abolished in the rural districts as in the larger towns and cities, but peaceful and cleanly inns brightened the country everywhere. Money-lending was declared a criminal profession. The parish council was fully empowered to assist proprietors on any deserving or exceptional occasion, with money grants upon the security of the properties. In every village there were lands set apart for recreation-ground, concert-hall, library, gymnasium, etc. Thus had England become a land of English *men*, and life was worth living to the masses. Perhaps one of the most valuable clauses of the land code was that which enabled the code to grow or change with the nation's growth and change. A special council was appointed, which met every fifth year, to consider and recommend any necessary modification or alteration in the constitution of the great land settlement. But no change could be adopted unless — after application of the Referendum*—three-fifths of the peasant-proprietors supported it. Any proposed alteration had to be set out in plain English to the people, every suggested alteration separately; so that the country's vote had to be taken upon every individual alteration. This provision had been made against the possibility of any future traitor of a Sorrypebble or his minions

---

* Page 426.

bribing moonlighting cut-throats, murderers, maimers of cattle, and dynamiters to vote for his Newcastle trickeries in order that he might induce the ignorant electors who believed in him to vote for their (Irish) separation trickeries.

The following excerpts from the code have reference to town and country tenancies:—

Every occupying tenant of a private dwelling and (or) trade premises had the right of acquiring from the State, where he did not already enjoy such privilege, the permanent lease of his premises. The system was practically one man, one holding; but such holding might comprehend a private dwelling, and trade premises, provided that such premises were in the immediate occupation and control of the would-be purchaser. As already set out, no owner could sub-let his premises, or add to them, except through the State Department.

All land in individual ownership had to be farmed and occupied by the owner, just as any dwelling or trade premises had to be in the owner's occupation. Practically a peasant proprietary was established throughout town and country.

Blocks of artisans' dwellings, middle-class dwellings, flats, and such like premises, or commercial offices in the occupation of various tenants, were made acquirable by such tenants in common, if they wished it, their management being reposed in a committee elected by themselves from the occupants, and assisted by a salaried secretary, as, for instance, in the case of proprietary clubs.

Wherever it happened that a living owner had been a just landlord, and had done his duty by his tenants, such owner received the same treatment as were he owner by purchase.

With regard to the acquisition by the State of the mines of the country, all capital expended in machinery, etc., was paid back to the owners, but, except where they had been acquired by *bona fide* purchase, all mining properties were annexed to the State.

It will be perceived in all the foregoing land regulations that mere equality of size or value of holdings was never contemplated or aimed at. Order is the first law of Nature, but not regularity. Irregularity is rather the second law of Nature, true of men and minds, as of all animal life or inert matter. The revolutionary code, therefore, afforded every facility for great and little alike to acquire complete emancipation from any landlord whatsoever. No farm was diminished in size if worked by its immediate owner:

but the new labour conditions tended to bring the size of all agricultural holdings into moderate and handy dimensions. Large farmers found it to their advantage to sell to the State those portions of their farms which, owing to the increasing desire of the labourer to work his own land, were left without sufficient hands to cultivate up to the average prevailing in the county, and which cultivation the local councils had to care for.* So it was in the villages, towns, and cities; no limit was placed on the size or value of individual holdings; the only condition was that the owner should be the immediate occupier and employer; the land to be maintained in a high state of cultivation, the dwellings in a perfect condition of repair. The only limit anywhere drawn was with regard to private residences and pleasure gardens. The latter were limited to five acres, as has already been set out,† and the former to one country and one town house.

Every facility was given for extension of trade and trade premises. The Revolution established something better and broader than had previously existed, not anything worse or narrower.

---

* Pages 127, 128. † Page 117.

CHAPTER IV

FINANCE—REVENUE.

LET it at once be grasped that the Revolution was in nothing more vitally and utterly revolutionary than in its measures of finance.

It found existing a system engendered by party feebleness and expedience—inanity, if not insanity—as subversive of every principle of justice and of wisdom, as it was in application, the very opposite of practical common sense and commercial integrity. Taxation pressed everywhere heaviest not on those best able to bear it, but upon the hardest worked and most moderately paid portion of the community.* An analysis of the burdens borne by the humblest country farmer, town occupier, or petty trader would show a proportion of rating and taxation for local and Imperial purposes of revenue often exceeding fifty per cent. of their actual net incomes,† whereas the proportion borne by the wealthiest would have to be expressed by some very minute fraction of their incomes. That such a system could ever have existed and endured so long may well prove a source of metaphysical speculation for future historians. Doubtless the origin of it all will not be far to seek: Conceive a great commercial enterprise directed not by a wise, experienced, and successful leader of industry, but by an intriguing, loquacious, word-chopping, law-confounding, political legal adventurer. The whirl of ruin would soon rid the commercial world of such a bubble-directed enterprise, of its capital and its captain. Yet Great Britain tolerated such captaincy of its finances for generations; hence it found itself, at the end of the nineteenth century, with a national business spinning, in an ever rapider ruin-vortex, towards bankruptcy and perdition.

---

* Page 119. † Page 121.

The national system of finance was one vast pyramid of political injustice and make-believe. It might be likened to a sort of commercial pyramid reversed, not a pyramid fixed with its base upon capital, whence, through myriad gradations, it led to the ether spaces of honest credit; but cunningly and expediently poised, by lawyer-jargon, on its square-pointed apex. Chancellor Bacon, with his fine-spun unveracities, his turmoil of fraudulent indebtedness, was a worthy father to most of the Chancellor crew. Nineteenth Century Politico-Party finance worked *not* upon a strong foundation of capital, but upon an inverted apex of unending debt, which it counted by the hundreds of millions, so that the nation was perpetually confronted with a millstone dead-weight of debt-interest, involving taxation of over a score of millions annually, a charge which fell largely upon the working classes. This term is literally employed, in contradistinction to the land-owning peers and gentry, who lived on their rent revenues and interest from investments, twenty-six millions of which were produced from the National Debt. The vast freeholders with their unlimited revenues and estates escaped comparatively free; the National Debt interest went directly into the pockets of the capitalists and wealthy classes, who mainly held the stock. At the commencement of the twentieth century the National Debt stood at six hundred and seventy-five millions, bearing interest at two and a half per cent., and required an annual interest charge of about seventeen millions sterling. This amount did not include enormous local loans, which brought the interest up to a considerably larger amount.

Carlyle Democritus at once converted the National Debt into terminable annuities, which provided for its extinction within a period of fifty years from the date of conversion, and which involved a total charge, for interest and sinking fund, of some forty millions annually. This large annual charge was but a light burden on the enormously increased State revenues, as we shall shortly see. Meanwhile, let it be realised that the old ridiculous theory, yet nevertheless widely held, as to a National Debt forming a satisfactory means for the investment of a nation's savings, got itself well exploded. It has been previously remarked in this history that innovating reform, the more new, the more real, and the more absolutely necessary it is, has ever, and inevitably, provoked a militant and exacerbating opposition. The principle of National Debt involves the perpetual bleeding of a nation, and was urged upon the people by the political quack doctors with as facile and ready a word-argument as it is the peculiar province of the genus quack to be ever able to furnish abundant store. That an ignorant public should accept such nostrums need scarcely be wondered at; such public never has had the opportunity, or capacity, to examine for itself the truth, or the untruth, of quackeries in general or particular. Said public only starts up in opposition to such "remedies" when the draining and exhaustion of their political, or other, system brings unending pain and death-spasm; then comes the question, "A lingering death, or violent and spasmodic opposition to such death?" "Death rather to the quack torturers," answer brave men. Comparisons are proverbially said to be odious, nevertheless they are useful, and even necessary sometimes. Here is a very appropriate sort of comparison which shows how an innocent world submitted, through generations, to a process of exhaustion, brought about by a system of medical treatment, happily now obsolete, once very real. The process peculiarly illustrates the national debt quackery, because—in both cases—the bodies that suffered submitted to a very similar course of treatment, namely, a process of blood-letting, which produced in the political and in the human bodies syncope or insensibility. It curiously happened about the time of the political discovery that "debt was evidence of the wealth of a nation," instead of national reserve; that medical practitioners also discovered, or practised, as a means of strengthening and preserving the human constitution and curing it of disease, the tapping it of its life-blood. The circulating systems of the political and the human constitutions were to be kept healthy by a regular process of periodic bleeding of the toiler's gold in the case of the national body, and of from twenty to fifty ounces of human blood in the case of the natural body. In the following extracts, taken from quite a monumental medical work of the before-mentioned period, the technical phrases are put into plain English, as our readers will not all be doctors:—

(75) "General bloodletting is of all our remedies the most powerful. . . . The most important standard of judging how much bloodletting the patient can stand is to draw his blood until he faints. The principle of this standard of judging appears to afford the PRECISE MEASURE to which that bloodletting should be carried. The

principle may be stated thus :—(1) Some diseases enable the system to bear a greater loss of blood than in health; (2) other diseases, on the contrary, cannot stand [medical: induce an unnatural susceptibility to] the effects of loss of blood. You determine the two points by placing the patient perfectly upright, and let his blood run out from a small hole [medical: moderate-sized orifice] until he commences to collapse [medical: until incipient syncope be induced]. The quantity of blood which flows denotes the power of the patient to stand the operation. It is important to remark that if at the first bloodletting much blood should flow before the patient faints, *it must be received as a proof that an early and efficient repetition of the remedy is required*. . . . Having stated the general principle, it only remains to add that we must not be deceived by that kind of fainting which occurs from timidity in regard to the MERE OPERATION."

By process of analogy this will perhaps account for the quick bloodletting of the British national millions, whereby in one century British "statesmen" bled poor England of eight hundred millions sterling, and called it "National Debt." Was ever analogy more exquisitely exact? It might indeed be followed up *ad infinitum*. But we will rest content with this one last comparison: The patient, in both instances, was to be bled until he collapsed; and the readier he could be bled, the more often was the operation to be repeated. The good medical doctors have long since acknowledged the error of *their* ways. But the political doctors were still practising their quack arts at Jubilee period, and bled the people to the extent of twenty-six millions a year for interest on debt, and hundreds of millions a year by way of rent. The more gold blood the people poured out, the more did the political quacks repeat and increase the operation, *quite ad infinitum.*

Indeed, was it not time for a fearless Carlyle Democritus to arise and warn the people that their period of syncope and exhaustion was past, and that national death was dangerously nigh to them? That, if further bleeding was necessary, they had better turn sharply about and try the process upon the political and other bloodsuckers, otherwise there would be no British nation left at all. "Shall ten thousand land-leeches draw out the national life-blood, O my people," said Carlyle Democritus, "or will you awake and confront those ten thousand with your forty millions?"

Carlyle Democritus quickly enlightened the people, and showed them that, in spite of lawyer and party jargon, a State was but a collection of men : That no man could hope to endure commercially upon a basis of perennial indebtedness, neither could a nation of men. Furthermore, that a reserve of capital was the very soul of life of any would-be successful trading, manufacturing, or other commercial body, whether that body might be called company, community, corporation, or nation. The Revolution would therefore substitute for former *in*debtedness, future *ex*debtedness, and would provide a permanent national reserve fund. Carlyle Democritus counselled the people no longer to be blinded by the ancient, cowardly, and specious argument that a National Reserve, in the place of a National Debt, would lead to Revolution by destroying the people's hold on the regulation of the country's finances. The existing Revolution and the French Revolution might prove to them that the curse of unlimited debt was no particular palladium against civil uprising ; but quite the contrary, since Revolution was now to destroy perennial debt and replace it by perennial reserve. Nor would future Chancellors and Parliaments less wisely, or tightly, control the national purse, because it was perennially full instead of being perennially empty. The tendency would work entirely the other way.

The New Sources of Revenue.

The six hundred millions furnished by the great Jewel Requisition, that had been levied in order to deal with an exceptional condition of things which had been brought about by ages of wanton neglect, will be separately dealt with. We are now concerned only with permanent reforms in the taxation of the country. A common error with statesmen in dealing with this subject is to separate Local from Imperial burdens. So far as rates and taxes are extracted from the pocket of the citizen, they need only be considered, and should only be considered, as a whole. We have not to deal at the moment with the application of the national revenues, but with the sources whence they were derived.

The first source of revenue under the Revolution was from the land. The rentals from land and houses, hitherto swelling the bursting pockets of a few individual peers and landowners, produced to the State for the first twelve months succeeding the abolition of landlordism upwards of one hundred and thirty millions sterling. This revenue, vast as it was, by no means represented the actual rent value to accrue from the land, which, according to a preliminary return made by the Revolutionary Land Commission, would most probably exceed three hundred and twenty millions annually. But, in numerous instances, existing occupiers had already acquired their premises, either by purchase of the leases or of the freeholds, so that the hundred and thirty millions by no means represented the full land revenue, which in course of time would accrue to the country's exchequer. (76)

The next source of State revenue was *not* that derived from the sale of intoxicants. In Jubilee time the country depended upon the extension of drinking and drunkenness for more than a third of its Imperial revenue. The net Imperial revenue was roughly about ninety millions, of which the drink tax—through excise and customs—furnished about thirty millions. The Revolutionary Legislators cut down that villainous upas trade in a manner dealt with elsewhere.* The healthier establishment of the liquor traffic produced only fifteen millions to the revenue, and that in spite of an almost prohibitive spirit duty. On the other hand, the old fetish of unlimited "free" trade had been tried and had *not* proved the universal lion-lying-down-with-lamb-panacea which Jubilee political doctors and quacks had overlong prognosticated. In theory, the doctrine was simply delightful; in practice, it was simply suicidal. So much of it as commended itself to actual wisdom, experience, and fact, the Revolution not only confirmed, but widely extended; but the mad exaggeration of the doctrine, the mere crazy bigotry and fanaticism of it, had to adapt itself to living facts and experiences. Every article of food was made free of duty, and was only charged enough to cover the bare cost of entry and examination as to purity, etc. The old Free-Trade quacks, whilst they taxed many articles of the people's food, such as coffee, cocoa, tea, dried fruits, etc., to the tune of some six millions annually, not only admitted free every conceivable article of manufacture to unfairly compete * with Home Industries, but they actually paid from the public pocket the cost—some million or so sterling—of their examination and entry at Customs. Nor was this in itself the most cruel feature of the lunatic system, but they helped Foreign Governments to ruin English industries by welcoming the free entry of goods which the said Governments manufactured in their prisons, or supplied bounties to their manufacturers. Now let it (77)

---

* Pages 203-207.

be at once repudiated by the veracious historian of Carlyle Democritus, that taxation as a method of protection could ever recommend itself to so wise and discerning a statesman. Never. Carlyle Democritus was as far removed from the political incompetencies who advocated protection as he was from the old political mud-gods, who "proved by irrefragable process of arithmetic that Great Britain's Colonial Empire was a ruinous bargain, and a mere matter of pounds, shillings, and pence; and that our glorious Empire of India was a calamity and a curse to the English people." That was the actual dictum of an ante-Jubilee chief of a party of political extremists, who abetted that doctrine of Free Trade. As described under the Colonial portion of this History,* Carlyle Democritus brought about a Pan-Anglican Customs Union, whereby between Great Britain and her Dependencies, Colonies, and Settlements, absolute and unrestricted Free Trade was established. But outside that magnificent Empire, which, be it remembered, brought into intimate commercial union a population exceeding four hundred millions of people, the following system of import duties was established throughout the Empire: Upon all foreign manufactured articles was levied a duty equivalent to the ratio of difference of labour conditions prevailing in this country, and that whence the goods emanated; no more, no less. Where any country admitted English articles of manufacture free, and its industrial laws were just, that country's goods received reciprocal advantage. Where a country sent us manufactured goods, differing in nature from those we exported to them, and where they taxed our manufactures or exports, the mean was established by a reciprocal *ad valorum* duty, levied on whatever goods they sent us. In no case (except as necessity compelled) were raw materials, used in manufacture, taxed. All raw materials entered the British Empire free. But even this wise rule had to have exception, viz. Those countries who sent us raw material, or grain, and no manufactured articles, and where such raw materials, or grain, were obtainable from other countries, or within the Empire—then a tax was levied on those foreign countries' exports to the Empire. For instance: One country taxed nearly all our articles of manufacture to an extent varying from twenty-five to sometimes a hundred per cent.—that country might send us in return only grains of one

---

* See Book III., chap. i.

description or another; upon such grain a full reciprocal duty was levied. This did not appreciably augment the price of the grains generally; it simply induced the trade into Canadian, Indian, or Australian channels, and closed it against the Protectionist State, and very rarely failed to bring the unreasonable Protectionist country, or countries, quickly to their senses.

The result to the revenue was that instead of the six millions formerly levied on food stuffs, twenty-five millions were levied on imported foreign manufactured articles.

The political arithmeticians, "anxious to cut India and the Colonies adrift," cast up their hands and eyes, shrieked vociferously, but happily in vain, for the practical amongst the four hundred millions of British subjects remembered that their panaceas had not made, but had gone nigh to unmake, England. " With us, or against us, O Foreign Nations?" No longer do political poison-quacks, spawned of party caucus, rule Great Britain, but a little of the Eternal Wisdom has to shape British Policy in future.

The next great change was in the income-tax, which was graduated, and divided into three categories: (1) Non-productive incomes (from dividends, investments, etc.); (2) trade; and (3) profession. The income-tax commenced on incomes of £200 a year, which paid two per cent., up to £500; these paid three per cent. up to £1000; these four per cent. up to £5000, which paid five per cent.; and all incomes above that figure a tithe. Professional incomes paid only two-thirds of the above rates; traders and manufacturers, three-fourths; and all others in full.

Considerable extension of the powers and duties of income-tax commissioners rendered fraudulent returns a dangerous and very unprofitable enterprise, and finally stamped out the evil altogether. Let those who deem a tithe levied upon incomes of extreme wealth an exorbitant assessment destroy their Bibles and keep away from church, for that tithe was the ancient conception of man's duty towards God and the State; and England declared itself to believe (*vide* the Thirty-nine Articles) that the wisdom of the Scriptures is the especial revelation of Deity. But on lesser grounds its wisdom and justice may be easily set out. With a few exceptions, which need not here be gone into, these taxes and the death duties constituted, after the land and property rent or tax, the principal sources of revenue for Local as well as Imperial purposes. In pre-revolutionary times, the poorest workers had paid to the State not a tithe of their poor income, but practically a quarter to a half of it, and often more.*

This tax did not approach the old system of local taxation, which had drawn from the nation annually seventy millions. The new income-tax—remember that it now included practically all charges for Local as well as Imperial requirements, because the revenue arising from the State rents could by no means be deemed a tax, (since in the past it always had to be paid in one form or another to private owners)—produced thirty-five millions. It was a variable quantity, and Parliament could either raise it or reduce it, but any alteration had always to be in the ratio and the graduation required by the new Constitution as given above.

Probate duty was also revolutionised. The Tax Commissioners were the most august body in the land. They were very highly paid, and were drawn from the most trustworthy citizens of the Kingdom. Neither directly, nor indirectly, could they be connected with any trade, profession, or company. This Commission consisted of fifteen members, who were nominated by the Upper House and appointed by the Commons. Just as the ordinary Local Assessment Committees throughout the Kingdom knew the value of every building in their respective districts, from a cabin to a castle, so the Tax Commissioners, who had local branches throughout the country, knew the actual capital value of the owners of cabin or castle. But whereas the House and Land Assessments were publicly recorded, the capital and income records were available only to the Government and the Commission itself.

Not only had such a Board or Commission become imperatively necessary to overcome the scandals of false and fraudulent returns, which were rampant at Jubilee period, but as a measure of mere even-handed justice it was necessary. Thus, in the old system, an employer was constrained to furnish the names of his clerks and assistants to the Income-Tax Commissioners, and to name the salaries he paid them. Their humbler incomes were thereby known, to the last penny, to the Tax Commissioners. Why should not the same justice be meted out to the wealthy master as well as to the poor dependent? Common justice, and Carlyle Democritus, determined that there was absolutely no reason. Accordingly, the

---

* Pages 119, 121.

returns of all persons, after the Revolution, were made equally exact. The value of such a system was abundantly proved by the results of the first twelve months' returns from probate duty as well as from the income-tax, under the new code. Jubilee officials returned as the average net annual capital value of estates assessed to legacy, probate, and succession duty, the colossal total of about three hundred and fifty millions sterling. It was soon found that numbers of the wealthiest of the deceased Jubilites had evaded probate by what was euphoniously called in those times "Deed of Gift" (or in legal jargon, "disposition *inter vivos*), but which the Revolution called by its true name of downright cowardly fraud, whereby soulless Mammonites, in order to evade (78) probate duty, transferred, before their decease—Carlyle Democritus reckoned the only vital part of them, their national integrity and patriotism, already dead—the greatest portion of their huge fortunes to their successors. After the Revolution was established, the first year's probate returns exceeded five hundred millions. How? Because the old deed-of-gift dodge availed no longer. The Tax Commissioners proved the actual value of the deceased's estate, and it rested with the successors to disprove it; and since any false or fraudulent evidence carried with it a penalty of total sequestration, millionaires had to be as honest as the humblest folk. And now let us see what the death or probate duties realised. Mammon Parliaments considered they had done ample duty in taxing their three hundred and fifty millions to produce about eight millions, or two-and-a-half per cent., and *their* system bore lightest on the wealthiest. All Mammon legislation seemed based upon the principle of—"A tithe of my income to Thee, O Lord, whilst I'm earning a poor or moderate income; but Thou wouldst not have me give a tithe of, say, a hundred thousand pounds; that would be *too* much; would it not, O Lord?" This was the new Probate Law: At death, never mind of what the property consisted (other than *bona fide* household furniture, goods, and chattels), the State levied one per cent. on all estates of the net value of one thousand pounds; exceeding that amount, and up to ten thousand pounds, they paid two-and-a-half per cent.; above that, and up to one hundred thousand pounds, five per cent.; and above that figure a tithe. The first year's death duties gave to the Exchequer twenty-five millions sterling, a sum destined to be largely exceeded in future years.

One year after the establishment of the Revolution, and after Parliament had confirmed all its reforms, the total British revenue showed no less a figure than three hundred and thirty millions. The land revenue from State rents, land allotment sales, etc., produced a hundred and twenty-five millions. This was destined to increase for several years, as the old leases either fell into the State, or were converted, by purchasing occupiers, into permanent leaseholds. The spirit and liquor taxes produced only fifteen millions, as against the Jubilee sum of thirty millions. On the other hand, the new customs or import duties netted twenty-five millions, as against the Jubilee twenty-one millions. Death duties produced twenty-five millions, as against the Jubilee eight millions. Stamp duties on share certificates, bill-stamps, etc., brought in six millions, as against the Jubilee five. Unmanufactured tobacco was admitted free, and manufactured tobacco, including foreign cigars, were treated in a somewhat similar manner with foreign wines, viz. the duty on them was in proportion to the duties levied on British exports by the countries from whence they came. The whole duties from tobacco produced rather less than they previously did—two millions annually. The surplus of revenue from the Post Office no longer fell to the general revenue, for the simple reason that, after the Revolution, the whole of such surpluses were devoted to improving the postal service generally. Thus there was a universal British Empire Postal Union rate of one penny. The cost of telegrams was reduced to sixpence for twenty words; and telephones could be hired at every Post Office at the rate of threepence per minute. One-half of any annual surplus, which rarely fell below two millions, was set aside for the establishment of permanent branch Post Offices, in place of the ancient variegated assortment of temporary agencies. The revenue from mines and quarries, now the property of the State, produced ten millions, in spite of the diminished coal output, and of the lower prices at which the produce was sold.* The Suez Canal shares dividend produced one million. Minor rates and taxes produced a total of six millions. And last, comes the new house and land tax. This tax was a graduated one, levied on all house and land property. It commenced at sixpence in the pound on land and houses under an annual value of £20; went to two

---

* Pages 219-225.

shillings on property from £20 to £50 annual value; to five shillings on properties from £50 to £100; and rose one shilling (*gradatim*) for every £100 on properties above that value. It produced in the first twelve months after its imposition £75,000,000. This tax rose or fell according to the requirements of the Government, but the graduated scale could not be altered. As the national income from the State rents increased, the taxation upon house and land property would *pari passu* decrease, as would also all other taxes. One generation after the establishment of the New Code, when nearly all landed property had fallen to the State, the State rents * produced two hundred and fifty millions sterling annually, the total house and land tax was reduced by two-thirds, and the income-tax by one-half.

One year after the establishment of the Revolution, on quarter-day, the twenty-fifth of March 19—, the total net revenue of the British Isles reached three hundred and thirty millions sterling. For simplicity of reference, these are the tabulated returns:—

State rents from land, house property, etc.	£130,000,000
State revenue from mines and quarries.	10,000,000
Liquor Taxes	15,000,000
Customs	25,000,000
Income Tax	35,000,000
Death Duties	25,000,000
Stamps	6,000,000
Tobaccos	2,000,000
Suez Canal Shares	1,000,000
House and Land Tax	75,000,000
Minor Taxes and Sundries	6,000,000
Total,	£330,000,000

Deducting the amounts produced by the house and land rents.

---

* Wherever a lease of house property was purchased outright by an Urban occupier, the purchase price was funded, so that the interest remained in lieu of rent. But after a time the security of tenure was found to be so absolutely safeguarded under State rental, that perpetual leaseholders of Urban property became a gradually diminishing quantity. No limit was fixed on the number of years of a lease for which an occupier might purchase. But as the gradually disappearing rate of interest made the purchase of a lease almost equivalent to the laying down of so many years' actual rental in advance, only those availed themselves of the system who desired to leave their wives or children rent free.

and taxes, together two hundred and five millions, this leaves a sum of one hundred and fifteen millions of revenue from all other sources as against the total ninety millions of Imperial revenue raised at a Jubilee period. But this ninety millions of the Jubilee period was mild as compared with the seventy millions of local taxation levied at that time, which pressed almost unendurably upon the lower middle classes. The Revolution entirely abolished local taxation. There was no penny raised beyond the revenues above described. They comprehended everything. The reform of the revenue system may be thus briefly summarized:—

JUBILEE TAXATION:—
Imperial £90,000,000
Local 70,000,000
Total, £160,000,000

CARLYLE DEMOCRITEAN, OR REVOLUTIONARY TAXATION:—
From all sources, other than land £115,000,000
State rents and taxes on houses, land, and mines . . . 215,000,000
Total, £330,000,000

As the taxes on land and house property were in lieu of rent, the new system was actually a relief of taxation to the extent of about forty-five millions annually. All taxation beyond the hundred and fifteen millions was provided from the natural resources of the land, enhanced by the labour of the nation, which a blind, party-ruled people had hitherto permitted a small fraction of perhaps their most worthless to absorb.

We shall see in another chapter how the new revenues were applied.

CHAPTER V.

FINANCE—EXPENDITURE.

BEFORE proceeding to deal with the revolutionary expenditure, it will be necessary to explain the new Stock which had to be created. And it is to be remembered that it was made a part of the new Constitution that no money should ever in future be borrowed which did not at the same time provide a sinking fund for the loan, based upon a minimum period of twenty-five years, and a maximum period of fifty years, according as the purposes of the loan were productive or non-productive; the shorter period applying to non-productive loans, the longer period to the productive. For the purposes of the State acquisition of the land and mines, the new Parliament authorised a land-loan, which was to be issued in instalments as required. It bore interest at two and a half per cent. Owing to the immense proportion of the land which fell to the State by natural sequestrations,* there was never more land stock floating at one time than required an annual interest charge of eleven millions sterling, including sinking fund. This land stock was divided into three categories to meet the requirements of the Lands Department's assessment of value. It is to be remembered that the Revolution classified the landowners who were to receive compensation into various life periods :—

1. Persons who owned land which had been purchased by themselves or by their predecessors.
2. Persons who owned land, the gift of the State for actual service by them or their predecessors.

---

* See pages 116, 118.

3. Those who, without original adequate title, had yet dealt worthily with their existing tenants and with their property.

The last class was, after careful examination, found to contain just thirty-seven representatives.

The first, who, for convenience of classification, were called "Commercial Landowners," after the value of their holdings had been determined by the Land Assessment Committee, received land stock to the full value of such assessment—such stock bearing, in addition to its interest of two-and-a-half per cent., a further one per cent. sinking fund, whereby the stock terminated after fifty years. The second and third class received land stock bearing interest at two-and-a-half per cent., terminable after one, two, or three lives, according to the finding of the Revolutionary Court, or of the Land Commission, which finding was dependent entirely upon the original merit of the State donee, together with the condition of the property and its management at the time of the establishment of the Revolution.

The new Parliament also issued a Consolidated Stock of several hundred millions, terminable after fifty years, for the purchase of the Gas, Water, and Electricity Works in the kingdom, held by private companies. But as all of these loans were levied at the current rate of interest, *plus* a sinking fund of one per cent., which combined amount was made a first charge upon the respective undertakings, they none required additional taxation, as in no instance could compensation be given beyond actual earning value. The method of working the various enterprises is dealt with elsewhere.*

The national expenditure after the Revolution has to be divided under two distinct heads, the one including the temporary annual charges, for half a century, of eleven millions for land purchase, and forty millions for interest and extinction of the National Debt—together, fifty-one millions. Further, a special provision (extending over a lesser period) for increasing the strength of the Navy, fortifying our coaling stations, building harbours of refuge, and generally making amends for centuries of past neglect and *laisser-faire.*

For years after the establishment of the Revolution the **expenditure was** therefore a thing by itself. After that period the

* Pages 221-3.

expenditure became normal. It will be remembered that the *Jubilee Imperial Revenue* was about ninety millions.* Its expenditure was roughly as follows :—

National Debt Interest	£26,000,000
Cost of the Army	16,000,000
„ of the Navy	14,000,000
Civil Service :—	
Education, Science, and Art .	6,000,000
Law, Justice (Jubilee Justice), and Courts	7,000,000
Colonial and Foreign Service	1,000,000
Public Works and Buildings	2,000,000
Royal Family, including the waste flunkey payments, Cornwall and Lancaster Duchies, etc.,	1,000,000
Sundry other Disbursements	4,000,000
Cost of the National Services: Customs, Post-Office, Telegraph, etc.	13,000,000
Total	£90,000,000

These figures are stated broadly, so as to convey a rough idea of the National Expenditure before the Revolution, in order to facilitate comparison with the new expenditure. Thus, in fixing the cost to the Nation of Royalty at one million in the Jubilee finances, there is no doubt that the figure is substantially correct, and is probably *under-* rather than over-stated as regards the amount which the Nation actually paid in one way or another to foreign princes, and by land and mining revenues to the Royal House. But only a portion of that amount really benefited Royalty in any way.† A large portion of it was squandered on keeping up empty palaces and paying hundreds of sinecure officers. The cost nowhere figures directly in the particular accounts; they were purposely mutilated and made misleading, but the sum named may be taken as well within the actual total.

As to the seventy millions of local revenue, or taxation, raised

---

* Page 137.   † Pages 73, 74.

annually at the pre-Revolutionary period. It was expended roughly as follows :—

On Workhouses, and the Relief of the Poor generally	£15,000,000
By School Boards of Education, on Police, the Maintenance of Roads, Drainage; carrying out the Sanitary Acts, etc., .	49,000,000
By Burial Boards . . .	1,000,000
On Harbours, Pilotage, etc. . .	5,000,000
Total .	£70,000,000

THE ANNUAL EXPENDITURE FOR FIFTY* YEARS AFTER THE REVOLUTION (INCOME, THREE HUNDRED AND THIRTY MILLIONS, see page 143).

On the National Debt, and Provision for its Extinction	£40,000,000
Land Stock and Sinking Fund . . .	11,000,000
New Ships, and perfecting existing ones .	10,000,000
Navy, normal expenditure . . .	20,000,000
Coaling Stations and Fortifications . . .	10,000,000
Harbours of Refuge	2,000,000
Increasing the Number of Sailors, and forming the New Reserve	2,000,000
Army, normal expenditure	20,000,000
Improvement of Barracks, and General Reforms .	10,000,000
CIVIL SERVICE—	
Education, Science, and Art . . .	10,000,000
Law, Justice, etc. (including the various Guild Courts †)	7,000,000
Colonial and Foreign Service . . .	4,000,000
Public Works and Buildings (including new Post Offices)	5,000,000
Carry forward,	£151,000,000

* The fifty years only applies to the National Debt and Land Stock Charge, etc.; the Army, Navy, and other great Reform charges lapsed after much shorter periods, varying from twenty years to twenty-five years.

† Page 209.

Brought forward,	£151,000,000
Royal Family (including cost of State Palaces and entertaining Imperial guests)	500,000
Various	4,000,000
Poor Law, including State Contributions to Fund for National Insurance against Old Age, etc.	12,000,000
Bounties to Trade and other Unions	3,500,000
Reclamation of Waste Lands, including cost and maintenance of Penal Labour	6,000,000
Re-afforesting	1,000,000
National Improvement of the Dwellings of the Working Classes and others	2,000,000
Colonisation and Settling of the people on the land	10,000,000
	£190,000,000

LOCAL EXPENDITURE—

School Board, and Grants in aid of Education	£12,000,000
In aid of Technical Training	6,000,000
Police and Street Keepers	22,000,000
County, District, and Parish Councils for maintenance of roads, drainage, and carrying out the Sanitary Acts, etc.	35,000,000
The same Bodies for planting trees, and architecturally improving the cities, towns, etc.	12,000,000
Burial Boards	5,000,000
Harbours and Pilotage	8,000,000
Total Expenditure, Imperial and Local	£290,000,000
Total Revenue*	330,000,000
Balance to accumulate as National Reserve	£40,000,000

In the above figures the cost of Customs' collection, of Post Office, etc., have not been included, inasmuch as Jubilee dodges are dispensed with, and only the NET Revenue is entered on the Credit side.

With regard to the funds of the National Insurance against Old Age and Accident, when the reserve reached one hundred

---

* Page 143.

millions by the joint accretion of the State bounties and of the accumulating subscriptions, the State bounties ceased.

The National Debt of Great Britain used to be eight hundred millions. The Revolution, having provided for its extinction, had established, as we have seen, a National Reserve instead. The limit of the National Reserve Fund was fixed by the new Constitution at five hundred millions, and the new taxation could not be reduced until that reserve was attained. The amount would only accumulate gradually and was not to be left idle. One tithe of it was to be in bullion, the rest to be employed in the extension of remunerative Imperial works in any part of the Empire, such as railways, irrigation, reclamation of waste lands, opening up new territories, etc., according to the decrees of Parliament; and a special sub-department of the Imperial Executive was appointed to deal with this matter. It will be seen that the entire revenues of the country became collected by direct taxation, with the exception only of the Customs and the Spirit Duty, and no distinction was made between Local and Imperial rating. The people exactly and justly shared the burden in proportion to their wealth.

Under the Jubilee system the Vestries or District Councils collected the whole of the local rates, although only a very small proportion of them was actually expended by those bodies. They included the School Board, the Police, the County Council, and the Poor Rates, over none of which the collecting authority had any control. After the Revolution, each of these different bodies received their rates direct from the one central Taxation Department. Their expenditure was restricted to a certain maximum rate per head of the populations over which they had control. Any desired expenditure beyond the normal maximum had to receive the sanction of the Superior County Council or Local Government Board. The greatest change in the Local Government was the disappearance of the Poor Law Guardians. They were no longer required, as will be seen on reference to the chapter dealing with the measures affecting the poor, the unemployed, and the labouring classes generally.*

NOTE.—No separate account has been taken of the Jubilee National Debt Sinking Fund, because, like all Jubilee measures which had any wisdom in them, it was for ever abused by the lawyer-Chancellors, and its fund diverted to hide their free trade deficits, etc.

* Pages 156-60.

CHAPTER VI.

THE CONSECRATION OF THE GREAT REQUISITION.

How some of the Six Hundred Millions were employed.

THE QUIETUS OF PAUPER IMMIGRATION.

BEFORE any great lasting social reforms could be brought about, Carlyle Democritus and the Revolution were confronted with that vast, inert, seething mass of misery, the product of generations of legislative incompetence, neglect, ignorance, and cupidity. But it did not dismay them. On the contrary, like the slums which had to be removed before wholesome dwellings could be rebuilt upon their sites; like the debased and soulless legislators, who had to be rusticated before a new franchise could be evoked to establish a worthier set of Governors; like the carnal, priest-ridden, Mammon-controlled Church, outraging the very name of religion, needing Augean-stable treatment before purity of worship and the pastorate of Christ could be in any manner wisely introduced—so there was necessary a fearless, manful grasping of the terrible social nettle of pauperism before any possible lasting labour-reform could hope for success. The fearful pauper problem was twofold: on one hand was an insidious poisonous inflow of dank and festering foreign beggars; on the other was a widespread so-called "sub merged class"—a nigh hopeless mass of pitiful, suffering human beings. With these two classes Carlyle Democritus had to deal, and thus he dealt :—

Pauper immigration had been allowed to dump down upon Britain's narrow shores for years and years endless thousands of the waste beggary of Europe, in spite of loudest protest. The Revolutionary Government would tolerate no cowardly turning of the back to a problem by means of so-called "Royal Commission."

Jubilee-Parliament dodge of evading legislation by smudging and burying the issue of a problem in mountains of hollow twaddle and make-believe.* The extent of the evil was known to those who cared to know it only too well, and Carlyle Democritus had caused a rough and effective classification to be laid before him of the actual state of this pauper immigration. It showed that there were in Great Britain one hundred thousand foreign poor or unfit labourers, so utterly broken and sweated as to be scarcely removed from the lowest depths of pauperism, adding to the want and misery of the great centres of population throughout the

---

* One of the last of these Royal Commissions and mockeries appointed by Sorrypebble was a so-called Labour Commission. It consisted of some thirty Honourable and Right Honourable word-spinners. They sat for three years, and laid wind-eggs in the shape of sixty-five volumes of bulky Blue-books, and issued two reports—a majority report (majority of words, since it consisted of over one hundred foolscap pages), and a minority report (minority of words, consisting of some dozen or so foolscap pages). At the waste cost of between fifty and sixty thousand pounds sterling, they had scraped together information and facts which had been in the possession of every poor and wise student, or any other, for years previously, and they discovered—

1. That there were at least five millions of British people on the brink of starvation.

2. That more than 25 per cent. of the population fell below the "poverty line."

3. That two millions of British souls were driven every year to seek Poor Law relief from hunger and unbearable misery.

4. That horrible destitution was not confined to the poorer classes only.

5. That in London alone 100,000 little children were brought up in incest dens (mother, father, and entire family "living" in one room); [the clergy at their Mansion House Conference, the year before, declared 300,000 children to be nearer the truth].

6. That the landlords, or devils, sucked in rents, royalties, etc., from the oppressed British nation, five hundred millions sterling annually.

7. That public bodies bought their uniforms, etc., from the vilest sweaters.

8. That overwork and under-pay and the filthiness of Slumland were rife everywhere.

9. That boys were condemned to work in underground mines, and remain there ten and eleven hours at a stretch.

10. That cheap and incompetent foreign seamen were being increasingly employed in British ships whilst brave British sailors were increasingly starving.

11. That agricultural labourers and their families were "living" on wages below eight shillings a week, cooped up like pigs, in styes and mud-cabins.

12. That women and children laboured like slaves from twelve to

kingdom. The hundred thousand his officers had classified as follows :—(1) Fifty thousand foreigners, speaking or understanding a little English, partly skilled, all capable of field work, provided they were placed under adequate supervision and determined discipline—most of them political, or religious refugees. (2) Thirty thousand foreigners, speaking little or broken English, mere food for sweaters, unskilled, and ousting poor English labour. (3) Twenty thousand foreigners, knowing a smattering of English, for the most part beggars, and following waste employments, such as organ-grinding, street hawking, and ice-selling, German band " musicians," and a motley crew of paupers of the most hopeless type.

---

fifteen hours a day, for wages insufficient to provide decent maintenance—and under sanitary conditions utterly damnable. That hundreds of thousands of females, demoralised to the lowest possible depth, were thus engaged in the manufacture of inferior boots, shoes, and saddlery, slop-clothing, " cheap " furniture, iron nails, cutlery, etc. And . . . they did *not* find that Mammon was riding his devil-horses of "progress of the species," "survival of the fittest," " political-economy-party-word-spinning, devil take the hindermost " —upon the racecourse of "free-trade "—to hell and eternal perdition.

Nearly the whole of the information adduced in that period of three years in those sixty-five bulky blue volumes, at cost of fifty to sixty thousand pounds, had been similarly compiled only a very few years before by a similar Royal ''Sweating" Commission, which had also wasted three years of valuable time, unending number of thousands sterling, and a whole library of volumes blue. Jabber, jabber, jabber, and only jabber. Let any sane mortal try to examine the huge wind-egg of that Royal Commission—called majority report—and he will be fit afterwards for no other place than Hanwell. The above findings are from the minority report, for at least the minority report is honest : humanly, from the heart—though tremulously, timorously, the still small voice in the Babel of Cant, endeavours to suggest remedies. Three true men out of thirty—all honour and God-speed to them. But that other—the majority report—is a mere confused mass of cowardly futilities, asinine stupidities, and Parliamentary vacuities—leading nowhere, touching no general reform worthy the consideration of gods or men, fit only for the party asses and cant wind-bags who had evolved them— a vast, mad, cruelly expensive and wasteful illustration that "ex nihilo nihil fit": "Out of Sorrypebbles you will only get stones—stones which by futilities, company-mongering, eternal political party-cant, Mammon-mumbling worship, he, and the likes of him, will persuade you to be not only bread, but actual manna from Heaven. O poor heavy-laden English people! Well might the starving multitude cry before the face of high Heaven : " We asked them for bread and they gave us stones ; we asked them for wisdom and they gave us but wind."

For the last two orders, the twenty thousand foreign beggars and the thirty thousand pauper labour, quick arrangements were made. Ten of the largest transport ships, thirty cruisers, and forty large vessels hired from the merchant fleet, were ordered, without any one but those concerned being made aware of their purpose, or intended destination, to prepare to receive and transport fifty thousand men, women, and children. Within ten days of those orders the ships were victualled and ready for sea. Three days before the ships were ready to sail, short notices were served upon the persons to be deported, apprising them that they would be given free passages to their respective countries, good food on their journey, and a gift of twenty shillings to each person, together with seven days' free rations for every man, woman, and child upon leaving the ship. As each ship was filled with its live cargo, it quickly left the port and steamed, as the need might be, to Italy with its organ-grinders, its vendors of ice, and sundry assorted beggars; to Germany with its itinerant minstrels and beggars; to Russia and to Poland with *their* respective beggar squadrons; to each nation, in fact, its pauper-due.

Our consuls at the various ports had apprised the various Governments of the act of the Revolution, and no difficulty arose in any case. Tents were supplied with all the ships in order to provide temporary encampments for the poor emigrants where necessary. The instructions of our consuls, or ambassadors, included a written notice to the Courts to which they were accredited, which courteously explained that Great Britain had found it imperative to adopt the steps which it had done, as she found it already a sufficient task to care for the poor of her own people.

For the remaining portion of the foreign poor a different method was adopted. Many of them were political refugees, or religious victims, and they implored to remain under British protection. For these, settlements were acquired in South Africa, on terms agreed with three of the chartered Companies.* Upon these settlements the people were as quickly as possible provided with land allotments, shelter, tools, seed, and live stock. Superintendents, with absolute authority, were established over each community, all under the control of one of the wisest and most experienced of British Governors, a Viceroy entrusted with

---

* See pages 290-2.

supreme responsibility. Penal settlements were set up in each colony to deal with refractory persons; free schools were opened in every community, where the English language was compulsory. In later years these settlements became important communities of English-speaking]; to England grateful, agricultural landowners; and they eventually paid off the whole cost of their emigration. But at the time of which we are writing, the first cost to the Revolution of the entire emigration of the hundred thousand foreign poor, and paupers, absorbed nearly twenty millions from the great requisition fund. The details of the organisation of the settlements need not here be gone into, because they were as nearly as possible identical with those described in the chapter on Colonisation.* One great caution Carlyle Democritus impressed upon the Governors, and upon all those concerned in the gigantic scheme, viz. not to expect, and not to take any steps towards enforcing payment of any sort for the first five years after the settlement of the people. But, in every instance, the most careful accounts were to be kept, so that eventually, when the people had become established, the cost of settlement should justly fall upon each head of a family.

Great Britain, thus freed of its first great incubus, one of its great poison-sewers cleansed and sanitated, was not allowed by cowardly no-legislation to fill up insidiously, or in any wise again. Every ship-owner was made responsible for his passengers. Any non-self-supporting foreigner imported after publication of the edict which peremptorily put an end to pauper immigration, not only was obliged to return whence he came, at the expense of the offending ship-owner, but rendered the said owner further liable to a fine of £100 for every offence. These fines were intentionally made prohibitive. At the same time, compare the noble impetus and support that Carlyle Democritus afforded the mercantile navy in all their glorious province of legitimate trade and enterprise.†

Pauper immigration was killed. Within three months of the edict, not one foreign pauper or unfit worker was to be found on British soil.

---

* See page 250. † See pages 281-2.

CHAPTER VII.

WORK FOR THE WEAKEST AND THE WORST.

NEXT came the yet heavier problem: The caring for the "submerged" of British origin. One of the gravest Councils appointed by Carlyle Democritus was that on poverty. It consisted of five members, the five bravest and most experienced men, whose names were respected by all men but "statesmen," who in Jubilee period merely ignored them. A characteristic interview between the Revolutionary chief and this Council took place the day following their first assembling. Happily the record of it is yet extant, and here is a portion of it. The House of Commons' Committee Rooms were alive with State Councils actively engaged in carrying out reforms already devised, or providing the mechanism for future edicts. They were no mere talking, time-squandering, lawyer-jargoning, bigwig idiocies; but they were ardent, active, practical, business-like directorates. The "Council on Poverty" was one amongst many, and its composition affords a clue to understanding the methods of them all. Carlyle Democritus once having selected the best and most practical men in the kingdom to serve on these various committees, whose numbers he always left as small as possible, his next great care was to leave them entirely unhampered by red-tape rules of any sort. Their duties once clearly and tersely set before them, they were one and all zealously besought to consider only the cause they were called upon to serve; to keep steadily and unerringly before them no other consideration, but to manfully and fearlessly fulfil their duty, with God and their consciences for guiding-light. Upon his appointment to serve on one of these great committees or councils, each member received a thousand pounds. Whether his council sat many days, or few days, mattered in no way. The fee was for invaluable *service*, was not measurable by time-service, or by windbagism. The five members constituting the Council on Poverty were:—

Colonel Andrew Black, who, for many years before the Revolution, had slaved to better the condition of the unemployed, had times out of number headed deputations to Jubilee Ministers, only to be scoffed at, jeered, and grinning-Pilate-questioned, "What is truth?" Colonel Black knew a little of the people he was now at last called upon practically to work for; he had with rare devotion lived the very life of the roughest and the poorest, had left for a time his gentle wife and home, disguised as a navvy, and had at one time actually starved with the hunger-stricken. To Carlyle Democritus Colonel Black was one of God's own workers; he would entrust such a one with almost indefinite power in the direction of his appointment. (83)

Another member was Harley Tent, also an indefatigable worker amongst the suffering multitudes, and who had published perhaps the most complete history of poverty ever compiled by man—quite an anti-Giffen sort of person; one who used figures to enlighten the world, to explain the truth, and not to obscure it. (84)

A third was Pastor Truslove, adored by the people. Rumour said that it was he whom Carlyle Democritus visited in an awful London slum-hell many years before. Truslove had since that time lost his only son, a little child of ten years or so, victim to the stench of Slumland,—eternal sun-ray of the poor Pastor-life gone out into far-star radiance. The Pastor's countenance of subdued resignation and sorrow had little of earth in it: "For the sweet child whom God has taken from me," he would say, "that same God has laid upon me the care of many other children. And He has said to me, O Pastor, as thou lovest these little stricken ones, so will I love thy son; finish thy task, O beloved Pastor, and I will call thee to Me as an Angel of Eternal Light, thy golden darling here awaiting thee upon My right Hand." . . . The small, gentle Pastor, embodiment of Christ-like love, raised to the highest post of veneration by the Revolution, had starved in a slum vicarage at the Jubilee Period on a salary of some thirty shillings a week, unheeded and unknown. When they lifted his poor flock out of the slum-hell into Christian, helpful worksomeness, and told the gentle Pastor, now growing old, what had happened, and that the loving people and their great Leader had made him Chief Pastor of the Church, the poor old man sank down upon his knees, and the devoted ones around him heard his sigh-prayer to the Great Father: "Thou hast answered Thy servant, O Eternal One. Now take me, I pray Thee, to Thee and my lost one." And as the soft silvery waves of the old man's hair fell like the down from an angel's wing upon his recumbent breast, they lifted him half-unconscious, reverently, lightly as a dormant child, and brought him to the Leader of the people. This poor, little wasted Love-man, a living saint upon earth, when they, in reverent worship, looked into the way of his life, and found how, from his Church-pay of weekly thirty shillings, most had gone to his flock—and the Archbishops all that time in their palaces, with their ten to fifteen thousand pounds a year, and the Bishops and the Articles Thirty-Nine! It was *then* that the people vowed they would sweep all priest-craft away—and have no more gilded Bishops —but servitors of God, like this saint. And they printed the tale of his life, of the love he had lost, and of the love he had gained, and down into the slum prisons they sent it, and there, on the Sunday morning, in the barn-church provided there, the simple story was read by a rescued son of toil to the fallen kings of the Church and the broken lords of the State.

Next to the Pastor Truslove in the Council sat a working farmer of large experience. Next to his own farm he had seen, in the old Jubilee time, fifty acres of rich land cleared of its tenants for sport-shooting; and when the Jubilee sportsman tired of his toy, the farmer bought the land for a kindly experiment. He hired ten broken Irish peasants, who, with their little families, he had seen evicted one winter's day from a Jubilee lord's estate, turned adrift by bailiff and bayonet to starve.* The old farmer divided his land, set those ten families upon it, and bade them work, with a promise of the land to each family, with the hearth, and the sheep, and the pigs, as each one should perfect the wasted soil—he remaining there to counsel and direct. In three years the fifty acres waved with golden corn; fat cattle and woolly sheep fed on the hill slopes; pigs and poultry thrived on the waste. Bright, happy children outvied the merry flowers in the corn; brave and sturdy peasants lustily directed the plough, every man of them owning his own plot. Carlyle Democritus had a long list of such men as Farmer Tried*itt*, and they

---

* Page 100.

became infinite powers for good under a system which, quietly and unerringly, sought out merit in action, instead of rotten *pretence* of merit and political word-mongering.

The fifth member was another such farmer, only a younger man. And to this Council of five Carlyle Democritus entered. They had made Pastor Truslove their spokesman, though Colonel Black was their chairman.

"Gentlemen," said Democritus as he entered, "though we may know little of each other personally, except our dear Pastor here, we have each one of us an intimate and well-understood knowledge of the Cause which you are here gathered together to help forward with your loving counsel. Let us be as brief as we can— time is so short, the misery so wide."

Pastor:—" General, we come here at your bidding, to serve with our hearts and our understanding the great Cause which God has entrusted to you to establish. We have longed for this time to come, longed—until now—without hope. General, we can utter no idle words to tell you our devotion and our love; we will not return to our homes until our work is done that you have called upon us to do; we fervently thank the Eternal Power that He has raised up a trusty servant to work His Divine will and way. General, we pray you to accept our service unpaid. We would prefer that our work be a labour of love."

General:—"Pastor, I, too, cannot speak my heart's reverence for you here assembled, nor is there need of it; your loving presence here, my prayer to you to come, are our best, our only speech on that. Beautiful indeed is that to me and to you. As to the State payments, do what you will with the money, but it must not be returned. Let us bravely regard this one thing, and not confound State work and personal regard. Your independence, your desire to serve gratuitously, does you honour, but all cannot spare their time ; many that I have had to call are, indeed, as poor as those they are called to work for; our dear pastor here is not a millionaire. For the sake of all, therefore, I pray you keep what the State but too cheaply requites, for true service is unpayable. And now, to sterner things. Do you need other directions than the printed sheet affords ?"

Col. Black:—"Yes, General. We are entirely agreed that we shall be able promptly enough to lay before you the information and the scheme you desire. Nor are we at all dismayed by its probable cost. All we would ask is how that cost is to be met, and are we to treat that part of our scheme as though it did not concern us?"

General:—" Precisely that, Colonel. But I will at once reassure you as to cost. Apart from the fact that the Revolutionary funds are ample for all purposes; even were they not we should *make* them so. We are resolved, Colonel, that the same Britain which could free black slaves for twenty millions sterling shall not stop even at ten times that cost, if necessary, to emancipate their white slaves. Nay, more, we say that the Britain which hesitated not to squander seven hundred millions in mad wars of butchery and folly—for remember, Colonel, the greatest of England's conquests were not the cause of that foul and accursed political expenditure—we say that were another seven hundred millions wanted to save our poor from their wretched sufferings, we would *have* those millions. But enough; we have ample funds in hand; we now ask you to furnish us with fearless, thorough, practical, and most speedy counsel how to mitigate, and finally remove, the burden which presses out the life-blood of millions of God's creatures, our flesh and blood."

All stood as the General prepared to depart. The old English hand-shake of each one stirred his heart-blood into warm and uncontrollable emotion. As Democritus took the gentle pastor's hand, he raised it reverentially to his lips.

. . . .

Within twenty-four hours of that interview the Council on Poverty laid before Carlyle Democritus a brief outline of the approximate numbers of the actually suffering poor with whom it would be necessary to deal. They explained that whereas the total number of the submerged class had been variously estimated by experts—in figures ranging from two millions to five millions, not including mere political statisticians, whose figures were absolutely worthless—they felt justified, after the deepest study of the facts, in naming the sufficiently sad figure of ,four millions. Whilst it was tolerably certain that there had been far larger numbers in the direst straits a short time previously, yet the large numbers of men drawn into employment by the recent measures of the Revolution had very materially reduced them; they referred especially to the great activity in all the ship-building yards;* the

---
* Pages 319-20.

immense number of men employed in rebuilding the slums,* and the further impetus in the building trades everywhere which would result from the barracks they were about to propose to erect for the penal colonies and other settlements. The four millions whom they named they divided into three classes :—

1. The most abject class, loafers, semi-criminals, drunkards, and the worst portion of the inmates of workhouses, they estimated at 200,000.
2. The honest poor, so demoralised by semi-starvation, casual work, or absence of work, as to be broken alike in will power and in physical power; this division included a portion of the inhabitants of workhouses, partly able, and wholly willing, to work—and was estimated at 1,000,000.
3. The hard-working, or would-be hard-working poor, weakened but not spoilt by the evils of casual labour, under-feeding, bad housing, and general neglect, but anxious for and highly capable of healthful work under wise superintendence and direction; in this class was also included that proportion of the workhouse inmates not coming under the first and second divisions. The total number under this division was set down at 2,800,000.

Four millions of neglected labour! The figures seem appalling. (85) They are, nevertheless, rather understated than overstated; nor is this the place for a wise historian to enlarge his difficulty. For the wider the maze of misery, the more insuperable must appear the possibility of its solution. Yet it *was* solvable, *should* be solved— swore Carlyle Democritus. Let us discover what he and his brave Council ordained :—

Throughout England, Scotland, and Ireland, wherever there was marshland, moorland, waste land, or foreshore, or rivers to be embanked, or wherever there was fallow and waste, like the poor 200,000 abject ones—there, everywhere, on the confines of such places, as quick as willing hands could build, huge labour barracks were erected—not inelegant ; they were staunchly constructed, well warmed, drained, and lighted, brightly and strongly decorated.

---

* Page 176.

There was always provided within them resources for genuine human comfort, cleanliness, and recreation. Each barrack had its club-room and library. There was one thing never to be found in any of them—spirits of any sort. Good beer was included in the rations, one pint per man per day, no more, or any means of obtaining more. Good warm clothing, wholesome food, perfect human shelter, rough but manful labour were all there. That labour was compulsory; God had made man to work. If he could not work for lack of will, the strong and wise will of his brother man must direct him. There was no escape from that great law. The work of those penal colonies was the reclamation of waste land. Each colony or settlement worked like the regiment of an army under duly provided officers and generals, with *tools* instead of arms; ploughing the bosom of mother earth with spade, instead of a brother's heart with lacerating lead or steel. Women were there too, and in abundance, set to work on lighter and more domestic matters. Each colony had its four great divisions: There were the single men's quarters, the women's quarters, a division for married couples, and the officers' headquarters. Did a man wish to marry, he had but to emancipate himself from laziness, prove steady even in the poor labour he could perform, and he might win, if he could, a wife from the similarly reformed women labourers. Into infinity of detail we need not descend; suffice to say that Carlyle Democritus knew and understood human nature well. He was no party-seeking minister, content to see a few hundred anarchists sporting his effigy on a gallows' rope in Trafalgar Square, and considering that action and the talk that accompanied it "liberty of speech." Carlyle Democritus knew well the difference between liberty and licence. Man's first and highest command and privilege in this world is WORK—" Work, that thou mayest eat."

If any man could work, so that his superior industry could raise him from a penal or reclamation colony to the agricultural colonies, or to other labour, he was at once free to go, but he had to *prove* that power. And in this manner: As every acre of soil was reclaimed and rendered cultivable, the best labour was rewarded by transference thereon; once on the cultivable soil, his labour was assessed; and where, without exceptional superintendence, any man could prove his capacity to earn a wage as a free labourer, such assessed wages were allowed to accumulate for him, and when an independent sum was reached he might command it and be free. But in the first years on the penal settlements this class of labour showed but a sadly poor percentage who were able thus to emancipate themselves. The cost of establishing these reclamation or penal colonies drew twenty-five millions from the great Requisition Fund. But as the land was reclaimed, it not only became valuable, but men commenced quickly to realise that former mere poisonous idleness, contaminating and harming wherever it spread, was not only set to useful work, and by its absence from slum filth rendering healthier town life possible, but that the money expended upon the food and clothing of the former waste labour was in itself now productive of further industry.

For years to come these penal settlements required three or four millions annually to support them, but two hundred thousand loafers converted into even the poorest of workers is to a Carlyle Democritus God's own labour, compared with the old cruelty of do-nothingness, starvation, and criminality.

With the next order of the submerged there was greater hope, large as the numbers were. Upon analysis it was found that more than half of the 2,800,000 of the Third Division had been originally agricultural labourers. The best of these were at once settled on small farms and allotments, under the conditions set out in the Land chapter.*

Here the cost was at first very large, but not unexpected, the principal cost in both the first and third class being the need of building, supplying tools, seed and cattle, and providing adequate superintendence. One million and a half of men were settled back upon the land, every allotment whereof would become a man's holding upon his proving himself capable of satisfactorily working it. In Ireland alone, within two years of the restoration of the people to their land, and the granting to them of their own peasant proprietories, inalienable and non-subdivisible,† over three hundred thousand Irish families returned to the soil. To the purpose of the re-settlement of the people upon the land one hundred millions of the Requisition Funds were set apart—not that the whole of such a sum was likely to be required, but the provision was made large in order that, at any future time, any worker desiring to settle upon land should not lack the opportunity.

Of the second class of suffering labour, and the remaining

---

* Page 126.   † Page 128.

portion of the third class, a very large proportion were found to be aged workers over sixty, or bodily infirm. These became provided for by the National Pension Fund, as will be explained in a subsequent chapter.*

The workhouses were eventually converted into almshouses for decayed workers over sixty years of age, and for those whom infirmity prevented working upon the reclamation colonies or labour settlements. But in no case was any possible worker permitted to lead a life of mere idleness either inside or outside a so-called workhouse.

After the Revolution had completely provided for all the terrible arrears of waste labour, and had lifted misery into decent protection and comfort, there remained of the great Requisition Fund one hundred and fifty millions, *plus* the plate which had since been coined, and had produced fifty millions more. How the Revolution dealt with these remaining two hundred millions will be seen in the chapters on the Navy, Labour, etc.

---

* Page 254.

CHAPTER VIII.

WASTE HANDS ARE WEDDED TO WASTE LANDS.

THIS fragmentary record of an interview between Carlyle Democritus and his Council on Poverty, which took place after the Council had drawn up its report, and was shortly afterwards adopted by the Revolutionary Tribunal, will serve to explain the working of certain of their propositions, which were little more than referred to in the preceding chapter :—

Col. Black :—In setting the numbers of neglected labour requiring help at only four millions, General, we have taken into account the several important considerations notified in our instructions, or referred to by you in our last interview. Thus we find that the eight hours' labour day which you have introduced in the Government factories, workshops, and municipal employment throughout the country, together with the permanency of the men's employment and the new order of keepers* that you have established, the increase in the Navy, the old age pensioners—all these will remove from the hitherto congested labour market at least a million men. In the mines now worked by Government on the six hours' day and permanent engagements, at least half a million men will be required.

Then we have had to reckon a large increase in the number of men employed throughout the country in private shipbuilding yards as well as the Government ones, consequent upon the immense increase of the Fleet.† Indeed, we have every reason to hope that by the time all your great measures are thoroughly established that the figures we have worked upon will be found beyond the provisions required. We need only observe that we have adequately arranged for any possible requirements; and if, as indeed we hope, it be found that your noble reforms have lifted

---

* Page 196. † See Chapter on Navy.

out of penury into manful employment half the masses we have hitherto had to deal with, no waste will result, inasmuch as our reclamation colonies will be established only as required.

Furthermore, it must be remembered that when any colony is reclaimed, and the land rendered fertile, the buildings which at present are designed to serve as labour barracks will, without any material alteration being necessary, be available as labour dwellings, inasmuch as they are being built on identical lines of comfort and convenience with those designed in all the urban settlements. We start with fifty colonies at first in different parts of the country, each capable of employing five thousand hands, not including the labour required to erect the various buildings, nor the permanent staff of officers and men to drill and superintend the settlers and colonists—a staff which, of course, will be larger the more worthless the men they have to deal with. Have we understood you rightly to determine that in this matter of drill and discipline you require almost identical rules to those prevailing in an army?

Carlyle Democritus:—Entirely so. In no other way could the waste masses we are to deal with ever be made available. A *Labour* Army, Colonel; and you are right to provide no lack of officers for the lowest workers, practically no-workers. We recognise facts, and are not pretending to blink at difficulties. Your first division—the loafers, and I am not using this definition other than pityingly—worthless as these poor wretches are, we here at least agree that the old infernal social system must be held responsible for them; but they, being there, must be made as useful as their desperate condition will permit. They will not prove babies or baa-lambs to deal with, nor as such are we contemplating them.

Col. Black:—Assuredly not, General. Not only will these men *not* readily work, but they will imitate the Jubilee Governors, and declare any attempt to make them work "an interference with the liberty of the subject."

C. D.:—Most decidedly will they, for we mean very much to interfere with the liberty of such subjects, have indeed interfered broadly and deeply in that direction already. We mean to stop the "liberty" of many thrice-damned abuses; of that have no fear, Colonel.

Col. Black:—By no means any fear, General. We have given

orders for notice to be served on every out-of-worker, informing him that worthy labour is now ready for him; the Revolutionary patrols have already cleared the streets of all touts and do-nothings. In any case where a man objects, he is taken before the Revolutionary Magistrate's Court, and, after due examination, an order in legal form is obtained, authorising the action of your officers. Acting upon your decree, we have already started the preparation of five reclaiming stations, and our contractors promise us that within three months they shall be ready for occupation. We shall be also ready by that time with twenty thousand men already undergoing daily drill, well cleaned, clothed, fed, and sheltered. We have also made arrangements with the County Councils' Sludge Stations, and you may be sure, General, that before twelve months are over, waste hands and waste lands shall have been put together not in vain. Although we have not considered cost, we are absolutely convinced that before seven years we shall have converted some two hundred thousand idle vagabonds into workful men, converted also as many acres of swamp and sand wastes into richest soil, at infinitely less cost than a Marlborough War, and whose eventual return will bring a rarer glory to England than any Marlborough war ever did.

C. D.:—Now that you have completed your report, gentlemen, I have to inform you that the Revolutionary Council have appointed you permanent officers of the Department, and the fullest powers will be entrusted to you to carry out the practical application of it. Your annual salaries will be two thousand pounds each member. You must confess that such service as you are rendering to the nation may reasonably compare with the Jubilee "services" of over five thousand of our slum prisoners, of whom an interesting list some fifteen furlongs deep hangs on the posterns of the various slum-prisons. Lest your Modesties have not perused those lists, let me quote from a few of them:—One Jubilee palace had a Department called "Green Cloth Board," served by some threescore peer-, and other flunkies at a cost of at least nine or ten thousand pounds a year. Then, gentlemen, another palace had sinecure and other officers of the peer-flunkey order exceeding several hundreds in number, and that vacuous, do-nothing peer-crew got more out of this snob-ridden Nation than all my devoted Councils, working with hearts, heads, and hands from morning to night, in spite of our edict of an eight hours' day, put together. Therefore no word, my brother labourers. After ten years of our service, let us stand before the tribunal of our people, and render them account of these great doings, side by side with the doings of those Jubilee creatures, and then let a just Nation judge between us and them.

Col. Black:—Before you quit us, General, we should like to lay before you the plan of our engineer for working our first estate, and also the methods we propose adopting with regard to the social side of our Reclamation Colonies. We have had to look some angry questions well in the face; questions which cowards sneak by, but which we mean to face, for they will not be over-*looked*, but must be over*come*. You see, General, there is the old Adam in these men, debased as they are, and there is *more* than the old Eve in the women amongst them. There has been no difficulty in regulating work for either the women or the men. To briefly explain the method we intend to pursue, we will lay before you our plans of the Great Hope Colony. We have purposely taken a tract of marshland of the most repellent description. Its very air of hopeless reclamation, and, as far as eye can reach, dismal swamp-appearance, determined us to make it our first undertaking. In times of drought only sullen mud-fissures are visible; for nine months in the year it is practically an unending silurian bog. We have had to fix the camp and barracks at two miles from the scene of operations, as we required a high and healthy site to counteract the conditions under which the men will have to work. The barracks will be erected upon the summit of a small range of hills or slopes, and will, when complete, afford permanent accommodation for five thousand men, with provision for double the number in temporary camps in case of emergency. Our engineer has carefully surveyed the place, and it is certain that within ten years this vast waste tract will be converted into one of the fairest farm areas in England. A light railway will run from the foot of the hills to the marshes. At a spot a thousand feet from the base of the slopes whereon the barracks are being erected, excavations will be made to a depth of ten fathoms, and the basin of a lake completed, having a diameter of fifteen hundred yards. The soil removed by the excavations will be used to form a double embankment one hundred feet wide, between the banks, leading from the lake basin in a slightly undulating course towards the marshes. The lines of rail will run at the inner bases of these slopes. As the lake-basin becomes completed, the ground between the slopes—at a distance of twenty feet from their bases—will be excavated to a wedge-shaped bottom, with a slight declination towards the lake-basin, the canal thus formed having a width of sixty feet. As this artificial river-bed approaches the marshes it will gradually drain them, and locks being provided, the water-course will be used to facilitate transport. When the lake and the canal are completed, we shall then connect our railway with one of the lines in direct touch with the nearest Municipal Sludge Station, and thenceforward the work of reclamation, drainage, and enriching the soil will go forward until completion. We shall plant young trees and shrubs around the entire sides of the lake and along the embankments, from base to summit; and for that purpose, and also because it will afford additional strength, the slopes of both canal and lake will be built in gradually ascending terraces, three feet wide. So far the plan of the colony. Now as to the labour drill. The men will not use the railway; it will be devoted entirely to the transport of materials. The men are being drilled absolutely upon army conditions. Discipline, obedience, and order are rigorously enforced. The men are provided with strong working uniforms, in addition to their home or barrack dress. At bugle-call every morning they will assemble, armed with their implements, on the parade ground, according to their various companies and under their respective officers. Each company will then march to its alloted field of labour. Precisely similar regulations will prevail in their ranks as in those of a regular army. The humblest worker can, by brave conduct, raise himself to the highest post, that of commander of a battalion. Orders and badges for faithful service and good conduct will carry with them pecuniary and other reward.

The women will have the care of the laundries, cookshops, repairing wards, etc. Discipline with them, General, has to be even sterner than with the men. They are women mostly in name only. Some of these poor unsexed things are not to be dealt with by touch of velvet.

As regards hours of work, these fall into three grades. First comes the generally adopted revolutionary order of the eight hours' day; but we are compelled to provide for recalcitrant workmen. First offenders will have to work nine hours, second offenders ten hours, for periods longer or shorter according to the nature of the offence. Our penal code compares generally with the regulations provided for ordinary military offenders; perhaps with a few additional severities to meet exceptional cases. Flogging will not be resorted to except in extreme cases, and we have provided that in the first instance any such extreme cases shall be tried before a jury drawn from the nearest town, or later on, we hope, from the good conduct men—if found practical—in the respective settlements. But in any event we leave to the Governor and Council of each settlement the amplest power of discretion. As for the relations of the sexes, that has been a matter of no small difficulty. These men and women, well fed, well clothed, in honest regular work—never mind how low they may have fallen, often because they have so fallen—are mortals of passion, perhaps beyond the rest of us. They will meet in their concert-halls, at their various social gatherings, in the parks or gardens we are laying out in each of the settlements, for—except that they are tied to the colony until, by their own industry and capacity to stand alone, they may gain their independence—perfect freedom will prevail in all the colonies, and as far as possible the Revolutionary laws and customs on this subject will prevail. We have therefore decided to encourage marriage, but not indiscriminately, and our pastors, all married men, will previously convey that necessary and wise instruction to a colonist, impressing upon him the duty of incurring no greater responsibility than his means and his station enable him to fulfil. No marriage will be permitted until a pledge to this effect has been subscribed to by the intending contracting parties.

Before we separate, General, we would add that every care has been taken, and every provision made, to elevate and ennoble as much as possible the lives of these poor people. A band will play in their gardens every afternoon when weather permits, or in the concert-hall in winter and bad weather. Educational classes for intellectual and moral training will be compulsory upon all the men and women. Every care will be taken that the reasonable labour hours are not misunderstood, nor the leisure misapplied or wantonly dissipated.

Work will begin at nine in winter, and at eight in summer; the "Out Lights" bugle will sound at eight-thirty in winter evenings, and nine-thirty in summer.

Such, General, is the brief sketch of the first Great Hope Colony, which will start work within three months, and upon similar lines all the Colonies will march. We have only to add that should economy, and the interests of the scheme, recommend any increase in the number of the labour settlements on this first land reclamation scheme, our site affords us barrack room for extension in three directions, totalling a capacity of twenty thousand men and women.

Book II.

LABOUR

CHAPTER L

SLUMLAND REGENERATED.

However elastic the term "slum" may have been, the Revolution quickly gave it a definite and by no means narrow meaning. They included within the scope of the measures of reform they were introducing not only the rebuilding of the foul courts and alleys, whose utterly brutal condition rendered them unfit for decent human habitation, but also those streets which had been from time to time debased by the jerry-builder, and the mercenary grasping of the old ducal and other freeholders. Included also in the building reforms were all those new blocks of flats situated often in the most fashionable centres, whose rear spaces admitted neither sun nor air to the rooms which were relegated to the servants of the premises. The Revolution would not tolerate any of those blocks whose courtyards gave not an area open to the light and air equal in breadth and depth to the height of the buildings abutting upon such area. As nearly all these flats, never mind how magnificent their design, or how "fashionable" their locality, had been built by the soulless landowners without any other consideration than how many human beings could be crowded into them, they were one and all treated in a similar fashion, viz. the interior small rooms were demolished, and a wide, healthy, asphalted courtyard substituted. The work was done gradually, and as fast as one block was re-modelled another was immediately taken in hand, until all of them were transformed. There was no difficulty in arranging the necessary transfer of the residents, as they were all compensated, as were also the various companies who had owned the buildings, and who were not responsible for the infamous overcrowding, inasmuch as they were but the victims of the freeholders, just as absolutely as were the tenants. As for the cost of the alterations, they were amply met by the fact that the entire freeholds were sequestrated to the State, and the accruing rents and ground-rents more than requited the outlay; indeed, such reforms, pressing and necessary as they were, would have been impossible, because of the expense, had it not been for the wise and just law of the Revolution, which treated all these mercenary freeholders precisely in the same fashion as of old were treated the

(88) swindling purveyors of foul or adulterated food, viz. by confiscation of their poisonous property. How utterly futile it had been to attempt any other method of dealing with the infamous abuses of the old land system may be quickly seen by referring to the experiences of the London County Council, before the Revolution discovered to them the only possible method of dealing with long-established abusedom. The Council, after demolishing one of the filthiest slum areas in the Metropolis, and erecting thereon, with utmost economy, healthy artisan dwellings, found themselves (*i.e.* their ratepayers) burdened with an outlay more than double the value of the new buildings; and this notwithstanding the fact that they had substituted comparatively rotten pig-sties by

(89) wholesome and worthy labour dwellings. In the Chapter on Land Restoration has been described the method of dealing with the acquisition of property by the Revolution. This is how they dealt with those portions of Slumland *not* comprised within the areas reserved for slum-prisons. Commencing in the south or south-east of London, they first converted the empty Bishop's Palace at Lambeth into commodious quarters for workmen; the grounds were then laid out as a building site, and blocks of magnificent dwellings were, with utmost despatch, erected upon them.

Why commence at South London, and why at the Archbishop's Palace? Because, O reader, South London, although flanked by an Archbishop's park and palace, was one of the very cruellest slum and poverty areas in the United Kingdom. The humble historian cannot expect that statement to be accepted at his bidding. He proposes, therefore, to introduce the evidence of the Church itself, as offered by a Bishop and a Canon; further, the evidence of the Lambeth Local Authority; and, as also worthy of consideration, —the stern authority of fact—the damnable fact, viz. that the horrors here following—the rats and the incest, the quintessence of misery, filth, and degradation—were all rife at the very skirts of the Lambeth Archbishop's Palace itself. . . . So far had it rome in Jubilee period 1894; and not only were Christ's vicars preaching to the starving multitude that "the Kingdom of Heaven was for the poor," but they were practising the doctrine which was *not* Christ's—that "the Kingdom of Earth was, meanwhile, for the Bishops." And now silence for the Bishop of Rochester, who, at Corpus Christi College, in the year of Jubilee 1894, speaks:—

"It is a curious fact how very little the area described as South London is known to the people of England; but the region contains one and three-quarters of a million of people, and is the largest consecutive poor area in the British Isles, and probably in the British Empire. The poverty which exists in it is something terrible." So spoke the Bishop of Rochester, at Body-of-Christ College, Oxford, in the year 1894. And in the midst of that terrible poverty lived the Fifteen-thousand-pounds-a-year Archbishop of Canterbury, with his park there at Lambeth, and his other—Addington Park—at Croydon.

Whilst the Rochester Bishop was eloquently preaching at Body-of-Christ College, Oxford—at that very time, down there at Lambeth, hard by the Archbishop's Palace—home of the supposed representative of the *Spirit* of Christ—the Law Officers of the Lambeth Local Authority were applying for the payment of rates at some slum dens, property of "a lady [Jubilee lady] living in the country." Listen:—

"The Local Authority found most of the occupiers unable to pay the rates, and distresses could not be levied, as the goods of the occupiers were worthless. The parish constable and three members of the Local Authority visited the premises, and they found—in the neighbourhood of the Lower Marsh there [just at the back of the Archbishop's Park and Palace]—a six-roomed house, occupied by six families, every room in the house in a filthy condition. In another house in the same street, with underground rooms overrun with rats, twenty-two people were living. Another small house in the same street was inhabited by twenty-six people. In an underground 'room,' seven feet by nine, a man and two children slept on an old box. When the authorities called, they found the man preparing, in this filthy room, baskets of comestibles for sale in 'first-class' houses. The officers say in their report that the stench in the room was unbearable." [Put even an Archbishop, with his wife and two children, in an underground room, seven feet by nine, swarming, or not swarming, with rats, with a box for bed for them all, constrained to prepare comestibles for bodies instead of for souls, and even an Archbishop might not keep clean.] "In another house twenty-five people 'lived.' One underground room, a mere scullery, was occupied by a man and his wife, his daughter of seventeen, and his son of fourteen. . . . In another room, nine feet by nine, lived and slept a man, his wife, and four children. Upstairs a piece of sacking was nailed to divert the rain which came through the ceiling in a stream down the stairs. 'It would seem to indicate '—[happy Jubilee phrase]—' It would seem to indicate ' that Lambeth stands much in need of a house-to-house inspection."

(90a) —*Jubilee newspaper of the year* 1894.

Preaching at the Church of St. Edmunds, in the City of London, at the same time, within the same week of the year 1894, as the before quoted authorities, Canon Scott Holland thus addressed his congregation : " The clergy has arrived at a point where it stands convicted, by the outraged conscience of its fellows, of the most inhuman injustice, harshness, cruelty, greed, and ambition. The Church of Christ, founded in mercy and pity, has suffered itself to arrive at a position where it has become the very byeword for arrogance and merciless ambition. Is there not evidence on every side, far and wide, to make us suspect ourselves?" Is it necessary to further inquire, O British people, wherefore Carlyle Democritus commenced to rebuild Slumland in

(91) the South of London? And wherefore he selected the Archbishop's Lambeth Palace site as the most fitting corner-stone for the rebuilding? The worthy Canon who fired the above quoted rhetorical blank-shot at the Jubilee Church was quite a fashionable Canon ; for he who can pour forth tuneful abuse, and not propound a remedy, is never feared, and the sound of mighty words fascinates some men—and more women. And now we will return to our history.

The Revolution, as we have said, converted the Archbishop's Lambeth Palace into a commodious artisans' block. The park of his Fifteen-thousand-pounds-a-year Grace was laid out in building sites, and blocks of labour dwellings were erected upon them. The external architecture was as beautiful as artist could devise, and as the whole of London (and indeed the country generally) was treated upon a similar plan, it will be as well to enter somewhat fully into the Lambeth Building Reforms. The National

Council on Buildings, public and private, having examined and selected from the designs submitted to them by the various competitors that one which, by virtue of its external beauty and internal fitness, best recommended itself to their judgment, the Government immediately proceeded to have their plans carried out. As under the new Labour Code employment was now permanent,* and no labourer was engaged upon the barbaric Jubilee system of pay by the hour, not only did the men work with a will, and a real interest in their labour; but, knowing its purport, and also the unending boon their fellow-workmen would enjoy from its achievement, they laboured to prove themselves worthy of the great future which the Revolution was opening up to them. Upon the debated question of size of building we need not enter; the centre of employment at Lambeth was much in request, large buildings were a necessity, nor was there objection so much to the size of the old artisans' dwellings as to their wretched air of dismalness, dirt, and depression. That "living in common" was not objected to may be readily proved, because even in the most fashionable neighbourhoods, where cost was not a consideration, flats were everywhere sought after. It was just such structures that here were erecting; the internal accommodation was in keeping with the bright and beautiful exterior; suites of rooms were complete in themselves; not only had each set, or flat, its own domestic offices, bath-room and kitchen, with hot and cold water supply, but there was also provided a general kitchen from which all the tenants could be served if they desired it; there was a large club-room and library, ample laundry accommodation for the women, healthy playground and gymnasium for the children, and either bowling alley or tennis court for the men. Throughout the whole building the same care and regard had been displayed as if they had been in Mayfair instead of Lambeth. If the rooms were smaller, they were also cosier. No reasonable invention of modern comfort and convenience was omitted. The premises were warmed throughout by means of steam pipes, and lighted by electricity. We must not forget to mention that, in addition to the bath-room attached to each set of rooms, there was also a number of baths provided in the basement of each block,

---

* Page 194.

and having separate entrance from the rear, for the use of labourers whose calling required especial attention to cleanliness.

Each block had also a crèche, or common nursery, under the charge of a matron, who for a small fee looked after young children and infants whose mothers had to leave their homes for work. Add to what has been described, that experienced superintendents were appointed over each block, and that a committee of nine, selected from amongst the tenants by themselves, managed the affairs of the dwellings generally. One of the duties of these occupying tenants-committees was to care that only those workers were admitted to tenancy for whom the buildings had been erected. This precaution was necessary, because it frequently had happened that, after the clearance of a particular area, and the substitution of improved accommodation, a class superior to the residents, for whose requirements the improvements had been designed, would rush in and raise the rents against the poorer class of labour, who often thus were forced into thoroughfares more overcrowded than the ones they had left. To protect the tenants of each locality, therefore, directly a new scheme was put in hand, a number of the best conducted men in the area under improvement were nominated by the Department on the Housing of the Working Classes, and from this number the people affected were allowed to select the nine referred to. It must be remembered in this place that the worst, or loafer class, had been removed to the Penal Settlements.* Where any of that very difficult, or rowdy element remained, do not let it be thought that they were allowed to destroy the peace of the general body of decent labour. There was none of that infinite cowardliness of misrule existing in the twentieth century which the leading paper of the year 1894 described as characteristic of the nineteenth century:—" Civilisation must be pronounced rather a stupid affair if it is not capable of devising efficient protection against its domestic enemies. There is a flabby and sentimental condition of the public mind which refines away the distinction between right and wrong, between good and evil. A large portion of the British public is steeped in a sloppy and slushy sentimentality. It shudders at applying the lash to the shoulders of some brute for whom hanging is a great deal too good. Any knave or charlatan

---

* Page 162.

obtains toleration," etc. Now those are really brave words, and (92) worthy of the great "Thunderer." And, moreover, they accurately described an immense proportion of Jubilee people. On such lines a Carlyle Democritus is *not* constituted. We have seen, and shall further see, how he dealt with the villainous Jubilee swindlers of all sorts and conditions. We have not seen him start or stagger at any fetish, be it called Free Trade Fetish, Survival of the Fittest Fetish, Political Economy, Rights of Property, Progress of Civilisation, Liberty of the Subject, or any other fetish. The truth is, that a Carlyle Democritus sees in mere names absolutely nothing, but in FACTS absolutely everything. What Jubilee lunatics called "Free Trade," he saw was mere "Unbridled Licence of Trade." Their "survival of the fittest" was the corruption, starvation, maceration, of the entire manhood of Britain, in order that some few thousands of idle, sport-loving, ancestor-selling peers, or worthless mammonites, might live in fulsome luxury. What the ruling class called "rights of property" was a huge stench-bladder which, when pierced by the Revolutionary sword, poured out the stolen and misappropriated national wealth which a few land-robbers had fraudulently stolen from successive generations. Their "progress of civilisation," he saw, was a progress to Hell and Eternal Damnation. Their "liberty of the subject" was the license of might over right, of pretentious ignorance over innocence, of stalking quackery and fraud over retiring integrity and worth. High or low, rich or poor, strong or weak, let them, if they value their souls, conform to the rule of Justice and of Wisdom. Abuse of any sort met with instant punishment; no dead fly was permitted to make the Revolutionary ointment stink. A Carlyle Democritus spares *not* the rod. There was no difficulty found in dealing with the management of any of the labour palaces. The superintendents were everywhere in proportion to the requirements of the places. Order was not a more absolute law of Nature than it was of the conduct of the Revolution everywhere.

With regard to the assessment of the blocks of labour dwellings they all had to accommodate themselves to the rates which had prevailed in the old hovels, which were in some proportion to the earnings of the tenants. The question as to whether these buildings "paid" can be safely answered; for in place of unending filth, degradation, misery, and disease, starving and mud-covered children, and filthy men and women, there were bright and merry little ones playing in protected asphalt courts, away from mud gutters and general contamination, and there were clean and self-respecting men and women. There was health where there had been disease; there was pure air and water where before had been unending stench and impurity. It was not the "pay" of a bishop's ten thousand pounds a year. But it *was* the pay of duty done, of godliness and justice, in place of former infamous and merciless neglect. Another essential feature in the assessment of these beautiful labour homes was the wise provision which the Revolution had caused to be added to the general Assessment Laws of the country, and which was to the effect that, after the assessment of every block had been completed, the following system of rebates should apply to all artisans' buildings, viz. :—A reduction of from five to ten per cent. was to be allowed off the rent of any tenant whose rooms were certified by the Committee and Superintendent to be kept in an exemplary manner. Ordinary cleanliness and care were secured by the regulation and discipline enforced in all the dwellings; but the rebate referred to was an inducement to more than mere cleanliness, it sought to raise a spirit of worthy emulation in the tenants, and to induce them to brighten and beautify their tenements. In addition to the conveniences already mentioned, lifts were provided in all high buildings; and, in a word, the exterior beauty and the interior comfort of the new labour homes throughout the country were not to be distinguished except, perhaps, for superior solidity of architecture, from the best quarters of the towns and cities. Directly the Lambeth Palace buildings were complete, which afforded accommodation for over two thousand people, an area of corresponding population was cleared; and after permanently housing the quondam inmates in the new buildings, similar magnificent labour palaces were at once built over the sites of the former slum wastes. In this manner was the whole of London and of the country generally in course of time gradually dealt with. Wherever temporary buildings could be obtained to remove the people into whilst new buildings were being erected, there the great work went on apace, as fast as willing hands and eager hearts could carry it. Nor let it be thought that there was the slightest difficulty in acquiring temporary buildings to house the workers in whilst new labour palaces were being erected on the old slum sites. The 1891 census proved that there were no less than 372,184 empty houses at that time *in England and Wales alone—*

a fact not a little notable when compared with this other fact, that the same census returned 481,653 tenements of the poor as overcrowded. That is precisely one of those vivid characteristics of the whole Jubilee period, of the whole political economy, supply-and-demand, devil-take-the-hindermost civilisation. Wanton, idle waste on the one hand, and crushing, maddening misery, wretchedness and suffering, on the other. Jubilee Government Census, Progress of the Species glorification, Pinnacle of Civilisation theory; Sorrypebble, universal prophet of the whole civilised world; and yet, declares the official record, over three millions (3,258,044) of English and Welsh subjects crowded into pig tenements, whilst there lie absolutely empty more than a quarter of a million of houses.

But damnable as those records are, they are as angel-figures compared with Scotch or Irish House Census Returns. The Scotch returns show that *their* four millions of people consisted of about 874,000 families, or an average of about five people to a family (in England and Wales the average family is rather higher). Of those eight hundred and seventy-four thousand families, more than three-fifths (to be exact, 535,566) lived in one or two rooms, some of those "one or two *rooms*" not having even a window in them. Over sixty per cent. of the entire Scotch nation were rather to be described as kennelled than housed. With our poor Irish brothers and their mud-cabins it was yet worse. As to the cost of re-housing all these neglected thousands, Carlyle Democritus never let ¦the work stay for funds. "The soldiers of peace should be as dear to the State as the soldiers of war," would he say; "issue land loans, if need be, but house my people worthily and without delay; they have waited long enough." It must not be imagined that there was any unnecessary costliness in the style of architecture adopted; anything like meretricious ornament was rigorously eschewed; so also was the old deliberate ugliness of mere bricks (and they generally bad ones) and mortar (and that, for the most part, mud). Indeed, it was not only in the architecture of workmen's dwellings that Carlyle Democritus introduced and insisted upon an outward beauty of form and style, as well as an inward regard to cleanliness and comfort; he had instituted amongst his other councils, one on the "dwellings of the people," as well as one "on public buildings;" and to this latter body, consisting of the ablest artists and architects of

(93)

(94)

the day, was referred the plans of all buildings proposed to be erected. And whilst the County Councils determined all matters of construction from a sanitary and local point of view, the Art Council protected the land from desecration such as prevailed in Jubilee times, when a money-grubbing duke and his agents, or a jerry-builder, could run up whole streets of mere brick walls with square holes in them, and call them houses. It was not only the slums that were rebuilt and beautified; the unending miles of jerry-built hideousness were also reformed and beautified, either by the new landlord—the State—or inducements (mitigations of rent, and other facilities) were given to occupiers to improve the frontages of their houses in conformity with the requirements of the Art Council. Throughout London and the country these great reforms in the housing of the people went forward; nor did the improvements draw largely on the requisition fund (they were nearly all defrayed out of the improved and sequestrated properties); but large loans when required were at once forthcoming, and were always promptly recouped. After ten years of this treatment Slumland in the United Kingdom had disappeared, except in those parts still incarcerating the old tolerators and abettors of it—the peers, bishops, legislators, slumowners, etc. All prisons in large towns and cities had disappeared. Upon their sites had grown labour palaces, their centres wide courtyards, where clean and merry workmen's children could play untrodden by sewer-carts, uncontaminated by gutter mud. There was not a street in London but showed unmistakable evidence of the wisdom of the new land laws. Nearly every man practically owned the house he lived in. In place of one peer owning ten thousand houses, and sucking the life-blood of the people in oppressive rents, ten thousand householders enjoyed an undisturbed possesssion. Streets which before had been but long-drawn miles of dreary bricks and window-panes, now shone forth in tasteful architecture. Jerrybuilding had had *its* day; the jerry-builders and the swindling, grasping abettors of all that infamy had paid their penalty by sequestration of property, and, in some cases, of life. Throughout all the cities, towns, and villages, young trees beautified the streets, and in summer-time flowers from the park greenhouses were added also, and gave a brightness and freshness to them which was everywhere reflected on the national life. All the parks were lighted by electricity, and remained open until ten at night. Bands played in them, and order was everywhere preserved by the widely organised system of park-keepers, who were set to protect all parks and gardens in the proportion of three men to every two acres. A similar class of men were appointed to superintend all the streets of the great cities, a system which not only afforded an enormous and worthy outlet for pensioned labour, as is explained elsewhere,* but which effected a long needed-reform in the general condition of the streets. Street-keepers were appointed in the proportion of one man to every fifty houses; they were in direct communication with the police and fire-stations and the various councils by means of telephone stations provided on their respective beats. They thus afforded a great protection against disastrous fires; they reported any cases of accident; and they helped to preserve perfect order in the streets. It was their duty to call the attention of their District Council to any street whose condition required repair or cleansing; and they assisted the authorities in superintending the carrying out of all regulations as to street traffic. The old abuses of street cries, street fights, street advertisements, street mud, street organs, and street nuisances generally, had disappeared as effectually as the slums and the slumowners. When in years to come the people saw the noble labour palaces which Carlyle Democritus had caused everywhere to be erected, and when they saw the bright, merry children playing in their broad, clean, well-sheltered playgrounds, and the cheerful, contented women, and the strong, reliant men, they admired the cleanliness and the beauty and the godliness of it all, for they had not quite forgotten the old order of half-naked gutter children, reeking in mud-filth and starvation, cramped in worse than pigsties, and the women distraught with hunger and misery until the Godlikeness was forced out of them, and they would "insure" their little children in Jubilee Insurance Companies, and then slowly murder them for the few shillings money-gain which the law of Jubilee England winked somnolently upon.†—there was indeed much wonderment, and some of the descendants of the old political economical crew asked the Revolutionary General if it would all "pay." Then Carlyle Democritus told these people that they could get their question quickly answered, for he had caused to

---

* Page 196.   † See Chapter on Women.

be prepared a brief special report upon these questions, not in the form of the old Parliamentary Reports by Royal Commission, for it was contained on one page, instead of on one thousand pages, and had been compiled in only a few hours instead of a few years. And the burden of the report was this :—

"The Revolutionary Council having at various times been asked through the public newspapers, and otherwise, whether the new system of the housing of the working classes 'pays,' as compared with the old, the said Council have caused to be prepared a statistical table of the life and death rate in the slum prisons, as compared with the new labour centres. The said table shows as follows :—

The Arctic and the Antarctic of Slumland:

A Table which shews the Injurious Results of Existence in regions where it is not meet for Man to dwell, and where the Divine Laws of the Great God to Man have for generations been set aside :—

DEATH RATE PER 1000 OF THE POPULATION.*

AMONGST THE POOR IN SLUMS BEFORE THE REVOLUTION.	IN LABOUR PALACES AFTER THE REVOLUTION.	IN ARISTOCRATIC PALACES BEFORE THE REVOLUTION.	IN ARISTOCRATIC SLUM-PRISONS AFTER THE REVOLUTION.
Owing to the tainted and poisonous air, semi-starvation, overcrowding, and general wretchedness, deaths in the slums ranged from 45 to 60 per 1000 of the population.	The annual mortality, owing to purity of surroundings, has become reduced from the old massacre - figures to between 15 and 20 deaths per 1000 of the population.	The annual death-rate, owing to healthfulness of surroundings and, in spite of excessive feeding, and of other intemperances, was very low, and varied between 18 and 20 deaths per 1000 of population.	The annual mortality in the slum-prisons, due to the filth and misery of the surroundings, varies between 45 and 60 persons out of every 1000 incarcerated.

* The *average* death rate in London was about 20 per 1000 of the population, but it varied more than the above figures set out as between a Park Lane and a Seven Dials.

"To that Table the Revolutionary Council have only to add that it is open to any earnest and enthusiastic advocate of the pre-revolutionary doctrines to prove his belief of the old Jubilee Political-Economy-Gospel by changing his present mode of existence, and adopting that still prevailing in the few remaining slum-centres. The Revolutionary Government here again make it generally known that they will not permit the question of amnesty of the slum prisoners to be brought under public discussion.

"They feel that there is the less necessity for such discussion, inasmuch as owing to low birth rate amongst the prisoners, and the high death rate—which remains the same as in the pre-revolutionary period (and is therefore 'not exceptional')—it will not be many years before death will have naturally amnestied all the prisoners. The Revolutionary Council remind those interested in the question that already the original twenty-seven slum centres, which were reserved for the slum prisoners have been reduced, by the natural means before referred to, to eleven; and as the populations of the various remaining sites gradually diminish, their inhabitants will continue to be transferred to other centres, as it is part of the sentence of the Grand Tribunal of the Revolution that all the conditions of the old slums shall be rigorously preserved; and as over-crowding was an essential feature of the Jubilee slums whilst the poor were compelled to occupy them so is it maintained now when their only remaining occupants are those, who formerly owned, tolerated, condoned, or abetted them.

"By order of the Revolutionary Council on the
Housing of the People,
"JAMES CUSOLE, Colonel,
"*Presid* *.*"

CHAPTER II.

STATE EMPLOYMENT AND NEW AVENUES OF LABOUR.

INNOCENT people are prone to accept indiscriminately as truth, with an ease amounting to conviction, the assurances, or even the opinions, of those in authority; and they are still more prone to adopt those assurances and opinions if they are supported by their daily newspaper.

Were a modern Galileo to arise and tell them that the political world-system they had hitherto believed in was as false and unreal as the old-world theory that our earth was square, it is tolerably certain that such a daring new Galileo would share the fate of most wise teachers who have been also innovators. How many would regret that we have no torture inquisition to drag his limbs and his opinions out of him, and vow that such was the will of God. O good people, you are by no means so far removed from mad and ignorant superstition as the complacent amongst you comfortably imagine. Has this present history not already shown you how a GREAT AUTHORITY, one Giffen, Statistician General to Britannic Majesty's Government, had assured you that the "world was nearly full," as far as the purpose of emigration was concerned, and how the "greatest newspaper in the world" had wept crocodile's tears over that awful revelation, commenting upon it that: "It is sad to think that an outlet for poverty which has existed all these years of the World's History is coming to an end." This is indeed a remarkable doctrine of Messrs

(96) Giffen, Times & Co. But is it more remarkable than this other: That it is unreasonable on the part of British working men to demand that the wage accorded them by their employers should be a living wage? Yet that is also the doctrine of the "greatest

(97) newspaper in the world." In spite of the formidable Government Statistician, and the leading newspaper in the world, Carlyle

Democritus determined that the planet Earth was *not* yet full, and that every Briton *should* be able to live by the honest labour of his hands. And he also determined various other equally astounding principles of humanity and natural justice, not hitherto recognised by Political-, Giffen-, or Times' Economy.

Having duly provided worthy human habitations for worthy human beings, the Revolution next took steps to obliterate the degrading public-houses, which, in the Jubilee period, diverted seventy millions of the Nation's savings annually from thrift to waste, washing along with its bestial poison-flow tens of thousands of men, women, and children into the slough of poverty, pauperism, misery, and crime. One brave worker amongst the starving children of the poorest of the poor in those times, who spoke with the written life records in his possession of some twenty-four thousand of these little suffering outcasts, has left it on record that the "most potent factor in the ruin of the young lives that came into my hands was DRINK." "Were it not for the drink," he writes, "MORE THAN EIGHTY PER CENT. OF THE CASES THAT COME INTO MY HANDS WOULD NEVER HAVE NEEDED MY AID. THIS IS A STRONG STATEMENT, BUT I SPEAK THAT WHICH I DO KNOW." Another great authority, in an address delivered before the Royal Statistical Society on the subject of "The Perils and Protection of Infant Life," stated that: "Deaths (of young children) from suffocation in bed were found to have a *definite relation to intemperance*. By far the largest number, over twenty-eight per cent., occurred during Saturday night" (refer to page 84 for a full description of a slum-hell, drink Saturnalia), "and on that night about thirty-five per cent. of all the apprehensions for drunkenness take place." (98) (99) (100)

The consumption of spirits was narrowed to near vanishing point by means of an exceedingly high duty, which practically confined their sale to chemists for medicinal purposes. Malt liquors could only be procured at eating-houses, restaurants, and general provision sellers, or (for consumption *off* the premises) from the brewers. The quality of the beverage (which had to be made from pure malt and hops) was jealously superintended by Government inspectors, and any adulteration by a brewer or dealer rendered him liable to enormous fine and loss of license for a second offence. The old abuse of "drinking clubs" was cured by their suppression, immediate and complete. With regard to working-men's clubs, it quickly followed upon the general improvement in the condition of the working-classes that their clubs became raised in tone along with those who resorted to them; and, furthermore, the loathing with which the crime of drunkenness grew to be held and punished, after the establishment of worthy labour laws, tended to stamp out the filthy vice altogether. Though before the Revolution drunkenness was allowed, in numerous cases, to extenuate guilt, *after* the Revolution it was made an aggravation of offence. Furthermore, on proof before a magistrate, or judge, that any man, never mind what his condition of life might be, had been three times drunk, he was liable to a minimum period of six months' incarceration in an inebriates' prison, and to a minimum period, after one conviction, of two years. The old Jubilee theory of "liberty of the subject" was most piously "considered," but it was not permitted to mean *licence* of the subject. Also a faithful Government considered more the innocent wife and the tender children than the bestial and depraved drunkard! Remarkable, is it not? Probably, for did it not require the Revolution of a Carlyle Democritus—a social Galilei Galileo—before a party-ridden and beer-governed nation could be induced to even recognise that the claims of maternity and innocence, of outraged women and suffering children to protection, were superior to those of the besotted beast-thing—God forbid, we should call him man!—mad with drink, ready to commit on them, or on any one, murder, or other crime? As for the so-called music-halls—as such they were allowed to continue, but their old filthy trade of drink *plus* vulgarity was instantly suppressed—the drink—not the vulgarity; *that* was not suppressed, it quickly suppressed itself; for when once the besotted idiots who used to revel in those places could no longer become more or less comatose in those places, it transpired that neither could even *their* intelligence, when unfogged by liquor, tolerate the old class of leg and haunch exposure, set off by more or less silly or allusive "songs." No bar was allowed in any such hall, theatre, or kindred place whatsoever. Coffee restaurants were permitted for the ravenous frequenters who might otherwise perhaps have succumbed if left without means of other sustenance than that which the proscenium afforded between the hours of eight and ten.

The first great reform of the Labour Code was the abolition of casual employment, and the substitution of yearly engagement.

The hideous barbarity and folly of the old system needs only to be realised to be condemned. Even in the Government labour yards it was a common thing, in Jubilee period, to dismiss hundreds of men from work in the depths of winter, a proceeding which ensured misery and starvation to men, women, and children in the most trying period of the year. It requires no argument to convince any thoughtful man how infinitely superior must be the permanent workman—assured of his livelihood, rendered intimately familiar with his surroundings and his fellow-workers —to the poor casual labourer engaged for a fleeting period, paid by the hour, and dismissed, uncared for and unthanked, when his task is done. Carlyle Democritus introduced a nobler system. Throughout the country, in Government workyards and factories, and in all Government service whatsoever, from the post*man* to the post*master*, in all municipal employments, whether by County, District, or Parish Council, he ordered that all engagements should be by annual agreement. In order to promote harmony and goodwill between employer and employed, he caused to be established, in every centre of public employment, a Board of Reference, before whom all questions of estrangement should be submitted. This Board was constituted of nine members, one in every three of whom was a representative selected by the men employed. Its object was not to take sides in any labour questions which might arise, but rather to prevent their arising by affording the employers, or their managers, a permanent council of information as between masters and men. These Boards of Reference were required to meet in private at least once a quarter, and, if necessary, report to their respective public bodies, or departments, upon any matter requiring their attention. By this means the men were safeguarded against possible dismissal without cause, protected against high-handed action by unjust overseers; or, on the other hand, they could bring before their masters any question of reform, or of management, by virtue of their office, and without its assuming the nature of ill-will or complaint. No dismissal could take place until such a Board had heard and decided upon a case, but any workman guilty of misconduct could be suspended until their decision could be obtained. This establishing of permanent labour staffs throughout the country, together with the eight hours' work-day which accompanied it, again combined with the fixing of a minimum or living wage,

(102)

formed a strong starting-point from whence to promulgate the system eventually in all industries, private and public. Carlyle Democritus had always held that the Government, and its satellites—the municipal authorities—must be model employers of labour; it is they who set the great example to the Nation; indeed, if the matter is seen rightly, no universal and general improvement is possible until Government has set the ideal before the people. But, in justice to the great General, let not any loose poetic meaning be attributed to that word "ideal" as he interpreted it: "The worthiest, truest, most practical, and most just conditions of employment," those were the pure and simple conditions which he insisted should characterise State service. What were such conditions? These:—

1. Healthy, adequate homes; HOMES, not hovels, for the workers.
2. Permanency and regularity of employment.
3. Just and honest wage, in manful recognition of the fact that the man's LABOUR is to be requited, not the accidental circumstance that one other man, or one million other men, could be found to supply his place.
4. Insurance and provision against the worker's untimely death or disaster; assurance that his wife, children, or dependants should never suffer by reason of his service: "Be not to me as a servant, who serves his master merely for the sake of reward; serve me with all your heart and will, and I will protect you and yours, as a father his children." (Carlyle Democritus, in the name of the State, to the workmen engaged under the new Labour Code.) Pension and provision in old age.
5. Definite and moderate hours of labour, justly and wisely apportioned to the nature, conditions, and arduousness of the work.
6. Inducement and opportunity to worthy and elevating recreation in hours of relaxation and leisure. Not temptation of bestial gin-hells on all sides of the labourer, thus the Government encouraged in all directions: Well-laid-out parks, good music, public libraries, manly sports, gymnasia, etc.

7. The system of apprenticeship was introduced in all the Government workshops, mines, and laboratories. Especially were the sons of the workers welcomed.

8. In addition to all the wisdom of arrangement which the Government thus established in its dockyards, workshops, arsenals, and factories throughout the Empire, it also established in the United Kingdom "model workshops" in every branch of trade. These were not to compete with trade. Quite the contrary. They were formed to induce co-operation in all trades, co-operation, viz. in the determination to reassert Great Britain's lost prestige in the markets of the world for sterling thoroughness of work and material. Only the most perfect articles of workmanship were allowed to bear the Government stamp, and the prices fixed upon these articles were never less than ten per cent. higher than the prices current for the best manufactures of private makers. But the value of these State workshops was inestimable. They speedily caused the death of shoddy everywhere. People soon grew to appreciate the value of a good article, and the absolute worthlessness of the old fraud stuffs.

Manufacturers were at last compelled to supply genuine goods, and one after another applied to Government for the right to mark their goods with the proud guarantee of perfect workmanship which only actual fulfilment of the Government conditions could secure them. When once the object of Carlyle Democritus was attained, and a true standard of honest and thorough workmanship in all trades established, he transferred all the State model factories to trade guilds, but preserved them against future degeneracy by uniting them under the supervision of the Board of Trade, which department was represented by one Government Commissioner on the council of every guild. Wherever any of the old guilds existed, they were reformed in the following manner:—Their funds were declared liable to public audit; a special council of the Board of Trade was appointed to help in restoring the original purpose of their existence. All the mere dummy or feeding members of the guild, who were not connected with the trades they served, were at once expelled; in their place the foremost members of the respective trades were elected and on one was admitted to membership of any guild unless he was directly connected with the trade it represented. And not only the masters, but, in the proportion of one to ten, representative workmen were also admitted to the guilds, for it is ever an essential condition of any wise reform in trade or manufacture, that the conditions of the worker, as well as of the material, shall receive perennial consideration. All those ancient squanderings on fulsome banquets were stopped; not only that, but wherever responsibility could be brought home to those who had wasted the revenues of the guild, they were made to refund the corrupt and greedy waste of funds which had been originally devised for a noble purpose.

We have seen how the Revolution dealt with its workers. It is necessary to further explain some of the eight divisions under which the State dealt with its various grades of labour.

The First Division—that which provided good housing. The method pursued was upon lines similar to those described in the first chapter of this book.* It is only necessary to add that wherever cottages had to be provided within the vicinity of the workmen's factories—at the arsenals for instance—as much care was given to structure and design as in the case of the highest officials.

The Second Condition — Permanency of the Labour Contract. No difficulty was found in carrying out this reform; the branches of the Government Service were so various that if at any time one portion was slack, another would probably be brisk. The entire service was interdependent, and men could be transferred from one branch to another as might be required. In fact, the system was precisely that of an army, the men well drilled—with tools in place of arms. The various departments of labour were so many various labour regiments, and the men soon well appreciated the brave and independent position the new conditions of service established for them. As in the fighting army, so in the labour army, a worthy spirit of love and pride in their service engendered and spread amongst the men. Just as only the best men were selected for military service, so were only the best working men selected for State labour service, and it was not long before the uniforms of the State labourers evoked a splendid emulation in their wearers.

---

* Page 175.

The Third Condition.—An adequate wage carried with it the provision of a working uniform, appropriate to the different branches of the service. It is impossible to overrate the value of this innovation; the advantage to the men as an addition to their wages was its very least benefit—"the honour of the cloth" has a deep meaning in it, never mind whether that cloth be the black of the parson, the blue of the sailor, or the red of the soldier. The Labour Army of the State became the sturdiest and worthiest body of men in the country; there were few prizes more cherished than a good service stripe of a labour regiment, carrying with it as it did an addition to the wearer's pension. The National Insurance, dealt with fully in a later division of this book, covered all men in State employment, but they enjoyed besides a pension according to the length and merit of their service, which ranged from one-tenth to one-quarter of the sums detailed under the General Insurance System,* which addition to the ordinary annuity was paid by the State. With regard to the rate of wages paid by the State, they followed the rules laid down in the general trades, as indicated further on; but the men enjoyed the State pension and uniform in addition.

The Fifth Condition—Hours of Labour. These varied considerably. The mines, it will be remembered, were now all owned and worked by the State. Amongst the changes which this brought about was an absolute cessation of competition between mine and mine; and, as the fundamental condition of all employment after the Revolution was the wellbeing of the people, all labour underground was restricted to six hours a day. The rest of the miners' time was devoted to the cultivation of his agricultural holding— every miner having his own allotment of from one to three acres, or, where the position of the mine did not afford facilities for small allotments, larger areas were worked in common. Before proceeding further, it will be well to remind the reader that under the term "State Employment" is included all public service of what nature soever. From the earliest days of the Revolution Carlyle Democritus had come to an understanding with the municipal authorities throughout the country; therefore let it be well grasped that, from the smallest Parish Council to the greatest Metropolitan County Council, the new labour code in

---

* Pages 181-4.

every detail applied. The old cruel form of Vestry labour, with its wretched rags-and-tatters decrepities, was for ever abolished. No more were those ignorant bodies permitted to degrade the name of employer by filling their filthy roadways with half-starved, half-paid, worn-out beggar labour. In a word, only the best men were selected for parochial and municipal, as for Government employment, and the rules as to pay, uniform, pension, hours of labour, were identical.

To revert, then, to the hours of labour. The maximum was eight, but it was not the minimum; all labourers in unwholesome trades, such, for instance, as workers on sewage stations, furnace-stokers, miners, etc., served fewer hours, according to the decision of the Labour Councils, who regulated all matters arising out of the new code. In all those employments where work was required during long periods, such as road cleaning, from five in the morning till ten at night; gas-making (all the gas, water, and electric light works had been taken over by the State or municipal authorities), park superintendence, etc., there were double relays of men. And it may be incidentally mentioned here that the result of this wise policy was as evident in the perfect cleanliness and safety of all the roadways, whatever might be the condition of the weather, as it was in the bright, manful, and worthily independent bearing of the labourers everywhere. The men no longer bore that sluggish, hang-dog, sullen air of listless misery which in Jubilee times too often characterised them. Work and workmen at last were worthy of one another. With regard to the men employed to superintend the parks and public gardens, and to preserve order in the streets of large towns—this branch of service, light and healthful, was reserved entirely for pensioners, not only those of the State, such as soldiers, sailors, and workmen, but for all pensioners over sixty, who, under the National Old Age Insurance scheme, were already fairly provided for, and (by the large avenue here opened to them) could for five years, or for a longer period if they desired it, and if their health and strength warranted it (a matter which the Labour Council decided), further increase their pension by a wage which was based upon an addition of one-half to the amount of the annuity they were entitled to. They received also the uniforms pertaining to the Services. This Service must not be misinterpreted as any infraction of the minimum wage. It was a part of the National Insurance scheme, and afforded a worthy opportunity for those who, whilst compelled to retire from the ranks of active labour, still desired an outlet for remaining activity of a light and not exhausting kind. This outlet for pensioned labour had been reserved by the authors of the reformed code as a valuable means of supplementing the Insurance Pension to those workers who, by good service, deserved recognition. Both the Street and Park Corps were available only to those pensioners who had earned their employers' or the State's good-service certificates. The number of street-keepers thus absorbed was immense, nor was the number of park-keepers inconsiderable. At the commencement of the twentieth century London alone contained about 750,000 houses, with a total street area of about 4000 miles. This vast city was ridiculously undermanned. Street pests abounded everywhere, but rarely was a policeman discoverable when most required. It was not so much an increase of police that was necessary as the institution of a subsidiary force, similar in constitution to the private keepers provided, even in Jubilee times, by the residents of some of the richer neighbourhoods, who patrolled their squares or streets, and kept away loafers, beggars, organ-grinders, and other nuisances too numerous to mention, which were the unending torment of London residents in those times. The corps of street-keepers established from the good service pensioners called into requisition nearly fifty thousand men in London alone—viz. one man being allotted to every fifty houses, required fifteen thousand men—or three times that number on the eight hours' system for night and day reliefs. Shelters were provided somewhat similar to those which had prevailed for cabmen. Where cabmen's shelters already existed, the street-keepers used them in common, the local authority duly paying for such accommodation. The total number of these keepers required throughout the kingdom for similarly patrolling all the cities and towns, large and small, including those men already enumerated, afforded an outlet for 650,000 pensioned labourers.

A slight digression may be here made to explain one central feature of the organisation which characterised the entire force, and which characterised also the entire municipal service throughout the country. Variety in detail of management was not wanting in the different country towns and cities; but there was one dominant feature particular to them all. We shall confine our illustration to London, but it will be understood that the discipline and regulation was common to the whole Service. The Revolution left to the various Municipalities and Councils the nomenclature of the streets, but they insisted upon the universal adoption of a system which was independent of mere street names—which in the metropolitan city was almost chaos itself. The new system consisted in the numbering of every street, small or large, in addition to its name or postal division. The tortuous construction of many of the streets did not permit of an absolute approach to exact consecutiveness of street numbering sufficient to directly guide an erring pedestrian in search of any one of the score, or twice a score, of similarly designated London thoroughfares; but it materially assisted even him. The value of the street numeral system as a postal and telegraphic facility it would be difficult to over-estimate. It was enacted, therefore, that underneath the name of every street its number should also be added. For instance, one of the numerous "High Streets" of London appeared written thus:

High Street,
Kensington,
S.W.
(1376.)

The advantage of this system to colonial or foreign telegrams and cables need not be urged: 9, 1376, would be all the address that was required to designate the inhabitant of No. 9 High Street, Kensington, London. There is only to be added that the enumerating was entrusted to practical experts, who took steps to make the system as simple and scientifically accurate as possible. Wherever vacant land existed, numbers were missed to allow for future street extension without disturbing the local consecutiveness of figuring. Every street-keeper bore upon the collar of his uniform his street-number; *plus* an *a*, *b*, or *c*, in the case of streets which exceeded fifty houses. Nor was it any longer left to a small local authority to neglect its duty * of properly marking up the street names on buildings and lamps. It had to carry out the law,

---

* One system of road-cleaning was compulsory throughout all towns, districts, and parishes. Instead of the old no-system of the Vestries, with their gangs of twenty to forty inefficient poor labourers, under-paid, under-fed, miserably clad, getting in each other's way, without responsibility of any sort—strong, well-paid, well-uniformed, and properly trained men were engaged. One man, or two men, had a definite length of streetway to keep

and the law now compelled it to have the names and numbers of streets plainly and legibly marked on the corner house of every street, and upon the corner lamp-post of every street, or turning; furthermore, in the case of long roads and streets, the names had to appear on every twenty-fifth house, on both sides of the street, and upon the street-lamp-glass nearest such twenty-fifth house. It was one of the duties of the street-keepers to report any such name which required renovation or repair to the District Council, and in default of remedy within seven days he had to report it to the County Council, who would compel the delinquent smaller body to take action.

The London and Suburban woods, parks, and public gardens covered an area of about twelve thousand acres before, and about fifteen thousand acres after, the Revolution. (The parks were cleared of private houses, which had been erected in some of them, new gardens had been laid out in centres requiring such air spaces, and the existing gardens increased in area wherever possible.) Three park or garden keepers were appointed for every two acres of ground; a double staff was required to work the eight hours' shift, for although only one shift was necessary in the short winter days, the summer seasons required double relays, and some additional numbers were required for the smaller gardens, numbers of which were only one acre or less, but which all required better superintendence than they had hitherto received. With regard to the fewer hands required in the parks in the winter months, this was also the time when more men were required in the streets, because in the inclement weather the hours of service were shorter; therefore the street-keepers and park-keepers were made interchangeable. This was a feature of all State and Municipal employment after the Revolution. None of these keepers in any way dislodged the existing gardeners, as their duties were strictly confined to the maintenance of order. In London a permanent staff of park-keepers required, and found an outlet for, twenty thousand hands, and the number similarly employed throughout the kingdom, including London, absorbed altogether sixty thousand

---

clean, varying, according to the density of traffic and width of thoroughfare, from ten house-lengths to fifty. For his portion of the road and footway each man was made responsible, and with the two shifts of eight hours, the system made London and all British towns and cities the cleanest and best-ordered of all Municipalities in the world.

men. There was thus provided an outlet for future pensioners—in a service honourable to the employer and employed—placing at least seven hundred thousand men in a situation of worthy service. However, the requirements of the State could not wait until a sufficient number of workers, under the new Labour Code, had passed through the various grades which were to entitle them to fill vacancies in the keeper service as they might arise. The first places were therefore allotted to all those men over sixty years of age whose health, strength, and good character recommended them to the Labour Council. The staff of men already serving as park-keepers remained in their places; but in future no keeper under sixty years of age could be so employed. Such employment was not fitted to young, active men, whose work was required in sterner places. Before leaving this section of State labour, which deals with the number of hours of all servants in the employment of the Government, there remains only to be added that in certain branches of the Civil Service a system of average was continued to be observed, as in pre-Revolutionary times; in such cases, for instance, as officers and clerks to Parliament, which only sat during a period of the year. All salaries were annual, and all engagements were permanent, even to that of the humblest charwoman, but the hours of attendance depended upon the sittings of the House. It was provided, in all cases, that the *average* work hours must not exceed the statutory eight.

The Seventh Condition of State labour—the System of Apprenticeship—calls for some elucidation. As it was the determination of the Revolution to put an end to incompetent workmanship in all trades, it was essential that the State should set the example in a reform which the State was inaugurating. It was enacted by a law—which naturally only applied to persons less than ten years of age at the date of its enactment—that future employers should only engage workmen who had obtained a certificate of competency from their respective **Trade Guilds**. All that was necessary to obtain such certificate was a due period of apprenticeship in technical and theoretical training as the nature of the trade required, and the certificate had to state whether the finished apprentice was ordinarily skilled or highly skilled in his craft. This wise law protected men and masters alike, and prevented any incompetent foreigner—as in the old Jubilee period—ruining the price of labour by offering his unskilled services at mere starvation wages.

A foreigner could obtain service rightly enough, but not unless he was able to pass the Guild test of the trade he wished to work in. The Labour Unions which, after the Revolution, were not only countenanced, but supported by the State, by an addition, or bonus of one-tenth to the sum subscribed by its actual members (on condition that any cause of complaint or dispute should be referred to the Boards of Conciliation, or other arbitration, for settlement), welcomed the system of apprenticeship, and fostered it in every way. The Government welcomed apprentices in all branches of its service, and it was seldom that a Government apprentice failed to obtain the highest-class Guild certificate. As will be seen under the division of this History which deals with child labour, fourteen years was the minimum age for admitting a child to apprenticeship or service, and the rate of wages for lads who had passed out of their apprenticeship was regulated by the Guilds at a minimum of one-quarter the adult rate for lads below seventeen years, one-half between seventeen and nineteen, and three-quarters between nineteen and twenty-one. At twenty-one years the worker came under the laws governing adult labour. One reason that had weighed heavily with the framers of the Labour Code in fixing their wages rates liberally was to enable and induce young workers to early marriage—that is to say, after their attainment of the statutory period of twenty-four years of age.* The proposal of the Revolution to inhibit young men from marriage before their twenty-fourth year, and women before their eighteenth, had been adopted not only by the workers but by the whole nation, and had been made a law of the land. It is dealt with elsewhere and is only here referred to, because one of the many recommendations which induced Carlyle Democritus to urge all employers to foster the apprenticing in their works of their labourers' children was the steadier influence which such a method exerts on the fathers, the consequent stimulus by example and emulation that the fathers exert upon their sons, and the certain impetus that hereditary employment gives to improvement in all crafts.

---

* Page 354.

CHAPTER III.

MASTER LABOURERS.

THE last chapter dealt with the State employees of Labour, the next chapter will deal with the ordinary employees of labour. This is an apt place, between those two chapters, to record the institutions and reforms which the Revolution adopted on behalf of employers as well as employed. Carlyle Democritus was too just and wise a statesman to invest industrial legislation with that mephitic atmosphere of ill-will, distrust, and antipathy which characterised most of the Jubilee measures. He knew that the masters had suffered from the old cruel social system often as deeply as the men. He knew that it was not a question of men against masters, but of men *with* masters. Their interests were as identical as those of a sea-captain and his ship's crew. He knew that there never could be any true benefit to a working man which did not also, and as truly, benefit the working master. Then let it be realised how this identity of interest was recognised by the Revolution. For, if Carlyle Democritus had an unbounded sympathy for the suffering working men, he had also a deep admiration for the working masters, who had fought the world in arms, as of old the naked Britons fought the cuirassed Romans, because the modern—like the ancient—Britons fought after being beaten. For, in spite of ever-increasing loss and suffering—loss of trade and merciless competition—they fought on until branch after branch of industry was killed out by the operation of the infernal Jubilee system. If any mortal doubt this let him probe the life-records of thousands upon thousands of the small manufacturers, merchants, and tradesmen who suffered in the Jubilee period. There were master victims as well as men victims, only less numerous because officers must ever be in a minority to men. If any there be who doubt the reality and the extent of the evils from which the great and the small traders and manufacturers suffered in Jubilee Period, let them ponder over this record :—

1. Just as there was no adequate provision for the labourer against the evils arising from untimely death or accident, old age, or decay of vigour, inadequate protection in dangerous trades, etc., so there was no provision for the vast numbers of small tradesmen and masters, who also were liable to those evils, and seldom had opportunity of guarding against them. An analysis of the broken-down paupers inside or outside workhouses showed always a considerable percentage of men who had been employers. And of that vast number who lived in a perpetual struggle against the demon of poverty, their lives one long slavery to feed and maintain their wives and children, only those know who submitted to or witnessed the struggle. Scores of thousands of such middle classes wrestled with poverty in a grapple which only ended with their death. For ever let those who wish to understand and help in solving the great social problems of modern civilization discard that narrow, cruel division, fostered and bred by Jubilee Sorrypebble and his like, which would make irreconcilable enemies of what he and they called the "classes and the masses." The greatest cause of the failure of his and their cowardly legislation was mainly due to that brutal doctrine. This is a far truer one :—Any legislation which benefits (causes good to) one section of a Nation, and malefits (causes harm to) another, contains in itself the ingredient of danger and death to both. It was in recognition of this principle that Carlyle Democritus, when he introduced his National Insurance against old age, accident, and death, made it include the whole Nation—masters *and* men.

2. An evil which beset the honest trader and manufacturer on all sides was the unfair competition which quackery, in all its myriad fraud and swindle forms, was permitted to offer against him unopposed. Jubilee laws rightly enough tried to prevent the master employing his men in unhealthy factories; they got as far even as proposing to forbid—or at least reporting upon—the cruelty inflicted by the use of dangerous ingredients in the manufacture of pottery and glazed ware, match-making, lead-smelting, glass-blowing, chemicals, etc. Extreme politicians dreamt of the

wisdom and necessity of compelling the provision of expensive, but highly necessary, accessories in the shape of ventilating machinery, baths and wash-houses, in all the lead, paint, and other injurious industries, and of forbidding altogether the use of such poisons as arsenic as an ingredient of glazed ware, white phosphorus in match-making, etc. Indeed, the Government *Gazette* went so far as to one day announce that "the following processes carried on in factories are declared to be dangerous to health: The manufacture of red, orange, or yellow lead; lead-smelting, tinning and enamelling of iron ware, certain electric works, flax mills, and linen factories." They restricted and sought to further restrict the hours and the ages of women and child employment. How righteous all that as a step towards protection of the workers! As will be seen in succeeding chapters, all those, and far wider, wiser, and more merciful provisions and protections were made absolute law after the Revolution.

But your Carlyle Democritus is not a crazed Jubilee party ranter, forcibly stripping naked his own son, and pitting him mercilessly against a thrice "protected" rival. He knew that the English master and the English man, like any wisely wedded couple, were one—not to be treated separately, but to be united in one strong bond of just-dealing. "An English potter shall not use arsenic to glaze his ware with, must use a less dangerous, if costlier, ingredient," said Jubilee "Free Trade." "But the foreigner shall be allowed to send *his* poison-made glazeries free and broadcast, to compete with your honest English ones." And so English potter-masters and men alike may starve, so long as our fine Jubilee idiocy of unrestricted "Free" Trade totter hellward on its Cobden-apex of word nonsense. Carlyle Democritus protected labour more righteously than ever a Jubilee Word Parliament even proposed to do, but he knew that there was no justice for men which did not protect the masters also. An eight hours' day; no poison-ingredients; healthily ventilated factories; complete and worthy provision for the workers; absolute prohibition against employing women and children in dangerous trades. Right godly all that. But how are you going to preserve those noble conditions? How are you going to preserve *any* conditions whatsoever, if your shilling article made under righteous conditions of manufacture, of true purity and fineness, is to be left unsold, whilst a foreign poisonous one made by slave and sweated labour is, by "Free Trade" Jubilism, saleable for some ninepence-halfpenny?*

Now upon that matter let there be no manner of doubt whatsoever. The extra cost of an eight hours' day over a ten hours' day is precisely calculable; of cheap poison-ingredients over healthful and more expensive ones also calculable; of little eight-year old Sicilian children slaved to a cruel death in dangerous industries at two shillings a week wage, whilst innocent English children are protected from labour until their fourteenth year,† that is also calculable. (106)

And the eight hours work-day has to be reckoned upon machinery as well as upon men. In the latter case the cost may be redeemed by the superior fitness and energy of the workers; in the case of the machinery additional cost must be allowed for. Foreign and English manufacturers employing a thousand horse-power of identical machinery for, say, fifty hours a week by British restric-

---

* Listen to this short extract from the record of English trade, published in 1894:—"Owing to the American Prohibition Tariff, manufacturers of Axminster carpets were much concerned by the introduction of low-grade American carpets. Worsted-spinners have naturally [Jubilee naturally] suffered with carpet-spinners, and the output of the mills has been reduced twenty-five per cent. below the average." "Hopes have been raised by the prospect of a reduction in the American duty" [no hopes from a mad, party-ridden, license-of-trade-to-foreigners, whilst we hamper English manufacturers on all sides Government]; "but," continues the report, "the hopes are practically futile"; and so the great carpet industry of Kidderminster is oppressed. In Leeds also, says the same record, "foreign trade has been unsatisfactory. The United States have taken next to nothing [send us their inferior produce 'free,' or even plus a bounty, whilst it taxes our best British goods up to eighty per cent.]. France formerly used to take considerable quantities of Leeds cloth, but last year scarcely any. The clothing trade has been the worst ever experienced; manufactures have declined twenty to thirty per cent.; the United States' demand has run down to almost nothing." It is the same story everywhere, even down to poisonous spirits. The same report says: "Foreign plain spirits would appear to be quite thrusting home distillations out of the market. Owing to the operation of the American Tariff, which practically prohibits the importation of molasses, it is made into rum *chiefly of inferior quality* and shipped to this market." For is not anything, from low grade soft goods to poisonous spirits, good enough for Jubilee Parliaments, so long as they, and everything, be cheap and nasty? That the British workmen starve, that British mills stand idle, what is all that to word-mongering party factions, so long as license-of-trade spins merrily on its apex, whirling British Trade into limbo? (105)

† Page 262.

tion, and seventy hours a week by foreign no-restriction, would run an unequal race, a sort of Jubilee-race, survival *not* necessarily to the fittest, but perhaps most-sweated product of labour. Shall no wisdom of justice step in between the British freed labourer and the foreign enslaved labourer? Shall only Jubilee blindness prevail— Jubilee oppressed trade for the much-enduring British manufacturer, and universal license of trade for the foreign manufacturer? Good English people, open your eyes, take your brave but ostrichised heads out of the free-trade sand, and see! For the sake of truth and wisdom, let not political party idiots longer blind you with rhetoric twaddle. If indeed you are to be eternally affrighted by a lie-word, a catch-phrase, Heaven protect you—which indeed Heaven will *not* do, Heaven having set its great law upon mankind, which commands that mankind shall help and protect itself, and not hide its head in catch-words and rhetoric-idiocies. Let all the Radical Jesuit party fanatics in creation roar themselves hoarse against unswervable Fact, and yet shall Fact abide, and not the Jesuit-Radical party-fanatical sham fact! It is true that some of the largest manufacturers might economise both machinery and workmen on the eight hours' day, and survive all the many restrictions of the Factory Acts, etc. But the best proof that the generality of manufacturers stood no chance against such one-sided competition is the Jubilee trade-return for the year 1893, which showed how the iron machines and iron-ware of England were fading in export, whilst, from Germany alone, in that one year, England *imported* iron machinery and iron-ware to the extent of nearly two millions sterling. That is not a light record, for we find in the latest Jubilee census return that 800,000 men were employed in the engineering and ship-building industries alone, all of them riding those iron steam-horses upon that strange Jubilee free-trade race-course. The foreign manufacturer running his iron horses seventy hours a week, and your British manufacturer to run his only fifty hours a week! Could a wise and truth-loving man promise you victory in such a race?

FREE TRADE! you mad, party-ridden, Jubilee word-governed ones? Free Trade? Yes, upon just and equitable conditions; it is *no* free trade else. Mad, party-governed England gave cruel, unbridled *license* of trade to the foreigner, whilst it hampered, restricted, and shackled trade for the Englishman.

Among the interesting articles of commerce admitted from

Germany by Jubilee "free trade," free to compete with British goods, we find "hardware, hosiery, brushes, lithographic-printing, joinery, and other articles, stamped with the English words 'Perfection,' 'Reliable,' etc., with a view to deceiving the British purchaser." Naturally the British Trade Unions protested against the competition of such prison-made goods. But the British Jubilee Radical Government, intent only upon Disestablishment and general disruption, in answer to the usual "question" said:— "There is 'no power' to prevent the importation of such goods, and we [supine, idiotic, free-trade-Radical-Government] do not think the German Government would 'like' to have their goods marked 'prison-made,' etc."

No more of that infamous Jubilee idiocy for sane men, for Heaven's sake! Unbridled murder-license on both sides, if you will. Work your babies from their mother's womb; slave your adults from sunrise to sunset in poisonous sweating dens. Work young girls in white lead factories till they fall palsied, or dead, after a few months or even days.* Steep your women in phosphorus fumes till their bones rot as they stand, and death seizes them in its most ghastly form, and the corpse can be buried at night by the light of its own disease. All that and more was practised wholesale at Jubilee period, and if any more righteous manufacturers, as a few endeavoured to do, discarded the cheap and deadly poisons, they were nigh ruined because "free trade," with its lunatic devil's pass, welcomed the poisonous things *free* from abroad. Aye, do all that, and more. Put your tender women to the cruellest drudgery, even from babehood unto puberty, and from puberty to pregnancy; for all that is *freedom*, of a sort—of the hell and the devil sort—*Jubilee* freedom that. But, by the eternal Heaven, if English laws are to protect English*men*, so shall co-equal laws protect the English *masters* of those men.† Of that a Carlyle Democritus permits no doubt.

---

* See page 341-2.

† As far back as the year 1879 the German Parliament petitioned its Imperial Chancellor to take steps to prohibit the use of white phosphorus in the manufacture of matches, and simultaneously with this prohibition to impose an increased duty on them.

Is not that but mere justice for German, as for all manufacturers? Protect workmen from cruel disease—yes, indeed! But protect masters also, from a not less cruel disease, ruin, brought about by free import of the very goods they are forbidden to fabricate, which ruin would overwhelm the workmen too.

Distinguish well, O English people, between godly *freedom* of trade, or of anything else, and mere brutalising *license* of trade, or of anything else. The Revolution inaugurated quite an unequivocal law against quack manufactures of any sort. Mere lying advertisements made their owners responsible for every word they printed. No rival house, or enterprising newspaper, had to do the dirty work which a corrupt and cowardly lawyer-party-government had neglected. All such cases were imperative upon the board of public prosecutors. What a man advertised, that had the man to make good, or take himself and his quackeries off. The trade guilds preserved and watched over the purity of all manufactures. Only those goods which reached the level of true excellence were permitted to be marked " best.' As every quality receded from the true standard, each article had to record indelibly upon it, in unmistakable plainness, " second," "third," or further removed from " first," or best quality, as the case might be. " Caveat emptor " (" Buyer, beware, for I may delude and swindle you according to my ingenuity, cunning, and power of infinite lying ") got changed into " Caveat venditor " ("Seller, beware, I give you my honest coin ; in exchange, I demand your honest ware ").*

That law did not alone protect the buyer against fraud ; it protected the honest manufacturer even more, and the able workman most of all. That it utterly squelched the fraudulent quack called for no explanation from the fearless Revolutionary leader, only evoked from him, and all true men, such infinite pæan that the bellowings of the quack genus were little heard, and not listened to. As for the remedy against foreign quackery, the method was similar, *plus* the indelible mark of the originating country ; and *plus* also the duty levied on any foreign article manufactured under conditions inferior to those obtaining in English factories and workshops. The exact margin of such inferiority was imposed as import duty. And where wise English laws forbade the use of poison ingredients to English manu-

---

* It is worth noting that the old Romans distinguished well between seller and seller ; they had a very different word for the seller of honest goods and the seller of trash and trumpery. The former was " venditor," the latter "scrutarius." The scrutarius tribe was very numerous and assertive in Jubilee period ; their altar was " Free Trade," and their religion " Political Economy."

facturers, so were all foreign goods, made with such ingredients, debarred admittance into English markets, or taxed according to the requirements of the Guilds.

3. Another sore evil of the Jubilee manufacturer, trader, and farmer, was the preferential rate which the railway companies afforded to foreign goods. That was at once determined by the Revolution by a law which compelled the companies to treat the humblest English trader on "the most favoured traffic rate," even although he was an Englishman. Any railway company levying a higher rate per mile, or per anything else, on any English goods, than was levied for the same class of goods, even though foreign, rendered the offending company liable to a fine of from £100 to £500 for each offence.

4. Next, Carlyle Democritus remembered the Jubilee law humbuggeries, and herein he worked a great reform. He established, or assisted and subsidised such as already existed, Trade or Guild Courts of Arbitration in every branch of industry, with an appeal to the central or county Chamber of Commerce. Members of such Courts were elected by the traders and manufacturers, through their committees, or other central bodies, and after ten years' service they were eligible for selection by the Government as judges of the State Courts, for trial of commercial causes.* It will readily be grasped how far superior were such practically trained men, understanding every detail of the cases that came before them, to the old Jubilee judges with heads stuffed inside and outside with mere horse hair. These trade Arbitration Courts were supported by the State; in no case did either plaintiff or defendant have to pay any portion of the cost of the Court or trial. Justice cannot be had on such terms, for the rich has thus ever the advantage of the poor. But it was in the power of the Court to impose a fine upon either party if, in the Court's judgment, there had been needless litigation, or obvious right or wrong on either side, as the case might be. Still, neither party was allowed to incur any expense in connection with the case in Court. Law was *free;* there never can be true justice where law is a matter of toll. The trade Arbitrators were appointed always in sufficient numbers to be able to deal freely and speedily with the cases requiring hearing. Neither party

---

* See Chapter on Law.

was allowed to appear by proxy. The Court provided any aid that might be necessary to both plaintiff and defendant. This wise and merciful system was the end of all litigiousness.

Not one case in a hundred but was settled in a day, often in an hour or two. All hearings of the Arbitration Court were private, and only appeal cases came before the public. Cases of *bona fide* litigation, as has been said, bore lightly upon plaintiff or defendant; but any attempt at mere litigiousness, often another word for blackmail in its most insidious form, was punished with a heavy hand. It was seldom, indeed, that an appeal case became necessary, for with the end of lawyers had come the end of dissension.

But there arise in the course of trade, and men's dealings and intercourse with one another, questions and problems nicer than a legal court can be always called to adjudicate upon. It was to meet this want that "Courts of Honour" were established in every trade and calling, both among masters and men.* They formed the inmost and most honoured section of the Guilds, trades, and professions throughout the country. Ten members constituted each such Court, and the members were entitled to use the initials M.C.H. after their name, meaning Member of a Court of Honour — a more meaningful thing than the Jubilee Bath or Washtub Order, Garter, Fleece, or other empty strap nonsenses which the Revolution had abolished, together with every other title which had been conferred without real merit, and served no worthier purpose than to perpetuate frothy names of characters without substance; and it may be incidentally mentioned here that all the peerages which had been conferred for mere party, money, or royal favour considerations were cancelled. Any act of dishonour perpetrated by the holder of a title or of a judicial office, or indeed of any office under State, caused the immediate extinction of the title, and the rustication of the offending judiciary or office holder. A judge, or magistrate, selling fried fish in prohibited hours, would not be the object of admiration and justification by a minister in a Revolutionary Parliament, however sweet such an ornament of Justice might have been to the heart of Jubilee time-servers. With regard to the severity of the order which extinguished a title for an offence against honour, Carlyle Democritus and the Revolution had not hesitated to determine

---

* See page 249.

that either an aristocracy means the noblest and the best, or it means nothing. They therefore remorselessly snuffed out the titles of bankrupt peers, ancestor-selling dukes, divorce-court marquises, and such kindred gentry. In the twentieth century "noblesse oblige" had its pristine and beautiful meaning restored to it. After the Revolution a title in Great Britain got to mean something more than prostitution to party for many years, or money amassed by swindling the public. *After* the Revolution, instead of 150 titles being created in a year, it was more common to find that quantity (of the old ones) cancelled.

5. Of the loss, often ruin, brought upon traders and manufacturers by the arbitrary and unscrupulous action of the Jubilee landlords abrogating the leases of old tenants, much has been said in the Chapter on the Revolutionary Land System. It need only be emphasised that by the granting of perpetual leases, with right of the tenant to compensation for improvements in the event of removal, the State protected the trader and manufacturer against disturbance or dislocation. Again, it was a great benefit to all tenants, but especially to commercial men, that every practical means was employed under the new land code to prevent the growth of anything like red tape, which was the curse of most official bodies under the old *régime*. It was to defeat the Jack-in-Office tendency of all weak people, dressed with a brief authority, that—at the quinquennial assessments—and wherever land or house property came before the land courts or councils, any trader might employ the services (in evidence) of his particular trade committee, or Chamber of Commerce, in questions arising out of the assessing of his premises, or other matter concerning his relation with the State or any local body. Good laws have often been rendered harsh and irritating by ignorant or arbitrary interpretation or application. To prevent any such abuse by officialdom, the Trade Corporations were endowed with power to protect the rights of their members in the manner indicated, and the case in dispute had to be put in a straightforward business-like method, no wiggeries were permitted on either side, to confuse words and confound justice.

6. Of the vast new markets opened up to English trade, and of the restoration of England's lost supremacy, the Chapter on the Pan-Anglican Union * gives further record. In passing may be

---

* Page 287.

mentioned the simple but wide-reaching edict which compelled the plain marking of all provisions from the countries whence they came. The British colonies produced the best and purest butters, cheese, and meat; yet in Jubilee time the poorest foreign stuffs were fraudulently sold as theirs. Two convictions for such a fraud, and the provisioner was turned out with ignominy from the Trade Guild, and forbidden to practise provisioning any more. Butter, cheese, or meat, or any provender, had to bear the plainest impress of its origin. No cavilling with *that* law.

The prevention of waste of English capital by Government repudiation abroad and by fraudulent directorates at home are all dealt with under their respective chapters.* They are all measures protective of capital, and therefore beneficial to labour; for labour is not of two classes, but only one and indivisible, even as is an army. From the Commander-in-Chief to the last private in the ranks, throughout the great diversity of officers and men, an army is one great living machine, only valuable as it is mobile and united. Its structure may be precisely likened to that of the human body, which, though built up of many distinct organs, subordinate to one supreme brain or nerve-centre, is in itself one complete whole. Whether labour-army or fighting-army, thus must the national structure also be. No clash of opposing interests then, the cruel invention of Mammonism—*quâ* selfishness—but one, undivided, the poorest wounded soldier as of deep concern as the strongest and the sturdiest. With the commercial or working army thus must it be—one great inter-dependent living mass.

7. Let us now advert to the working of the mines. Of all the far-reaching boons which masters and men enjoyed from the patriotic and wise government of Carlyle Democritus and the Revolution, none exceeded in value the reforms they introduced in the working of the State mines. It has been previously stated in this chapter how, amongst the other madnesses of political economists, the Jubilee unrestricted Free Trade was helping to ruin the country. At first glance this may scarcely seem the place to enter into a slight detail of figures to establish that conclusion; but inasmuch as Jubilee England, amongst her other delusions, was, after having cast her hands and arms to the all-devouring Free Trade dragon, parting with her very entrails also, her great and

---

* Pages 265, 266.

last resource of coal, this is precisely the place to insert the record which will prove how limb after limb of her great superiority was withering and falling away.

THE JUBILEE CONDITION OF BRITISH TRADE.

Taking first of all some of the articles which were England's chief source of manufacture, we find that where they remained not stationary, or almost so, they had fallen largely away. Thus the value of her imports of raw cotton, which stood in 1880 at £43,000,000, had fallen in 1892 to £38,000,000. And her exports of manufactured cotton, in the same period, had fallen from £64,000,000 to £56,000,000. This fall is not to be attributed to the disastrous cotton strike of 1893, which practically stopped manufacture for three months, for the figures deal with the year 1892 only. In the linen manufacture the position was worse; for whilst in the same period our exports (which employ British labour) had diminished from £5,800,000 to £5,200,000, our imports (which employ foreign labour) had increased from £246,000 to £381,000. Similarly, our manufactures of haberdashery and millinery—this includes the Nottingham lace fabrics—showed a decline in export from £3,800,000, in 1880, to £1,800,000, in 1892, or of more than half. The silk industry showed a falling away in imports of raw material of £2,000,000, viz. from £3,000,000 in 1880, to £1,000,000 in 1892. Wool and woollen manufactures showed a falling off in exports of £600,000, but an ominous increase in imports of £2,200,000. Our great hardware and cutlery industries fell in exports in the same period from £3,500,000 to £2,200,000, and our exports of telegraph wires and appliances fell from £1,300,000 to £910,000. "As a matter of fact," declared the electrical trade section of the (110) London Chamber of Commerce, on the occasion of their declining in the year 1894 to take part in a certain International Exhibition, "as a matter of fact the Continent is very largely closed against English firms who manufactured electrical apparatus, owing to the duties, which are very heavy in Germany, France, and Austria." (111) The leather trades suffered still worse; for whilst we imported nearly £2,000,000 less of raw hides (which in 1880 British labour converted into leather), we imported over £2,000,000 more of the manufactured leather and leather goods made by foreigners. Our export of manufactured iron in the same period fell from £28,400,000 to £21,800,000; whilst, on the other hand, our imports of manufactured iron increased by £1,600,000. Foreign bounties reduced our sugar industry by nearly a half; and England imported in 1892 manufactured sugar (which used to give her labourers employment) to the extent of £4,500,000 more than in 1880. In another leading British industry—the tin-plate trade—the *Times* reported in 1894: "The American tariff is working with disastrous effect; one-third of the productive capacity of South Wales has been at a standstill for the last six months, and some of the mills for the last twelve months, and even longer. More than 5000 tin-platers"—that meant, with the men's families, 25,000 souls—"have been thrown out of employment, besides a large number who depend upon the industry indirectly for their living. The *direct* loss to the wage-earners is computed at £12,000 weekly. That of the employers, at a low estimate, is £4000 a week. Out of a total of 500 mills, 160 are idle. In addition to this are many mills running at a loss, in the hope of the dawn of better times. Great distress prevails amongst the tin-platers, and many families are living ["living," O ye Jubilee Free Trade fanatics], living upon two shillings or two shillings and sixpence a week."

Twenty-five thousand Welsh working people "living" on two shillings a week per family. And the masters continuing "in hope of the dawn." *

---

* SYNOPSIS OF THE ABOVE REFERENCES TO JUBILEE TRADE.

IMPORTS.		ARTICLES.	EXPORTS.	
1880 £ Sterling.	1892 £ Sterling.		1880 £ Sterling.	1892 £ Sterling.
43,000,000	38,000,000	Raw Cotton	......	......
2,500,000	2,800,000	Manufactured Cotton	64,000,000	56,000,000
269,000	790,000	Linen Yarn	......	......
246,000	381,000	Do. Manufactured	5,800,000	5,200,000
3,000,000	1,000,000	Raw Silk	......	......
13,000,000	11,000,000	Manufactured Silk	2,000,000	1,655,000
		Haberdashery and Millinery	3,800,000	1,800,000
1,200,000	889,000	Goats' Hair	......	......
108,000	133,000	Do. Manufactured	......	......
27,000,000	27,500,000	Wool and Woollens	5,100,000	5,450,000
9,500,000	11,700,000	Do. Manufactured	17,300,000	17,900,000
......	......	Hardware and Cutlery	3,500,000	2,200,000
......	......	Telegraph Wire and Appliances	1,300,000	910,000

Amongst the many other victims to the insensate craze of unrestricted licence of trade (called "free" trade—meaning literally freedom of foreign nations to ruin English industry) fell the great works of Saltaire, whose labour homes had been models of (113) perfection. In addition to all that ruin and disaster, English (114) trade with her own colonies and abroad showed everywhere the same ominous shrinking. Taking first her own colonies and dependencies, we find for the same period, 1880-1892 :—

With Canada, her imports nearly stationary, in spite of the immense increase of population on both sides.

British West India, our exports stationary; our imports fallen in value from six millions sterling to three millions.

India, imports stationary; exports fallen in value two millions.

As to our trade with foreign countries, it was a record of shame :—

With China, England's imports had fallen from twelve millions in 1880 to three and a half millions in 1892.

With France, whilst our imports within the same period

The trade returns for the following year (1893) were still worse. Taking raw materials altogether—or textile goods, tanning, dyeing, etc.—the imports (which employed *British* labour in manufacture) showed a further fall of over ten millions sterling as compared with 1892. But, as was usual in Jubilee period, the import of manufactured articles (which employed foreign labour) showed an *increase*. On the export side, the figures (for goods of British manufacture) also continued the decline, and the total values for 1893 were less than those of 1892 by over six and a half millions sterling.

"The falling off in the exports for 1891 was seventeen millions; in 1892 there was a further decline of twenty millions; and in 1893 there had been a further decline of eight and a half millions."—*The President of the Association of Chambers of Commerce of the United Kingdom, at the Annual Meeting of the Association,* 1894. (115)

In 1894 the figures were growing yet worse. This is an extract from the *Board of Trade Labour Gazette,* volume 2, 1894 :—

"The total value of imports in March 1894 was more than in March of the previous year by £1,281,552, . . . but the exports were £1,334,001 *less,* and over two millions sterling less than the average for the last five years. . . . This decrease would have been greater if the exports of coal [the disembowelment and ruin of England, page 219] had not increased by £1,052,091. . . . Nearly all the other groups of articles have decreased. Metal manufactures have decreased in three months (1894) £1,307,714. . . . Re-exports have also decreased during the same period (three months) £1,467,999."

increased in value one million and a quarter, our exports fell one million and three-quarters.

With America, our imports increased one million, whilst our exports decreased four and a half millions.

Germany sent us nearly two millions more of her "made-in-Germany" articles in 1892 than she did in 1880. We sent her seventeen and a half millions sterling of English goods, and took from her twenty-five and three-quarter millions of her German goods.* Thus was limb after limb of Britain's old supremacy withering and falling away. Even the Parliament, whilst shackling every avenue of home industry, imposing necessary Factory and other Acts upon manufacturers of all sorts—necessary, indeed, for the protection of the workers—but necessarily enhancing the cost of manufacture, that same Parliament was obtaining its national supplies, if not directly from foreign countries, certainly
(116) indirectly, as witness the use of German pencils in the House of Commons itself; she subsidised foreign fleets — all this
(117) on the political economy "buy in the cheapest market" theory. Tie up the hands of the British giant, loosen the toils of the foreigner, and then the British Parliament, who has tied her own children's hands, will encourage and subsidise the unhampered foreigner. That worse ruin had not overtaken patient England because of the worthlessness of her governors is simply because other nations were yet more worthlessly, incompetently, or corruptly governed. Germany alone seemed to stand pre-eminent amongst the nations, blessed with a manful, fearless, truth-loving, cant-hating king—or emperor, a worthy descendant of the Great Frederick. But her enforced swollen armaments chained even *her* in the shackles of financial difficulties. The Germans were marching step by step under his leadership into that commercial pre-eminence which Britain under her mud-gods was gradually relinquishing. France, with her toy-governments spilt like round-bottomed skittles by the silly breath of folly and faction, had no stability, and divided her energies pretty evenly between no-legislation and over-legislation, very much in the British Jubilee fashion. Russia, a huge giantess, all grossness of body and microscopic smallness of head, floundered over the political world

---

* The Report of the Collector of Customs in Calcutta shows that trade with Germany had increased threefold in the last five years, while that
(117a) with England—in the same period—had *decreased* from 65 to 57 per cent.

like a mad whale on a surf-beaten shore. She was so intent upon cutting off the small remaining portion of head left to her by ruthless persecution of the only intelligent portions of her population, that such a blind colossus was becoming only dangerous to herself. Italy, Portugal, Spain, with *their* Parliaments spinning in chaos and inanity, were only cognizable by the comity of nations. As Governments, they were mere expressions. The great American people stood aside, whilst a vile fraction of them played at so-called Government, which meant merely robbing, cheating, and swindling the nation just so long as infinite courage and nobility would tolerate infinite loathsomeness and corruption.

The lion will *not* lie down with the lascivious ape, nor will he even hunt after him; a time will come when the filthy thing, become over bold, will approach too near the silent, much enduring lion-king, who will then turn and squelch the jabbering ape. Meanwhile, the universal corruption was the sole reason why England's sun had not for ever sunk. Where there is universal solar system of lurid brimstone and hell fire, those whose eyes are fixed upon it are likely to be more attracted by the flames than by the smoke; they become aware of the smoke only at a later stage. Lest any may think we have over-coloured the American villainy of Government, let America herself be heard. One Wilson of the American Parliament, Chairman of its Ways and Means Committee, spoke to the world of mankind these words in the Year of Grace 1894 :—" The Republican Government during one administration (a period of three or four years) converted an overflowing Treasury into a bankrupt Treasury, dissipated in one short administration three hundred and fifty million dollars (£70,000,000 sterling) of the national resources." (118) One need not be astonished to discover that the great American people were the first not only to acknowledge, but to enthusiastically welcome the British Twentieth Century Revolution. America joined hands with Carlyle Democritus across the seas, and entered the great bond created by him of all English-speaking nations, of which more in the Pan-Anglican chapter.* There was a wisdom in Carlyle Democritus which could distinguish between a nation and its government, as between a man and that man's shadow. And which knew how to discover whether the shadow was the

---

* Page 292

cast of a luminous sun-ray or of a lurid brimstone stench-fire. To Carlyle Democritus one heart beat beneath the true American and the true Englishman. Father and son had quarrelled; the son had been outraged, not by the father so much as by his vile and incompetent advisers. The Revolution abolished the corrupt politicians of *both* nations, and the people at last *saw* one another, and became reconciled. And now let us revert to the Revolutionary reforms in trade. We have seen how, on all sides, English manufactures had suffered; how steadily and surely Britain's pre-eminence was passing away. But there was one line in which she showed a great increase of "industry," an ever-growing immensity of export; but the line was a terribly fatal one. . Fatal, for England was pouring forth to the foreigner, as fast as mad Government could allow the mother-womb to be destroyed, the one resource which her politicians had left to her. England's rich store of coal was disappearing under the constantly increasing reckless export of it, which in one generation (twenty-five years) had increased from ten millions of tons to twenty-four millions of tons. One last record, and we are done with this awful Jubilee indictment. And that last is a reference to the great shipbuilding industry of the United Kingdom. We will condense as briefly as possible from the official return for 1893, which shows that in 1876 eighty-eight per cent. of all ships engaged in the carriage of British goods which entered and cleared British ports bore the British ensign. Twenty-three years later (in 1893) a large portion of that great shipping industry had gone over to foreigners, and Great Britain's shipping had fallen off twelve per cent. That represents the decrease in our own carrying trade only. Our loss in the ocean carriage of foreign trade was still greater, and year after year fell away as fast as that of foreign nations increased. Between 1880 and 1893, in the case of Germany, our total steam entrances and clearances fell away some thirty per cent. In the case of the United States, in the same period, we fell away over fifteen per cent. Well might the great and the thoughtful in those troublous ante-revolutionary times tremble for England's supremacy. It was indeed already departing.

. . . . .

HOW CARLYLE DEMOCRITUS COMPLETED THE RE-ESTABLISHMENT OF BRITISH TRADE.

THE MINES OF THE UNITED KINGDOM.

The Nineteenth Century mining figures stood somewhat thus:—

1. The value of all minerals raised in the United Kingdom in each year was about eighty-five to ninety million pounds sterling.

2. About eleven or twelve millions of this amount was declared to Income Tax as profit or income from the mines. Most authorities agreed that the sum of ten millions was a low estimate of the royalties, or toll, which the British people paid to the landlords of those mines.

3. In all mines taken together, 560,000 men were in one way or another employed, that is to say Jubilee-employed. In actual receipt of permanent work and full wage, such as the Revolution established, one-half that number would be nearer the mark; because the 560,000 miners returned in the Jubilee statistics included such of the poor agricultural labourers who had been ejected from their homes, and evicted from their lands all over the country, and who flocked to the mines to *seek* work, but rarely to adequately find it. Of those 560,000 men, who after the Revolution became fully employed and paid, and worthily housed—either at the mines, or resettled on their old agricultural farms—517,000 were in the coal-fields alone.

4. The yield of coals from English mines was increasing by "leaps and bounds" in that mad Jubilee period. It stood at sixty-seven million tons in the year 1856, and had risen to eighty-six million tons in 1863, and in the year 1892 stood at the enormous total of one hundred and eighty-two million tons. Wise and far-seeing statesmen, like Carlyle Democritus and his followers, viewed with far other than a rejoicing spirit this disembowelling of the national wealth. For in the same period, viz. 1856-1892, the export of British coals had risen from four million tons to thirty million tons; many of the mines were let on lease by the landowners to capitalists or companies, whose only idea was to force out of them as much coal as they could during the period of their lease; only one mad, State-destroying idea being in the brains or brain places of those Mammon-worshipping Jubilites: "To make them pay." Exhaust the invaluable coal resources of the country, sweat labour, ruin anything and everything so that a

few more gold coins may cram Mammon's already bursting pockets. All this infamous waste was made to end.

The Revolution stopped the export of coal. In Jubilee period that export had given occupation to a large fleet; it had been held to be a necessity for the adequate exchange of English goods, and as a means of effecting the carriage of produce from abroad to these shores at a nominal or very low rate. Certain authorities held the opinion, and widely disseminated it, that England's coal export was the great means of her salvation. With regard to the ships engaged in the coal-carrying trade, it will be seen in the chapter which deals with the navy that not one of these in any way suffered. With regard to the men employed upon them, all were absorbed into the State service, where they were not required to replace the foreigners,* who, on the Jubilee cheap or sweating system, had been engaged to man English merchant ships. As for the contention that the exhaustion of England's coal-fields was the necessary saviour of English manufactures, the whole history of the Revolutionary Charter with regard to trade will abundantly disprove it. The Revolution, then, absolutely stopped the export of British coal. Except for the service of supplying our coaling stations in all parts of the world, not one ton of coal was permitted to leave British shores for sale outside English dominions. And where the coaling stations could be supplied with convenience and reasonable economy from our vast colonial coal-fields, the British stores were spared. Immense coal reserves were established at home in the neighbourhood of all the mines for use in war or other national purposes. In these, as in all kindred matters, the Revolution left it not to future political degeneracy to risk the national welfare; but made it an article of the Constitution that at every naval, and military, and home coal depôt there should be a minimum reserve, to be certified as sufficient by the Board of Admirals for the time being. The export of coals having been stopped, and the mines being entirely the property of the Nation, directly worked by the State for the benefit of all, not for the benefit of a few hundreds, to the detriment of all, it became necessary to regulate the supply.

There were altogether about 3500 collieries working, most of which, at Jubilee period, were in wild competition with one

---

* Page 276.

another. *After* the Revolution they worked absolutely in co-operation. This great national industry was no longer a throat-cutting process of fratricidal trade warfare. The six hours' work-day adopted in all the coal mines absorbed all the 517,000 miners. But in spite of the full wages they were paid, and the shortened hours of labour, it was found impossible to keep this number attracted to the mines; the opportunity which the new Land Code afforded to the men to get back to their old and healthier calling gradually reduced the numbers to a considerable extent. But notwithstanding this, and the shortened labour hours, it was found that the average cost of the coal was considerably less than it had ever been under the land-owning and royalty system. The average cost of coal at the pit in Jubilee period, down to 1894, had averaged about seven-and-threepence a ton; in the latest period it had reached nearly eight shillings a ton. There can be no doubt that the rise in wages had little to do with this figure. There *had* been a time even in the land-owning period when coal at the pit's mouth had cost less than four shillings a ton. As worked by the Revolution with full wages to the men, the most merciful labour hours, (120) provision of palatial homes in place of the old colliers' slums, the maximum average cost of coal at the pit, taken for the United Kingdom, was under five shillings a ton.

One prolific source of waste, before the Revolution, had been the quantities of coal burnt for heating purposes in all the large towns and cities. By concentrating the consumption in all the great blocks of labour dwellings erected by the Revolution, by means of one central heating service, the saving of coal was as considerable as was the space gained in all the rooms by the abolition of flues and fireplaces, and the cleanliness occasioned by the absence of smoke and dust. Wherever a furnace was erected, if it was worked by coal, it had to be absolutely smoke-consuming; but in the end, when the gas manufactories of the State were completed, as will be indicated later on, gas engines and boilers took the place of coal in all these great dwellings, and in an infinite number of smaller dwellings as well.

In private houses, gas as a heating power in stoves, or for water tubes, was encouraged in the place of coal, by supplying the gas at a cost far below that of the dirtier article. The result of this policy was, within a very few years, to completely cure London and all great cities of their baneful smoke-fogs. The average cost of coal at the pit enabled it to be sold at a profit on the working at five shillings a ton. These were the methods of its disposal:—

To all British manufacturers who adopted the profit-sharing scheme,* which eventually they all did, as will be seen, coal was supplied at six shillings per ton at the pit. That might be called the basis price, and the varying qualities were duly adjusted by a Committee appointed by the Coal Guild, in conference with the Mines Department of the Board of Trade. To any manufacturer who had not adopted the profit-sharing scheme, the price charged was the market price of the day for coal as it stood in the general foreign markets. With regard to the smoke nuisance, a somewhat similar method was adopted: All factories were required to have smoke-consuming furnaces. This formed a clause of the coal contract, and any breach of that clause by a manufacturer subjected him to one month's increase of price by ten per cent. on his next contract, and a repetition of the breach to three months' increase for each additional offence. To prevent any abuse of the coal supply or its diversion from British manufacturers, no tenders were entertained except those from the manufacturers direct, and a clause in their coal contracts prohibited the use of such contract-coal except in the contractor's factory. An abuse of this clause subjected the offender to a twofold increase of price for three months on his next contract.

The next great step was the gradual abolition of all gasworks (it will be remembered that all these were taken over by the State) † in or in the immediate vicinity of towns. For lighting purposes electricity was almost universal, and, wherever possible, in large cities and towns, or even in small ones, gas was the motive power. The gasworks were erected in the neighbourhood of the mines, but not so near that in the case of accident in mine, or gasworks, the one could affect the other; gas reservoirs were erected in isolated districts, whence a double set of underground mains at sufficient distance from one another as to be entirely unharmed in the event of either one suffering disaster, conducted the gas to the towns and cities all over the country. What with the reduced price of coal, the absence of land-rent, the perfection of the State labour, and the general improvements in every field of invention and organisation connected with the works, the cost of the gas produced

---

* Pages 243, 244.   † Pages 146, 196.

by the State works enabled it to be sold at a profit at one shilling per thousand cubic feet. The Jubilee charge varied, according to the nature of the ownership of the works, between 2s. and 3s. 6d. the thousand cubic feet. In order to induce the adoption of gas as a heating power, either by means of gas-stoves or gas-engines for heating water-tubes, etc., in place of the old dirt and smoke-producing coal fires, the minimum price at which coals were supplied for private consumption was forty shillings a ton. But gas for heating purposes was charged only at 1s. 3d. the thousand feet. And for lighting purposes — with a view to encourage the adoption of the healthier and purer illuminant— electricity — the charge was made of 2s. 6d. for every gas-burner per annum. This charge will be found to have brought up the lighting charge for gas to about its old rate of 3s. the thousand feet, and, as has been said, was intended to act—and did in the end, act—as a deterrent to the use of gas for any but machinery and heating purposes. The immense saving effected by this great system of gas production at the mines, together with the cessation of the foreign export, reduced the annual output of coal from the mines from the old one hundred and eighty millions of tons to about eighty-five millions of tons. Nor did there seem any probability that the Constitutional limit which had been fixed at a maximum of one hundred million tons per annum was ever likely to be reached. The average of many years post-revolutionary working proved that quantity to be well within the requirements of the country. With regard to the railway companies, the same rules applied to them as to manufacturers, both with regard to the profit-sharing and to the smoke consumption ; but it may be here stated that, before many years, electricity had so developed that most of the engines in the country were worked by this means. The system had long been enforced in all underground railways, the State having temporarily subsidised the companies to enable them to adopt the change. This subsidy was provided for by a lien upon the various companies so assisted, and was to be repaid according as the profits of the working would permit. It may here be said that, inasmuch as the general feeling of the community was averse to the taking over of the railways by the State, the Revolution contented itself with the enforcing of certain necessary legislation which will be dealt with elsewhere. It would be difficult to exaggerate the value to manufacturers of coal at a uniform price, the supply of which, let it not be forgotten, benefited the whole nation directly by the profit that was put upon the cost price, and indirectly by the cheaper production—and, therefore, sale—of the manufactured goods, though, of course, it benefited those more who used it—viz. masters and men. It would be as difficult to exaggerate the beneficial results produced by the permanence of the labour contracts, and the humane regulation of labour hours, not to mention the new avenues of labour. The result of all this was that the old cruel cry of "want of work" was getting fast changed into the happier one of "want of workers."

And indeed it required all the wisdom of the Revolutionary laws to prevent an influx of foreign labour attracted by the godly conditions of the new code. What were those laws will be found fully set out in various portions of this work. But the Guild Examinations were effective in themselves alone; for, although the Guilds were never allowed to become monopolistic or merely exclusive, their rules were justly rigorous with regard to requiring the thorough efficiency of the labourer and his complete understanding and speaking the English language. Most of the Colonies adopted on their own initiative the entire code of the Revolution; indeed, several of them had been beforehand with many of its wisest provisions — notably the land laws and the farm, or agricultural settlement, factories.

(121)

Britain's next great mining industry was iron. The iron mines employed 18,000 men permanently, at the six hours' day, and full wage, with the provision of agricultural farms such as were allotted to all miners.* The annual production of raw iron had risen from three and a half million tons in 1856 to six and three quarter millions in 1892, and was estimated in the latter year at a value of seventeen and a quarter millions sterling, or about £2, 10s. per ton. It is more than probable that from a quarter to a half of that sum went into the landlords' pockets in some form or other. After the Revolution had acquired all the mines, and had abolished land rents, and land renters, and royalties, and had substituted permanent labour, good wages, and merciful work hours, it was found that the cost of the smelted iron was under thirty shillings a ton; indeed, left a fair profit to the State at that figure. As with coal, so with iron. No raw iron was allowed to be

---

* Page 126.

exported, nor was any sold to middlemen, but only to manufacturers, upon guarantee of use in their factories only—and a breach of this understanding was punished as fraud against the Nation in the severest manner. The iron was sold by tender at a minimum price of thirty-five shillings a ton. Small manufacturers were allowed to tender, and no difference was made between the largest or the smallest buyer. This was a humane principle which the Revolution enforced in every branch of trade, as in railway carriage, or other means of conveyance of goods throughout the Kingdom.*

Similar regulations were adopted with regard to the tin, copper, and lead mines, the prices differing according to the value, *i.e.* cost, of the material. The produce of the gold and silver mines was not sold, but was retained by the State for the purposes of coinage. The value of the precious metals raised from British mines before the Revolution was under £50,000 annually; but a large increase of output from the Welsh and other gold mines followed the humane conditions of employment introduced by the Revolution. Every miner felt that he was working for his personal welfare as well as for the general good, and no longer for merely a landowner's fortune at the cost of his strength and health; he to be cast off like a squeezed orange when no longer squeezable. The value of the gold mines increased rapidly, and early in the Twentieth Century a large portion of the English mintage was fed from them.

Most of the British quarries were worked at Jubilee period in much the same manner and under similar conditions as the mines had been; and with few exceptions, the workers were treated with as little, if any, consideration.

According to the Parliamentary Report of a Committee appointed to inquire into the dangers to life, limb, and health of workers in quarries, issued in the year 1894, there were upwards of 120,000 men employed in quarries and kindred works of the United Kingdom. The said Jubilee Committee found that "the quarryman's life is shortened to a remarkable degree by diseases of the respiratory organs. The excessive death-rate from these complaints is attributed mainly to the inhalation of dust. It is a most important duty to protect a quarryman against," etc.

And the Jubilee Committee drew up a code of rules. And the Jubilee Committee duly added the inevitable Jubilee BUT:—"But

---

* Page 209.

under the existing state of the 'law' these rules cannot be enforced, as the quarries are neither 'factories' nor 'workshops.'" Amongst the significant recommendations of the Committee (which Jubilee law enabled *not* to be enforced) was this one :—

(122) "We advise that a person before becoming manager should have had practical experience in a quarry for at least two years." How *could* any Jubilee Parliament sanction such a law as that? A law to prescribe that a fit and capable man should be put to command over the well-being and lives of his hundred thousand subordinates? Was not such a recommendation a running counter to the whole principle of Jubilee "law," custom, and Articles — thirty-nine, or other number — altogether? Jubilee system, from its legislative machine downwards, pursued a quite opposite course :—Senile washerwoman, Commander-in-Chief of the British Army; more senile chief, mud-god of British Parliament; legal word-chopper, Commander-in-Chief of Jubilee Finances; titled or untitled incompetencies, bottle-washers-in-chief at head of *all* departments; worthless landsmen at the head of the navy; old women magistrates; horse-hair wigs for judges; and so on to the very end of the chapter. Let not quarrymen, dying of overwork and condemned to breathe dust instead of air, expect relief from a legislative machine spinning on its apex to corruption and bottomless perdition. Nearly double the old quantity of men were found to be required to work the quarries under healthful and safe conditions such as the Revolution insisted on. In other respects the quarries were dealt with much in the same way as were the mines; but the material had to be disposed of somewhat differently. All quarry material, required for State or municipal purposes, was supplied at the net cost of production, and all such requirements were considered first. Afterwards, the general demands were supplied by tender, as it was found impracticable in any other manner to regulate values. There was one notable exception to the general method as above described; and the exception is of such interest, both in itself and as another indication of the corruption and utter worthlessness of the Jubilee landowners, that a complete record of the case is worthy to be laid before the reader.

Claimants of certain valuable soil, situate over the marble and other quarries of Dorsetshire, were preparing to turn entire populations adrift, to starvation, misery, and wretchedness, as ruthlessly as the Sutherland, Glengarry, Strathglass, and other hags —peeresses and non-peeresses—had evicted their crofters and farm hinds. The record which is to be given is taken with slight alteration from the *Times* of the year 1893. The *Times* was not (123) a paper to deal untenderly with the property-classes, so it may be accepted as a moderate view of the situation. The force and eloquence of the article, in its bare statement of fact, demands citation, and the historian admits it into his history with unqualified approval and appreciation: "Quarrying is a very ancient industry in the isle of Purbeck. *By some happy chance it has never fallen into the hands of any large capitalist or joint-stock Company.* [Mark that expression; it is of immense value, coming, as if unaware, from the greatest representative newspaper in the world.] The industry has always been carried on by the native population, each quarry being worked by a single man, or a group of two or three men, with the assistance of apprentices. There is a tradition that the right of quarrying was given by Royal Charter to the men of Purbeck, in acknowledgment of their services in defeating the Danes in the time of King Alfred. Many facts seem to render the former existence of that Charter probable. Beyond doubt the quarrymen of the island have from very early days been organised as a Trade Company, called the 'Company of Marblers or Stone-cutters.' Not only has the Company of Marblers existed, but it has exercised, and still exercises, its power in a very distinct and stringent way. From time immemorial, only members of the Company and the sons of members duly bound apprentice [mark that wise provision, reader—no incompetent, worthless hands admitted to those quarries] have been allowed to quarry stone or marble in Purbeck. Articles of the fourteenth century are, or were till recently, extant. Hutchins, in his 'History of Dorset,' prints a code of the year 1551. They are full of interesting and quaintly-worded provisions. Thus, only one apprentice is to be taken on at a time, and apprentices are to be kept in the house of the master for seven years. Not only are all their rules laid down in ancient documents, but they are observed to the present day. It seems almost a necessary conclusion that an industry so privileged *must* have its rights against the owners of the land in which the stone is found. *In later times the Crown sold its lands to subjects, who gradually bought up the small freeholds, reduced the quarrymen to the position of tenants, and then began to question their rights.*

[Mark the insidious creep of the land-devil-serpent, here, as everywhere, intent upon gorging himself upon the heart and entrails of the noblest labour.] As is so often the case, it seems to have been the prospect of turning their land to account for building purposes which first led the 'owners' into a position of hostility towards the quarrymen. A Mr. Morton Pitt, lord of one of the manors, with a view of making Swanage a rival watering-place to Weymouth—then basking in the smiles of Royalty—turned his manor-house into a hotel, adding two large wings. *It may be merely a coincidence, but about the same time the quarrymen and land-owners came to issue.* ["Merely a coincidence," of the sort which befel the lamb at the stream, whom the wolf was eager to devour.] Some years after that Swanage event, Swanage [or rather, Swanage land-grabbers] again aspired to make a watering-place. A more potent ally than Weymouth had arisen, viz., Bournemouth, only eight miles by sea from Swanage. Two or three times a day during the summer season hundreds of visitors land from the Bournemouth steamer to see some of the lions of the old quarry lands. Some of the visitors find *the quiet and simplicity of Swanage* [which the land devils are intent upon destroying] a pleasant contrast to the crowded town which they have just left; others are attracted by the grand coast. They come for a longer stay, and recommend the place to their friends; and so by degrees Swanage is acquiring a considerable summer population, and setting up a 'Season.' *These are the accidents which land-owners recognise as their chances.*" [Chances, O reader, of turning adrift to starvation the old pious, worthy labourers, who had earned an honest livelihood, and established themselves and their families in the heart of a beloved country since the days of the Great Alfred.] "*The few persons*" [mark the *few*] "*who 'owned' the hills of Swanage wished to turn their pastures into building sites. The right to open quarries, and to work them when open,* against the will of the landowner ["landowner" not from the days of King Alfred, only from the days of Devil Mammon] "*hampers the estate-agent, bent upon laying out roads and cutting up 'his' land*" [*his* land, not God's land, not the quarrymen since King Alfred's time's land] *in rectangular plots.* We hear, therefore, of the 'vexatiousness' of the quarriers' customs, of the absurdity of the claims they make [verily, absurd, to the land-devil's heart, or pocket, that the brave labourer of a thousand years' inheritance should love to work on the field that his ancestors had owned since time out of memory], of the damage they do to the land, *and there is a tendency to deny* [thou wilt remember, reader, that the great German poet has defined the Devil as the Denier] *that usages of centuries have any legal existence at all.* [Carlyle Democritus flashed that argument in the face of every scoundrel landlord who attempted to urge the 'usage of centuries' as a proof of his title to lands stolen from the people, and *not* given by Charter of the great King Alfred.] On the other hand, *the quarrymen*—we had almost said commoners [why not *quite* said it, O *Times* newspaper?] the analogy is so close—*though numerous, are individually poor, and shrink from litigation with all its risks.*" [Mark that *too*, you British readers, who have any heart for human justice; the poor shrank from litigation against the rich, and well they might, for it was not a risk, but a certainty of ruin.] "*And so, the quarry industry being discouraged, a class of independent workers may be gradually shouldered out of the district, and sent, one by one, to swell the labour market of our overgrown towns.*" [Do not pass lightly away from that paragraph, for in it is the keynote of all the diabolical misery which the brutal landlord class have inflicted on British toilers since the first day when Mammonism and Landlordism first commenced to usurp the place of justice, human or divine, in this Britain of ours.] "We find numerous and large villages in the stone-producing parts of Purbeck:—Swanage, numbering a large proportion of quarrymen; Herston, Down, and Langton. 'Longtown' undoubtedly, for the stone cottages of Langton seem never to cease. Up and up the long hillside they range, till we arrive at the very summit of the wind-swept ridge, only to see another and more compact hamlet forming the centre of more quarries. [All these homes to be destroyed, all these brave, patient quarrymen and their wives and little ones to be turned adrift from their pure stone cottages, to herd in the slums and sweating dens of Jubilee Britain's great cities.] Between the high road and St Alban's Head is the quaint, out-of-the-world village of Worth, with its fine Norman church, and again with its surrounding quarries. Very near is the model village of Kingston, solid with Purbeck freestone, and gleaming with Purbeck marble. And at Kingston we are close to Corfe Castle, the ancient metropolis of the quarrymen. *A pleasant race they seem to be; intelligent, independent, well mannered, and amiable.* HERE IS JUST THE CLASS OF MEN WHOM ALL STATESMEN WOULD AGREE IT IS MOST DESIRABLE TO SEE IN OUR RURAL DISTRICTS. [Let the reader again ponder over those words; for they are not the words of a revolutionist on fire with divine wrath and indignation at the intense misery brought about by the infernal wickedness of men, which he had to see on all sides of him in Jubilee period; but all that has been written of Purbeck is by the representative newspaper of the very class whose infamous devilries it describes in so able, calm, and gently unenthusiastic a manner.] Yet, *those of power and influence in the quarrymen's neighbourhood look askance at them, and the probability is that they will gradually decline in numbers, that* THE ISLE OF PURBECK WILL LOSE ITS SELF-SUPPORTING PEASANTRY, AND THAT LONDON WILL RECEIVE A FEW MORE COMPETITORS FOR WORK." For NO-WORK, thou shouldst say, O great *Times* newspaper. Is it possible to add one word to that straightforward record of right, on the verge of outrage by wrong? Is not the record in itself an appeal for justice against devilish and heartless Mammon oppression? Often have these pages had to condemn the lapses of the greatest newspaper in the world, but here it is worthy of the worthiest praise. It was such outspoken support of honest right against mere brute might, grasp, and greed; of the rights of labour against the soulless thieving, the heartless greed and grasping of those accursed Jubilee landowners, that saved the great newspaper when the fury of the Revolution, at its outbreak, burst upon so many of the worst trucklers of the press. The revolutionists remembered that the *Times* with all its sins, and they were heavy enough, had never wavered in its intense patriotism. And madly as it had often fallen in with the mammonish and plutocratic crazes of the Jubilee period, it had stood alone on many a historic occasion to save the Empire from the cowardly, lying, and shifty dodgeries of both political parties. England's fleet had sunk into ingloriousness, but for the *Times* and England's self, but for the crusade which had been led by the great newspaper against the soul-desecrated Sorrypebble, intent only on selling, for party votes, the unity of Great Britain to the foullest party scum which ever in the world's history had risen to the surface of a universally rotten political corruption—a gang who, to use the words of the would-be betrayer of England himself, had endeavoured "by rapine and murder to bring about the dismemberment of the

British Empire." If the infamy of the servile crew and its chief have carried the historian for a moment beyond his immediate range, he returns at least purified by that fire of righteous indignation which, be it God's will, shall never forsake the breast of any true Englishman. Those Dorset quarrymen, though poor, so brave and so worthy, shall *not* be turned out to starvation by land thieves, be they headed by ten thousand times a manor-lord, turning his private home into public hotel by addition of wings— not angel wings, O reader, but devil mammon-wings, of infernal selfishness and greed. Carlyle Democritus cleared that whole Dorset quarry district of its prowling land-grabbers, settled the people for ever on their land, and improved their homes and holdings on the lines of the land and labour codes. This was one of the few districts in which the landlord party made an armed stand against the Revolution. Carlyle Democritus was a great believer in Providence being on the side of big battalions. He knew well enough that his picked troops could stand against any odds, for the fire of Revolution will burn through any injustice or any representatives of it, however numerous be their legions. Here was an opportunity for the war dogs of Terence Grey.[*] At the head of twenty thousand men he marched into Dorsetshire, and on the field of Purbeck, after five hours' sanguinary engagement, in which only a part of his forces had been engaged, there remained not one live man of the landlord party. For quarter had neither been asked nor given on either side. The record of this event is still to be found on that old battle-field of Purbeck. Engraved upon the base of a towering mass of Purbeck marble may be read these words:—

"To the Glory of God and the memory of His servant Carlyle Democritus, who did, here upon this battle-field, cause to be made manifest the power of wisdom and justice over evil and oppression. It was upon this field of Purbeck that 7000 men of the Revolutionary forces, disdaining the use of artillery, since their opponents were without it, after five hours' mortal combat, finally overcame and slew every one of the oppressors—the flower and fruit of Mammonhood. The numbers engaged on either side were equal, but the cause for which each side fought was not equal. The Revolutionists fought to defend the sacred rights of the

---

[*] Page 36.

people, their homes, and their means of livelihood, which they had inherited through many centuries; whereas the landlords fought to rob them of those rights, and to enrich themselves at the price of the people's misery."

A local History of Dorset gives some curious details of the Purbeck battle, from which this may be transcribed: "They who saw the Revolutionist soldiers on that bloody day, ere they commenced their attack, as they knelt and swore that not one of them would leave the battle-field alive whilst there breathed a man of the oppressors, still remember the fire of those maddened soldiers, as, after a brief fusilade on both sides, they, at given signal, burst with a mighty onrush upon the landlord troops, callous of the shot which mowed them down as they advanced. Seventeen hundred men of the Revolutionary force had fallen before they reached the enemies' lines, but few fell afterwards. The oppressors broke when they met the terrible shock of the Revolutionists' attack, and their yet more terrible look. History tells a similar story of the British Troops of Revenge in the Indian Mutiny time. Of the 7000 upholders of Jubilee landlordism who stood upon that Purbeck field at sunrise, not one but whose mortal remains lie buried beneath the field marked by the marble pile. The mountainous monument is without ornament or carving of any sort. It is wild and weird, yet artistic in the massing of its great marble blocks. The field, in later years converted into a garden, was dedicated for ever to those who fell in the popular cause, and whose names are inscribed on the walls of the white marble church which commands the entrance to the old battle-field. The first name on the death record which meets the eye of the visitor is that of Terence Grey, to whom is also dedicated a memorial statue of rare grace and beauty, the pedestal of which bears this short inscription:—

TERENCE GREY,

25TH DEC. 19—.

EXPECTANS EXPECTAVI.   ILIAS MALORUM.

"Tradition says that those words were superscribed on a torn letter found on the dead man. He had been shot through the heart. The bullet which had pierced him had cut through the letter, and when extracted from the wound, the doctors found a small tuft of golden hair adhering to it. This relic is enclosed in a recess of the tomb, and is regarded with some superstition by the villagers. When they carried the news of the victory to Carlyle Democritus he expressed no surprise. 'The world in arms will never defeat Revolutionary troops with a noble cause in their heart,' said he. And when they told him that Grey had fallen, he seemed also unmoved, but that the paleness habitual to him seemed to deepen. And the messengers said that when they left him they heard a groan as of a strong man in agony.

"The beautiful memorial church was built by the men of Purbeck, with glistening, snow-white marble, the gift from their own quarries. They were a brave and noble race, and were worth preserving."

That Purbeck uprising was the last stand which the Jubilee Party made against the Revolution. Landlordism was already dead, but upon the field of Purbeck its remains received final burial. The result of the peace which followed was that the brave Purbeck people had their lands granted to them in perpetuity; and to prevent any possibility of future land-devilism, Carlyle Democritus caused the grant to be recorded in the Constitution of the United Kingdom. Thus met the giant spirits of the Great Alfred and the Revolutionary Leader. And therewith may fitly end this notable chapter.

CHAPTER IV.

"TOOLS AND THE MAN."

THAT, and no longer "Arms and the Man," shall be the burden of the great future epic, has said the superlatively wisest of all England's sages. Honour and everlasting glory—and not ignorant contumely—shall be the eventual lot of that sage, when the turmoil of idiocy shall have subsided, and the Sun of Truth shall have risen high above the fog-mists, which its divine brilliance, radiance, and fire-heat, inevitably draw up, in temporary dense clamour-cloud, from the dank rottenness of intellectual bog-depths and marsh mud, the accumulation of centuries of corruption and injustice. *They*, once desiccated, and well burnt up, and the sun of England's wisdom shall appear—his sorrow-cross and his thorn-crown, converted into halo of worship and of love—of reverence, and of veneration. The longer delayed such popular incarnation of esteem, the diviner will the apotheösis be. As the sun in the Heaven's arch is hidden to the valley throng, buried in dense fog exhalations, and is seen brilliant in its effulgence by those on the mountain-top, so was the great Carlyle seen by his reverent worshippers, and by none more clearly than by Carlyle Democritus. Supremacy of wisdom and supremacy of action had met. "Tools and the Man" had been written. "Tools and the Man" should be enacted.

. . . . . .

"LABOUR!—Is that a thing of the hands only, O my people? Is there no labour of the heart, nor labour of the head? O my brothers, workers of the hand, or heart, or head, not until all these have become one, and you can say of Labour that it is of the hand, *and* heart, *and* head, then, and only then, is there true Labour of any sort. Labour of the hand, without head and heart, is the monotonous cruelty, bred of work by the hour, for starvation wage, upon dog or swine conditions. Such was Jubilee labour. Labour of the heart, uncontrolled by the head, is but unwise and baneful; it is unthinking, harming where it would soothe, and is destructive of justice. Such labour was called philanthropy, or Jubilee 'Charity.' Labour of the head without the heart is the culmination of all evil; and, as in the neglected field, the thorn and thistle are supreme, so in the Jubilee Social field the thorn and thistle-class were supreme, to wit — the lawyer-, politician-, political-economist-, party-, caucus-class. I have come to emancipate you from all such Jubilee Labour, and in its place establish the only possible, worthy labour for mortal men, labour of heart and head and hand, one and indivisible. Where all those are conjoined, the worker is ennobled by his work, and the work is ennobled by the worker.

"A fallow field is the crime of the legislator, its thorns and its weeds are the tears of the workers, which bear witness before high heaven of his neglect. A field waving with golden corn, with the flowers nestling at the roots, like calm joy in the peasant's heart, is the glory of the free and unburdened farmer. Only such farmers will I have," said Carlyle Democritus. "The worker, whatever may be his task, can delight in the labour of his hands, when he knows that his industry and skill will bring him, and all he loves, healthful food, joyful home, lasting peace; and he will love the calling which brings him love. The workman true, and the work also true; only such workers shall be ours," swore Carlyle Democritus and the Revolution. Not only then are manual workers included in this chapter. The great Labour Code affected every class of labour, from the humblest to the mightiest.

THE EIGHT HOURS' DAY.—So many instances were known of the most important directors of great industries having, even in Jubilee period, successfully established the eight hours' day, that no difficulty whatever was experienced in making this law universal. Many employers declared they had long been in favour of it, but were debarred from its adoption by fear of the competition of other firms. The greatest difficulty occurred amongst the shopkeepers. Nowhere were the labour hours more cruel or the condition of work more inconsiderate, and the smaller the shop, often the more thoughtless the employer. Poverty constrains its victims to submit to almost any hardship; and it was as true in British Jubilee period as when the words were written

(124)

three thousand years before that time, that "the destruction of the poor is their poverty." But after those three thousand years, Carlyle Democritus thought it was time to deal a definite and enduring, and indeed deathblow to that destruction. And he said to the people : "Let us destroy poverty, and no longer be destroyed by it; poverty, as it exists in this world of Mammon, is *no* good thing, but is an accursed and an evil thing, whatever the Mammon parsons say. You shall believe the parsons, my people, when you see the ten-thousand-a-year-parsons *acting*, as well as preaching, their cant-doctrines and articles."

Thus spake Carlyle Democritus to all the people; and it may be observed from the World Chronology—upon whose vast inheritance Carlyle Democritus, and all wise men before him drew—that the king to whom is attributed the poverty proverb lived on this earth some thousand years before the beginning of the Christian Era. The Thracian Democritus, in whom it was regarded as a crime that he chose poverty and rejected wealth, came into the world some four hundred and sixty years later; and, after another four hundred and sixty years, was born the Latin poet who wrote the Æneid (Arms and the Man). Yet seventy years, and He arrived in the world of whom Saint Paul has said that "He was rich, yet for your sakes became poor." Christ, in His lore of love, had said to the poor that "theirs is the Kingdom of Heaven." But the rich had abused the teaching. Seventeen hundred and ninety five years later arose Thomas Carlyle to propound a fiercer doctrine, and to warn mankind that they were not to interpret that beautiful poverty-phrase as meaning also the converse, viz., that "earth was the kingdom of the rich;" and he warned them—the rich—and mankind generally, that either wise statesmanship would have to overcome the poverty of the masses, in a just and merciful way, or Poverty would overcome Mammon in a terrible and a merciless way. After them all succeeded, some two centuries later, Carlyle Democritus. He disturbed not the "Kingdom of Heaven" theory for the poor, for he would not deprive the Mammon peers, plutocratic bishops, and Shylock landowners, languishing in the slum prisons, from the only consolation left to them, and which, in their turn, they had duly afforded to the previous occupants. Therefore he left the Kingdom of Heaven *theory* a free and harmless circulation. But he very thoroughly destroyed the Kingdom of hell *fact* which Mammon had, meanwhile, created for the poor in this material world. And we are about to learn how he did it. Those who have seen in every individual reform, from the abolition of drunkenness to the restoration of the people to their land; from the abolition of sweating to the establishment of an eight hours' day, the panacea to cure all the evils of humanity, must have discovered from this veracious history that any *one* of those reforms would have been utterly futile but for the comprehensive wisdom which had learned and taught that each one of them was but a stone in a mighty structure, which on completion was to form the noble palace of human justice and well-being; that any one of them singly was only a stone, though of purest marble, of the whole structure, and in itself *no* panacea, only an ingredient of the panacea. The eight hours' day once established, it became difficult to believe that there ever could have been resistance to its adoption. But let it not be forgotten that no amount of legislation could ever have established it, had not, side by side with that law, gone other measures to enable the workers to enforce their rights. Surplus of labourers had given way to surplus of labour. And when one contemplates this marvellous world, and the work which is to be ceaselessly done in it, one realises that—in every naturally ordered State—labour must ever be in excess of the labourers, and that only the folly and corruption of men could have ever defeated—no, blinded themselves—to Nature's law in that direction.

The abolition of casual labour was not a matter to be effected by an edict. Abundantly good as the thing was in itself, it required more than philanthropic theory to establish it. Let us briefly run through some of the preliminary conditions necessary to have rendered possible the permanency of the labour contract. The Revolution was confronted with at least five millions of men and women on the verge of, or beyond, pauperism. Their numbers (125) were steadily increasing as more and more of the land was year by year thrown out of cultivation, as day after day shiploads of foreign paupers dumped their waste freights of human misery to further swell the already choked British slums and sweating-hells. Their numbers were further and continuously increasing with the ever-increasing exactions of the urban landlords or land-devils. Two other prolific causes helped to fill the ranks of the unemployed. One was the wasteful system of paying labour by the hour, day, or week. Thus were painters, bricklayers, builder-carpenters, paviors, masons, and a host of other workers, engaged, and liable to dismissal at any time. Wages in all those, and many other callings, followed the senseless course resulting from all evil systems. The labourer would be paid during the fine open weather full wages; good workers could earn from thirty to forty shillings a week. But in the winter, for months together, masses of them would be turned out to worklessness, and consequent wagelessness.

It was hopeless to expect that the jerry-builder, the jobbing contractor, the sweating middleman, could ever inspire enough confidence in any honest working-man to induce him to accept a year's contract at a settled average wage. Such was the state of Jubilee "law" that the workmen would have found themselves fully employed during the summer months at the average wage, but remorselessly turned off in winter, the jobbing middleman having "gone smash," or something of the sort. The jerry-builders, in common with the whole legion of quacks, were utterly stamped out by the Revolution. No builder or contractor was allowed to practise unless he was properly qualified and certified by the builders', architects', or other Guild. And an essential qualification for all would-be employers of labour was their capacity to pay their workmen. Every one such had to find adequate surety for the wages of the labour he sought to control; and not until he had satisfied the Guilds concerned, could he start as a contractor. If it be fraud to purchase an inanimate thing for which you cannot pay, how infinitely more cruel a fraud is it to purchase, or hire, human labour and defraud it of its pay, which means suffering to the labourer and all those dependent on him. Mark again the application of the Revolutionary "liberty of the subject," as against the Jubilee "licence of the subject." There would be no slaves if the State did not tolerate and encourage slave-drivers; be sure of that, all men, and beware of all false cries. Beelzebub is not God, though political economists and radical caucuses roar themselves hoarse in wild screeches asserting that he is. And licence is to liberty what Beelzebub is to God. Another factor in the increase of the unemployed was the crowding into such avenues of labour as city offices, and refreshment-houses, of German clerks and German waiters. The attraction for employing the foreigner was twofold: superior education and training of the German over the English, and greater "cheapness" of the foreign wage. The first cause was remedied by the more practical education inaugurated by the Revolution* and by the proper apprenticing of both clerks and waiters which those classes enjoyed in common with all labour. The second, "cheapness," was overcome by the minimum wage law. Germans serving for next to nothing, whilst they were learning English, could cut down British service. But when no man could be employed below the statutory twenty-five shillings per week, the influx of the foreigner ceased. "Made in Germany" is decidedly cheap when it costs next to nothing, but "made in England" has its value in comparison, when the voice of Justice ordains that not by "pressure of poverty," but by honest wage for honest work, shall British labour-pay be determined. Difficulties and trials awaited the Reformer on all sides. From the starving gutter child to the worn-out city clerk there filed before the piercing eye and much pierced heart of Carlyle Democritus one gaunt, unending skeleton army of despair. It seemed unending in its numbers, insoluble in its depth of misery. Temptation in myriad forms beset the General, not St. Antony was more sorely tried, Venus was not dead, nor Midas, and they united all their powers to allure the much-suffering man to yield up a task which they declared to be beyond his strength; and they waved the soft silky banner alluringly before him whereon the Earth Spirit for ever weaves the enchantment: "It will last your time." But the banner waved in vain. The gaunt army of Want dismayed not the servant of Man, for he felt in him the power of a living spirit which would marshal that army to glory.

Carlyle Democritus closed his eyes to none of the difficulties that confronted him; he raised the veil boldly! He faced God's Light! He knew that the privilege of the ostrich to hide its head in the sand, and to remain stolid against disaster, was not extended to man. A nobler, a loftier duty was Man's: To *face* disaster, stand undismayed before it, fearlessly wrestle with it, and finally die, or overcome it! The main causes of the artificial dearth of work, and the consequent compulsory starvation of the workers, were:—

1. Landlordism, *i.e.* the ejection or eviction of the worker from the soil, and its fraudulent absorption by the nonworker.

---

* Pages 359-65.

2. A consequence of No. 1. The absorption of the earnings of the workers, compelled—by ejection from the agricultural lands—to herd in congested centres, by the said landlord, who, whilst he starved an acre of corn-growing land, was able to exact an exorbitant rent for a square yard or two of urban land.

3. Unrestricted immigration of the waste and worthless paupers of foreign nations.

4. Suicidal, commercial, industrial, and trade laws and regulations, which fettered home manufactures, whilst they admitted and invited foreign goods *un*fettered into unjust competition.

5. A waste and extravagant legal system, made by an interested class, sustained by that class, and fatal to every other class but that one.

6. Overwork of one section of labour, and underwork, or no-work, of the other section.

7. There had resulted from all the above-named evils and abuses a residuum population of drones and of criminals exceeding in number three hundred thousand men and women.

(126)

. . .

1. The death of landlordism, whereby there suffered a few thousand persons who "owned" millions of British acres, gave freedom to the entire remaining thirty-nine millions nine hundred and eighty-five thousand, who had previously suffered not only in pocket, but, multitudes of them, endless life torments. Sixty-five millions of cultivable British acres in Jubilee period—of which some forty-eight to fifty millions only were cultivated—afforded work, at starvation wages, for only some one and a quarter of a million of agricultural labourers (those are the official figures of the Jubilee census published in 1893). After the Revolution, under the merciful provisions afforded to settlers, there flocked back to the land which they loved seven millions of people. Ireland, which, since the year 1841, had decreased in population from eight millions to four millions within one year of the free grant of her soil to her people, upon the terms already described in the land chapters of this history, reabsorbed nearly two millions of her old lost population. For the first year after the restoration no fresh grant of land in Ireland was permitted to be made to any

applicant other than of Irish birth. The six millions of population to which Ireland had increased within twelve months of the Revolution consisted entirely of free, hard-working, contented, and cheery Irish people; as indeed they ever would have been, had not cruelty and misgovernment driven them into crime and exile. Had that return of a free people to its land stood alone, it would alone have tended to exhaust the ranks of the sad army of want, but it did *not* stand alone. Those seven millions restored to agriculture were but as a balm-drop in the ocean of Revolutionary justice. The Highlands and Crofts of Scotland alone reabsorbed over a million of its brave people, who had been brutally and mercilessly evicted by the land-devils of Jubilee period.

2. The freedom of the town holders from constraint to hand over their earnings to the non-workers (landlords) lifted out of penury, or the verge of it, yet vaster numbers, who though not unemployed had been almost a drag upon industry, whereas they now became spenders on home manufactures, where before they were mostly spenders on landowners. The neglected land literally sucked up the people. In some of the great cities every third house was abandoned. In some of the mining districts—in spite of the high wages and short labour hours—not a man was to be found where before there had been a thousand.

3. The stoppage of pauper immigration. The return to their own country of foreign paupers, or their emigration to beyond the seas, caused a further lightening of the strained craft of the State.

4. The new laws of commerce, trade, and manufacture called into life all Britain's former supremacy, and so keen became the demand for labour that deputations of merchants and manufacturers waited on the government of the day to petition for the importation of foreign labour. The only avenue of labour which showed a decline was the old profession of jabber. The old windbagocracy was burst, and presented but a terribly shrivelled appearance. What with the burnt-up wigs, and the superannuated Cokes and Littletons,* there were some forty thousand of the lawyer class seeking employment. They soon righted themselves, however. The Revolution would not grant the importing of foreign labour, unless each labourer could pass the Guild trade test. But the manufacturers were not left long without hands; the legal, clerical,

---

* Page 387.

and publican classes, which had long been superabundant, gradually betook themselves to useful work, and instead of lawyers spoiling paper, parchment, and horsehair, they took to assisting in the preparation and manufacture of those articles. And instead of publicans and their men converting good corn into bad spirit, they learned to grow the corn for good wholesome bread.

6. The eight hours' day called for no increase of labour as far as factories were concerned; on the contrary, and as was long ascertained by the wise and practical who had tried it, *more* work as well as better work was obtained under the eight hours' day than had ever been before. But there was an increase in the number of men employed in State and Municipal service, because of the double shifts necessary in all street employment, and in sundry other avenues of public service. Altogether, where there had been a total of 150,000 labourers of all sorts employed in the public service before the Revolution, the new regulations required a permanent staff of some 250,000 men, not including the street and park keepers who, as State pensioners beyond the age of sixty, relieved the labour market of nearly three-quarters of a million of men.

(126a) The number of extra hands which the eight hours' day brought into requisition in the railway service, where overwork in Jubilee period was the order of the day, raised the numbers employed to nearly half a million of men. Entire staffs throughout the country had to be, on some of the lines, nearly doubled. Whatever was the actual increase, it was sufficient to bear very beneficially upon the labour market. About three hundred and thirty thousand men were employed on the railways of the United Kingdom at the time prior to the Revolution. A census of the Twentieth Century found that vast railway service increased to four hundred and seventy thousand men. An increase of traffic rate followed so great a change. But the extra rates were as nothing compared to the improved service and the improved servitors. Moreover, the real prosperity of all classes of the population enabled them to bear increased charges, since they possessed increased means to meet them. In the increased demand for workmen must be taken into account the many minor avenues of labour, such as those for carmen, bus-drivers and conductors, cabmen, dockers, etc. It was no uncommon thing for those (127) workers to have to toil, in Jubilee slave-times, from twelve to eighteen hours a day. Then the shop-assistant class had to be materially augmented; although, in a large number of instances, the hours adopted by the tradesmen's Guilds, for opening and closing shops, brought them all into line with an eight hours' day, still, very many of the larger establishments had to increase their staffs considerably.

7. The would-not-work and the criminal classes were definitely dealt with by the Penal Colonies.* *Their* withdrawal did more than merely unburden the labour market of their thousands. It purified the whole of their surroundings as well. If we add to the above figures the number of pensioners over sixty years of age (500,000), and who were provided for by the national and other insurance funds, we find taken away from the Jubilee flooded labour market several millions of hands. It is now easier to convey to the reader how very naturally and facilely the permanency of the labour contract adjusted itself. In fact, the difficulty was not with the masters. Such was the demand for labour on all sides, that inducements were offered to men beyond their union wages to accept a year's contract of service. The Labour Unions who, through their chiefs, were in constant communication with Carlyle Democritus, suggested to him to complete his great reforms by drawing up a scheme of profit-sharing, which would offer a counter attraction to the land, and which would finally cement masters and men. The Unions worked to a man with the Revolutionary Leader. Of the immense Revolution he had wrought, and the good it had effected, they so abundantly testified that by an unanimous vote they determined, with the approval of their men, to abide by the conditions of the Labour Code, and confine their entire attention to its universal establishment, and not seek to go beyond it unless Parliament and the country should first sanction the change (128) Upon this great question of profit-sharing, Carlyle Democritus determined not to attempt any law which was not the dictate of necessity, because any such unwise policy would tend to destroy the value of other reforms. He, therefore, called a meeting of the Guilds, and requested them to appoint a Committee of five to friendly conference with him. The great difficulty in obtaining labour, and the keen attraction which the land offered to the

---

* Pages 162, 250.

people, supported his case more warmly than any eloquence. He showed the merchants how there was only one counter-attraction to offer to the soil, which gave to its tillers a just share in the benefits it produced, whilst the healthy and cheerful surroundings of a country life would day by day render its appreciation livelier to the people. He suggested that they should select one large manufactory to be conducted somewhat upon the principle which had been established in the agricultural produce factories,* which had proved such a marked success. Pending the manufacturers' decision upon such an experiment, it was decided that the Government should take no further steps with regard to the matter. Meanwhile he reminded them that it was the experience of them all that the eight hours' day had increased efficiency, had improved the relations between masters and men; that not only the work was found to be better, but the quantity produced by each worker had likewise increased. After considerable negotiation on both sides, it was agreed between masters and men to try the system for one year, upon the condition that if, at the end of twelve months, the result did not commend itself to either party, the *status quo* should be established, and the code, minus the profit-sharing, should prevail as before. A majority of employers was to determine the question. After a year's trial, the result was declared a success by a majority of three-fifths of the employers. Thereupon profit-sharing was incorporated in the Labour Code. The division of profits was somewhat as follows:—Interest at five per cent. was a first charge on the capital employed in any undertaking, and a further two and a-half per cent. as a sinking fund for the redemption of capital. The Code labour wages remained as before. Any profit remaining, after the labour and interest charges, would then be equally divided between masters and men, that is to say, one-half to the capitalist or capitalists interested in the enterprise, and one-half to the labour engaged in it. The permanency of the labour contract was already assured by the great demand for labour, and now the union of interests between masters and men became finally cemented by the identity of interests of both parties. But the union of masters and men was not permitted to induce any relaxation of the rules of the great Labour Code. The eight hours' day could not be infringed. An

---

* Pages 126, 127.

average was permitted, times of stress might draw upon the daily hours a certain overtime, provided that these hours were remitted at another period, and that the average annual work hours did not exceed the eight hours' day. In the event of a national demand for labour arising—as in war-time, for instance—that was provided for in the reserve army; for the Government had its labour army reserve, just as it had its reserve in the fighting force. And they were furnished from the ranks of the pensioned Government employees. This reserve could not be called upon except in time of war, and it was this liability which secured to them the extra pension.*

We now come to the question of a living or minimum wage. It may seem strange to the student of Jubilee labour; but it is true that, although the Labour Code made twenty-five shillings the minimum weekly wage, and the labour contract an annual one, with a minimum of three months' notice on either side, or an equivalent money indemnity, such was the absorption of labour on the land and elsewhere, that, even at considerably above that minimum, it was difficult to obtain hands. Yet let it be recorded to the honour of labour, that such was the loyalty and gratitude of the unions to the Revolutionary Government, that picked men in all branches of trade offered themselves in all the Government yards and factories, in spite of the temptation which the profit-sharing scheme held out to them in private industries.

It would be difficult to find a more honourable tribute in the history of industry than that. Let only your brother man feel that you are his in sympathy; that he is more to you than a thing to use and to be cast away uncared for when worn out—and conflict will die away, and harmony succeed to it. Besides the eight hours' day and the annual labour contract, the new Code required a two weeks' holiday in the year for every labourer (not necessarily at any particular period) in addition to the religious festival days, such as Christmas, etc. Bank Holidays were abolished, as being no longer necessary. Wages were not allowed to be stopped during the holiday periods. The two weeks' rest a year was a minimum requirement of the Code, and no more difficulty was found in arranging it for labour than had attended its adoption for clerks or domestic labourers in previous times.

---

* Page 195.

National life, or the opportunities of worthy relaxation and recreation:—In the chapter on State employment some idea has been conveyed of the measures adopted by the Revolution to substitute something better for the people than the diabolical gin-hells which they had destroyed. Public libraries, which were particular to some parishes in Jubilee period, were general after the Revolution in every parish throughout the kingdom.

The management of the public-houses, which had been converted into restaurants, or inns, was made over to the Guilds which represented the provision-sellers and dealers. By them these establishments were conducted as public clubs, and were largely used as workmen's exchanges. The ground floor was a large refreshment-room, abundantly supplied with the daily and weekly papers, above was smoking-room, commercial-room, and other rooms which could be hired for trade meetings or otherwise. Except in the refreshment-room, at meals, no alcoholic drinks were sold.

And as the people increased in well-being and prosperity, the old drink curse of Great Britain so completely disappeared, that within a very few years after the establishment of the Revolutionary era, there remained only one inebriates' prison for the whole kingdom. The parks were the chief centres of attraction. All museums, gardens, and societies of Zoological and other collections were nationalised and made free to all. They were lighted throughout by electricity, as were the parks, and kept open until ten at night. The parks were cleared of all buildings other than the recreation and refreshment pavilions for the service of the public. Every athletic sport had its field allotted to it; and cricket, football, tennis, cycle, and training-grounds were all provided. There was also a reserve field for women, where gentler exercises could be indulged in. And in every park the little children's field was never forgotten, with its miniature pond only twelve inches deep for toy fleets to sail upon, its sand and shingle reserves for tiny delvers to mine upon, and always a grass lawn of exquisite richness. Soft and safe was the emerald carpet, as carefully and daintily kept as ever was the best of palace lawns. Also there were lawns of daisy and clover flowers for the little chain-makers. The children's garden was always the sweetest and brightest nook in the park, sheltered by a hedge of beech and chestnut trees, and from the wind by a triple shrubbery of flowering plants; it was alive with banks of merry flowers.

That feature of the parks was so dear to Carlyle Democritus that he personally examined the plans of nearly all of them, and visited many after their completion—the only recorded instance where the great General had been known to actually interfere in any mere detail work. He told the people that it was the sufferings of the little children in the cruel slums of Jubilee period that had called him to deliver them or die; and that in all the Gospels there was no more penetrating depth of Divine nobleness and poetry than the Christ words, "Suffer the little children to come unto Me." It remains in the records of those times that he exacted a promise from the great ones of the State that when his work time should cease in the world—if, when that time came, he was not to share the fate of earlier reformers, and be stretched on cross beams, or hung in gallows' chains—they would permit no other memorial to him but a little marble effigy in some of the children's grounds with that one Christ-line engraved upon it, and a little lad, emblematic of innocent confidence and love, close by him. But is this History? To return: In all the parks military and other bands played almost daily in fine weather. And there is a last mercy to be recorded—the regulation of park preaching. This was a terrible thing, and quite unregulated in the Jubilee period. Gangs of stump-orators, from the crazy nigger missionary to the more crazy white missionary, and an unending assortment of other demagogues of all complexions and fadderies, stationed themselves in the main avenues of the great parks, and there set up a cacophony of squeaky hymns, denunciation of everything and everybody (not of the mental or physical complexion of the specially illumined one); and altogether rendered the parks intolerable to sane men. The Revolution had a great veneration for "free speech," though a less veneration for free lunatics. Still, they were anxious not to spoil a harmless occupation so long as it did not interfere with other people's comfort. Accordingly, a special field was set apart for the preaching gentry, and to prevent unseemly altercation between these instructors and exhorters of mankind, the preaching-field was made circular, and divided by radii into exact portions, one of which was allotted to each various sect who might apply for it. There was the Nigger section, the End-of-the-World preaching section, the Mission-to-Timbuctoo section, the Psalm-singers, Rights-of-Man, Political-economy, Rights-of-Property, Pope-infallibility, Amnesty-of-slum-prisoners, Restoration of Jubilee landlords, sections. Also there were unending Societies: The Society for the Propagation of the Thirty-Nine Articles, of Laisser Faire; a Society for the Restoration of Bigwigs and Little-wigs, of Jubilee lawmongers; and a host of other societies and sections dear to such remaining Jubilee folk as might be found to exist after the establishment of the Reformation which this history is endeavouring to describe, and whose Park laws it has described in some detail in order to do justice to the great tolerance of the Revolutionary Government.

Some months after the period described, the circular fields fell into disuse by any except the lecturers, and by them also, before a year was over. The fields were then converted into general playgrounds, but their circular form was retained, in case of future word-saviours arising, who might require such safety-valves for the release of their surplus gas, without disturbing or offending the peace of those who preferred not to listen to them.

LABOUR COURTS OF ARBITRATION OR CONCILIATION.
(See also under the Chapter on Law.)

The Courts of Arbitration which were such a valuable feature of the commercial world were not less so in the world of workers. In every trade centre such a Court was instituted. The arbitrators were elected by the various branches of the Trade Unions through their committees. The members of these Courts were called Arbitrators (M.C.A.), a title which after the Revolution became one of great honour, and from the various arbitrators throughout the kingdom some of England's greatest magistrates and judges came to be chosen.

There were mixed Arbitration Courts for the hearing of cases between masters and men; such mixed Courts consisting of the three senior members from the Labour Court of the particular trade concerned, and three seniors from the respective commercial or Guild Court. The rules and regulations in all these Courts were similar. Plaintiff and defendant appeared in person; no one was allowed to represent, or misrepresent, either side. Each Court or group of Courts supported and provided officials, whose duty it was to assist either side when required on points of detail or of law, and to generally facilitate the routine of the Courts. Common civility and absence of red-tape were the distinguishing features

of these officials, for the times of Jubilee had ceased to be. As in
the case of the Trade or Guild Courts, so with the Labour Courts—
the State upheld them, and no expense fell upon either worker or
trader. No difference was made in the scale of remuneration
paid to the Labour, or the Guild, or the Professions' arbitrators.*
The Revolution determined that justice should only have one
scale of remuneration—that pertaining to the office, and irrespective
of the status of the candidate. In every instance it was of the
utmost importance that the greatest honour should lie in the office
and title of arbitrator, and no effort was spared to realise such a
consummation. No member was eligible, or could continue to
hold office, against whom any offence, social, political, pecuniary,
or other, had been publicly proved. Thus was it also with the
Courts of Honour, which were instituted with the labour representatives, as with other employments and professions. In every
profession, trade, and labour centre, these Arbitration Courts, and
Courts of Honour, were set up throughout the kingdom ; and as
from their members were drawn the magistrates and judges, who
became so renowned in later times for their wisdom, practical
common sense, and often Salomaic judgments, it has been necessary
to explain somewhat in detail the practical system upon which
these—so to speak—judges' schools originated. It is perhaps
impossible for a post-revolutionary reader to realise the infinite
idiocy of the Jubilee system. No mortal who had any element of
practical knowledge in him could ever be made a Jubilee judge.
" Reading," to wit :—Addison on Torts, Williams on Personal
Property, Chitty on Contracts, Jarman on Wills, Williams on Real
Property, Oliphant on Horses, Roper on Husband and Wife,
Woodfall on Landlord and Tenant, Russell on Crime, somebody
else on Executors, etc., those are samples of the law jabberies
which, together with hundreds or thousands of volumes of
" Reports " (Coke upon Lyttleton jargonings), and sundry millions
of " leading cases," and of *mis*-leading cases, went to train and make
a Jubilee judge—a stuffed wig-block, nothing more nor less, a mere
thing of unending words and bottled nonsense. But let us not
anticipate the Law chapter of this history. More pertaining to
this division is the question of Labour Unions. These were no
cause of dread to a wise legislator. Quite the contrary. The

---

* Page 384.

ingenious and wonderful organisations which could bring the State at once and intimately into touch with any great branch of industry, through its self-appointed chiefs, were things to foster and support, not to oppose and ridicule. The Revolution subsidised every independent Labour Union, upon condition that its doctrines or acts did not interfere with the liberty or constitution of any other Union. The State support took the form of a money grant.*

In common with all public bodies, the finances of the Unions were subject to independent Government audit periodically.

Agricultural Colonies and Settlements.

In various parts of this history, many of the Revolutionary Measures dealing with the land have been referred to; and here we shall only briefly recount them, in order to dwell more carefully on such portions of them as have not elsewhere been fully explained. Expressed in its most concrete form, the Revolution partitioned agricultural lands into three great divisions:—

1. Peasant Proprietories.
2. Penal and Reclamation Colonies.
3. Military † or Reclaimed Lands.

The first, or peasant proprietories, were sub-divided into—(a) Allotments of from one to two acres, available for factory hands, for cultivation as garden or agricultural plots. (b) Allotments of from three to five acres for miners and others, whose shorter hours of labour in dangerous or unhealthy callings afforded them and their families opportunity for healthier industry during a portion of their work-day. (c) Allotments of five acres and upwards for co-operative farming, afforesting, etc. All these holdings were granted, held, and protected under the land laws, as set out in the land and other chapters.

The second, or penal and reclamation colonies, were subdivided into four classes:—(a) The would-not-work-if-they-could-help-it—a large class, the sad result of generations of neglect—these were set to work, which has been fully described on page 168. Nor was this class permitted again, in any form, to assert itself. Any person discovered "without visible means of support" was forthwith led before a magistrate, and failing to afford evidence of his means

---

* Page 255. † Page 303.

of honourable employment, was relegated to a reclamation colony. Idleness is a vice which no righteously organised social system dare tolerate. Whatever may have been the Jubilee *theory* of the "liberty of the subject," the Jubilee *fact* was that thousands of loafers teemed in every thoroughfare of the kingdom. That order of things departed after the Revolution. The prime liberty of man then became liberty to *work*, not licence to no-work. Loafing, cadging, street-touting, became forgotten industries under the *régime* of a Carlyle Democritus.

(*b*) The Criminal Class. This was also a not inconsiderable element of Jubilee society, and was to be counted by the tens of thousands.* To this class—after the most careful assorting of goats from sheep—was allotted such tasks as the embanking and dredging of rivers and harbours throughout the kingdom. With the increase of justice and well-being this class tended materially to decrease, if not altogether to disappear. Accordingly, all the prison sites chosen, and the structures designed and erected, were upon plans facilitating their easy conversion, at any time, into such buildings as the locality might require. In the meanwhile, each prison and penal labour depôt received a distinct order of offenders. For first offences the prisoners were sent to a penal depôt nearest the place of their conviction, and their labour day was nine hours. For second offences, the sentence was not only doubled, but the labour day was increased to ten hours. For third offences the minimum period of compulsory labour was ten years, with a labour day of twelve hours. After a fourth conviction an offender lost his liberty for ever. In Jubilee period it was everyday experience for prisoners to be brought before magistrates scores and even hundreds of times, for the same petty offences. With regard to the crime of drunkenness, which, after the Revolution, was made in fact, as it was in act, one of the most bestial offences in man—it has been explained † that inebriates were condemned to loss of liberty for various periods. The first offence rendered them liable to labour in the home-work of a penal depôt; a second conviction condemned them to labour, for a day of nine hours, on outside work; and a third conviction made them permanent prisoners, where they were compelled to labour according to the regulations of the Governor and Council.

---

* Pages 387, 388.   † Page 411.

Every prison, or depôt, was ruled by a Governor appointed by the State, and a Council of three appointed by the County Council of the division in which the prison was situated. The criminal law of Carlyle Democritus differed widely from what had prevailed in pre-revolutionary times. Such scandals as were rife under the Jubilee system were not possible under the Revolutionary Code. Jubilee criminals were quite a recognised * and even fêted class. They had their "criminal suppers" fostered by the heart-without-head, or philanthropic class; and untold numbers of old women in petticoats, and other old women in male attire—and magisterial old women especially—smugged and snuffled over the "hardened criminal" whom they were never tired of trying to "reform." Carlyle Democritus reformed both the "old women" and the hardened criminals out of existence, that is to say, out of that particularly prominent and public existence which they had occupied in Jubilee times.

After five years of the Revolutionary treatment of criminals, the repetition offenders absolutely disappeared. A second experiment in hard labour on mud embankments sufficed even for the "hardened criminals;" for there were no longer any criminal supper parties, no delicate ass-pattings for "hardened criminals," in any shape or form. Humane treatment, wholesome but very plain food and shelter, the sternest of discipline, and the hardest of work. Early in the twentieth century such a thing as a third offender was become as rare as a barrister's wig, or an old woman magistrate's apostrophising an incorrigible rogue and vagabond before him for the seventieth or seven hundredth offence: "I am sorry to see you here again; when I see the same faces again and again it shows that the 'remedies' I try have no effect; there now, go and don't do it again." That was an actual and by no means exceptional Jubilee case. The scoundrel referred to had spent some twenty years in prison. The next day you would find a Jubilee magistrate sentencing a wretched starving woman, with five children to support on three or four shillings a week, to seven days' imprisonment, because one of her three-year-old children had stolen a rag from a pawnbroker, and in spite of the fact that the poor, half-starved creature had, upon her own initiative, taken back the rag to said pawnbroker.† Cases were so numerous of this

---

* Page 387-389. † Page 368.

description that one of the Jubilee Society slander papers used to indulge the class of readers for whom it catered with a column devoted entirely to the infamous "judgments" of magistrates throughout the country. These judgments, read in the light of these civilised post-revolutionary times, seem like the ravings of some court of mere mud-imps. Hundreds of cases of men fined a few shillings for almost bashing their wives to pieces; whilst women, and often young children, were mercilessly sentenced for stealing crusts to feed their hunger with. Such was Jubilee justice—capped by the liberty of any number of Society thieves to rob the poor of their earnings by means of endless quack nostrums and "Building" or other "Society" scoundrelries.| Carlyle Democritus defined Jubilee law as "Freedom for the rich to rob the poor, crime for the poor to beg of the rich." In the Revolutionary penal colonies that barbarous law was somewhat reversed, and you would find on the penal mud-banks hundreds of the old Jubilee swindling directors, side by side with the other common thieves, housebreakers, etc. The longest sentences were not any more for the wretches brought to crime by ignorance, evil example, and want, but for the soulless gold-thief, hatching, in comfort, his devil's plans to despoil the hard workers of their thrifty savings. All that of the criminal law, whereof more anon.

There is one last division of the agricultural colonies too memorable to be passed over—the issue of the reclamation works—*i.e.* the reclaimed lands. Thousands of acres of lands reclaimed from waste into rich and beautiful labour settlements were becoming year after year available for permanent colonisation; and a notable use was made of them. They were reserved by the Government as national or military settlements, upon which were drafted regiment after regiment of the military and naval troops, with their families and belongings. The management of these colonies differed only from that of the peasant proprietories in that the tenure of the lands was temporary instead of permanent. After payment of outgoings, all the profits of the farms were divided amongst the men who worked them, and in this manner a worthy field of labour was provided for the army and navy time-expired men, reserve drafts, etc., as will be more particularly explained in the chapters dealing with the Army and Navy.

CHAPTER IV.—(*continued*).

NATIONAL INSURANCE.

WHATEVER was the importance of the many reforms and institutions introduced by Carlyle Democritus, he regarded them all as subordinate to this one. The right to labour and live may be regarded as the very bone-structure of a social system, upon which all its parts are built. Man who has been born into a world without pre-knowledge or assent is entitled to a portion in that world. He finds it occupied by others who have arrived before him, with not a superior, only a similar title. In a rude age his strength would command a share, or his weakness invite destruction. In a civilized age justice has taken the place of mere brute force; and requires that, upon equitable terms, the right of every man to work be recognised. What the skin is to the human form, holding its parts whole and perfect, and protected by a mysterious sensitiveness, called pain, against injury, must the national protection of a people be in a complete and well-governed State.

No man, woman, or child was exempt from the operation of the far-reaching system of national insurance. "Time and chance happeneth to them all," and regard not age or sex. It is not more impossible for Fortune to bring the high-born into the gutter than for the fickle thing to raise up the poorest beggar to Mammon heights, or depths. Jubilee Era had her broken rich as well as her broken poor. The motto of the State Insurance Scheme was: "From each according to his means, to each according to his needs;" thus St. Simon, thus also Carlyle Democritus. The National Insurance was comprised under three great divisions, which dealt with accident or misfortune, old age, and death. But before going further into the matter, it is essential to observe that the Revolution not only provided against this scheme interfering with individual effort, but it took precautions against interfering, otherwise than beneficially, with any existing insurance or benefit society. By clear and plain-spoken manifesto it explained to all men that the National Insurance would but create a minimum provision for decayed citizens, and that it behoved all prudent and forethinking men to add to the necessarily narrow State provision by individual thrift and insurance. It was to encourage such thrift that the State subsidised every Labour Union and Friendly Society, to the extent of paying to them a bonus of one-tenth of the net annual subscriptions they collected from their members for insurance against accident, sickness, old age, and death.

How the State Insurance Rate was levied, collected, and paid.

To the National Insurance Fund was devoted the balance which remained (after the Navy additions) of the great Requisition; but as the many other reforms had drawn heavily upon that great gold harvest, a terminable loan known as the State Insurance Fund was raised to assist the scheme, until it had become long enough established to be self-supporting. This State Insurance was the only rate which was not a graduated one, the reason being that those contributors who paid on the larger incomes would be likely to be the less frequent callers upon the fund. Not only was the Insurance rate payable by every adult without exception, but every father had to pay one-tenth of the rate due from himself for each of his children, from its first year up to such time after its fifteenth year as the child should become a wage-earner, when the rate, one per cent., would become leviable on his own earnings. It was only by making the Insurance rate thus universally applicable that the old evil of unmitigated poverty could be absolutely conquered. That poverty which consists in being less rich than one's neighbour, or in being not rich at all, is beneficial rather than harmful. But Jubilee poverty, which meant starvation, or its near approach, was an order of cruelty to be overcome at any cost. It was also an advantage, and no disadvantage, that a parent should be responsible for the insurance of each child he brought into the world. Small as the payment was, it helped to remind all men of their responsibility, and tended to modify the unwisdom of indiscriminate philoproductors.

As has already been stated, the rate was levied upon all, because it could never be known how fortune might forsake even the wealthiest, and find him unprovided for. But although the rate was leviable upon all, it was not always payable to all, any more than every householder who pays for the insurance of his house against fire can claim compensation if his house be not burnt. The Insurance rate was collected by the State at the same time and by the same method as prevailed with regard to all other rates and taxes. But the payments made under the scheme were—as far as concerned accident, sickness, or disaster—made through the Trade Unions and Guilds, as well as through the agency of permanent committees of the various Local Authorities. It was of vital importance to this valuable measure that it should not be abused, and stern punishment fell upon the malingerer, or other fraudulent applicant. The minimum punishment for such an offence was heavy fine, and three months' imprisonment and labour in a penal settlement. Applications to the Insurance Fund in cases of disablement had to be made to one of the authorities mentioned, who, upon due proof, assessed the amount of relief to be paid to the applicant. The maximum weekly allowance was ten shillings. The Board had to inquire and decide as to the means of the applicant, as well as his ailment. Cases could only be entertained where the normal wages, or earnings, of the applicant were less than double the minimum legal wage. None of the State Insurances in any way touched the liability of employers, or others, for the due care and protection of their men. Nor could any money paid to an injured person, under the State Insurance scheme, be considered in estimating the compensation due to him by those responsible for his injury. The old-age pension came out of the same fund, as did also the provision for widows and children in case of a worker's untimely death by accident or disease.

It was not many years after the establishment of the Revolution before this class became almost the only one to draw to any large extent upon the National Insurance Funds, the high rate of wages and the profit-sharing system having lifted the great majority of workers above the need of State help. Somewhat similar rules applied to the payment of Old Age pensions as has been explained in reference to the disablement funds; but every worker over sixty years of age was entitled to a pension, if his means required it. The pension commenced at 8s. a week, which was the amount paid to workers whose wages had varied between 25s. and 40s. In order to encourage thrift, sixpence extra was paid for every half-crown additional insurance which a labourer had either, through one of the Trade Unions, Societies, or Insurance Offices, secured by his personal effort. The maximum payable on the incomes referred to was ten shillings a week. Although at sixty years a worker was entitled to the Old Age pension, it was not compulsory upon him to give up active service and become a pensioner. The improved physique of post-revolutionary workers found many men strong and desirous of continuing active service after their sixtieth year; but directly a man became an Old Age pensioner, he had to relinquish work altogether as far as the general labour market was concerned, otherwise his competition would necessarily have tended to injure the wages' rates. There were two exceptions to this rule: The park and street keepers,* the remuneration for whose service doubled their allowance, supplied them with uniforms, and freed them from payment of rent; thus bringing their income up to that of fully paid labourers, in a field apart from competitive employment. The other exception was the labour employed in Government yards and factories. These men received from the Government an additional Old Age pension equal to one-half of the amount paid to them under the State Insurance Scheme. In exchange for this extra rate, they were liable to be called upon to serve up to the completion of their sixty-fifth year in the event of any emergency. They formed the labour army-reserve of the State. In the event of their services being required, they received the full wage of the department they were allotted to. With regard to the insurance remuneration afforded to those who, in the higher ranks of life, fell into indigence, their cases were examined by the Local Insurance Board, or the Guild, or Professional Council, to which they might belong; and according to the decision of those bodies the award was fixed, from a weekly allowance of 15s. to a maximum of £3. All insurances were personal and inalienable, and the severest penalties attached to any attempt at infringing this so necessary protection. Any person attempting to barter with, or bartering for, or in any way

---

* Pages 196-199.

anticipating or attempting to anticipate, a State Insurance, was liable to a minimum fine of ten times the amount involved, and a minimum period of three months' imprisonment with penal labour. The limit of age in the public service was not voluntary on the part of the server. At sixty years, or in exceptional cases, sixty-five years, all public officers, high and low, had to retire. All public salaries carried pensions with them. Those pensions were really deferred pay; for it had been found that improvidence was by no means confined to the humbler workers; some of the best paid officers of the State in Jubilee times were not only penniless in their old age, but cribbled by debt as well. Their salaries, therefore, were rather less in post-revolutionary times than they had been before. But their Old Age pensions were fuller. And it should be here said that with regard to all pensions, or payments from State Insurance Funds, any case of proved waste, or incompetency on the part of a pensioner to deal rightfully with his pension as regards those dependent upon him, caused the amount to be payable to the wife, or other responsible party, according to the judgment of the Insurance Board or Honour Courts. With regard to the compulsory retirement of all officials, it may be said that if the State might chance to lose the service of some exceptionally late-budding genius, it gained on the other hand the life-stirring effect of brisk and healthy circulation in the national body, the invigorating influence of fresh blood, the sinewy strength produced by adequate opportunities of promotion. Set all that off against the Methuselahs who filled high offices at Jubilee period. Let us take the year 1894. Its list of senilities included a Minister of eighty-four, a Privy Councillor of ninety-five, a Commander-in-Chief of the British Army of seventy-five,* a Member of Parliament past ninety-two, a Judge of seventy-seven, many other judges past threescore and ten, bishops of ninety-one, eighty-three, seventy-three, and a host of others long past the age of usefulness, more fit for a nursery than any position of command. No law was more inexorable than the State service retirement law. Only by a two-third's majority of his peers voting in secret ballot, upon their own initiative, could any officer of a Government or State department, civil, military, naval, or political, continue his service beyond the completion of his sixtieth year, and, even with that sanction, never

---

* Page 307.

beyond the completion of his sixty-fifth year. In war time only was any modification of this law, in emergency, permitted. With regard to child-life insurance, the fruitful cause of cruel neglect and murder in Jubilee period,* any such insurance other than that provided by the State was by law forbidden. And the State-Insurance could not induce the most soulless parent to crime, since a child's death brought loss, and not gain, to its parent. The old excuse for child-life insurance, viz. expense of burial, was removed by this service having become a national one. Most of the burial grounds had, even in Jubilee times, belonged to the Municipal Corporations. After the Revolution they were *all* taken over by these Bodies, who also carried out the service connected with the removal and burial of the dead. There was one law for poor and rich alike in this last office. No burial grounds were permitted inside large towns or cities; the distance of the grounds compelled mourners to meet at the cemeteries, and not at the houses of the deceased, as had formerly been the custom, an excuse for wasteful display of all manner of hideous black mummeries through the public thoroughfares, a wasteful tax on the rich, and a ruinous one on the poor. Individual superstitions were not interfered with, and each various religious sect was allotted its separate portion of a cemetery, if it desired to have it, where it might perform its genuflexions and mummeries as it listed. But gradually the pure and simple State service recommended itself to all classes, and " God's Acre " came to be recognised as the peace-home where for ever ended childish differences. In any event, no difference was permitted between the poorest and the richest, as far as record was concerned ; over each grave a small, simple, white marble headstone bore the name, birth-, and death-place, date of birth and death, of the deceased. No other memorial was permitted, nor was any difference allowed in the position of the graves. They followed one another as the people died, and the rich lay side by side with the poor. The English cemeteries after the Revolution became known as the great Republics of the dead.

Not the greatest in the land was permitted burial in a church, were he king, or Carlyle Democritus himself. Indeed, this giant spirit had exacted a promise from his ministers that when *his* time should come, they would lay him beside the poorest who should

---

* Pages 395-398, and 401.

chance to depart on the same day. Terence Grey, buried at Purbeck, was the last man buried in a church, and the explanation seems to be that he died before the law was passed, but more probably that the Purbeck folk built the church over his tomb.

Dangerous or Unhealthy Trades.

Wherever the risk to life and health, consequent upon working in dangerous trades, could be overcome by shortening the hours of work, precautionary arrangements within the factories, and open-air occupation for a portion of the workers' time—in such trades rules were enforced, some of which are about to be indicated. But such materials as white phosphorus and arsenic, whose baneful effects could not be overcome, were forbidden to be used in British manufactories. At the same time, an Import tariff upon any articles of foreign manufacture compounded of, or containing such forbidden materials, was imposed, its rate being determined by the Guild or Guilds representing the goods affected. In all trades and employments where the danger to health or life could be overcome by wise and merciful regulations and conditions, such were every-where enforced. At the same time, the working men (no women were under any circumstances allowed to engage in dangerous trades), and masters, were honourably protected against the competition of foreign goods, manufactured under conditions which ignored the value of the worker's life, and considered only the cheapness of the thing produced. The list of trades, declared even in Jubilee times to be hazardous to human life, but nevertheless permitted to sacrifice the health and lives of untold numbers of women as well as of men, included such industries as lead in nearly all its branches, pottery, linen, glazed wares, matches, etc. In some of those trades two hours was the maximum which a strong man could work without detriment to his health. In none of them was the number of work hours allowed to exceed four. In reasonable proximity to all manufactories of the before mentioned articles, co-operative farms were established, upon similar conditions to those described elsewhere,* and no labourer could be employed in any dangerous trade who was not fitted to complete his daily occupation in the field. For, strange as it may seem, legislation of the twentieth century regarded human life as a

---

* Page 126.

sacred trust, held it more in regard than the most venerable doctrines of political-economy Banshees. One life saved from degrading misery, phosphorus torture, or lead palsy, out-equalled, to a Carlyle Democritus, a whole world of "buy in the cheapest market and sell in the dearest" doctrines. He imbued all his followers and every earnest thinker in the kingdom with the divine conviction that man was made in the image of God; and woe unto him or them who dared to desecrate that Eternal likeness.

In the cruel times of Jubilee it was a common thing to see a few hundreds of bedizened women at a Court reception, the upper part of them half naked except for bits of silly stones or shells out-costing an Empire's ransom. And jibbering at the side of these undressed things silk-stockinged men, plastered in gold braid and such trappings, the cost of each one of these Jubilee ape-things out-vieing a whole season's slave-wages of any dozen half-starved slum-folk huddled in sacks and rags. And *those* were the rulers of these! "Be not misled, my people," said Carlyle Democritus; "I tell you as a gospel of God that the jewelled nakedness of those Jubilee women was an outrage on the modesty of all womanhood, and the ape-men were a scorn and a reproach to the dignity and wisdom of mankind. But beyond all infamy, deeper than all disgrace, was the state of the Jubilee toilers, the slum-victims, dying for food. Whilst there is one neglected child in all a country, there lives a reproach to that country. What then is the corruption and foulness of that State where tens of thousands of children pine, and millions of women and men nearly starve whilst all that mummery stalks in broad daylight? It shall end, or it shall mend, shall that State."

There was no difficulty in establishing the two hours' shifts for dangerous trades. Large farms were reserved in the neighbourhood of the factories carrying on such trades, and, upon the regimental labour system, the various drafts were changed with all the simplicity of discipline which such a system admits. Three acres of land were reserved in each farm for every worker in the "dangerous trade" factories, and the whole farm was let upon special terms by the State to the factory-owners; they contained in all cases ample reserve allotments in case of future extension of any individual manufactory—the reserves in the meanwhile being left as pasture-land for sheep or cattle. Where any trade could not be rendered innocuous even on the two hours' system, it was forbidden.

APPRENTICESHIP.

The rules of apprenticeship in all trades were so nearly the same as those which had been established in the Government and Municipal factories and employments, that further reference might have here been dispensed with, were it not that the system was made applicable, not only to trades and manufactures, but to all professions and occupations. To have insisted upon an architect, a doctor, a pastor, or a dentist, an electrician, or an engineer, or any professional man, accepting from one to three raw youths for a period of five years would have been impossible. But to prevent any wight entering any profession who had not previously served a five years' practical training—that was possible. And *that* the Revolution made law. And in order to prevent any future dearth of training schools, where masters declined to accept apprentices, the State provided—in conjunction with the Guilds—ample means of apprenticing lads to all professions as well as trades. And these State apprenticeships were free, as were all avenues of education. It was left to the Guilds, in conjunction with the various Unions, or professional Associations, to decide upon all details of apprenticeship; but great precautions were adopted by the State reserving to itself powers of representation on the various Boards, in order to preserve the free admission of apprentices who were unable to obtain private teaching. No Jubilee quack could be tolerated in any calling.

To him who was without the needful outfit the wide field of labour was open, where training awaited him in that to which he could set his hand. There was no limit to the age at which a man might enter an apprenticeship; the youth entrance limit was the completion of his fourteenth year. For one year after a lad's service there was no pay: the second year he was paid one-quarter the minimum adult wage; the third year one-half of the minimum; the fourth and fifth years and until his majority three-quarters. The necessity for such an apprenticeship law was too manifest to require much setting forth in these pages. The unanimity with which the law was approved by masters and men in every avenue of labour is its best justification. Or, if better is required, it is to be found in the unending wail of the quack doctor, quack pill-maker, quack electrician, quack engineer, quack everything and body, who—as is usual in such cases—yielded not up their muddy ghosts without huge noise of bladder bursting in all directions.

One result of properly paid and equipped labour was to render unnecessary a great many of the products of Jubilee philanthropy. Thus there quietly died out untold number of almshouses, ragged schools, charity schools, and hospitals. Do not start, reader. The hospital, the most honoured of Jubilee achievements, really died, a slow and gradual, but sure and unresurrectionary death. It came about quite naturally. Every artisan's dwelling of large dimensions had its own properly salaried medical adviser, male *and* female; it had also its own infirmary, isolated not only for the sake of the others' health, but in order to ensure for the sufferer entire quiet and continuous care. It thus came about that with the improved housing, feeding, and general environment of the workers they became as healthy as the most favoured of Jubilee folks. Or, if they fell ill, they found not only a decent home and loving hands to tend them, but a wonderful sick-fund provided by the State Insurance, which their own thrift in many cases further increased, so that the hospital, in the course of time, became no more necessary to the poor man than it did to the rich man. With the disappearance of the hospitals the fine old custom grew up again of doctors personally training their own students. It was no longer possible to practise only on the poor, as in Jubilee times. That species of philanthropical vivisection had become a thing of the past. Hospitals were not killed; they died. They were the least of all the Jubilee sins. But do not let there be any mistake in classifying them as the result of an evil system—for that they were. In an altered form the best of them were remodelled as colleges. Where necessary, a division of them continued their valuable aid in cases of street accidents, but no longer as charitable institutions. After the Revolution they were uniformly managed by the Guild of Physicians and Surgeons, and supported by the State.

Labour Savings.

The Revolution numbered the halcyon days of the chartered thieves and scoundrels whom Jubilee laisser-faire let loose in all directions to gull and feed upon the public.* " Caveat emptor:"

---

* Pages 367-376.

"Purchaser, beware, for I am licensed by Britannic Government to delude, defraud, debauch, and gouge thee utterly. For one penny-halfpenny the British Government will 'protect' my grain of poison plus twenty grains of soap, and authorise me to sell it to thee as Pill of Paradise warranted to cure all the ills that thou, and the rest of foolish mankind, are heir to." For such a trivial fee the British Government let Italian thieves sell plain, undiluted water as "certain cure for cancer," at 3s. 6d. for one ounce. "It must be right," thought poor Jubilee folk, "and not a fraud, for upon the bottle is the British Government stamp." And well-paid British newspapers, one of them conducted by quite a holy and pious man, declared the water to be of marvellous, and of even miraculous power.* Bogus-building Societies, as fraudulent as the grain of poison plus twenty grains of soap, robbed the artisan of his life-long earnings, members of Parliament "directing" the scandalous things.* Everywhere Barrabas King and Jesus stoned. O most damnable and iniquitous state of things! The shilling pickpocket pounced upon and punished, but the ruiner of thousands tolerated and let go free. Fraud for a penny quickly caught in the toils of the Jubilee law meshes, but fraud for a million rewarded with a peerage. Enough, enough!

Company promoters under the Revolution had to satisfy the Committee of the Financial Guild that they were solvent men; that—for each one of them—three sureties were forthcoming to answer for the capital they required to be intrusted to their hands. The law laid down that every person concerned or interested in the formation of a Company should be held responsible for every statement appearing in the prospectus, or other document, which heralded its inception. No director, or other managing person, was eligible to serve upon any Company until he had furnished security, personal or real, with the Board of Trade to the full value of the share which—taking the whole number of directors of the Company as an unit representing the capital of the Company—in his person he represented. It is interesting to contrast such laws with the evidence afforded by the "Permanent Secretary to the Board of Trade" in the Victorian year 1894. Said that worthy gentleman: "Joint Stock Companies were created with the intention of producing shares and

---

* Pages 372-373.

nothing else. In one year (just passed) two thousand six hundred and seventeen Companies were registered with a nominal capital of one hundred and twelve millions sterling. An enormous number of Companies had gone to smash. Year after year Companies were floated of which the object was merely floatation." To float, viz. the earnings of toil into the pockets of chartered thieves, protected or tolerated, by Jubilee Board of Trade, or other section of Jubilee Political-Economy "Government." Not only those villainous Joint Stock thieves were brought to book, and their brutal trade quenched utterly, and for ever; but instead of Members of Parliament and Ministers being able to sell their names to such concerns, in order to entice poor folk—who were simple enough to think that common honesty was a desideratum of high office—after the Revolution it was forbidden to any man, holding public office or representation, to be connected in the management of a public Company.*

More will be seen of these laws under the chapter which deals with the Legislature. With regard to Foreign Loans, the Government also stepped in to protect the Nation. The Revolution divided Foreign Loans into two categories—one industrial, which fell under the ordinary Company law, and rendered the Directors individually and collectively responsible to their shareholders (and only responsible men were permitted to serve as Directors) for the capital they were inviting; the other concerned State Loans, and required the Foreign State, who desired to borrow, to guarantee due payment of its interest to the British Government, as well as to its shareholders. The Revolutionary Leaders would not consent to tacitly see hundreds of millions of British capital squandered by Greek, Portuguese, Turk, and other fraudulent Foreign Governments; and it took, moreover, a step to recover much that had already been lost. What that step was will be found under the chapter on Foreign Affairs. Here need only be cited, that ample measures were taken to prevent fraudulent dealing by British Stock Exchanges, or Stock personages, in defiance of British laws, protective of common honesty. Such measures ran upon somewhat similar lines to those established in the general trade market, which prevented the importation of foreign shoddy to compete with pure Home manufactures. The dealer in any stocks or

---

* Page 423.

shares not held to be *bona fide* by the Financial Guild and the Board of Trade, rendered the dealer liable in full for subsequent fraud or repudiation of the stock dealt in. *Caveat venditor* was universal in finance as in British Trade, and the gangs of Home and Foreign Company swindlers, who in Jubilee times could "float" an acre of African mudland as a "gold mine," found their occupation gone. The trade of sharks and exploiters upon ignorance and innocence had an end. *Bona fide* enterprise was not restricted, quite the opposite, was in every way encouraged.

The State was a very Queen Elizabeth to all true enterprise, just as it was an avenging Nemesis upon all that was *not* true

CHAPTER V.

TOILERS OF THE DEEP.

IN Jubilee Period—some time in the year 1894—close by the Board of Trade Shipping Offices, a party of great Jubilites and philanthropites "opened"—a process common in those times—a house of refuge for stray seamen. Said house was not new, was indeed a good half-century old, and had, during that long period, furnished "straw beds and broken meat to destitute sailors." But £400 having converted a decayed philanthropic Institution into more decent philanthropic Institution, new "opening" became necessary, and the great ones of the land "interested in shipping" did duly attend and blow trumpets, more or less loudly, in praise of Philanthropy in general, and the present specimen of it in particular. The Head and Chief of the British Chamber of Commerce, M.P., addressed his brother-M.P.s, and the other notabilities assembled there, and the destitute sailors also. And he said, amongst other things, that: "Seafaring men added to the national wealth from between seventy millions to one hundred millions sterling a year, consequently it was obligatory on those who stayed at home to look after their welfare. At the shipping offices close by fifty thousand men were annually 'paid off.'" (132) "Paid off!" Whither?—"Many of the fifty thousand will answer you if you ask them," said a voice from the ranks of the paid-off ones. "But you must seek them in the dens of Slum-land, or in the Government annual returns of deaths from starvation, or in the suicides' grave." Shouts of "Turn him out." Decorous silence is restored, and Philanthropy speaks: "We who are here to-day representing the Government, the Chamber of Commerce, and the British people generally, having tacitly agreed to close our eyes on such old-world theories as human justice, and adopted the more modern theories of casual employment, survival of the fittest, devil-take-the-hindermost—plus Philanthropy—now make proof of our keen sympathy with the 'fifty thousand men annually paid off at the shipping offices close by,' after having enriched the country by some hundred millions or so a year, and we do now, by the item four hundred pounds, propose to quit us of our admitted responsibility." After a pause, during which faint murmurs of applause struggled for utterance in the throats of some of the men, but sounded more like the death-rattle of choking sea victims, there rose from the assembled crowd the same worn, sorrowful-looking, but passion-inspired son of the sea, who had before interrupted. He bore upon the cap which he held in his clenched right hand a small red cross, not unknown to readers of this history. With a voice which commanded attention, partly by virtue of its terrible earnestness, partly by the spell-binding surprise which his sudden speech created, the man boiled forth: "Be damned to your broken meat, your straw beds, and your four hundred pounds; give us justice!" He could say no more. Half-a-dozen policemen—not then members of the Revolutionary League—put the maddened sailor out, and he continued his address that night, and other nights, to an audience less philanthropical, with the results already known to the readers of this history. The total audience which the seafaring branch of the Revolutionary League had to arouse numbered in Jubilee time about four hundred thousand men.

The Merchant Navy accounted for two hundred and fifty-five thousand of all grades; and the fishermen, boatmen, and others attached to the water-industry, some seventy-five thousand. Say altogether three hundred and thirty thousand toilers engaged in an industry perhaps the notablest and noblest of all the callings of mortal men. If omnipotence of word-deluge and immensity of legal and other verbosity could afford a proof that the Jubilee legislative machine also regarded the seafaring classes as worthy of something better than mere philanthropy, such proof is not wanting; for there exists amongst the wastepaper archives of the Jubilee Era, preserved in the Revolutionary Museum, room 793, reference number 25,987, a Jubilee Parliament "Bill," which the encyclopædic catalogue thus describes: "Merchant Shipping Consolidation Bill, specimen (13,796) of Jubilee legislation. Exact period of incubation uncertain; authorities vary between thirteen years and seven years; probably exceeded a decade. Was reported to Parliament Anno 1894. Contains 800 clauses, in addition to the usual quantity of whereats, bys, wherefores, moreovers, and inasmuches. Of its 800 clauses, 690 are lawyer-jargoned and sense-smothered, so that their precise meaning cannot be ascertained. With the exception of twenty-three clauses,—each clause affords and invites opportunity to litigation, varying from seventy-three opportunities in some clauses to thirteen in others. A careful examination of the actual practical value of the measure was made by a Committee of naval and business men, appointed by Carlyle Democritus in the year 19—; and they reported that what was material and valuable in the Bill could be printed, in plain English, on a single folio sheet. A copy of the Bill was kept in the 'House of Detention for legal prisoners,' who attempted to 'practise' after the New Code was established. The punishment consisted in the legal prisoners being compelled to read from 100 to 200 clauses of the Bill without stopping, but the punishment had to be discontinued, owing to the remaining reason of the prisoners giving way. Nine-tenths of the Bill is mere clotted nonsense, or law chopping. This was only a Jubilee *BILL*; before such a Bill could become a Jubilee *LAW* it had to be set upon by at least 200 more lawyers in the two Parliaments, after which process it would be called an *ACT*. Such process would probably occupy from thirteen to thirty-three months, by which time the 800 clauses would be turned into some 900, and any accidental plain English, unproductive of litigation, appearing in any clause, be purged out of it. The cost of Jubilee legislation would sometimes run into hundreds of thousands of pounds, most of which went into the lawyers' pockets." (133)

The sea does not always give up its dead, else were there many *Port Yarrocks* to horrify the just, and answer why one sailor out of every seventy was drowned in British ships, and only one out of 350 in foreign ones.* The *Port Yarrock* was "wrecked" in the Jubilee year 1894. Wrecked, by the "Hand of God," or by the hand of man? She was a large vessel of 1300 tons, carrying 5000 yards of canvas, to be taken in if a storm or a squall arose. To man that British vessel there were twenty-one "hands," including the captain; six of the twenty-one were mere lads, five of whom had never been to sea before. One of the men also had never been to sea, another committed suicide on the

---

* See page 314.

(134)

voyage. Of the remaining thirteen it is enough to quote the last written words of one of the poor drowned boys—the voice from the dead—without whose letter this sea tragedy had never been known. For three months they were without fresh meat of any sort. From October in the year 1892 until the wreck in 1894, wrote the lad: "We have not had one properly cooked meal, and if our crew had been a British one there would have been a mutiny. Exhausted by overwork and semi-starvation, all the hands suffering from scurvy, the Captain nearly dead, and every one of us either lame or footsore, hungry, and without food," they were driven on a lee shore in Ireland in a winter storm, and there released from further misery, by death. That was in Jubilee England in the year 1894. "At night, to watch the vessel and control those 5000 yards of canvas, if a storm came on, there were one man, and four boys, who had never been to sea before." Do you wonder, reader, why five times more men went down in British ships than in foreign ones? Why, by one English firm, 400 foreigners "who would not agitate" were taken on in one week and 400 British sailors discharged!*

Like the coroner's inquests ashore, the sea at times gave up its dead, and revealed, by death, the iniquity of Jubilee Mammonism:—

(134a)

(134b)

(134c)

Towards Jubilee year 1894 six steamers disappeared in a storm; some inquiries showed that one of the vessels was 2700 tons' register. At three men to the hundred tons, she would require a crew of eighty-one *men;* her entire crew actually consisted of twenty-four "hands." Hands, reader, is a Jubilee word not implying able seamen, but too often including "absolutely incompetent foreigners," "boy apprentices, and others who had never been to sea." Like the poor little Jubilee insured children, who were "worth more dead than living,"†—that 2700 ton ship and her undermanned crew, who may yet appear at a Judgment Court *not* of Jubilee type, was very well insured. But not insured were the widows and orphans of the drowned "hands." Another of the six "lost" vessels was 1868 tons' register. She had a crew of twenty-five "hands" on board; three men per hundred tons register would have required fifty-five men. A third of the lost vessels was 1933 tons register, requiring, at three men per hundred tons, a crew of fifty-eight men; instead, she had only twenty-three "hands."

---

* Page 314. † Page 396.

Remember, reader, that the requirement of three men per hundred tons is no fancy figure. It is not only the proper requirement for a thoroughly well-appointed vessel; but a noted ship-*owner* tried to convince a Royal Commission that the number of men in our merchant steamers actually *was* in that proportion. Nay, (134d) that worthy gentleman waxed quite indignant when the Mariners' Society* gave his evidence the lie. (134e)

One of the many foreign sailors employed in British ships, a Turkish sailor, a Turk probably in more ways than one, sent a letter to his masters, which was no doubt a very wicked letter, and had not a word of truth in it, but it is nevertheless worth quoting :—

"He asked for payment for the loss of his clothes, and stated (134f) that he and others knew that the steamship——which had gone ashore on the Indian coast and become wrecked, was allowed to drift for the purpose of being wrecked. A number of the men could swear to hearing the second mate say that the captain was bribed by the owners to lose the vessel. The letter was signed by the Turkish sailor and two other sailors of the ship." All that is but evidence of the poor sailors. Let us hear the evidence of the masters. Here is the signed statement of an officer of the Royal Navy Reserve, written from the offices of the Shipmasters' Society in late Jubilee times :—

"With ample means of judging before me, I do not hesitate to (135) assert that undermanning of sailing-ships and steamers is of frequent occurrence, and is rife to a very large extent. To send or take a ship to sea insufficiently manned is not an offence against common or statute law." [It is an offence against common and uncommon law for a starving child to steal bread, but for a rich shipowner to murder his seamen is no offence. Dost thou commence to understand why one out of seventy British sailors was annually drowned at sea, O British reader?] "The Board of Trade" [with the ministerial chief, Right Hon. M.P., anxious *not* to be examined under Clause 8 of the Companies Winding-up Act†]—"the Board of Trade returns in respect to ships' crews are unreliable. Look at their evidence before the Royal Commission. Whilst the then President of the Chamber of Shipping of the United Kingdom was asseverating that there were three men put on board ship to every hundred tons' register, at that very

---

* Page 272.   † Page 369.

moment, in London alone, there were more than thirty steamers whose articles of agreement provided less than one and a half men per hundred tons' gross register, and in eleven sailing ships the proportion was just over one and a half men per hundred tons register, but *that included apprentices and boys.* In the greater number of these vessels the undermanning was of a serious character. In the *Port Yarrock* there were just over one and a half men per hundred tons register, but only a few days ago the *Liverpool Journal of Commerce* named four sailing-ships whose crews were only just over one and a quarter men per hundred tons register."

That is evidence from the Ship*masters'* Society. Now hear the evidence from the Ship*mariners'* Society (also of the year 1894):—

(137) "Undermanning is general. On board sailing-ships and steamers the manning is disgracefully inadequate. At this moment lying in the Mersey are eighty-nine vessels representing 123,425 tons register (a ton register is only one-half of the carrying capacity). On all those vessels there is a total of 2028 men engaged (or *less* than one man per hundred tons register), and that number includes boy apprentices, as many as four or five of whom are on board many a ship, and also a considerable percentage of foreigners unable to speak or understand the English language, and generally incompetent, men shipped because they are cheap. The wonder is, not that so many lives are lost, but that more lives are not sacrificed through undermanning."

. . . .

"The sea has claimed its victims, and the widows and the children starve. Help, O ye charitable, help! Brave fishermen have been overtaken by the storm and drowned. . . . In the whole of Ireland there are not a more industrious, hardworking, honest set of men than the Kilkeel fishermen. These brave fellows went out to sea in bad weather to get food for their women and their children, and the deep has claimed them . . . and now there is neither food for the starving women and children, nor return of the husbands and fathers evermore. Charity! O British people, charity!" . . .

(136) Thus in the Jubilee Year 1894 sounded the appeal in the daily papers, hid amongst quack advertisements, which, to name as they appeared side by side, were almost blasphemy. "O England," said the stern Democritus, "not the cold, chance hand of Charity

to save my orphaned ones and widows from the terrible grasp of starvation and endless misery. No appeal of that sort shall any more prevail. Not *appeal* any more, but an eternal *demand* shall there be, the demand of justice, the demand of right. The victims of those sea-heroes shall be the first and dearest care of their people, not any more the last, or the neglected altogether. Justice, Mercy, shall be the eternal law of Man as of God."

The Reforms which this chapter is about to record were completed and enforced within three months of the day of their inception. They occupy about four pages of the great Revolutionary Codex. And although the Mariners' Court was empowered to decide any disputed matter in connection with them, or to interpret any doubtful clause, such was the honesty, straightforwardness, and plain English of the drafting, that never was a single clause questioned, so far as its actual meaning was concerned.

THE MARINE LAWS OF CARLYLE DEMOCRITUS.

The Water-lords who, in Jubilee times, strange as it may seem, held "Rights" over the water of British coasts, disappeared after the Revolution in the same manner as the landlords had been made to do. British waters belonged to the nation, and for the benefit of the nation they were worked. The Marine laws were divided into two sections. The first dealt with the Fishing Fleet; the second, with the Merchant Navy. As the Revolutionary Government had established model factories in all trades as the most practical method of inaugurating staple qualities in all manufactures, so it organised model fishing fleets composed of the staunchest craft which modern science had developed. The fishermen engaged on them were the best of their kind. Their contracts of engagement were optionally either permanent, or for a minimum period of one year. Uniforms were supplied appropriate to the service. In addition to the full wages ruling for the best men (the minimum wage applied here as in all trades), one-half the profits of each ship went to the fishermen who manned it. Fisher Guilds were instituted analogous to those elsewhere explained. To each fleet was attached a steamship, which took the place at sea that the workman's club or library afforded to men ashore. A doctor and attendants were attached to each "Havenscraft" (the name given to the club steamers which were distinguished from one another by the addition of the name of the harbour, or port, to which each belonged). On many of the fishing stations the period between Friday night and Monday morning was closed against fishing. At such times, when the weather permitted, the "Havenscraft" afforded recreation of many sorts to the men. A well-stocked library, various ship games, rowing-boats, and athletic apparatus offered worthy means of recreation to worthy men. On Sundays pure simple services were conducted by the pastor of the ship. On all the fishing boats and the club boats rations were ample in quantity, wholesome in quality, and healthful in variety. Spirituous liquors were absent; but beer, brewed of malt and hops (no other decoction was permitted to bear that name, either at sea or ashore) according to regulations, was served on the recreation craft as well as at the men's messes. Ashore, factors and factories received the catches of the fleet, and cured, smoked, or dried the produce, and arranged for its disposal, as also for the immediate dispatch of the fresh fish to the various rural and urban markets. Free markets for all produce were established by the Revolution in all towns and villages throughout the kingdom. The old Jubilee wicked waste of food, when from one hundred to four hundred tons of putrid fish would be destroyed in London alone, in a month, was put an end to. Co-operation, instead of competition, amongst the fishing fleets, together with the national factories, disseminated the produce of the sea at less than a third of the old prevailing prices, and still left the men concerned in the industry better fed, paid, clothed, and protected than they ever before had been.

The profits of the factories (after paying for the fish at market value) were divided into three portions—one went to the seamen (the men divided equally, the captain, or master, counting three shares), one to the workers in the fish factories and distributing agencies, and the third to the improvement of the fleet generally. When the State fishing fleets and institutions had proved their success, and the men concerned in the fishing industry were united in a protective union to preserve the great reforms throughout their fisheries of the kingdom, the various establishments were made over to the Fisheries' Guilds, whose duties and powers were akin to those which prevailed in other centres of industry. The laws as to apprentices in the fishing fleets were similar to those which had been introduced in all other callings.

An important feature of the new organisation was the division of all those of the hundred thousand fishermen—the number so engaged in the twentieth century—who joined the Royal Navy Reserve (and there were very few who did not) into regiments of about a thousand men, or regimental companies of five hundred men or less, named according to the port, or county of their origin. The State paid to fishermen who joined the Royal Navy Reserve an additional wage of from one-tenth to one-half over and above their ordinary wage, according to the age, physique, and fitness by Navy drill of the reservist; he obtained also the benefit of one-half addition to the Old Age pension. The minimum period that a reservist was required to serve for annual training in a man-of-war was one month, and arrangements were made, wherever possible, to secure that such service should be in the vessel of the fleet to which the reservist was allotted. Every reservist was entitled to wear a badge on the right breast of his sailor tunic and reefer, bearing under the imperial crown the letters R.N.R. over the name and number of his regiment, and the ship in which he received training. Every facility was afforded the men to reach their training ship and to return from it, and they received full pay during the period of training. The labour code which protected the fishermen at sea did not forget them at home. The labour homes throughout the kingdom had been a great care of the Revolution, and none were more dear to sea-girt England than those of her sons of the sea. The fisher villages were conspicuous for their charm; not alone were the cottages fair to look upon, and fairer still to live in, but especial provision was made that each should have attached to it its garden and field, inalienable as the land-laws could make them. Provision was made for paying the seamen's wages, part into the savings-bank of his Guild or Union, and part to his family, as he might direct. Courts of Honour and Arbitration were established amongst the sea-folk, as everywhere in trade. The Lifeboat Service was amalgamated with the State, and each fisher company or regiment supplied in turn a crew of men to each boat. The State paid £10 for each occasion upon which a lifeboat's services were requisitioned, and added £1 for every life saved. A powerful and specially constructed steam-tug was attached to each port and harbour, to assist the lifeboats, or for general service when not so engaged. The number and possible speed of these powerful little steam craft made them valuable as scouts in war time, and they formed an organised division of the Navy Reserve. Their machinery was so constructed that when required for tug-service their speed was diverted to hauling power, but for Navy purposes they could attain a speed of twenty knots and upwards. They were all built with steel rams, a torpedo tube, collapsable funnel, and a turret for mounting a swivel gun.

The Mercantile Marine.

First-class seamen of the Naval Reserve, at Jubilee time, were driven out of employment, and so forced to relinquish their retaining fees, whilst 44,707 cheap and more or less incompetent foreigners were taken on to fill their places (see Vol. IV. Jubilee Census, 1893). Circumlocutory, lying Jubilee minister, in reply to questions, thus explains from his place in Parliament (year 1894):—

"The latest return of foreigners engaged in British ships shows an increase [increase on 44,707]; but I have *no reason to believe* [no votes to gain by believing] that any appreciable number of first-class Naval Reserve men have been unable to obtain renewal of their retainers; *perhaps* they are in better employment ashore,[*] etc." Merely to have to quote the garbled falsehoods of those Jubilee vote-catching things maketh the Historian's heart grow sick. The Divine Jesus was confronted with one Pilate grinning at Truth, but, O heavens, to be confronted by a whole element of grinning Pilates, not content to inquire "What is Truth?" but only intent upon circumventing truth. To have to search the Jubilee records of those political desecrations is, to any truth-loving son of Adam, the all-cruellest, heart-despairing business yet laid on suffering man. The Parliamentary Records of those Jubilee times are one vast charnel house of falsehoods, cowardice, and unending verbosity.

.   .   .   .

---

[*] Vol. II. of the *Board of Trade Labour Gazette* for 1894 recorded the continued out-of-employment of British sailors at all ports of the United Kingdom, and at the same time recorded the continued "immigration of foreign sailors to the extent of more than one thousand in one month above the immigration of foreign sailors in the same period of the previous year."

At Jubilee period Great Britain's Merchant Navy employed some
235,000 men. To restore the glory of sea-faring England was the (1381)
summit of Carlyle Democritus's ambition. Not by cold and
selfish neglect of the brave seamen, nor by screwing down the mail
subsidies to the last competition penny, and invoking the foreigner
in the Political Economy race for mere cheapness, was the old love
of the entire people for its sea-heroes to be restored. The lifting
of the submerged classes into work and independence was the
foundation of all the Revolutionary reforms. The keystone of the
entire superstructure was the restoring the British sailor to his old
shrine of honour in the nation's heart. To render his calling the
highest, to bring about for him the very worthiest conditions of
employment, were objects to which Democritus devoted his untiring
energy. He felt that he had no time to lose, this giant Saxon
Mirabeau; the spirit was gradually sapping the colossal strength of
the man, day by day he felt the nearer approach of the Eternal
Angel of Rest. He had made his Faust-Covenant—" Let me overcome poverty; then overcome thou me, twin brother of sleep!" It
differed only a little from the Goethe one, perhaps differed not at
all. "Oh moment stay, thou art so fair," was not the time
moment, but the moment of supreme achievement. To no great
poet-soul was material Eternity ever an aspiration, for the poet-soul
is itself a ray of the Eternal God-spirit, and in its supremest
infatuation of Venusberg, or other enchantment, base mundanity
could never hold it, could only passingly fascinate it. " In the
midway of this our mortal life," Carlyle Democritus had found the
world astray; had, by the inspiration of the Eternal One, redirected
the errant and the erring. And the wild longing for his Master's
peace was absorbing him. Finish his work he must, finish it he
did, and then—in mercy—it finished him.

"Jamque Opus exegi. . . .
Jovis omnia plena. . . .
Jubilate Deo."

" Thou hast overcome poverty, thou hast destroyed the oppressor,
thou hast set the lowly in high places, and everywhere justified
God. . . . A sun ray from the Spiritual Sun has penetrated
humanity to its core, ripened the divine in man, and hied home
to its spiritual source." (Pastor Truslove on the Life-work of
Carlyle Democritus.)

But wherefore have these words entrance in this place? Because of the answer of Carlyle Democritus to the praise of his people, which it is good that men should hear: "Give me no praise, my brothers. Him who shall record the history of these times, I implore never to ascribe to the servant the glory which belongs to the Master. God's purpose has been set before all men since all time. Those who blindly would not read may be blamed; those who have but done their duty and obeyed Him, and carried out His Divine purpose to man, are only pained by praise not theirs. Your love is my meed, my brothers."

Now let the record of the Revolution proceed. The 2300 men annually lost by shipwreck no longer left their families to swell the suffering masses as at Jubilee time. The State Insurance Pension to those dependent on a sailor lost at sea was made equal with the full wage of the victim, and continued to be paid to the survivors until, in the case of children, they attained to years when by labour they could earn their livelihood; to the indigent widow it continued through life. To the thousands of men annually disabled in the performance of their duty, whose numbers Jubilee statistics do not record, in addition to such compensation as they might be entitled to from their employers, the State Insurance accorded three-quarters of the full wage they were in receipt of at the time of the disaster.

The "Able Seamen" (A.B.) qualification, once a condition of sea service in England's palmy days, had died out in the merchant navy, except in the best conditioned fleets.* In the same way that capability and training had ceased to be a necessity in the various trade callings. That was the first reform of the Revolution with regard to the merchant service. Both the minimum wage and the permanency of the labour contract facilitated the adoption of the law. But the establishment of a State training fleet prepared a class of men for service who, in time, restored to the British sailor all his old prestige.

With regard to the manning of all British vessels, three men per hundred tons gross register was the *minimum* statutory requirement laid down by the Revolution. Nor could that number include apprentices or foreigners. In Jubilee times there were no less than 44,707 foreigners employed in British ships, in spite of the fact that at all ports throughout the United Kingdom British

---

* Page 272.

seamen were idle and begging for work. But "British seamen were prone to agitate," said the Jubilee minister, prone to agitate against (139) being sent out in water-coffins, called ships; prone to require a little of God's justice on sea as well as on earth, but bereft of both by Jubilee Governments. Death by drowning at sea, or by starvation ashore, was the brave seaman's alternative in Jubilee time. O British seaman, shall a Carlyle Democritus call thee to arms in vain?

THE NATIONAL TRAINING FLEET.

There had been much over-building of ships in the Jubilee period, and the vessels no longer required for coal export left many ships idle.* All that were seaworthy were purchased by the Government, and after being duly refitted were converted into training ships. As there had been no lack of men idle, so was there no lack of strong lads idle. Thousands of these young fellows were equipped and started on a new career as sea recruits. The training fleet was divided into three sections: The first section received the lads for one year's training in ports, or harbours, or short coast trips; the second were all sailing boats, and in them the recruits served three years; the third section consisted of steam-ships, provided also with sails, and in this division the apprenticeship was completed. The period of service in the last division depended upon the efficiency of the recruit. The minimum period was one year. It might extend into several years, as this division was intended to supply a reserve for both the Merchant and the Imperial Navy. Wages were paid in proportion to the years of service and the efficiency of the apprentice. The training fleet was open to receive any British subject, Home or Colonial.

Foreign sailors were not allowed to be employed in any ship carrying the British flag and receiving a British subsidy. But more effectual than any law, in this direction, was the establishment of the minimum wage, for no sailor in the world will equal the value of a British tar. It is not necessary to enter into details of the perfect training which the Revolutionary apprentice fleet afforded young British sailors. All of the ships were commanded by the best obtainable officers from the Imperial and Merchant Navy. In the third section of the training fleet the ships were required to enter and leave ports unassisted and without pilots. On all the

---

* Page 220.

ships anchor work and the management of sailing power was an important feature of the training. The tuition of the apprentices was looked after in all three sections by the pastor, doctor, and other lay officers attached to each craft, nor was physical drill overlooked. Swimming was compulsory upon every sailor, whether he had passed through the training fleet or not. The largest steamers of the fleet were mostly reserved for the training of engineers and stokers, and hundreds of the best men and officers were annually reared by this valuable branch of the service. The Navy Labour Code laid down strict laws with regard to stores. The best fleets had rarely been wanting in this respect, but in the cases of ships belonging to small owners, food had often been insufficient in quantity, and bad in quality. Especially was this the case in sailing-ships.* At a very late Jubilee period, a Government Minister had stated in Parliament that out of some thousand ships which had been inspected within a period of five months, stores had been rejected upon nearly four hundred of them. Doubtless the men suffered most from bad potted food. The indiscriminate import of tinned meat and other stuff—freely permitted at Jubilee time, regardless of quality—was stopped by the general trade laws, which required the marking of the quality of every article in absolutely plain English in common with all goods. Every tinned article of produce had to bear upon it the name of its manufacturer, the place of its origin, the date of its import, and the exact nature of its contents. The custom-house authorities sampled all these goods and tested the contents, and marked the tins according to quality. Nor was the question of the make of the tins overlooked. Whole families had been poisoned in Jubilee time for want of such a precaution. Any dealer selling or holding tinned foods not bearing the statutory particulars, or in any way falsifying them, was liable to a fine of ten times the value of the fraudulent goods in his possession, and a third conviction prohibited his trading as a provision-seller, besides subjecting him to a long term of imprisonment in a penal settlement. The provisioning of all ships was effectually dealt with by a tariff drawn up by the Shipping Guild, and by them enforced on all British vessels. And it must be remembered that the Guilds were composed of men as well as masters, with power of appeal to the Board of Trade; all interests

(140)

---

* Page 270.

were justly combined. It was this wise co-operation, in place of
the old cruel opposition and competition, which made every reform
of the Revolution work easily. The Labour question in the
Merchant Service was brought to an issue by the same method
which helped to adjust good understanding in all other employments, viz.—The universal demand for *workmen* in place of the old
devastating starvation cry for work. The State itself helped to
organise the union of all sailors and seafaring men. Organisation
is the thew and sinew of human achievement, of which righteous
labour is the outcome. Without organisation parts may be seemingly strong, but the whole machine is out of joint, and only acts
with ceaseless friction and needless wear, tear, and waste. Organisation will never be feared by any just man or men. Organisation
is a lever to the just and wise for the ennoblement of all labour.
It is only a ghost-drag to the ignorant, the selfish, and the unjust,
who falsely and cowardly fear that whatever benefits one man
must detract from the sweets of, or tend to the harm of, another.
Whereas nothing in all the world can benefit any man which does
not also beneficially affect another, or all others. Benefit other
than that is mere Jubilee-benefit, needless to be entertained by
right-thinking men. A Mr. Winans, in Jubilee period, probably
thought he was benefiting himself when he acquired two hundred
square miles of Scotch lands to hunt deer upon, turning out meanwhile Scotch peasants "made in the likeness of God" to starvation and misery—them, their women, and little children. Poor
Mr Winans, that it should need a Revolution to teach him, and
the likes of him, that murder, barbarism, theft, were truer defini-
tions for such infamously cruel self-indulgence—but never benefit.
The "Right" of a Mr. Winans to those two hundred Scotch square
miles of land lay upon the blasted lives of his ruined brother men,
maintained by Jubilee Parliaments, mainly composed of Winanses.
"God forgive them, for they know not what they do," need to
have been written high and large above that St. Stephen's Parliament, and perhaps *was*—in letters of blood and fire, visible to
those not morally blind.

The State and the Shipowners.

Capital and Labour being but two organs of one organism, true
benefit cannot be brought upon one of them which does not also
ameliorate the condition of the other. If labour is to be well fed,

well clothed, well paid, and well housed, it must also be well skilled.

And that which directs it must be able to bear the burden that all those duties imply and impose. We have shown how the State provided that the labour should be truly trained and skilled. No man could be taken into service in any British ship without the certificate of the Navy Guild. A wise Guild—State supervised —cared that the term "Able Seaman" should have a meaning in it. But could just statesmenship stop there? Were the great leaders of industry, the owners, directors, and builders of the noble fleets, to whom Britain owed her glorious sea supremacy, to (141) be forgotten by a Revolution, determined to achieve national justice and wellbeing? Jubilee appreciation of Great Britain's maritime supremacy consisted in subsidies for foreign mail services and foreign manning of English ships. Lying Ministers, smothering truth under verbiage, were yet compelled to admit the disgraceful poltroonery that they accepted foreign money-help to their mail service on the humiliating condition that all the (142) British sailors should be turned off the British boats and foreign sailors be substituted. Enough of those mud things! By virtue of the State-owning of the mines, it has been shown how—to British manufacturers—iron and coal were reduced in price. The first tenders for iron entertained by the State were always those of the shipbuilders for the construction of British vessels, for these benefited the largest number of men, both directly and indirectly, besides tending to the increase of Britain's lordship of the sea, which, under Heaven, Carlyle Democritus was determined should continue to prevail.

The Mail Subsidies.

The laws which determined that there was a minimum wage for labour determined that there was also a minimum wage for service which supported, employed, and protected labour. The nobler, stronger, England's Merchant Navy, the greater her power, always a power for good. Mere blind competition was a heresy to the Revolution. Their supreme orthodoxy was co-operation. Laws could do less to foster the nobler alternative than worthy State example, ushering in universal custom. The National Government did not invite competition tenders for its great mail services. but continued to the magnificent fleets which had long and ably served the country, the mail subsidies which they had long enjoyed, plus always the ampler grant which "Buy in the worthiest market" involved as against the Jubilee "Buy in the cheapest market." The Government mail subsidies required that the lines subsidised should keep ahead of the best existing of the world's fleets in speed, strength of construction, general equipment, complement of men, especially in the Engineering Department. This was not difficult, but it was imperative. Afloat, as ashore, the British name must mean the bravest, best. The estimates for the mail subsidies were prepared by a permanent Council, consisting of the Presidents, for the time being, of the Shipping Guild, the Shipowners' Association, the Association of Master Mariners, the Seamen's Union, the Chamber of Commerce, and the Board of Trade. The First Lord of the Admiralty presided. Parliament, but not the ministers, had power to amend the recommendations of the Council; but it was not often that they disagreed with the estimates of so experienced and practical a body. Do not let it be overlooked that these mail subsidies embraced also the Colonial fleets; the oceans did not divide the mother country from her children under a Carlyle Democritus, but united them. This will be better understood after the reader has examined the chapter on the Pan-Anglican Union.

Reserve Cruisers.

In Jubilee time many of the best merchant ships were already retained as cruisers for times of war, but many vessels which complied with the Government requirements were not. With the changing conditions of a great industry and an ever-improving sea service, the same Council dealt that had the direction of the mail subsidies. In agreement with the Government Department of Naval Construction, they laid down the lines upon which ocean steamers were admitted to the reserve. They established a scale which adjusted the amount of subsidy in accordance with the size, speed, and fineness of construction of the various reserve boats. Every Pan-Britannic vessel, built up to the requirements of the Admiralty, could enter the reserve. Details of the State contract need not be gone into. The subsidy was a liberal one on the Government side, and it required a substantial pledge on the owner's side that for ten years after receiving a Government subsidy, the vessel should not be sold to any foreign Government or service. Not only the vast ocean steamers were thus secured to the National Service, but fast small steamers, constructed to the satisfaction of the Admiralty, and capable of a speed exceeding twenty knots, could also be subsidised to serve as "look-outs" in time of war.

The Royal Navy Reserve of the Merchant Marine followed pretty closely the conditions described in the fisher fleets;* but the order of regiments, instead of following the county of origin of the reservist, followed the Line in which he served.

Throughout all marine ports and stations under British control, the old villainous crimp-shops were mercilessly abolished, and in any foreign port where those vile debauch hells were tolerated, no sailor was allowed to land from any British vessel. This law was accepted by all the great Unions and Associations connected with the Service, and was made imperative upon the Commanders of all vessels. In the commercial division of the Navy there were, in the Twentieth Century, a quarter of a million men, the sturdiest and bravest of British workers. The Revolution would not permit the voices of such a vital portion of the Empire to be mute when a General Election was deciding the Government of the Nation. Provision was therefore made for a ballot to be held in every ship. Every man who would have had a right to vote had he been ashore, enjoyed the same privilege afloat. The purser and doctor on large vessels, or the captain on small craft, counted the votes and telegraphed home the result from the nearest port. Here, as in all cases (see the Chapter on Parliament), the State bore all expenses connected with the Election.

---

* Page 275.

Book III.

NATIONAL.

CHAPTER I.

THE PAN-ANGLICAN UNION.

It has been commonly observed that the apple falls not far from the tree; also that the apple-pip, though put into new soil well away from the parent mould, will still produce an apple-tree—not a poplar, not a rose-bush, nor any other plant, bush, or growth, but an apple-tree. And also, say the naturalists, that with due neglect, the vermin who feed upon the apple-tree are everywhere found to be a kindred species of vermin, with a kindred object in life—viz., to feed and fatten themselves on the tree's strength and richness—other object, none whatever.

The same has been observed of the acorn and the oak—indeed, of Nature's handiwork generally — that the child differs not materially from the parent, and is subject to the same diseases bred of the same neglect. Thus, the sturdy British oak, made by the Great Creator, the ruggedest and most valiant of forest trees, can be gradually hewn, bled, stripped, and finally killed; but to its last life-flicker, to its last shred, it will be oak—oak branch, oak twig, or oak splinter—but oak, always oak. Why the Creator, in His wisdom, made the oak-tree stronger than the bramble-bush, or the bramble-bush other than the oak-tree, practical wise men do not inquire, for all men are not Darwins, any more than all vegetables are thistles. Man's province is to put the oak to worthy purposes, and to beware of making ships of bramble-twigs.

Amongst nations the children of Britain are as the oak amongst forest trees. Idle to inquire why, as idle to ignore the Divine message or fact. It is so. The world's history attests the fact, just as surely as the world's history attests this other fact, that the oak-man has a soul in him—a God-inspired soul to discern right from wrong; and only as the oak-man discerns aright, and acts rightly, can a nation of oak-men, or of any men, long continue as a nation to live. It has happened that the mighty British people have cast their acorn sons all over God's earth-planet; and, unfortunately, in every instance it had also happened that the merciless political economist woodlice had also planted themselves inevitably upon the new growing oak saplings. Thus it came to pass that, although the broad lands of Australasia offered unnumbered millions of fertile acres, pure and rich from the mother-womb, to the willing husbandman, and although in the year of Jubilee, 1894, there were less people in Australasia—about equalling in size and richness all the territory of Europe—although there were less people in that vast-as-all-Europe island-continent than there were in the one City of London; yet did the oak sapling which sprouted in that Australasian soil exhibit the same soul-and-body destroying vermin, in every branch and twig of her young strength, that were sapping the life blood of the parent tree at home. There, side by side with fabulous wealth in those Austral lands, you would find the fields neglected and the towns suppurating with filthy slums, starving women and children and workless men. For the British Colonies had imitated the British method of Government by party, caucus, and political economist insanities; and "buy in the cheapest market," "survival of the fittest," "devil-take-the-hindermost" was gospel in the Colonies, as it was in the mother country. Details of each colony cannot have place in this short history; but one picture will serve for them all. So we will take one small corner, one little island of the Australasian group—New Zealand—or rather, we should say, two little islands, for New Zealand consists of two, just as Great Britain does; and, to make the comparison more exact, it has a tiny splinter of a third island at its southern extremity, corresponding to our Isle of Wight, which it calls Stewart Island. New Zealand is somewhat the size of Great Britain, its climate averages nearly the same, is perhaps a little more favoured. This beautiful England of the southern hemisphere, at the mid-Jubilee period, had a white population of, not forty millions, but somewhat over half of one million; and it reproduced the evils of the old corrupt Jubilites as faithfully as a small mirror will reproduce a large picture. Out of its half a million of white people, seven companies—just

(143)

seven—were allowed to "own" about a million and a half acres of land. Thirty private people owned fifty thousand acres each, and thirty-seven other persons owned between one hundred and two hundred thousand acres each. Many people who never went near any of the Colonies were "owners" of the land, and made the new settlers pay rent to them, and give them of their earnings, just as if *they* had made the land and had the Divine permission to keep it, and only permit its cultivation after prayers, in the shape of gold rent, had been paid to them. Yes, there was one man, say the New Zealand blue-books, who never went near the place, to whom those innocent imitators of caucus-ridden British slaves paid eighty-five thousand pounds sterling a year. All those facts you will find, with many more of passing and permanent interest, recorded in the blue-books of the Little Britain of the southern hemisphere; and if you went to the mainland of the immense island-continent of Australia, you would find that exactly the same evils prevailed. Take, for instance, the beautiful Colony of Victoria, a territory also about the size of Great Britain. In the year 1894 there were 871 people who owned upwards of seven millions of its acres, about half the entire freehold land of the colony. They counted their holdings by miles, instead of acres. The soil and climate of Victoria compares with the richness of Italy, rather than of England. Of all that fine soil, only two or three million acres (out of fifty-six million acres) were cultivated, and yet almost a half of the entire Victorian population was to be found in over-crowded cities. The same madness recurred everywhere —starving people and starving land, and only a wise Captain wanting to wed the two together and breed prosperity from the union.

Two British Europes—Canada and Australasia—with a total population of about two Londons, had managed to dissipate their credit and their land as recklessly as their old grandmother at home had done. The total joint indebtedness of those eight millions of colonial people, after an average existence of about one hundred years, was half as much as that of Great Britain's forty million of inhabitants, after a national existence of over a thousand years. But some of the Colonies were commencing to awake from their nightmare. Particularly that little New Zealand colony. King Demos opened an eye, and saw a little of what this History has already described; and the awakened spirit caused no little alarm to the land investors. After a certain length of time the wood-lice who feed upon a tree get to think they are part of the tree's life and strength, and they cling so hard that it requires sulphur-fumes to dislodge them. Sulphur-fumes, often, of the French Revolution sort. Suffice to say that Carlyle Democritus sent emissaries to all parts of Great Britain's colonies, possessions, and dependencies. Slowly, gradually, the people saw the awakening at home; how the slums disappeared; how the starving came to be fed; how the workless found adequate work; how the giant force of right had overcome the quondam abuse of might The fearless devoted ambassadors of the Revolution were not diplomatists. They had not a lie, or a subterfuge amongst the whole lot of them. Not one of them could smile when he meant to scorn, nor flatter when he would condemn. But, then, they did not go to the powers that be, but direct to the people themselves. For months and months they worked patiently, even as they had striven at home, till at last democracy awoke. And although the result is now to be told in a brief and simple chapter, it did not occur all at once. Some of the Colonies held out more or less; some had already desired to go further than prudence advised; but in the end they became one huge power—one mighty family of self-supporting and mutually defending British men. It required three years after the completion of the English Revolution—three years of patient, brave, and ceaseless labour—before the last knot was tied to the great invincible bond which cemented in one Pan-Britannic union the parent country and her giant offspring.

The Colonial Land Question.

The principle adopted in the United Kingdom—abolition of landlordism, or dual ownership—was made law in all the Colonies. The notable differences in the colonial system were in the size of the holdings, which commenced at five acres, and were limited to fifty acres to any single tenant. All the other terms were, with slight modification, the same. Colonial Land Stock was issued under Imperial guarantee, in order to facilitate the loans at easy rates of interest, and all owners of land above the statutory limit were bought out at the market value of the land. The land, not occupied and worked, constituted a reserve for future increase of population. Emigration laws were made to prevent the influx of paupers and to facilitate the settling of desirable emigrants. They followed so closely the home conditions of the general land settlement that they need not be repeated here. The colonial slums were cleared and rebuilt exactly as the British slums had been. Penal colonies were founded, in every way conforming to the home regulations, except that, instead of reclamation land, large irrigation plans were devised, new highways were constructed, and other works provided, suitable to vast and unoccupied territories with overwhelming richness of forest lands. All details of government were settled by the participation of the Colonies in the Imperial Assembly in the manner described under the Parliamentary division of this history. The vast coalfields of Canada and Australia were worked for the benefit of their respective colonies, as were also the other enormous mineral deposits. The completion of the union was brought about by the amalgamation of all the military and naval forces of the colonies and the mother country. Each continued its separate existence for local requirements, but for Imperial services they became united. Similar laws and conditions were gradually introduced throughout all British possessions and settlements, small and large. All the coaling stations were fortified, and docks, wharves, and repairing basins constructed in all of them. Gibraltar, Malta, Cyprus, Aden, Socotra, Perim, &c., were made impregnable; the jut of land opposite Gibraltar, on the African coast (Spartel, Tanjier, Ceuta, and Tetuan), was purchased from the Sultan of Morocco; and Egypt was definitely taken under British suzerainty, and idiot Boy Khedives no longer permitted to imitate Jubilee Ministers, and play the fool with the British Lion. Nor was foreign interference with Great Britain's wise administration any longer tolerated.

In spite of Jubilee-Giffen-doctrine—"world nearly full"—the Pan-Anglican Empire had secured absolute reserves for untold hundreds of millions yet unborn. Instead of Britain's emigrants being cast off uncared for, and uncaring, whether they went to enrich Great Britain's settlements, or to foreign shores,—Carlyle Democritus made future emigrants their country's care. Precisely similar rights were held out to them as were conveyed by the home land laws, with the additional provision of free passage, food, outfit, and cross-country transit to any British settlement. In that way the tens of thousands of Britain's sons who yearly sought fresh fields and pastures new, and were in Jubilee times mostly lost to the Great Empire, were henceforth attracted to her own Colonies, which they enriched with their labour, while they repaid all cost of passage by love and patriotism, instead of hate and ill-will, which the old cruel "laisser aller" engendered. The African colonies and settlements reclaimed from Black barbarism by England's fearless sons, were united in the great bond, and made subject to the Pan-Anglican and other laws. Her hero-pioneers, no longer the scorn and scoff of filthy-souled radical denouncers, raised to co-equal governorship with Britain's best and bravest. One reciprocal Customs' Union completed the grand Pan-Anglican Union. Here, indeed, was "Free Trade" an absolute fact. Identical conditions of labour — the outcome of wisdom and justice—rendered the Freedom a godly reality, and no mere name to cloak unbridled licence and injustice. As was the British Code, so was the Imperial, and from one end to the other of the justice-loving Empire, from the smallest coaling island to the greatest New World continent — wherever the British rule extended—there prevailed, in all essential features, one universal, unvarying law, one land-nationalisation, one currency, one language,—one British people. The members various as the climes they worked in, but by the supreme all-pervading laws of mercy, justice, truth, and honour—one people, indivisible.

Fired by the high example of her great progenitor, the whole American nation shook off the political vermin who had also fed upon and nigh ruined her young strength. Purged of the poison, the two united nations saw that they were one in flesh, in blood, in love of justice, truth, and in mutual sympathy. The United States of America, with few modifications, absorbed the teachings of the mother land, and the result was an end to all old bickerings and jealousies. The Irish sore was healed, justice had made the Emerald Isle and her brave peasants a peace-loving, prosperous, and constantly increasing people. America and Great Britain became reconciled; and though each pursued its independent national existence, they became one people for mutual defence. The great issues which followed for the world need not be recorded here. The British American reconciliation was the dawn of an universal peace, arbitration having taken the place of war; but to treat of that will carry us beyond the point defined for the present History. There were generations between the Pax-Britannica and the Pax-Mundi.

INDIA.

"The English are a wise, practical and cautious people. They are doing a marvellous work in India, worthy of the admiration of mankind. . . . The czars have their eyes constantly fixed on Constantinople. Russia covets Afghanistan. She is already almost mistress of Persia. . . . Russia alone can arrest and annihilate England's civilizing mission in India, which would be a misfortune for the world."—*Barthélemy Saint-Hilaire.* (145)

"Why should we saddle the poorest classes in India to save putting taxes on the wealthy and well-to-do? It is the wealthy in India, such as are voiced and represented by the Anglo-Indian press and the Congresses, who at present, at the expense of the poorer classes, escape their due measure of taxation. It is well known that, owing to false returns on the part of the monied classes, . . . the Income Tax raised from the traders, money-lenders, zemindars, shop-keepers, and other parties forming the upper and middle classes in India, represents only a small fraction of its proper result. Why should not steps be taken to remedy such a glaring injustice before further burdens are laid on the poorer classes? A source of income is awaiting the Government in the pampered zemindars in the large areas in India under permanent settlement. When making the settlement the Government never intended that the rents of their tenants should be raised. . . . Since that time these properties have been enormously improved in value by the construction of railways, which have brought their produce within reach of extensive markets. Instead of sharing the resulting prosperity with their tenants, the zemindars have rack-rented them, and the Government has not protected the interests of the tenant. . . . Why should these zemindars escape Scot-free? . . . There should not be one rule for the poor and another for the rich; but as long as the Anglo-Indian Press and baboo-ridden congresses are deemed in this country to be the voice of India, the poor of that country will have little support, and will have to go to the wall."—*Holt S. Hallet.* (146)

"Of late years there has been a remarkable rapprochement

(147) between France and Russia. It is instructive to mark the successive steps of advance which have been made by the two countries. In 1863 the Russian frontier was 1680 miles from that of India. Russian outposts are now (1894) within 60 miles of Herat, which is under British protection.... The advance of France has been synchronous with that of Russia. It was in 1860 that she first made her way into Hindo-Chinese regions. Now (1894) she is advancing toward Bangkok, 95 per cent. of whose trade is in British hands."—*George Curzon.*

(148) How instructive for the British reader to learn from the history of its great feudatory a lesson identical with its own, and which had led to a similar catastrophe,—conquest and annihilation of British nationality,—but for the timely advent of the great Reformer. With utmost attention let the highest authority upon the Land System of British India be heard :—

"Oriental financiers held the limit of land assessment to be what could be extracted from the cultivator, short of reducing him to semi-starvation. Only a few rapacious revenue farmers killed the goose that laid the golden eggs [*à la* British Jubilee landlords.] The best rulers of India were averse to raising rents or rates on the land; they made the assessments perennial or for long periods. It was only as the Government declined in character and ability that annual rentings became the rule. Weak Governments at last introduced capitalists and large revenue farmers, estate holders or landlords (zemindars). As effeteness became more prevalent, the landlords became more cruel and exacting, until at the time when commenced British rule, their merciless exactions stole from the peasants *all* they could, whilst they yielded to the State of it as *little* as they dared. Unfortunately, these landlords having developed, as we have seen, into a grasping, evicting, all-powerful landlord class, and being found in possession by the British [instead of being crushed out as useless vermin, who had already over long drained the life-blood of the people], they were recognised by the British Government [a fellow feeling, perhaps, making them wondrous kind]. Many changes have, in the course of our occupation, been made, but the modern system is generally that of a rent assessment value *devised upon the payments made by the tenants to their landlord.* Never were assessments more merciful than the British. Mistakes have been made, and have caused trouble and suffering; but to England's honour be it said, she has ever tried to justly regulate and render as light as possible her Land Tax. *But the original evil of having recognised the landlords—the zemindars—has worked the same oppression in India as in Europe, and has required the same reforms—abolition of the middlemen."*

"Abolition of the middlemen!" Precisely. Landlordism had throttled India as it had nigh done England. The brown peasant slaved and starved that the brown landlord might idle and thrive. England's land taxes were generous and merciful as they could be made. But the landlord—the land-devil, the middleman—drained the peasants.

Very gradually were the Revolutionary troops—as their services were no longer required at home—drafted, regiment after regiment, fully equipped and officered, across to the Indian Peninsula until, spread throughout the great dependency, three hundred thousand British soldiers (in addition to the permanent forces), having freed their white brothers, were now about to free their brown brothers. The same marvellous organisation which had broken the tyrant's back in the white man's land, overcame, without possibility of resistance, the brown tyrant also. When every avenue of possible disturbance was outposted, any possible resistance anticipated, this notice appeared on every native building and in every peasant's hut; was put into every peasant's hand, or, by duly appointed officials, read out to the peasants:—"From and after this day the worker is the owner of the land which he tills. There are no more zemindars in India. In future the land of India will belong to the people of India—to those who till that land, and to no one else. The British Government will protect the ryot (the peasant) in the possession of his land and of his labour. Beyond a light and just land rate, which will be assessed at one-tenth of the produce value of the field, no other land payment shall be made by the new owners."

The Indian landlords were justly treated: For two or more lives, according to the finding of the Indian Land Court, they were paid the interest upon the value of the land they had "owned." The maximum was a fourth life; after that all payment ceased. With regard to house property throughout India, the conditions followed as nearly as possible (with such modification as the country required) those which had been instituted in Great Britain. The result is scarcely to be set out in the narrow compass of a chapter. Instead of annual deficits, the Indian revenue returned to the Government tens of millions of surplus, increasing annually. The land laws, duly adapted to the requirements of the country, followed the British laws to the extent of strictly limiting the size of individual holdings, forbidding agglomeration by purchase, gift, marriage, or otherwise, forbidding also subdivision. Money-lenders—the ruin of the Indian peasant—were prohibited. The local Land Courts made small advances to the peasants if the nature of the case required it. The homestead law protected the ryot as it did the British peasant. Let no unwise conclusions be drawn from the drastic laws of Carlyle Democritus, nor from the brief record of them in these pages. Just as Carlyle Democritus accepted no praise, reward or dinner-banquet eulogies for the great reforms he had established, so did he not waste time in eulogistic reference to good work achieved. To work well was man's duty, particularly the Englishman's. To the noble work that Great Britain had achieved in India, Democritus best bore witness by the wide extension of power he everywhere gave to the British local administrators, and the notable methods he adopted to prevent the sickening mission-washerwomen, white-livered radicals, State service by brown cram-examinations, and other noisy and ignorant fadmongers and fads interfering in any way with the Government of India, or any of Great Britain's possessions. No snatch "resolution" of ignorant demagogues could any more threaten the ruin of a mighty empire. Before three hundred millions of people could be made the plaything of brainless busybodies, their "resolution" had to get itself adjudicated upon by the Imperial Council of the colony, possession, or dependency* it concerned, it had then to be confirmed by the Upper House. Only after such an ordeal could frothy demagogues get their quack nostrums patented and compulsorily applied to the detriment of three hundred millions, or lesser number of millions, of subject nations, of what colour soever they might be. It is most notable that in no single instance did any Jubilee fad-gang ever propose a single useful piece of legislation. Did any of them ever attempt to give the Indian

---

* Page 432.

people practical instead of unpractical education? Listen to a Viceroy, in 1894, after five years ruling the great dependency :— "Education is spreading, and with it the restlessness engendered by superficial and imperfect knowledge, prolific of vague aspirations and ambitions." But, until Carlyle Democritus came, who had proposed to stop the mad cram *de*ducation, and substitute for it plain, practical, technial training, plus just so much true education as was comprised within the three R's? Never a one— cram-stuff prolific of "ambition,"—ambition of the brown lawyer and brown barrister class to imitate the white lawyer and white barrister class, and bring about universal Pandemonium by jaw-government.

Why did Carlyle Democritus ruthlessly exterminate the Indian money-lenders? Listen to the words of the same Viceroy upon the question of settled land tenure, which merciful land-laws (but unhappily inadequate and only half-measures) had tried to bring about for the brown peasants:—"Increased security of land has increased indebtedness;" and another high authority continues: "Land has acquired a value for the purposes of transfer, of mortgage, which it never possessed under native rule. Under British rule land can be mortgaged in many districts, or sold outright. It is suitable that a departing Viceroy should candidly point out the danger to which such increased indebtedness gives rise."

(150)

Danger—viz. of disappearance of the hardworking peasant— and reappearance of the ubiquitous land-devil. Of what good ever to give poor ignorant peasants "fixity of tenure" if you let a pack of cunning money-sharks loose upon them to exploit their labour, their earnings, and their land? Yet, that is precisely what *every* land system must do which does not peremptorily and for ever effectually stamp out and render his trade impossible to the money-lending vermin. It were wiser to turn timid sheep into an open pasture with wolves for collies, than to establish a peasantry exploitable by money-lenders, or other of the shark species. Better no peasantry at all. For, upon such terms, it is but a victim feast of the ignorant and innocent, prepared by fools, for the merciless, the heartless, and the cunning. Either no propounding of a land question at all, or this inexorable answer to it :—

The land is the people's—inalienable, unmortgageable, **unsellable,** non-subdivisible, non-agglomerable. Worse than foullest criminal shall any mortal be adjudged before the law who shall attempt to come between God's earth and its peaceful tiller. There is no other land-devil but such middleman: never mind though Jubilites called them landlords, land-agents, land-factors, land-dealers, land-mortgagers, or zemindars.* They were one vast vampire-class the whole of them, for ever to be extinguished by any wise ruler of men. The land and the land-worker acknowledged only one intermediary—the State, no other, no other for ever. As in the home country, so in the Colonies and in India, temporary help could be afforded by the Land Courts either in money or in kind, but by no middlemen of any sort whatever. The first annual return to the Government, after the establishment of the British revolutionary land system in India, showed a surplus of over fifty millions sterling. A gold standard was introduced which absorbed about twenty millions of the first surplus; ten millions were devoted to extending irrigation works; ten millions were put to general internal reforms; and the balance went to the Imperial revenues. India,—in common with all other states,—had her waste lands, which were all gradually dealt with as work for penal labour and for the settlement of vast numbers of half-caste populations,—till the revolution, a growing danger to the country. The poverty in India was as successfully overcome as it had been in all other of the British dominions similarly treated, and the troops of starving beggars—a reproach to any government—ceased to be. The educational system of the people was completely reversed. The old foolish cram-method which taught the Indian discontent, and little else, was abolished. Thorough technical training, plus simple reading and writing of his native tongue, and English, with a modicum of arithmetic—that, and no more. As for the ignorant radical dreamers who, under Jubilee party government, had raved for government by chattering Parsees, no more was heard of them. Another test than mere talk-capacity was needed to rule an empire of three

---

* Sir A. P. MacDonnell's minute on the cadastral survey states:—"The income of the zemindars (landlords) is now eighty times greater than at the time of the settlement, and the zemindars now take ninety per cent. of the revenue."

"If the increase in the value of the land were taken into account, the land revenue would be twenty millions sterling, instead of three and a half millions."—*Capital* (India Financial Paper), November 1893.

hundred millions of men of utterly conflicting race elements. White talk had nearly ruined Great Britain, brown or black talk was by no means preferable, and had to find other outlet for itself. The system of national insurances which had been introduced into all British possessions completed the Indian reforms.

The Native States were by wise and firm pressure compelled to introduce the land and other reforms into their territories, with a beneficial result to the people, their rulers, and the British Exchequer. Throughout India an income-tax was introduced leviable on all incomes over a thousand rupees a year.

How Carlyle Democritus counteracted the Russian March to India by a British March *from* India?

The honour and prestige of Great Britain under Jubilee Radical-Tory rule, as described by the historian Arminius Vambéry :—
"Party politics in England have so essentially injured the Imperial interests of that country, have done so much harm to England's position in Asia, that the most strenuous efforts of very many years to come may scarcely be able to heal the wounds and restore the respect and consideration for England, so wantonly destroyed by the selfishness of one party in its struggle against the other. The frivolity and short-sightedness exhibited by party of late years, culminating in the famous Egyptian Ophthalmy, was really of such a nature as to make people despair of the results of constitutional life. . . . One might have taken the statesmen, who have been deliberately deceived by Russia, step by step, in Asia, and who have shown cold indifference whilst the prestige of Great Britain was going to pieces all over the world, either as miscreants, or as men escaped from the lunatic asylum. Foreigners, indeed, entertain such an opinion. . . . It is the great misfortune of the country that their political views are biased by party spirit, employed even in cases where it becomes patent that it is not the welfare of the country, but that of the party, which is aimed at. . . . One party undoes the work achieved by its predecessors in power, the progress—nay, even the maintenance, of Imperial strength and power will become utterly impossible. . . . Whilst the English nation were quarrelling about the Why and the How of the measures under

consideration, the insidious bear was quietly trotting towards India."—*Vambéry*.

The duty of Russia as defined by her General Skobeleff :—
"It will be in the end our duty to organise masses of Asiatic cavalry, and to hurl them into India under the banner of blood and pillage, as a vanguard, as it were; thus reviving the times of Tamerlane."

(151)

The duty of the people of Great Britain, as defined by her deliverer, Carlyle Democritus :—" It will be *our* duty forthwith to wrench the banner of blood and pillage from the Skobeleffian Russian bandit host, and yield up to the Imperial Master of said host the broken staff and shredded rags, that he may bind up with them the wounds of his marauders."

When throughout India the domestic revolution which we have described was complete, the 300,000 troops, whose services had not been called upon, were quietly concentrated northwards. Once for all the northern frontiers must be settled, had Carlyle Democritus determined. Russia, marching Indiawards by stealthy steps, by "irresponsible battalions," must learn to comply a little with treaties. Pendjeh incidents, Pamir interferences, defiance of international obligations, must have an end. Hair-pulling from the British Lion-tail, plentiful contempt of the British Lion, all possible when said Lion is hedged in by white-livered Sorry-pebbles and mealy-souled party politicians, but likely to become a dangerous business with a Carlyle Democritus for a people's leader. Once again, not for the first time, have "irresponsible Russian battalions" defied frontier demarcations, and with Czar's approval, or not disapproval, knocked down "poles stuck in sand" on Afghan frontier. Remonstration produces for reply that said raids are " only temporary," " Russia not responsible" for action of ambitious Russian Cossacks, and more poles are tumbled down, and Afghan land encroached upon. The wily Bear-Czar deems the opportunity good : " the revolution at home, revolution there in India, also possible." And so the Afghan territory and other border places are " occupied." When lo ! there emerge from the mountain passes thousands of swarthy Indian troops, British officered, and other thousands of revolutionary British troops, who suddenly overwhelm and annihilate the "ambitious Cossacks, not responsible."

(152)

(153)

Nor do they stop there. Half measures were no feature of Carlyle Democritus's administration. With base and posts firmly established, the British, Indian, and Afghan troops move forward and reach the territory of Czar-land, finally seize Khokand, Merv, and Tiflis, and establish themselves there in force. Other thousands of British and Indian warriors filing double quick on to Russian soil. The despatch of Carlyle Democritus was not lawyer-drafted. It briefly told the Imperial Czar that 11,000 of his Czarship's Cossacks, "not responsible," lay dead, or prisoners around the Afghan "poles stuck in sand," cemented now, Oh, Czar, with irresponsible Cossack blood! British troops, *very* responsible, have retaliated, and now occupy certain of the Czar's territories or protectorates, and will continue to hold them until Russia pays to British Government the cost of repressing the irresponsible depredators tolerated by Russian Majesty, and until definite borderland be demarcated. Threats and manifestoes followed. "War imminent," said all the newspapers. More British troops, meanwhile, file through the Indian passes, the indemnity-money mounting every day. No war came. The cautious Czar perceives, this time, that there are no longer three hundred party things, howling at him on one side of a word-Parliament, and three hundred white-livered other party traitors (or lunatics, say the foreign nations) backing and stroking him on the other side. But in place of those old party curses, there is a united British people, with a non-party Government, loving truth, and determined to stand by their treaty pledges, and determined also that the Czar shall stand by his. And there is also a Carlyle Democritus prepared, if need be, to pour millions of Indian troops into Czar-land, or Czar-protected-land, to compel respect for treaties, even from "irresponsible Russian Cossacks."

The indemnity was paid in full, heavy as it was, and right across the Northern India frontier,—to be for ever impenetrable by British or Russian men-of-arms,—a border-line was defined with unmistakable precision. The line ran from Batoum, in the Black Sea, to Kashgaria, in the Chinese Empire. And the line depended no more upon "poles stuck in sand," but upon the unerring line of the world's fortieth degree of latitude. That famous Carlyle Democritean Treaty cut from recent Russian acquisitions a narrow strip of land taken by her from Persian territory, a larger slice of the South-Western Turkestan country, and a lesser portion of the southern extremity of Eastern Turkestan. That involved a slight sacrifice from Russia. But he who loses invariably has to pay. And it became evident to Russia that with two hundred and fifty millions of Indians, whom Carlyle Democritus would draw freely upon, with Persia, Afghanistan, and the great Chinese Empire, in one league against him, determined to maintain that fortieth degree of latitude as Russia's southern limit,—Czar could not but yield, and so the Treaty got signed, a clause wherein rendered Russia or Great Britain liable to the aggrieved nation in a fine of £10,000 for every armed soldier of either nationality who should dare venture, in defiance of treaty, within twenty miles of the declared neutral territory on either side of that fortieth degree of the world's latitude, which runs between the Black Sea and the Chinese Empire. That ended the march of the Russians towards India. Verily, under Carlyle Democritus, Great Britain was rightly pictured as a lion,—no longer a jabbering ape in shrunken skin of lion,—but a lion of Judah, a lion of truth and justice. No longer to be mistaken for the toothless party mongrel, all slime and crawlingness, of Radical-Tory-Liberal breed, led by Sorrypebble, Davidxhume, & Company. In the same fearless manner had the Egyptian and all other "questions" been overcome and definitely answered. Party diplomatist (lie agent) had spent, over one Egyptian "question," some £50,000, filled innumerable quires of foolscap (literally), wasted a year of time—and produced? Zero! Idiot Khedive boy, and half-a-dozen corrupt pashas and beys, led on by foreign riff-raff of the diplomatic class, for months insulted all British officers and tried to render Government impossible. Effete party contemptibilities looking supinely on, daring no manful act, because its party sicklinesses of the washer-women-missionary, rights-of-women, swindling-director sort,— pledged to evacuation of Egypt, &c., tied Government's hands. Carlyle Democritus sent a squadron of ironclads, landed reinforcements of British troops, and posted up short proclamation:—

"British men and British money have saved this country from anarchy, and the world from wrangling over the spoils of it. Great Britain declares the country under its sole protection, free alike to all men and all nations to honestly trade and sojourn in. Further impertinences from boy or man Khedive, Bey or Pasha, will not be tolerated."

The millions saved to Egypt by the wise British administration were no longer allowed to waste,* to please one or two designing foreign nations. The Government of the country was thencefor- (156) ward conducted entirely by British officials, the native ones having proved incompetent, or corrupt, or both. Wisdom was at Great Britain's helm, and not mere wordiness. Government had been found to have a meaning in it. Govern! Steer! Not "consider" to steer, O lying spirit of circumlocutory Jubilee statesmen.

---

* "The Egyptian Government accounts for 1893 show an effective surplus of £740,000. The Government reserves on Dec. 31st, 1893, amounted to £3,643,000—viz., £2,046,000 of the general reserve fund, £546,000 at the disposal of the Government, and £1,051,000 the amount of accumulated savings from the conversion of the debt. This last cannot be touched for any purpose until the European powers remove what is practically a prohibition of its employment. Proportionately, it is the same as if the English Chancellor of the Exchequer had ten millions in cash, increasing at the rate of three and a half millions, plus compound interest, yearly, yet could not use a penny of it for relieving the burdens, or ameliorating the condition of the country."—*Times*, 1894.

CHAPTER II.

THE ARMY AND THE NAVY.

1. The Army.

(157) SHORT service might have been an admirable substitute for the old system which it replaced; but, like most Jubilee measures, it was marred by its want of thoroughness, its callous disregard of the trained soldier suddenly turned on to an already overcrowded labour market (after the period of service with the colours), there practically to fall into no-work, or pauperism. This sad feature of the system was not altogether ignored, and the inevitable "question" may be found put to Ministers in Parliament, and duly followed by the inevitable Jubilee ministerial reply — a mixture of equivocation, circumlocution, and down-right lying. As an inevitable result, a system good in itself led only to evil for the men discharged. Death and despair let sometimes a sudden and lurid light into the dismal regions of dumb misery:—In Jubilee year 1894 they found the drowned body of a young Dragoon Guard, and brought it to inquest. Then it transpired that the deceased was one of one hundred and sixty soldiers who had endured great distress. In search of employment the hundred and sixty had gone to a Chicago Exhibition to fight in a tourna-
(160) ment there, but that means of livelihood failed, and for some time none of the men had money to bring them home again. How many of those hundred and sixty remained to starve in America, or returned to commit suicide in Britain, the record sayeth not. Charity had organised an Association to find work for the time-expired soldiers. Charity! Not in disparagement of the gentle souls do we speak who bravely did their best to fill the post of duty which the cowardly ministers avoided;—perhaps not altogether avoided, for we find that the British Government did, after plentiful appeal, subscribe to the Association, which had found

employment for 7000 men "paid off," or discharged, by the British Government, the munificent sum of £200. Two hundred pounds! That was Jubilee Party-Government's measure of its duty towards the brave defenders of the country.

(161) All honour to the worthy "Association for the Employment of Soldiers," but what word for the lying War Secretary daring, from his place in Parliament, to answer—by the usual Jubilee subterfuge and evasion—one who asked him: (162) "Will you make no provision to prevent the thousands of men to be shortly transferred to the reserve being turned upon the unemployed market in mid-winter?" Did not our brave Lord Wolseley say, with warm approval of the *Times* newspaper, "One of the most (163) serious complaints that can be brought against the system of Government as it bears on the army is that it does not tell the truth to the English people." "Does not tell the truth!" Far, far from it. Lies, lies, and only lies, everywhere. They cheated the soldier out of his pay, and turned him out to starve after his period of service.

A Lieutenant-General, speaking on the question of discharged soldiers, said that hundreds of them "failing to get work were driven to re-enlist. ... The consequence was that their prisons were full of good able-bodied men, whose chief offence had been that they preferred doing work to remaining idle. To give an idea of the extent to which the prisons throughout England must be filled with these men, at the cavalry depôt at Canterbury alone fifty-one men had been sent to jail since the beginning of the present year for fraudulent enlistment, and there were fifteen more awaiting trial. The greater portion of these men were tried on their own confession, showing that as honest men they preferred going to prison to retaining a secret which troubled their minds."

(164) Space forbids the setting out of all the abundant evidence in proof of Jubilee Party infamy, but this interesting excerpt from the great *Times* may be adequately inserted here:—"It is (158) beyond all doubt that public confidence in the competency of the officers entrusted with the charge of the supply of warlike materials to the Army and Navy has been very severely shaken, and that grave suspicion has been engendered even as to their honesty. Charges of conspiracy, corruption, and malversation have been publicly made by persons of repute and standing. It is no one's

fault but their own, if the officers responsible for the supply of warlike stores to the Army and Navy have fallen under grave suspicion. So far as we can see, they can only escape from the imputation of dishonesty by the admission of incompetence. Matters have assumed so grave an aspect that we should be wanting in our duty to the public if we did not call attention to the accumulating evidence of mismanagement and incompetence. We will take a few specimens from answers given by Ministers of the Crown to questions addressed to them in the House of Commons as to the quality of the rifles, bayonets, swords, carbines, or the ammunition as supplied to the troops under their command. One Minister replied that complaints *of the nature indicated* had been made, and the Department was making 'enquiries.' . . . This is surely a policy of 'immense consideration,' as the Chancellor of the Exchequer might say. Five years' complaints from commanding officers in the field as to the quality of rifles, bayonets, swords, carbines, and ammunition; AND THE WAR OFFICE IS STILL MAKING ENQUIRIES! Nothing is done apparently, BUT ENQUIRY IS BEING MADE. And for all we can see, enquiry will still continue to be made, and complaints will continue to be received, unless the public insist upon ACTION being substituted for ENQUIRY. The Secretary of State declines to publish such complaints as have been received. . . . The Secretary of State assures the world that statements made from the Treasury Bench are made in 'good faith,' otherwise we should be compelled to regard his answer as a *transparent subterfuge*. . . . Of course, publicity would stimulate the War Office into something more effective than a five years' enquiry into defects disclosed in the field, and this would naturally be very unpleasant to the barnacles of the public service. . . . It used to be said that the occupation of barnacle consisted in the cultivation of the art of 'how not to do it.' It now seems to have been developed into the art of *how to do the British taxpayer out of his money.* . . . Is all this the result of sheer incompetence or of something much worse? There is absolutely no escape from one or the other alternative." Those comments (from a leading article in the *Times*) have an especial value, as they apply to a Government not of the ultra-radical sort, but of the Tory description, and should be read by the thoughtful Briton in conjunction with some of the miles of adulation and processional magnificence which, a few months after they were written, illuminated London with their glories, and rendered the word JUBILEE a word of scorn and contempt to man. Those were the Ministers who were the *talking* chiefs of the army. This is a Jubilee newspaper's comment upon the *acting* chief of the Army :—" Who is it appoints our Field Marshal Commanding-in-Chief, and renews his appointment every five years? Are there no other men in England capable of commanding an army? . . . Have we no other Field Marshals for this lucrative post? Why is this septuaginarian gentleman continued at the Horse Guards? Is it for his gallant conduct in the Crimea, or for the exceptionally high state of efficiency to which he has brought the Army?" (15,,)

Will this perhaps explain why a fearless, outspoken, and tried British hero is *not* selected as Field Marshal Commanding-in-Chief, and an absolutely worthless seventy-six-year-old incompetency remained (still in 1894) glued to the post :—

Report of evidence of General Lord Wolseley before the Royal Commission on the Civil Service:—"The tools supplied to the army, taking them generally, are bad, extremely bad. You will find the picks, shovels, axes, and all those descriptions of stores are very bad. The Government of the day cut the prices down so low that inferior articles are purchased. For instance, when we sent out a large number of troops to Canada they took out a number of axes. The only purpose they served was to amuse the people. They were absolutely useless. The pattern was infamously bad. . . . The pattern, of course, was dense stupidity on the part of the people who bought the axes. . . . We buy articles of inferior quality; the price is scamped by pressure from above. I think that our implements have always been inferior. I can remember it is described in Napier's Peninsular War that in our sieges under the Duke of Wellington we used to try and break into the French mines in order to get to their tools, our tools being made of poor metal. From my own experience I can say that the tools we had in the Crimea were bad; and I am quite sure that if you sent to-morrow for an implement called the bill-hook—the common bill-hook that is used in the army—you will find it is made of very inferior stuff, little better than hoop iron. If you chop wood with it, the wood chops it." That is evidence not to be sneezed away by any, except by party-sunk corrupt mud-politicians and those who "think" with them. They neglected and ruined both the materiel and personnel of the British army. We will deal with the personnel first. (164a)

What the lying Jubilee Ministers failed to do, that the Revolution commenced by doing—they prevented the soldier from ever falling into the ranks of the unemployed. Part of the agricultural lands, it will be remembered, were reserved by the state as military lands. Not only were these retained for the reservists, or time-expired men, unable to obtain other employment, or not desirous of emigrating to a British colony, but they were worked by the soldiers during their period of service. It used to be the curse of the soldier that no adequate outlet was provided for the men after their period of daily drill. Some foolish officers tried to fill up spare time by excessive or unnecessary drill, which only provoked mutiny. Wise officers know that over-drill may be worse than no drill at all. Your strained bow is not better than your untried bow. The result was to drive the men for distraction to the public-house, resulting in crimes induced by drink. The public-houses having been abolished, some other means of occupation became imperative. Let it, then, be recognised how valuable was that institution which, whilst it trained the citizen soldier to as perfect a discipline as ever prevailed in Great Britain's army, protected him also from enforced idleness, and retained him as a productive worker, as well as his country's defender.

The minimum period of engagement after the Revolution was twenty-one years, whereof ten years had to be with the colours, six years in the first class reserve, and five years in the second reserve. During his service with the colours the soldier was trained to a trade, or to agricultural service, all the produce of his labour at the farm or factory being absorbed by the army or navy. After the completion of his ten years' service, if the reservist could not obtain employment—a rare event, with the ever-increasing demand for labour—the State offered him continuation of employment in the trade, or farm, he had served in, or free transport to a British colony and settlement upon a farm allotment, free of rent and rates for three years, and subject, after that period, to the rate prevailing in the colony he had selected— a rent or rate never exceeding one tithe of the net produce of the farm.*

If the reservist remained in the military farm or factory, the wages paid to him were only one-half what they were outside,

---

* *See* Land Conditions, pp. 117, 253.

for it was not desired to retain strong men in a service which was only designed to provide against waste of the soldier's time, and to prevent his suffering for want of work after his period of active service was past. As for the Jubilee pension system, it is but an insult to the word "pension" to call it so. Take this as an illustration :—

"William Rogers, aged fifty-six, formerly of the 2nd Dragoons, after eleven years' service, was discharged on a pension of sixpence a day. [Sixpence! Remember that sum, reader, and that the Parliament Minister retired, after a four or five years' course of party-lying and maladministration, on a pension of £2000 a year or upwards.] The old soldier received sixpence a day. He was able to supplement that British Government sixpence by a further half-crown a week, by serving in the Tower Hamlets Dispensary seven days a week from seven in the morning until ten at night—sometimes he had to serve all night. The old soldier, who had bled in the defence of his country, 'lived' for a time on the six shillings a week, but finally could not, and died of starvation. The jury said that that was the way the poor army pensioner often died, and that it was a disgrace to the country, and the coroner agreed with them."

Let the patient British subject contrast the sixpence a day pension, for life service in the defence of his country, with the Duke of Grafton's pension of £20,000 a year for "butlerage to Charles II.," continued down to late Jubilee times, and by a Jubilee Parliament commuted by payment to the Grafton Duke of the sum of £229,000. That is small in comparison with the Duke of Richmond pension, commuted by Jubilee Parliament in the sum of £630,000 odd. The Amherst people received in a similar way and for similar "service" £95,000. The Duke of St. Albans was paid by Jubilee Parliaments £1373 a year for filling the post of "Master of the Hawks," notwithstanding the fact that those interesting animals had ceased to exist in Great Britain; but that did not matter, for the Parliament lawyers decided that "the nation was bound to continue not only to pay the Duke his salary, but also to find him in hawks" which did not exist. For such were Jubilee lawyers. Those are a few of such pensions which Jubilee lawyers and Jubilee Parliaments paid—"memorials of corruption," said the *Times* newspaper, in a comment upon them. Can the British reader picture to himself the venality and utter foulness of the political things capable of the "sixpence a day pension for life service," and the £600,000 pension to a do-nothing duke for a corrupt service performed two hundred years before to a corrupt king? With all this hot in thy mind, O British reader, listen to the story of another State pensioner, for all State pensioners did not die of starvation; some of them died in the workhouse instead, like David Thomas, "a hero of the Crimea, who held the Crimean medal with four clasps, the Turkish medal, and the medal for distinguished services in the field. He fought and bled for his country for twenty-six years, and then was sent by his grateful country to die in the workhouse a pauper!" And your circumlocutory Jubilee Minister "has no reason to believe" (no votes to catch by believing) "that the thousands of reserve men to be turned off in mid-winter" will swell the ranks of the unemployed. He is ready to pension Grafton, Richmond, and other dukes. Let us ask no more.

(169)

Carlyle Democritus materially changed that quaint Jubilee system in every way. The National Insurance included all the forces of the Crown in its wide scope. But in the time of war the soldier's loss fell upon the Imperial Government instead of upon the Insurance Fund. The State pension to a soldier who suffered in the service of his country was to the full equivalent of his service pay, and in the event of his death those dependent on him received the full pension so long as their circumstances required it.*

The standing army was raised to 250,000 men, a large portion of whom were engaged in productive work, and all, on retirement, became workers, and strengthened the State in a double sense. The tone of the militia was raised by more attractive conditions of service, better pay, more efficient drill, and frequent camping with the regular troops. The volunteers were also a particular care of the Revolutionary Government. A system of capitation grant was instituted on a liberal scale, and was made dependent partly upon the efficiency of the volunteer and partly upon the efficiency of the entire regiment. The Government afforded facilities for volunteer regiments to camp and drill with the regular forces, and bore the entire cost of the men and officers

---

* Compare p. 278.

during such periods of training, including transit to and from the camp, etc. But the most notable change made by the Revolution in the military service generally, was the abolition of senile, or juvenile, incompetencies in high places, and substituting at the head of all Military Departments and Commands the ablest officers in the army. Titles, Royal or otherwise, ceased to afford any grounds for promotion. Merit, and merit only, could commend an officer to a post. And in order to prevent future degeneracy in this direction, the Revolution instituted a Military Council having very much the same powers in the army that the Guilds possessed in trade. They had their Courts of Honour, and notably the power—not to appoint but—to bring to the notice of their superiors the merits of any officers, or men, whom they deemed worthy of promotion. These councils enjoyed also the power to make representation against any appointment which sought to set over the army incompetent leaders, or officials. Promotion was rapid after the Revolution, as immense numbers of officers were required for the enlarged Indian, and other Native forces of the Empire; the reduced age of retirement was a further help. After Carlyle Democritus had given to the people of India, Burmah, and all British Dependencies their lands which they tilled, and had raised entire nations out of the extremes of poverty and oppression into independence and content, the loyalty of the subject populations grew beyond the influence of detracting agitators. Nor were these gentry at all tolerated by wise leaders. Native papers, which could not learn to appreciate freedom without degenerating into mere vulgarity of licence, were instantly quashed.

Listen to this excerpt from a very high authority indeed. "In (170) India the press is not representative; it is the creation of a set of instructed—not educated—men, who have obtained their instruction at the expense of the State, and use it for the purpose of vilifying and abusing every officer of the Government who will not fawn upon and flatter the class to which the writers belong. Their hatred of those who are trying to work for the good of the people at large, and not for the exclusive glorification of the Bengali Baboo, is betrayed in every page of their journals."

"Not garbage," my brown friend, said Carlyle Democritus, "can the British Government any more tolerate as adequate food for mind or body." No more of that, O brown or white baboon, (plural and general form of the chattering baboo-species of any colour). Yes, after the Revolution, brown lawyer, barrister, and able editor, had to seek other livelihood than the brown agitation business. Native congresses had to confine their debatings within the loyalties, or betake themselves to more useful work, provided for them in the farm and labour settlements. The age of talk— by white or brown tongues—had passed away. All the Indian troops were British officered, even in the native states, to a wider extent than had ever prevailed before. Similar steps were taken in India with regard to military lands, and the industrial occupation of the soldiers, to those which prevailed at home. The methods differing, in some cases, to meet Indian considerations of caste. Measures were also passed with the Colonial Governments by which their forces were incorporated with the Imperial Army. And when the Indian frontier difficulty—referred to in a previous chapter—came to a head, 50,000 Canadian and Australian men volunteered for service, 30,000 of whom took part in the operations. It was computed that had Russia at that time decided on war, Great Britain could have poured into her territories at least a million men without drawing on the home reserve, or including in these figures the Afghan troops—who had all submitted to British leadership—or the untold hordes of China. A few minor details of the army reforms may be touched upon before closing this chapter. The value of the thoroughness of British manufactures, in all departments of trade, was abundantly well tested during the course of the Indian campaign. The commissariat of the army was as remarkable for the excellency of its officers as for the good quality and quantity of the provisions supplied; and its consequent abdominal strength gave it a marching endurance which tested its boot-leather more than the Napoleonic maxim perhaps contemplated. Although it may seem a detail to add in this history, yet it should have place, as an evidence of the wisdom of the revolutionary leader, who had insisted upon exceptional care being exercised with regard to this portion of the soldiers' equipment. The old English thoroughly-tanned leather was practically a lost art in Jubilee period; but Carlyle Democritus restored it. And amongst the great military factories which he inaugurated, the most important were the military tanneries and boot factories for supplying the forces. Worthy to be remembered also is the law which forbade the wearing, or imitation, of the

Imperial uniform by any other than the Imperial troops. A very necessary law; and it supplies another indication of the miserable degeneracy of the Jubilee authorities that they permitted, in spite of protest in Parliament and out of Parliament, the proud uniform of the national forces to be literally dragged in the gutter by street clowns and advertisement hawkers. It was a common thing in (171) Jubilee times to see poor, half-starved wretches, dressed up in military helmets and tunics, parading the London streets, carrying advertisements upon their backs of some wretched music hall vulgarity. The designer of such brutal travesties was an honoured personage of Jubilee Government, and lifted by said Government, along with the beer-brewers and party politicians, into titledom, instead of being taken down to public whipping with cat-o'-nine tails. Military bands were forbidden to assist in degrading Saturnalia. In Jubilee time one might have seen the regimental band of one of Her Majesty's crack corps taking part in an advertising entertainment for the sale of a poisonous hair-wash. (172) " Ex uno disce omnes."

2. The Navy.

With all the glorious traditions of her fleets which had conquered an empire for Great Britain, compared with which the dear mother country was but as a pearl drop in an ocean of expanse, might not the British reader hope that political corruption would here have stayed its desecrating hand, its lying tongue, its cringing cowardice! But not even here. The palsy engendered by the party politician had touched the nation's heart. And, but for the Revolution, Great Britain's doom had sounded. If any reader of this history be not already convinced of the callous disregard which successive Governments betrayed towards most that was great and good, whilst they pandered to the time-server everywhere, that can only be because a long continued disregard of human worth, of national greatness, of human life, has sunk into that reader and has infected him by generations of political decadence.

But let the real evil be recognised and not mistaken. Let not the British oak tree be confounded with the wood-lice feeding on it. There were not forty millions of political vermin in Great Britain. They were but a class—a dangerous, spreading, much infecting class, but they were not the people. At the core of the nation still beat the pulse-throb of hope for a truer life. The nation longed for its true reformer. It was the calling for the man that brought the man into being. The world of Englishmen cried aloud for a Carlyle Democritus, and Carlyle Democritus appeared. Why did the British sailor in those Jubilee times go to his watery grave in thousands every year? Because the numbers engaged on the sea were large? Or because of unpunished crime, not detected because insufficiently inspected, and which has not a name? Lost at sea in the Jubilee years was one British sailor out of every seventy engaged in the calling. In the ships of Germany only one man was lost out of 128 so engaged; in the Dutch, Italian, and Norwegian ships the average sacrifice

(173) of life was only as one in every 350. Those figures belonged to the merchant navy. But it was the Government duty to remedy them. There *was* a remedy. Was there not also a remedy for another cruel evil of the merchant seaman, that which condemned them to perennial no-work? Read this from the Jubilee Government

(174) *Labour Gazette* of the year 1894: "The supply of seamen is in excess of the demand in nearly all ports of the United Kingdom."

Whereupon in Parliament followed a somewhat unusual "ques-
(175) tion":—

Fierce sea officer, M.P., a navy reserve man, knowing somewhat of the real sea life, no mere party jabbering ape, he, the salt of God's sea and God's truth well in him—"How dare the Government ask British sailors to enlist in the Reserve when no employment is found for them in times of peace because they ask for something better than a bare starvation wage? Only last week one firm of shipowners discharged four hundred of its British sailors to take on four hundred foreigners, and that firm is heavily subsidized by the British Government, but no word of protest, or protection, on behalf of the British sailor. How *dare* you ask the free British sailor to join your Reserve and then send him out to starve?" O fierce son of God and truth, Parliament is not *thy* place. Picture Jesus in Parliament with not one, but 500 Pilates opposite Him, enquiring, "What is truth?" Poor sea hero gets due Jubilee mud-lies for
(176) answer from Jubilee Mud-Secretary to Admiralty, listen:—

"'The Government can do nothing, British seamen are turned off and foreigners taken on because the British seamen 'agitate.'

"Cheap foreign labour is not so particular about sweating wages and bad food as your British sailor." Brave Naval Reserve man, leave jabbering Parliament, and stand by Carlyle Democritus.

The Governments who had languidly shut their eyes whilst Russia stealthily crept towards India; whilst misery, starvation, and disease crept upon her children in slum-courts; whilst the demon of drink besotted the people and soaked them in crime. Of such Governments dare any one hope that there could be wakefulness to the gradual and ominous growth of the war fleets of Great Britain's rivals? Vain hope if such were. Stealthily the nations crept on to the water, as Russia had been creeping on India. Jubilee Party-things, sunk only in lust for power and place. "Awake, my Country," shouted the lion Democritus, "and before it is too late *see!*"

And now let it be told, as briefly as may be, the naval works of the Revolution. The nation was aroused. It was indeed time. In the Mediterranean waters passed the great trade of mighty Britain. Think of the Mediterranean as a wide irregular funnel, through which British trade to India and her other Colonies took its shortest route. The handle to the funnel is Gibraltar, the spout the Suez Canal. All the ships collected in the wide mouth of that funnel passed through the Suez Canal to get eastward. As a measure of the importance to Great Britain to guard that Mediterranean Sea, let it be realised that whilst in the latest Jubilee year of which this history treats (1893–94), two thousand two hundred and sixty-two British vessels passed through the Suez Canal, there went only one hundred and sixty French and nineteen Russian ships. To guard shipping interests represented by her nineteen vessels passing in one year, Russia had, in the Jubilee year 1894, four efficient battleships in the Mediterranean. (177)

To guard her hundred and sixty vessels and their line of route, France had thirteen battleships. And, to watch over her two thousand two hundred and sixty-two vessels, Great Britain had eleven ships of war. But ominous as those figures are, they become more so if the total of war vessels large and small be taken. Of these, France alone had in the Mediterranean, in the year 1894, over one hundred, whilst Great Britain had less than forty. (178)

If we take the whole British shipping and compare it with that of France and Russia, the figures become curiously startling. The value of the merchant navy of Great Britain exceeded one hundred and twenty millions sterling. And the joint value of the French and Russian merchant navies counted for less than the odd twenty millions of the great British service. Add that Great Britain had Colonies and possessions all over the world* to guard and protect, whilst France had one or two, and Russia none. Yet Russia and France possessed a total of 107 ironclads against England's 77. And whilst Great Britain was expending some eighteen millions sterling a year upon her Imperial navy for the protection of that enormous and most noble sea service, the other two powers were within a small amount of the same expenditure on their comparatively insignificant interests.

(179)

(180)

(181)

Glance at this table taken from the Year-Book of the Chef de Bureau of the French Minister of Marine—

Ships.	France.	Russia.	France and Russia.	Great Britain.
Armoured Ships,	66	55	121	81
Unarmoured Ships,	160	72	232	280
Torpedo Boats,	230	180	410	155
Officers,	2,227	1,573	3,800	2,803
Seamen,	41,536	38,000	79,536	42,507

Or at this Jubilee-ministerial confession in a Parliament session of 1894, extracted from the Right Hon. Shuttlecock, M.P., under examination by Brother Radical, anxious for the waning British fleet, but nevertheless walking out of the House when the voting time came—more anxious for Radical mud-Party than British Navy and British Empire combined. Right Hon. British Secretary to the Admiralty :—" Yes, during the last twelve months the tonnage of battle-ships launched was as follows :—

(182)

FRANCE,	30,000 tons.
RUSSIA,	12,000 tons.
GREAT BRITAIN,	*nil.*"

Except to soul-sunk Party cowards, dead to all patriotism, dead to everything but their sordid truculences, could those warning figures be without significance? Here, as everywhere throughout

---

* The area of Great Britain is 121,069 square miles, and the area of Greater Britain is 11,000,000 of square miles, or three times the territory of all Europe.

Jubilee history, the same slime-track of the Party serpent presented itself, which only by crushing under her heel could Great Britain hope to save herself. Oak-tree of sturdy Britain sore beset by political vermin in every crevice of its rugged strength. On all sides the Russians and the French were building as fast as they could—not ships to do brave trade, but war ships. To what purpose, reader? France and Russia were not, and have not yet become, Island-Continents. All Britain was asking, imploring cowardly Party creatures to rouse themselves and build up the British fleet ere it should be too late. Tory and Radical word-machines, one was as worthless as the other. Thus had the British poet hissed at them :—

> "You—you—if you have fail'd to understand
> The fleet of England is her all in all;
> On you will come the curse of all the land,
>   If that Old England fall,
>   Which Nelson left so great.
>
> This Isle, the mightiest naval power on earth,
> This one small Isle, the lord of every sea, —
> Poor England, what would all these votes be worth,
>   And what avail thy ancient fame of "Free,"
>   Wert thou a fallen State?
>
> You—you—who had the ordering of her fleet,
> If you have only compass'd her disgrace;
> When all men starve, the wild mob's million feet
>   Will kick you from your place—
>   But then—too late, too late."

Aye, KICK THEM! No other word for them even from the gentlest and sweetest singer this England ever had. KICK THEM! For heart they had none to pierce. Their conscience was but a maw for gold pensions or temporary place and power. Their brains but diseased fibre, fit to sling empty words upon. What else to do? Where else to apply the brand of contumely, but there—the region emblematic of their utter baseness, utter senselessness.

The London Charivari spoke boldly, as has ever been its wont, of those dastardly Admiralty wizard-enchantments, and it bid the English people change their "Rule Britannia" into :—

"*FOOL*, Britannia, Britannia ruled by knaves!"

and change also its old heroic abnegation into new and craven determination of remaining EVER slaves.

(184)

(184a)

(184b)

Let no man be deceived by the momentary word-humbug of either party, when in what was called *opposition*. A party politician snug in office invented subterfuges, lies, crawlings of every sort. Often—within a few days of protestation that the navy was sufficient for all purposes — the first lords, or liars, of the Admiralty, the Prime Minister, or Crime Minister, would be driven by outraged public opinion to admit the truth, and propose to Parliament to build much needed ships. *In* office, only cowardly lies and subterfuges. *Out* of office, called "*in* opposition," the Party slime-things befouled the other side for not doing the very work they had neglected to do.

Take this as an instance, First Right Honourable Lord of the Admiralty, M.P., "in opposition":—" It is an act of recklessness amounting to madness not to keep the navy strong enough ; *when I was in office I did all in my power to bring before all classes and sections of society the paramount importance of a strong navy.*" That was the Tory Right Honourable M.P., First Lord of the Admiralty, addressing a gullible Jubilee public in the year 1894.

Now listen to the manner in which he *actually* performed his duty, as described by the great *Times* newspaper, in a leading article, at the time when the same Right Honourable First Lord, or Liar, of the Admiralty was "in office ":—"Official assurances are directed with exasperating persistency to points remote from the real issues. Every one is weary of the statistics which the Admiralty is always ready to present . . . *Omissions, misdescriptions, suppressions, and errors to such an extent that no two experts (unless they are in office together) can be found to agree upon them. They are absolutely worthless and deceptive* . . . It is a scandal and a disgrace to the rulers of this country that an official ring has been allowed to deprive us of the advantages of our unrivalled manufacturing capacity, and to enable foreigners to beat us hollow in our own staple industry. . . . *There are ships which have been waiting years for guns,* etc., etc." . . . Those are the *Times* comments on the Jubilee party liar, who, when in office, "did all in my power to bring before all classes and sections of society the paramount importance of a strong navy." That First Lord, or liar, of the Admiralty "in opposition," and his party, were the very persons who maddened the nation by their "omissions, misdescriptions, suppressions, and errors," said the *Times* newspaper, and who by their stolid refusal to strengthen the fleet (until public opinion finally drove them to do it) provoked those fierce Tennysonian lines :—

> "You—you—. . . the wild mob's million feet
> Will kick you from your place. . . . "

Be not misled, good people. Trace all the Party history through, and, except the one great Earl of Chatham (in his first period), they are one crew of waiters upon popular propulsion or compulsion. Away from them quickly. Consider the work of a MAN and turn to what Carlyle Democritus did to remedy the creep of dangerous foreign fleets after British commerce.

It is a pity that the pen can only record in gradual and extended manner actions which are not extended, except in their application to events. Many of the brilliant reforms which this history has endeavoured to describe have had to toil through chapters, in the way that pearls are hung upon a thread. But in the actual doing they proceeded not in sequence, but many of them simultaneously. Thus especially was it with the reforms in the army and the fleet. Long before the period we have reached in this recital, the new legions of the army and of navy men were already drilled and absorbed in the national forces. And the ships about to be recorded were built and speeding everywhere upon the mighty ocean ways. Seeing, then, that Great Britain needed warships for defence and not offence. Seeing also that the strangers were increasing their fleets, not in proportion to the requirements of their mercantile marine, but in ominous proportion to the swelling greatness of England's, Carlyle Democritus, within one day of his establishment in power, set all Great Britain's shipbuilding yards into fervour of construction. Let the puny-souled, of Jubilee-party-creature and peace-at-any-price sort, shudder in their timidness and time-servingness, and pass on, for the record of the Democritean naval building scheme will dement them. The Revolution determined that England's fleet should stand at least in strength as two battleships to one of any of the two most considerable foreign powers combined. But as to armed cruisers, which are only one of two things, protective of a country's merchant ships, or destructive of an opponent's merchant ships —the Revolution determined Great Britain should always be in the minimum proportion of five to one of any two other combined Powers. Accordingly, such the Revolution made law. The reformed Parliament in due course confirmed that Revolutionary law, and to prevent its desecration by any possible future degeneration, made the great rule a part of the Constitution. But Carlyle Democritus had provided that the marvellous little Island, which held an empire in wise sway, should not wait, should start with no possibility that the foreigner should mistake his meaning. Great Britain touched not, nor threatened any foreign nation's peace. Nor should any nation threaten hers. These were the ships which within five years the Revolution added to the glorious navy of Great Britain :—

> Twenty-five first class battle ships.
> Twelve second class battle ships.
> Ten third class battle ships.
> Twenty-five ironclads of the gunboat and coast defence class.
> One hundred small strong steel ram-boats.
> Twenty-five armed cruisers of the first class.
> Ten cruisers of the second class.

And of the torpedo-destroyer sort one hundred boats, besides two hundred of the torpedo type, according to the determination of the Admiralty. Of reserve cruisers we have already spoken. Every merchant vessel, small or large, built to the requirements of the Admiralty, at home or in the Colonies, received an annual reserve-pay of from ten shillings to fifteen shillings a ton. The sea, not the land, is the home of England; her land is the cosy hearth—the sea her work-a-day world. She bridged the seas with her fleets. The child loves its parent for his love; how impotent is that love without protecting strength. Only the just and the merciful should be strong. England had become just and merciful, and the same hand now made her strong. But the wisdom which created the giant fleet did not leave it in idleness, or lingering in ports, or vainly rusting. The great cruisers and the transport ships, when not required for military or naval services, were the "free bridge across the ocean" for British emigration.

Of improved ordnance the fleet at Jubilee times stood as much in need as of added ships, and the Revolution neglected not that grave matter. All the old obsolete muzzle-guns were replaced by breechloaders, and ample reserves were held in all the naval depôts. Ample armaments were also held in readiness for all the reserve cruisers. These also carried guns for training purposes, and periodic gun-drill was gone through by all the crews—that being one of the conditions of the subsidy, which varied from the maximum of fifteen shillings, down to a minimum of ten shillings, according to the class of the vessel, and the expertness in naval drill of her crew.

At Gibraltar, Malta, Cyprus, and all British ports and coaling stations available, docks were built and fortified, and large reserves of coal and provisions stored in them. And—to prevent any future laxness in these reforms—a joint council of the Admiralty and the War Office (no longer presided over by party apes, but by the bravest generals and admirals in the respective services) appointed a staff of ten admirals and generals, whose duty it was once in every year—never at the same period of the year—to visit and inspect every naval station, and report briefly and plainly the exact condition of the places. Their report had to be immediately acted upon and laid before Parliament. The party Inanities had allowed the Fleet and the national armaments, the coal and other stores, and the naval prestige alike to dwindle. The whole fleet was undermanned; but within two years of the establishment of the Revolution, there were over one hundred thousand officers and men serving in the navy, and a reserve, ready for immediate call, of at least fifty thousand, not including the great reserve of the merchant navy. Nor had the wise Democritus forgotten a class of men and officers, too much neglected by Jubilee people, given to forget and neglect the strongest portions of the social frame because not always or easily visible. In modern warships and steamships generally, serving under conditions more trying than those of any other division of the fleets, were a class of men—the engineers, stokers, and firemen—upon whom not only the safety, but the wise manipulation of the ships in large manner depended in storm or calm. Five hundred engineers were at once added to the navy. The pay of all engineer officers and men was raised to the highest scale prevailing in the service; and the engineer officers, according to their merit and and standing, were accorded equality of rank with the highest grades of the service. On all boards or Councils of the Admiralty the corps of Royal Naval Engineers was represented, including the council who carried out the annual inspection of all naval ports and stations. The same care which was extended to the food supplies of the merchant navy protected the Imperial navy also. A wise Government does not neglect the health and strength of the men upon whose valour the national existence depends. Promotion was secured in the inferior ranks by limiting the number of years' service in any one department to periods of fifteen, ten, and five years, for the three lower grades; whilst, in the higher ranks, an age-limit retired commanders, captains, and admirals at from forty to sixty years of age according to their degree. All were retired on full pay, if remaining in the reserve till their sixtieth year, or on half-pay if definitely quitting the service. One object attained by this system of retirement, in addition to the benefits of the healthy system of promotion, was the provision of able officers for the training fleet. Poor England had long expected men would do their duty. MEN *would* do it.

But party-jabbering apes? Of them let no wise man expect other than ruin and decay. Expecting duty from such as they, England had been cruelly enough disappointed.

CHAPTER III.

THE CHURCH: PASTORS OF CHRIST. PANTHEON PURIFIED.

PROEMIAL.

". . . It is the curse of making the Clergy a profession, a road to get on upon, to succeed in life. The base strain is apparent in their very language, too sad an index of what they are. Their '*duty*' what is it? To patter through the two Sunday services. For a little money one of them will undertake the other's '*duty*' for him. And what do they all aim at? Getting *livings!*"—*Froude.*

"The Marquis of——has been condemned by three judges as utterly unworthy to associate with gentlemen. His conduct is so scandalous that he is kicked out of sporting circles with every possible mark of ignominy. But no matter what disgrace has been inflicted, no matter what a flood of filth has been poured over the country, . . . this noble Marquis appoints clergymen to eleven livings. And the Bishops leave this question of private patronage untouched."—*Jubilee Jottings.* (185)

ECCLESIASTICAL INTELLIGENCE.

"Yesterday afternoon the Bishop of Lichfield was presented with a new cope. It is made of red stamped velvet, richly embroidered with gold. The gold band contains figures of six saints *specially connected with the diocese of Lichfield*. The cope cost £500, and was given *to supply a deficit in the Cathedral worship.*" In accepting the £500 piece of mummery, the Bishop said:—

"Considering *the weight of authority* on which the use of the vestment rested [not that I have been able to find any authority for it in Christ, or His simple history], considering also the

324 THE ENGLISH REVOLUTION OF

continuity of its use in the Christian Church [and not considering its utter uselessness, vanity, not to say vulgarity, and not considering that the £500 would have been more aptly bestowed upon the underpaid and half-starved curates, or the wholly starving children of the poor—not considering any of *such* things], how can I do otherwise than accept it? You have asked me to do nothing illegal, and I hope it will help you all, and help me also, to rise above Party. [Party, or a *certain* Party, very anxious to disestablish £500 copes plus six saints on the golden waistband, bishops, and all that belongs to them.]—The "*Times*" (bar (186) parentheses), *Anno* 1894.

(187)   MORE ECCLESIASTICAL INTELLIGENCE. ("*Times.*")

"Prayer was offered yesterday on the occasion of the appointments of the Right Rev. A. R. Tucker, the Right Rev. H. Evington, and the Right Rev. H. Tugwell to be bishops of Kiushiu, Japan; Eastern Equatorial Africa; and Western Equatorial Africa. Last week, the Archbishop of York in the chair, exhibitions were granted to promising divinity students in the Egyptian Ek-Tissad School, and it was decided to take steps for aiding materially the higher education of the daughters of the *upper classes of the Copts*, at a cost of £2000."

Brown and black Eastern people and the Egyptian upper classes thus accommodated with expensive new bishops and exhibitions, by no means wanted by, or necessary to, such people, there immediately followed, under that "Ecclesiastical Intelligence," a statement and appeal on behalf of Eastern *white* people, signed by the Bishop of London:—"The East End Church Fund is nearly exhausted. After anxious deliberation, and with a full knowledge of the sacrifices which its action must entail, the Council has determined to reduce all its grants for assistant curates and lay-helpers [although they were already reduced to about £36 a year!]. It is feared that many of them will be compelled to resign, and this, of course, involves the loss of valuable helpers. The only method of averting such calamities is to 'appeal,'" etc.

No method of diverting those expensive black and brown bishoprics to the salvation of the white slum-people, for whom, continues the "Statement and Appeal," "the demand for assistance is continually increasing, and upon whom terrible poverty is creeping [nay marching double-quick, O London Bishop] . . . for example, here are six thousand people in one parish, with one clergyman working single-handed because a second clergyman cannot be maintained," etc.

Small wonder that an eloquent Canon Scott-Holland in his sermon on "National Penitence," had to say:— (188)

"Nothing is more noticeable and startling than the discovery of the selfishness, recklessness, and cruelty with which even a Church is capable of acting." . . . For was not that Church, even then, that very day, in that year of grace 1894, there in mighty London, the centre of civilized humanity, intent upon Japanese, Chinese, African, Timbuctooese, Indian, and every sort of expensive coloured Bishopric, while its own white curates were starving? Was not that Church itself deriving "rents from slums (189) which were a sanitary disgrace, and from publichouses which fattened on the hideous drunkenness which their blazing gas or roaring heat fed nightly into fever? Was there no room for a plain, straight curse on such sins?" (190)

Veritably, yes, your Canonship, abundant room; and has not a Carlyle Democritus achieved it for you, and sent your archbishops and other panderers, "become the very by-word for arrogance and merciless ambition," down to the slums they fostered, down to the starved stipends they afforded their patient, long-suffering curates? Shortly after that Scott-Holland canonical fulminous, or fulminic maranatha, we find him, under "Fashionable Intelligence," instead of "Ecclesiastical Intelligence"—at a Jubilee dinner-party. And (191) readers may picture to themselves the eloquent divine, after the champagne and the multifarious courses have a little subsided, thus "returning thanks" for the Church, with more or less fuliginous magniloquence:—

"My dear brethren—I beg pardon, my lords, ladies, and gentlemen,—I have been requested to respond to the toast of the Church—so appropriately, adequately, liberally—I make no reflections upon the politics of our host—expensively, warmly, and enthusiastically proposed by the right honourable gentleman, recently at the head of Her Majesty's Government. If at a superficial glance you might conceive that I have any compunction in responding on behalf of an institution of which I said the other day that 'it had arrived at a point where it stood convicted of the most inhuman conduct, harshness, cruelty, greed, and ambition, that it had yielded to the impulse of self-interest, and had become the very by-word for arrogance and merciless ambition;' I can assure you that I have not. You must remember that I uttered those words in a church in the City, and the subject was 'National Penitence.' I appeal to the right hon. gentleman, recently at the head of Her Majesty's Government, who has so eloquently proposed 'the Established Church'—notwithstanding the fact that in another place he was prepared to disestablish what his sapient supporters, the centre and select of the civilized world, called an anomaly. I appeal to the right hon. gentleman to support me, when I say that there is a time for everything,—and that the marvellous compound of saltpetre and charcoal, called gunpowder, must not be blamed because it is used for brilliant effect in the display of fireworks, and for deadly effect in the breech-loader on the battlefield. Nothing in nature is consistent,—certainly not my right hon. friend recently at the head of Her Majesty's Government. He glories in his marvellous ability, which I am sure we all admire, and which enabled him to exalt one day that which he denounced on the morrow. My dear brethren—ahem, my lords, ladies, and gentlemen—that great, that hyper-superlative, that most absolutely essential, all-comprehending, ultraperfect, adoration-compelling attribute of a Jubilee statesman—inconsistency (*loud and prolonged applause*)—must not be thought to be the attribute of the politician only. Ladies and gentlemen, it is the sole deity of this modern world; it is the axis upon which our whole social system turns; it is the Alpha and the Omega of modern greatness. Without it, where would any of us be? I look around me on all sides, and I shudder to think what must occur were I to use that saltpetre and charcoal compound *outside* the Church, as I made use of it *in* the Church. Ladies and gentlemen, I spoke to the people God's truth within the sacred edifice, but—and the right hon. gentleman recently at the head of Her Majesty's Government will bear me out—you *dare* not speak that truth to the people at large. Where would modern statesmanship be if the truth were to be spoken, instead of dexterous platitudes? Ladies and gentlemen (in a deep and solemn tone, somewhat hushed), if we were to tell the people the truth, as the Lord Jesus required we should do, where would the social structure be? Could we uphold our peerages made out of public-houses and the sale of alcohol-poisons, our statesmen raised by tongue agility into power, our wealth and prosperity wrung out of the festering misery of the masses, our archbishops of £15,000 a year, and our starving curates of £35 a year, to be further reduced,—the £35 curacies, not the £15,000 bishoprics? Ladies and gentlemen, I say again, if the truth were told, if we spoke to the people, as we shall have one day to answer to our God, nothing hiding, all confessing— . . . (signs of impatience commence to manifest themselves) . . . Ladies and gentlemen, I will say no more (evident signs of relief). I will only ask you to bear with me, and remember that if I am a Canon in the Church, I am only a sort of toy pistol outside of it. (Loud cheers and soft laughter; music.)"

The Church.

Disestablishment! The political Jubilee Radical Party cure for spiritual, material, and political evils and abuses: a Church filled with ten-thousand-a-year bishops, fat, dual, triple, quadruple, quintruple, and other-uple livings; Christ's poor pastors left poor indeed, even to starvation poor; these doing all the work, those robbing all the honey. Church livings, priestships, advowsons, benefices, put up openly for sale or exchange in the same way as cattle, pigs, and stable refuse; offered for barter openly in the daily papers and special "Church Bazaar and Exchange Gazette," (192) as were they empty beer casks, superannuated pianos, bicycles, and such things. Overpaid ministers *not* ministering, filling pulpits with inanities, twaddle, and windbagisms, and pretending, with much unction, that those were the teachings of Jesus. Was there no cure for all that? No remedy but to cut the great Church adrift? Could no new Luther be found to cut the lies away, and leave the beautiful Christian faith divinely pure, and recognisable by mankind? Was the only possible way to cut the State adrift from the religiousness and the religion which had made it strong in past times, and should make it yet stronger in times to come? Could not we cut the *lies* away? Radical, Anarchic disestablishment panacea is an effective kill, but it is no cure. Was it not the same with the Jubilee Upper Chamber, no longer a House of Lords, only the house of the degenerate sons and grandsons of lords? Was there no wise means of reforming such a necessary second chamber, by wise rule of true lords, instead of no-rule, or misrule, by dummy-lords, or worse, money-lords? "No," said blatant Jubilee Radical Party brayers*—"easier to anarchise lords, second chamber, and national constitution—blow them *all*

---

(193)

* Lest it be deemed that a natural and patriotic abhorrence has unduly warmed the historian against the belittlers of all that was glorious in England, and perilled his impartiality, the said belittlers shall speak for themselves, through the mouth of their high butcher. It is not often given us "to see ourselves as others see us," but in the year of grace 1894, that power *was* given to the Jubilee Radical Party, and the following accurate description of the genus Political Radical was published, unsolicited, by the most typical specimen of them all, the Radical-in-Chief of the United Kingdom :—

"We are ever ready to grovel before a lord who will condescend to notice us. A Radical who has spoken to one of those lofty beings drags the act into his conversation, and would have it believed that he and his lord are intimate friends. We are a race of snobs, and we are never so happy as when we can indulge in an orgie of snobbism. Look how your Radical rejoices when he can get a lord to preside over some local festival, how he beams when he is talking to one, and how elated he is when he secures the smallest shred of a title for himself." We may complete that candid confession by adding other marked characteristics of the species; for, in addition to their tendency to grovel before mere wealth and titles, was a far more fatal tendency, indeed, the very fatalest of all tendencies—an inability to appreciate true merit anywhere. The mere sight or sound of heroic action amongst their countrymen sent them into fits of uncontrollable vituperation. In exact proportion to their fetish-worship of the foul was their abhorrence of true merit or greatness. The Radical-in-Chief, who drew the above faithful picture of his political crew, also defined his own methods of attacking British volunteers who sacrificed their lives on the battle-field in the service of the Empire. He deemed it his radical "duty" "to publish every statement calling his attention to any misconduct on the part of the British forces." . . . Such trifles as enquiring into the *bona-fides* of the lying statements, he held to be quite unnecessary ; he entered, therefore, into a "campaign of misrepresentation, malevolent guesswork, and anonymous, or unsupported slander ; adopted and circulated broadcast, in an undiluted stream of calumny, accusations of odious crimes by anonymous or irresponsible slanderers, whenever the pioneers of British colonization were concerned." This arch-type of the Jubilee mud-Radical M.P. boasted (all these excerpts are from the *Times* newspaper, which the Radical-in-Chief had himself declared to be without bias in the matter)—that "if none of the charges he had published against the brave men fighting under the British flag were true, he would still continue to call those British officers and men, murderers, marauders, ruffians,

(194) and riff-raff." Seldom indeed in this world has a foul-souled Jubilee politician so accurately illustrated the truth of the proverb : "The cuckoo calls its own name." We will not soil a history destined to live as long as English wisdom lives by quoting his other patronym. The Revolution relegated the whole Jubilee Radical crew to their proper place in the British Constitution, as a reference to the reformed Parliament will make abundantly clear.

up, that is easier than reform." Destruction is so easy, reform so difficult. Any fool, even a Radical fool, can destroy—but wisdom alone can reform—and wisdom was not in the Radicals' line of business. Need wise souls, or true souls, have to consider much upon such methods? Were it not more profitable to a pure heart to consider how far downward towards the abyss his nation was speeding, led by Anarchy in disguise? The Radical Anarchists used not a glass or an iron infernal machine; but they used an infernal machine beside which the iron and glass instruments were as children's toys. The Radical infernal machine bore the Devil's seal unmistakably upon it; it was a compacted imbroglio of futilities compounded by ignorance, cupidity, and often enough rascality, put up and packed in harmless-looking guise, and carried by the ignorant and dishonest—assisted occasionally, unfortunately, by the honest and well-meaning, but very simple—for a little time—until the internal mechanic clink startled them, and they cut their foul acquaintances and *their* methods of world reformation. Disestablishment! The patent Jubilee quack panacea for all evils: poor Ireland robbed, oppressed, down-trodden, bled by absentee partridge lords, the peasants evicted from their fields, left to penury and starvation generation after generation. Was no wisdom of just government possible for those poor Irish peasants, no settling them justly upon their land, and abolishing absenteeism for ever? No; that is the remedy of wisdom and of justice, not of Jubilee radicalism. Jubilee radicalism would "disestablish" Ireland, would give her a Government crew of pirates, of the political moonlighting, cut-throat, dynamite, dancing-master, publican class, and call it "Home Rule." No other method known to Anarchy-radicalism. Their cure for a nursery full of ill-treated children was not to punish the wicked nurses, and substitute just and wise ones, but to take away the nurses altogether, and let the children "rule themselves," with just a sufficiency of moon-lighting brigands placed at the doorway, with daggers for the parents' backs and thongs for the children. Must your noble oak perish because of the woodlice on it? Or will you not rather brush the vermin off, sulphur-smoke them off if need be, destroy *them*, but spare the tree? Bethink ye, O English Nation, it was not a little thing, that divorce, which Jubilee Party creatures were howling to consummate. Of all the desolation of inanity, ignorance, and corruption, national-spiritual-suicide, that of the divorce between a State and its religion is the saddest, fatalest. Anarchy, which reared its cowardly head in all directions towards late Jubilee times, knew but one method, one treatment for all diseases—and that treatment was death. Jubilee radicalism's one Gospel was comprised under the fatal watchword of universal Disestablishment. Remove your vermin by burning down your whole oak forest! That was the political-Jubilee-Radical method. Effective vermin cure, it is true, but— There is always that little word remaining; what about an after-forest of weeds instead of oak-trees? Verily a vermin-laden oak-tree is preferable to mere waste thistle-growth, or noisome poison-weeds. It was not by disestablishment that a Carlyle Democritus would cure anything. Rather by re-establishment. Under the Anarchy cloak of Church Disestablishment lies hidden the foulest fiend of all the Satan-crew—indifference. A friend, an enemy—the one for sweet counsel, the other to teach you many necessary things, wise caution, constant readiness, preparation; and to wean you from all soft indulgences, most of all from sick indifference. Neither friend nor foe, but the thing between, the lukewarm thing, the father of every evil over hell, he who stands on earth to intercept men's energies from producing righteousness; the ubiquitous steriliser; of that lip-smiling fiend, let all brave men beware! Indifference is a Jesuit robe, capacious, even wide enough to find temporary shelter for every evil under the sun. Indifference is the eldest-born of Disestablishment. There are some who are quietly fostering the Disestablishment fiend with considerable inward chuckle, viz. your Jesuits. They hunger for just that Radical garbage to feed upon. Given Disestablishment indifference for just one decade, and you may see resuscitate (for carrion easily breeds) popes and cardinals, monks and friars, to hack you once more in Inquisition torture-holes, *auto-da-fé* burnings, Smithfield bonfirings, and St. Bartholomew massacres; cowled Spanish fiends to hack your tender women and little babes, in order to impress God's mercy on them; Italian popes twisting maidens' hair into Cenci-ropes, drawing them limb from limb, all in the name of the Pope-God. Those are some of the things which stand waiting outside the door of Disestablishment.

Is there then nothing between the divinely simple Christ-teachings and the coalescence of abuse, lies, make-believes, hypocrisies, and cant which have crept into the Church of England? Fat and omniverous as the priest-lice are, cannot we mend *them* without burning down the Church along with them? Fifty thousand pounds, eighty thousand pounds, say the papers, in Jubilee times, easily found to start new bishoprics; sixty thousand little Board School children, say the same papers, were meanwhile starving, forced to the schools every day unfed. O Divine Spirit of the ancient Hebrew people, Thou who hast said "Suffer little children to come unto Me," what were the mockings of that ancient ignorant mob compared with the devil-cant mockings of these Thy pretended followers? Thy humble disciples turned into fifteen-thousand-pounds-a-year archbishops, plus palaces and parks, and Thy little tender children crying for food. "O Thou mighty Spirit of unending sorrow, whom to name by such as pretend to teach in Thy name is sacrilege, enlighten the people who suffer, to know the true teacher from the false one, for ever more." Thus spake Democritus as he opened up the purest book which the world possesses, the book which records the life and death of the sweetest Son of God who ever walked this earth. And he searched in vain in that book for the Thirty-nine Articles, for the fifteen-thousand-pounds-a-year archbishops, for the priestly palaces, for the . . .

Then he searched the English priesthood, and he found many exquisite souls, pure as the Master required them to be, poor, poorer than He willed they should be, some of them nigh starving. Also he found a motley crew of archbishops, bishops, archdeacons, deacons, deans, canons, vicars, rectors, curates, such a host of "venerables" and "reverends" that he wondered the Church branch had not fallen from the Church tree with the mere weight of such a host.

The Jubilee Church contained upwards of 20,000 of those assorted gentry, with salaries varying from £15,000 a year, with two parks and two palaces, down to £50 a year* and one slum tenement — the latter posts often occupied by the best of men,

---

* Here is an interesting excerpt from the *Times*:—"The speeches of the Bishop of Peterborough are always eagerly read for their combination of sound sense, eloquence, and racy humour. With regard to the impoverishment of the clergy, he says that this difficulty may be met by a distribution of Church incomes. He proposes to meet a glaring inequality which exists at present, when we have incomes of £15,000 at one end of the scale, and of £50 at the

who cheerfully sacrificed their lives for the poorest and weakest; true pastors of Christ they. One such died in the year 1894, quite a young hero-priest, from overwork amongst the diseased and suffering, and the Jubilee papers truly enough called him a modern martyr; he had asked in vain for help from stepmother Church. And there were many such. Was a Church which contained such martyrs to be destroyed, or were not the pure rather to be chosen from the impure, and not left to starve and overwork, whilst meaningless pomposities outraged their Master's teachings by their mere existence?

(198)

The Jubilee Church income from all sources was eight million pounds a year; some authorities put it at ten millions. But let us adopt the humbler figure. It accounts for the salaries which the Revolution established for its pastors. Twenty thousand pastors, and eight million pounds would give them all £400 a year That was the irreducible, and also the irre-increasable, pastor stipend. Not gold trappings, place-allurements, money prizes, may a Christ Church offer. Those are the prizes of Mammon-worship, not of Jesus-worship. The only "attraction" that a pure Church may offer to its servants is that divinely and humanly beautiful attraction: "Power to serve thy fellow-men." No nation worthy the name will ever lack such service. Great nations have always had those servants, with or without pay, oftenest the latter. Great Britain beyond all nations has had them, and will continue to have them. When the day can come, and England seek in vain for such service, there will be no longer a Great Britain, but only an infinitely Little Britain, a despicable and disappearing Britain. Never to come such a time, may it please the Eternal Guardian of mankind.

(199)

Not only was there only one stipend for the pastors, but only one title was there also. Could a better, nobler, be conceived? Pastor—a spiritual feeder *of* the people. Not a material feeder *upon* the people. Pastor—a shepherd of the people; verily, a pure and homely title. Not to be without meaning either. The Revolution estab-

---

other. He wants to see the Church funds treated as one united whole. . . . *Undoubtedly some scheme for the redistribution of clerical incomes must be undertaken,* either by the Clergy themselves, or by the State. . . . *What must be done is to establish some kind of relation between the work done and the money received.* It is monstrous that a clergyman should be condemned to work in a town parish of ten thousand souls on £200 a year."

lished Shepherd Guilds, very much as in all other callings there were Guilds. They had also their Courts of Honour. The whole subordinate to the Government, through its Minister of Public Worship. One inestimable value of those Pastor Parliaments was the prevention of rust or decay. It was through the medium of them that the Revolutionary Government finally brought about its great Church Reform. The Jubilee Church was quite hopeless as far as expecting reforms of it to come from within. Let us see what the new pastors, without palaces, with a Revolutionary Government at their back, were able to do. They inquired into those Thirty-nine Articles, and found them empty things, dried shells without a kernel; mere worn-out wrappings, serviceable to no man. For the soul grows as the body grows. It will not do to try and cover the full man's nakedness with mere infant swaddlements, nor the full man's reason, as for ever developing, in pristine dogma-futilities.

In the realm of matter much can happen in three hundred years; and no less change occurs in the human mind in such a period. Yet did the Jubilee bishops and parsons pretend that the "Thirty-Nine Articles," which the stress of furious religious warfare against the corrupt Cenci-torturing Romans rendered necessary in the years 1562-1571, required no change, and that they were "believed" by them, as facilely as they were subscribed by them— in the Jubilee year 1894. The great Universities had already, some years before (1881-88), revolted against the mummery, and were freed from them, but the bishops and their crew mumbled on, in the impossible nakedness of the threadbare Thirty-nine Article garments, no more able to cover their or any sane men's mind developments than thirty nine infants' swaddling-garments could cover their body developments. The Revolution cast them away for ever. Freed the human soul of such unrealities, and gave them healthier fare—the divine Article itself as in the pure, wise Book propounded.

They considered also the worn-out Trinity theory, and they got that and the Ghost well buried, for long since were they dead. They reverted everywhere to the pure and simple Jesus lesson, as it stood long before vain traditions spoilt the Divine MAN Jesus into the impossible God Jesus. Prophet he, Christian, Mahomet, Moses, Confucius. Not the Godhead, but His beloved servant upon earth. Teach *that* to the people, O pastors, Christianity that will be of the purest, loveliest. Can ye not see how warmer the heart can beat to human sacrifice which a people *can* understand, than to myth-jargonings which the teachers believe not, nor the people comprehend? Open the way of the people to communion with their God. Has not Luther broken the pope idol worship? Let us further his good work, said Carlyle Democritus, and break down the worst of all idolatry—book idolatry,—whereby from Trinity-myths and Holy, or unholy, Ghost impossibilities, a pure Christian deism may become again visible, realizable, and actually believable of men.

In Jubilee times there were churches never visited in centres (Cityward, and other), where the populations had disappeared, yet where a puppet bobbed to empty benches and performed, for huge pay, at stated intervals, sundry unrealities. All such churches were closed, and the sites sold. And where new centres of population had arisen and no churches were, churches, State built, arose.

In the church all pastors wore a simple gown of the college rector sort, but out of church they clothed themselves like other sane men. All monkey dressings of the lawn sleeves, coloured silks, and such woman fripperies had to get themselves effaced. Any conduct unbecoming a spiritual minister quickly relegated him to lay business. There was no appeal from *that* law. Preaching was not confined to the pastors. Earnest men of wisdom could be invited by the congregants, through their wardens and committees; or if no wise preacher, clerical or lay, was to be had, sermons were dispensed with. For poison is not better than no food, either for the physical frame, or the intelligent soul. The collecting plate was abolished—money collecting not being commended in God's temples; strictly forbidden, indeed, both by the Christian Book and Carlyle Democritus. The State made good any requirements in the money line. If a State cannot support its Church, that State had better abdicate itself.

The Revolution abolished all abuses of the Church, and restored to it its exquisite simplicity, as the Great Master taught it—pure, unselfish, without arrogance or ostentation, divinely just. No £15,000-a-year parsons shaving their flocks, but worthy £400-a-year pastors feeding them. It was required of the servant that he should follow a little the life-example of his Master, whose divineness of self-immolation, self-abnegation, self-renunciation, he elected to teach to his fellow-men. All so-called training colleges for priests were abolished; but in all schools and colleges there was a "Divinity side" where the young pastors were trained, not apart from, but together with, the men whom they would have always to live with. Other training may make cant-machines, but not fearless, free-thinking men. Religion is not a garment only for Sunday wear, but is the very atmosphere of the human soul, and requires of the spiritual doctor abundant acquaintance with humanity, and not mere dogma cant-acquaintance. Carlyle Democritus left to the new pastors and their flocks the whole business of reformation; and it was not he, but they, with the characteristic wise, sober, earnest manfulness of the British people, who cut away the old priest-cant from the Established Church. Carlyle Democritus had only cut away the cant-*priests*. They being gone, cant soon followed. All that jargon which had been characteristic of them disappeared as absolutely as if all England had been visited by another Luther. He who had knocked the bottom out of the lying popes, saints, virgins, relics, and other Macbeth witcheries, had his work consummated by the Revolution, until finally they laid make-believe stone dead. In all that concerned mere doctrine, neither Democritus nor the Revolutionary leaders interfered. They were satisfied to abolish the abuses of the Church, its sale and exchange of livings, its glaring and monstrous corruptions. *That* quite complete—an abolition of all titles and powers outside their immediate duties, and an institution of 20,000 worthy, pious, and righteously paid men, in sympathy with the people—he knew well enough that wise reforms could not but follow.

But there was one matter which the Revolution left not to the slow hand of a multitude. Carlyle Democritus having cleaned out the living abuses from the Church, next proceeded to clear out dead abuses. Great Britain had her Pantheons, but by misuse they had become far other than homes of gods, or heroes. In Westminster Abbey there were hundreds of allegorical insipidities in stucco, stone, or marble; hundreds of saints, apostles, virgins, and such articles; untold hundreds of Fames *plus* trumpets, heathen deities, negroes, Indians, dogs, dragons, and other grotesqueries. Read Sir Gilbert Scott upon all that. St Paul's and Westminster Abbey were crowded with lying epitaphs and muritaphs of not heroes, but mere **mammon-folk, politicians, and empty-title-gentry** generally. The Revolution clean swept away every one of them. It appointed a council of the wisest and best men in the land, and according to their decision it dealt with the London Pantheons and all churches throughout the country. Only truly heroic names and monuments were left; and some of England's best and bravest who had *not* been there were quickly and worthily given presence. Amongst the most notable of these were Cromwell and Carlyle. In Jubilee time the people thought the Pantheons full, but after the great "delivery" it was found that there remained ample room for many centuries of British heroes. A law was passed soon afterwards which prevented any interment in the Abbey, or St. Paul's, or the erection of any public memorial until twenty years after the death of a national hero. After that time your mud-god will cease to be resplendent, whilst your real hero shines ever brighter. With such a wise law a national Pantheon need not fear to become overcrowded. It need scarcely be added that the Church reforms extended to, or were adopted by, all British Dependencies, and that the bishops of the Otaheite and Borrioboolah-Gha type effectually disappeared. Missionary gentlemen were allowed to continue their harmless and useless enterprises, perhaps not harmless though useless, in common with the searchers after the North Pole, and other voyages to the great inane. But the State Church funds were not concerned. The State found quite enough to do in converting the wicked of its own people, and left better-regulated nations to tolerate missionaries if they listed. But on no account would the Revolution permit the misdirected energies of its fad-people to provoke it into war, or warlike attitude ; and it gave the Chinese and all other nations clearly to understand that the missionary persons were doing business on their own account, and not by any means on that of Great Britain, or with their approval:

CANT lay dead, but *not* lamented.

It may be mentioned here that not only were all Churches "jail-delivered" and all records of the Great Unknown and the Little Well-known scraped and scoured away for ever, but public street monuments were treated in like fashion, and all of them that did not commemorate true heroes well moved off. York Column vacuity, scores of political zeros, money dukes in stucco, stone, or bronze, in entire regiments, disappeared as effectually as their types in flesh had been made to do. On the other hand, many noble and worthy memorials of the truly great were added and multiplied. And where inadequate or inartistic memorials of good men existed, they were replaced by the best that good taste and high art could devise.

Complete tolerance was extended to all religious denominations, but they were not permitted to interfere with, or infringe upon the laws of the country. Thus, while they were free to teach the children of those who intrusted them to their care their various tenets, they were not permitted to fill the child's mind with lies by torturing History or Science to suit their futilities.* Even Jesuit nunneries, mummeries, and monkeries were tolerated, but they came under the merciful law of all private asylums—lunatic, dogmatic, or *any*atic. Government commissioners visited all such establishments and examined every individual inmate; and upon evidence appearing that any incarcerated person desired his or her liberty, such an one was forthwith removed by the commissioners, without any opportunity being afforded to the Jesuits, or such people, to coerce, or further mentally torture the victim. Such a released person was protected by the State, made its ward, whilst under age, and retained at a Government school and protected against "undue influence." For the first six months after release from one of those so-called religious establishments, no persons, other than the Guardians appointed by the State, were permitted access to the released victim. Any attempt by a religious, lunatic, or other asylum to evade the law rendered such asylum liable to immediate suppression.

---

* Page 364.

CHAPTER IV.

WOMAN.

I.—*Jubilee Women and Children.*

Is it well that, while we range with Science, glorying in the time,
City children soak and blacken soul and sense in city slime?
There among the gloomy alleys Progress halts on palsied feet,
Crime and hunger cast our maidens by thousands on the street;
There the master scrimps his haggard sempstress of her daily bread,
There a single sordid attic holds the living and the dead;
There the mouldering fire of fever creeps across the rotted floor,
And the crowded couch of incest, in the warrens of the poor.

 · · · · ·

      This is fixt
As are the roots of earth and base of all;
Man for the field, and woman for the hearth;
Man for the sword, and for the needle she;
Man with the head, and woman with the heart;
Man to command, and woman to obey—
All else confusion.
For woman is not undevelopt man,
But diverse: could we make her as the man,
Sweet love were slain.   —TENNYSON.

IN theory many things are beautiful which in fact are singularly unbeautiful. In theory the Jubilee woman was perhaps the most enviable creature upon God's earth. She was "free," "emancipated," had "rights," was redolent of adoration, the object of man's protection and veneration; was, in fine, that highly delectable being which theoretical perfection invariably is. "England," said the Continental people, "is the Paradise of women."

It behoves sane men to inquire what the status of the Jubilee woman *actually* was. In nothing anywhere in the world was the contrast between truth and semblance of truth, pretentious theory and sober fact, more overwhelmingly poignant and humiliating—unless perhaps in the Church—than in the condition of Jubilee womankind.

In the two centres of European civilisation representing the most polite and the most free of Christianised humanity—France and Great Britain—there were in Jubilee times some quarter of a million of women ostracised from all that was ennobling and pure, sunk in the social ban of irrevocable damnation. Condemned to a life of degradation unnamable. Was it love which attracted them thither? Passion? Inclination? Temptation? Or was it *WANT*—the grim, the terrible, the protean monster of "civilisation"? Jubilee misery forced the woman into the earth-hell—the Piccadilly mud-fires—and the Jubilee social system *kept* her there. Let us try and realise the alternative occupations which Jubilee civilisation offered to the poorer classes of womankind. And, remember, you of the lighter kind, prone to believe in the facile doctrine of "slums made by the slum-dwellers," remember that there are not two kinds of women in the flesh, though infinite in variety as education and circumstance may make them. In this they are all one, viz. — that the God who made them willed them to be the weaker of human kind, the weaker in order to invoke the protection of the strong. Be not misled by the ravings of Jubilee rant-idiocy of the political radical or any other type. True, they invented a hybrid variety of non-male monstrosity, by pumping the bosom nutriment into the brain organs, and called it strong-minded-woman class—tough of skin, voluble of tongue, but that was not a branch of *womankind*, only of abortive, radical-political-economy *malekind*, a type of infinite degradation.

It is essential to the right understanding of a problem that true men be got to look at fact, and be not misled by mere *semblance* of fact. You may paint wood so cunningly that it will look like iron to the casual observer, but yet the axe will cleave the wood as it will not cleave the iron. Those Jubilee things who could only demolish a Church and not reform it; destroy an Empire instead of govern it; pull down a Parliament instead of purge it, did not stop at trying to corrupt and unsex their women, in lieu of elevating and ennobling them. Let us glance at some of the trades that Great Britain put its tender women to. And we are not misusing the gentle adjective. It is the divine order of humanity. God's wisdom protected His Divine masterpiece with weakness and with delicacy, as He surrounded the sweet flowers of the mimosa with leaves of infinite sensitiveness; as He made the leaves of the aspen-poplar tremble before a warm summer breath. He turned the man's hard breast into the yielding woman bosom—the living child-rest and lifespring; the stern and fibrous man skin into velvet smoothness in the woman; the hard, irregular muscle of the man into the dimpled roundness of the woman. Such was woman as God made her. Look at her as the Jubilee governing classes made her:—

Upwards of twenty thousand young girls and women were employed in the manufacture of iron nails, anchor chains, cutlery, bolts, screws, rivets, and other iron and steel manufactures, from the age of ten years and upwards—at ages when the Jubilee bishop's child had scarcely emerged from the nursery; when the minister's child knew nothing harsher than to be deprived of a mother's kiss. At the mines there were 4,700 women at work; 26,000 women were to be found in the earthenware and glass factories (not only in the lighter departments). Three hundred thousand women worked in cotton mills, 89,000 as tailors—displacing men; 13,000 were cabinetmakers, upholsterers, French polishers, etc. Those are a few of the trades and manufactures in which women and young girls were employed in Jubilee times, in nearly all cases displacing men, "because their labour was 'cheaper'"—a rare consideration in Jubilee times. This fact is proved by the census return, which showed that whereas the percentage of female workers above the age of ten years had largely increased during one decade, the percentage of male workers had at the same time decreased.*

---

* "It is often stated" (says the *Census*, Vol. IV., page 58, 1893) "that women are, owing to the smaller wages they will accept, gradually ousting their male competitors out of their occupations, and there can be no doubt that in some industries such a substitution of female for male labour has occurred in the course of the last thirty years. Occupations that require great muscular strength are [*should be,* you mean, O Government compiler of the census returns] practically confined to men. There are, however, some occupations in which the opposite is the case. The following is a part of a list of the headings in which the female sex outnumber the males:—

"Bookbinders; pin-makers; steel pen-makers; fusee, fireworks, and explosive articles manufactures; worsted stuff manufacture; flannel-blanket manufacture; silk, satin, velvet, ribbon manufacture; cotton

But if we condemn the employment of girls and women in such delicate manufactures as ironware, glass, cutlery, tailoring, boot-making, etc., what measure of denunciation do those deserve who employed young girls in such cruel callings as match-making, lead and litharge factories, the glazing of pottery, and other such works. Let the civilised reader consider these things, taking as illustrations by the way these notes from coroners' inquests :—
"Frances Louisa, aged twenty, employed since her sixteenth year (201) at the Imperial Enamel Works. The girl had suffered on many occasions from lead-poisoning. The body was emaciated and pale. Verdict—Death from lead-poisoning." "At the Thames Police Court an Inspector of Factories summoned a Lead Company Limited for employing a girl of fourteen years. He said it was 'singularly unfortunate' for the said Lead Company Limited that within a period of six weeks he had attended the inquests of six persons who had worked for them." "Two sisters worked in (202)

---

goods manufacture; flax linen manufacture, fustian manufacture; hemp, jute, and cocoa fibre; net-makers, canvas, sackcloth, and sacking; machinist and machine-worker, hosiery manufacture," etc., etc., etc.

The Government of the day were aware of these facts, for they quote some of them in their *Board of Trade Labour Gazette*, Vol. I., 1894; also these further statistics :—

"EMPLOYMENT OF WOMEN IN 1881 AND 1891.

"It appears from the census returns that the number of women and girls returned as 'occupied' out of every 10,000 females above ten years of age in England and Wales shows an *increase* since 1881 of thirty-seven per ten thousand, which compares with a *decrease* of ten per thousand in the case of males."

"The number of young girls between the ages of ten and fifteen employed in 1881 were 1506 per ten thousand of the population, according to age periods. In 1891 the proportion had risen to 1626 per ten thousand. Between the ages of twenty-five and forty-five the employment of females had increased from 2900 per ten thousand in 1881 to 2960 in 1891; whilst during the same period the employment of males between those ages had *decreased*. In contrast with the increasing employment of young girls there was a corresponding falling off in the numbers employed above forty-five years of age, both as regards male and female workers."

Amongst the trades which were employing cheap girl-labour, and ousting male labour, the same authority quotes :—"Tailors, increase 25 per ten thousand, against a *decrease* in the case of males; increase of female labour in boot and shoe manufactures, against a considerable decrease in the case males; and similarly with regard to drapers," etc.

another lead factory for a few weeks at a time, and then succumbed. After recovery, they would work again, till one of them, at the age of twenty, could go no more, the lead-death having overtaken her. (203) They earned from twelve to fifteen shillings a week when they could work." "Another, a mother of six little children, went also to the lead business, driven to it 'because her husband was out of work; she knew the work was risky.' She must feed her children; but the poison attacked her, and she could go no more. The doctor told the court that he had at that moment under his charge five young women all so poisoned, one of them under sixteen years of age. He said a great number of such cases came under his notice, in which women were ruined for life. The coroner said the lead occupation was the most dangerous he knew of, and the jury said the state of things was most appalling," and . . . and all over Jubilee England the horrible toll was being exacted from tender girls and young women. Were it necessary, this volume could be filled with the cruel records of such ruined lives, the tribute of God's tenderest creatures to Jubilee mammon-worship. Between your lead-poisoning, phosphorous-torture, enamel-death, and the Piccadilly-pavements, was there not a way? Could you not starve, O children of the poor? Ye of the gentle sex, brought into the light of day in dens of Slum-land, knew *ye* of the "Paradise of women" which this England is said to be?

Now, if there is one authority in Great Britain who may be said to be unimpeachable on a question of this kind, it is the British Government (never mind how unconsciously it is incriminating itself); and if there is another authority as entitled to be heard upon such a question, it is the *Times* newspaper. When these two authorities are combined, they compel the attention of all thinking men and women. Listen, then, to these authorities upon (204) the condition of workers in the Jubilee period. This is an extract from a *Times* leading article:—

"The Board of Trade Report on the condition of the South Staffordshire and East Worcestershire nail-makers raises by its facts an imperative demand that something be done. From time to time every industry is subject to depression, with sad consequences to those engaged in it. Colliers may be ill off without any fault of their own. Weavers suffer for a period from a cotton famine or a glut. Coventry ribbon-makers may be brought to pauperism by a caprice of fashion. [Mark the comfortable way in which this is accepted: "the established order of things."] In the East-end itself penury practically is permanent. [That is quite a natural order of things.] But hunger, grinding toil, hopelessness, and an utter privation of the pleasantness and beauty of human existence are the enduring and constant characteristics of an unchanging population in groups of villages in the neighbourhood of Dudley. Cottage workshops might be supposed to offer the happiest aspect of manufacturing industry. But we find in the privacy of home, children under fourteen labour all day long without fear of or hope from legislative prohibition. Married women, with large young families, wield heavy hammers for twelve or fourteen hours a day. Their infants are left to themselves, or are cradled on the bellows or a rafter of the ceiling. For a pittance of four or five shillings a week mothers abandon their duties and instincts of affection, and do the work of slaves on a Cuban plantation. Their husbands, though they cannot work harder, are as wretched. Except drink, they have no variety in their lives. There is no grace. Their houses are gloomy and unspeakably dirty. Their wives generally are robbed of all feminine attractiveness, and are more ignorant of housekeeping arts than savages. Wages have been diminishing continually, and neither men nor women attempt to fight against the fall. They only toil the more without ceasing. They are born to be nailers, to blow huge bellows, and operate ten to thirty pound weight 'olivers' from morning to night; to be skinny, wan, flat-chested; to breathe fetid air; to account butchers' meat once a week a luxury; and to be deafened with the perpetual babel of rasping sounds. That is their fate, and they accept it. That is the nailer's life for a dozen hours a day from the end of infancy to old age. Old age for nailers commences soon after fifty. The nailer is forced to sell his ware at the price the nail-master will give, whether it be high or low. The nailers have to sell without a moment's delay, and are at the mercy of 'foggers' or factors—the Black Country equivalent for sweaters. The number of persons existing in this misery the report puts at *fifteen thousand*. The small chainmakers of Cradley and neighbouring villages vie in the severity of toil, and want of comforts of life, with the workshops of the Sedgley and Gornal nailers. For twelve hours' work a day a chainmaker may expect to gain ten or eleven shillings a week.

A woman receives from half-a-crown to eight shillings. On this her household lives in a ruined hovel, amid filth, on water-gruel. A man of sixty-eight, who has been a chain-maker for fifty-four years, and earns five-and-threepence a week, out of which he finds fire, shop, and tools, exclaimed to the Board of Trade representative, 'I often feel inclined to put myself away.' The whole of the industries are stained by these horrors. The enslavement of children and women in circumstances of the most frightful cruelty should be checked. The report concludes with instances of endurance under overwhelming difficulties, which prove nail- and chain-making villages to be schools of heroic courage and devotion. The pallid, horny-skinned young women who work from six in the morning to nine at night, and remain 'clean, civil, honest, and respectable' on five-and-fourpence a week; the man of seventy-two who toils from six in the morning to half-past eight at night for four shillings a week without a murmur; the woman with the paralysed husband and three children, who keeps a roof over their heads by earning tenpence a day; the young fellow 'working like a demon' for eighteen shillings a week; and the patriarch of eighty-three rejoicing in his ability to earn half-a-crown, are but specimens of a collection of cases which show that labour and privations may be heartbreaking and not demoralising."

In Parliament, in the year 1894, it was asked of a Jubilee Home Secretary, was he aware that young girls in paper factories were worked twelve hours a day, and for two hours additional as overtime, making fourteen hours a day on forty-eight days every year? "Yes," said the Jubilee minister, "he was *quite* aware, not only young girls of sixteen, but young boys also could work fourteen hours a day."* You have seen what some of their wages were; take these other examples: Seventy thousand women and girls,

---

* The British Government had attended an International Labour Conference in the year 1890, and there agreed to raise the age at which children should be set to work from eleven years to twelve—inadequate enough concession that to bare humanity; yet four years had passed, and the year 1894 was also passing, with its filthy olla-podrida of party-quackeries—Home Rule Bill, Scotch, Welsh, and Universal Disestablishment Bills, Moonlighter and Dynamiter Relief Bill, etc.—but no step was taken to relieve those silent, suffering, little children. . . . Had ye votes, like the cut-throat moonlighters, O poor little Jubilee children? . . . None? . . . Then was there no hope from a lying, swindler-director-ridden Party-Government.

mill-hands and others, in Ireland, working fifty-six hours a week in a damp, hot temperature of eighty degrees, productive of lung disease, could earn about eight-and-six a week. In the light, woollen goods trade of the Yorkshire West Riding, the weavers earned nine shillings and sixpence halfpenny a week, those poor wages being brought about by the influx of women into the trade. "Only those who have seen inside a mill can realize how exhausting both mentally and physically is the work at the looms. In the wholesale clothing trade, at Leeds, a woman by working from eight in the morning till half-past six at night, and then taking home bundles of work to finish until midnight, could earn fifteen-and-six a week. A great deal of overtime is worked in the trade, which means working from eight in the morning till half-past nine at night. The unskilled only earn from five shillings to seven shillings a week." "The match-box makers in Leeds earned from six shillings to eight shillings a week, working twelve and fourteen hours a day, and finding their own paste and their own fire for drying the boxes." ... "Girls in the fish-curing yards near Aberdeen could earn about eight-and-six a week, occasionally working for thirty-six hours at a stretch." ... In the rope-making trade, in evidence before a Jubilee Royal Commission, the women workers showed how they had to submit to an eleven weeks' strike before they could enforce a bare living wage—some ten shillings a week, or so. "In the sack-making trade, the women, by working long hours for two days, if skilled hands, could make one hundred sacks per woman, and her pay for those hundred sacks was one shilling and sevenpence. By employing three, four, or five, little children to help her, a sack woman could earn from ten to fourteen shillings a week. (206) (207) (208)

We fain would have avoided these details, but who can realize the crying necessity for the laws of a Carlyle Democritus who knows not the evils that required a remedy? Into the misery of shop-life we will not enter;* the curious reader may learn

---

* Poor girls employed as dressmakers' assistants were worked from twelve to fourteen hours a day, and turned adrift without redress if they protested. The Courts were worthless to protect them, the "Acts" more worthless still, and the magistrates yet more worthless. We find a factory inspector summoning one of the wealthiest and fashionablest ladies' establishments in Regent Street for employing seven girls from nine in the morning till half-past ten at night. ... The magistrate dismissed the summons on the ground that the Act "did not say at what time at night work should cease." That was a Jubilee magistrate administering Jubilee "law." (208a) (208b)

enough and to spare of all that species of Jubilee employment of girls and women from a brave little book entitled "Death and Disease behind the Counter." Surely, after all that, women in England were revered in a strange way. You could see some of them nightly dancing before wild beasts in a cage of lions, or jumping from the roof of a place opposite the Parliament of Westminster, and elsewhere into a small tank of water, or into a rope net. Jubilee minister, of the radical species, in the Parliament opposite, on being asked if Government intended to tolerate such brutal

(209) exhibitions, replied that he had not seen them. It was the Jubilee minister's ostrich-privilege not to see anything which did not produce votes. All else was mere political sand, wherein such ministers laid their political eggs, to be in due time hatched into mammon peerages or money pensions. Meanwhile, let women peril their life and limb, or betake themselves to Piccadilly street-walking. But let us be just to the Jubilee people; for although they protested not against the degrading folly and inhumanity of risking a woman's life "to make a Jubilee holiday," the Society for the Prevention of Cruelty to Animals *did* protest against the keeper whipping the lions to prevent them mauling and tearing the woman, and they brought an action against the showman in the Jubilee courts of horse-hair-wig-justice, but as the judges were not agreed upon a point of Jubilee "law"—to wit, as to whether lions

(210) were domestic animals or not, some of the sapiences deciding one way, and some another,* in the usual Jubilee fashion, and since no lunacies of that precise nature had been dealt with by M. and W., Vol. 3, 719, Ex. 2., Eliz., Mary, or Anne, present learned asses and antediluvian learned asses had no chance of comparing notes —the question remained undecided down to the time of the Revolution.

But who would wonder at the Jubilee reverence for women who knew the sufferings of the yet tenderer than women, the little Jubilee children? A visitor to some of the Board Schools of

(211) London gave this record to the world, "That after an exhaustive enquiry at a few of the schools he found 2600 children insufficiently fed, and 1400 usually in a state of hunger." They brought before a Jubilee minister (a Tory this time) the case of a little child who had had no food for twenty-four hours, and the

---

* Compare Chapter on Law.

minister replied: "He was afraid there were many cases of the same kind." "Not exceptional," by any means such cases to Jubilee ministers. (212)

Of the condition of little Jubilee children generally take this from a School Board Inspector's report:— (213)

"There are 60,000 families in London, whose 'homes' consist of one room only." One room: do you realize what that means, reader? Mother, father, sons, and daughters in one room, in one bed—like this, as an instance among a thousand such brought to light in the usual Jubilee way, by death and the coroner's inquest. "Adelaide B., aged thirty-three, wife of an engine-driver. Wife, husband, and five children living in one room; all the seven sleeping in one bed; children attacked by measles, mother dead, and the children playing around the bed nearly naked, mid-winter too." (214) 60,000 families in homes of one room, and your archbishops in two palaces—that is Jubilee London under the Gospel of Party Government and the Thirty-nine Articles. Let the School Board Inspector, a noble-hearted man, as every page of his report abundantly proves, continue:—

"In one school I found that 36 per cent. of the parents of the children were out of employment, 40 per cent. of the children came to school without breakfast, 28 per cent. without dinner. In another school 34 per cent. of the children's parents were out of employment, 10 per cent. of them were fatherless, 17 per cent. attended school dinnerless, 23 per cent. breakfastless. In another school 11 per cent. of the children were fatherless, 27 per cent. breakfastless, 20 per cent. dinnerless. I am in a position to say that the rents in the most overcrowded parts of my districts amount, as a rule, to about a third or a fourth of the *maximum* wages earned by the tenants.* I have more than once, when going my rounds, been accosted by a landlord in a state of abject terror, lest I might be arranging to rob him of his victims. A dilapidated house of ten rooms yielded to its landlord 54s. 9d. a week, or £97, 8s. a year. That did not include one of the cellars which was to let. The hungry little boys and girls who fill the Board Schools are not fit, either physically or mentally, for the strain that passing the Government examinations implies. Some means should be devised whereby one good meal a day [confess that our worthy inspector is

---

* Pages 119-123.

not unreasonable] could be provided for the breakfastless and dinnerless children of our schools, and saving the little children who are now rotting in heaps within sight of the porticoes of our churches.". . . . And those were not the worst cases. Those poor little starved things had dens of a sort. There were gathered together by one London Charity Home for Children in one year (214a) 2400 absolutely destitute and homeless children, and 3000 others only slightly less destitute. The same agency in one year supplied over 50,000 nights' lodgings to forlorn street wanderers, most of them young girls. Need more be said? Except, perhaps, this significant climax to those Hell-statistics: In the report of the School Board Inspector he records that in his division there were 429 bakers' shops, 350 milk shops, and 912 public-houses. Those figures speak for themselves. The public-houses debauched the poor, whilst their owners and caterers were the elect of Party England, the richest of them ornamenting the British Jubilee Peerage.

(219) There is no over-colouring in those tragic details, for we find the state of things more than confirmed at a later period by the School Board itself. Here is an excerpt from a *Times* leading article on the subject of how to deal with the semi-starvation of the Board School children:—

"No less than 43,000 children,* or more than 12 per cent. of

---

* And these 43,000 (or, according to Sir R. Temple, 60,000) little starving children were only of those who were upon the register of the London School Board. There were many more thousands who were too far gone even for the School Board register—little shoeless waifs who were to be seen in courts and alleys of Jubilee Slum-land at all times, and who, if all had been told, would have brought those already dreadful figures of half-starved children to (215) nearer 100,000 than 60,000. Indeed, the workers amongst the poorest, the Ragged School Union, sad and ominous title for a Christian civilisation, held *their* Jubilee in the year 1894, and published a book to commemorate the event. The poor little Ragged School children were altogether apart from those dealt with by the Board Schools, and the book declares that "the outcasts are as many to-day, and almost as needy, as they were fifty years ago, viz., 30,000 absolutely homeless children (in London alone) growing up in the most degraded, or even criminal surroundings. . . . Thousands of suffering little ones were left unhelped for lack of money." . . . On that (216) very day a London suffragan Bishop died worth £50,000, and the day before (217) a Dean died worth £34,000, and the day before that some millionaires had "dinner" at a cost of £20 a-head—"sixty of them," said the Jubilee news- (218) papers, "at a cost of £1200 for one dinner." Human pigs, with golden troughs!

the numbers in average attendance, come to school in want of food. Eight thousand of the little sufferers are in the Infants' Department. It is absolutely incontrovertible that starved, or half-starved, children can do little or no good at school. . . . It is not only barbarous to torture the brains of a foodless child, but it is useless as well. The money which is bestowed upon teaching starving children is wasted. It is 'clearly desirable' either that these children should be fed, or that what is called their education should be abandoned. . . . After a 'certain period of experience' it may 'perhaps' become possible to obtain help from Legislation."

"After a certain period of experience." "Perhaps!" Perhaps! Have 43,000 little children votes, O *Times* newspaper? Can 43,000 starving little children compete for legislation with Irish moonlighters? Will your Jubilee legislative machine stoop to the Christ-love: "Little children, come unto me,"—"we are rich, strong, powerful; you shall be fed"?*

Your Jubilee Parliaments have Parish Councils to create, Welsh Church to disestablish, British United Kingdom to dissever: how shall such Parliaments consider little starving children? The little wasted forms, the wide starvation eyes of those silent suffering children,—think of it, O women of England, intent upon platform oratory! Think of it, O Churchmen, intent upon "higher education of the wealthy classes of the Egyptain Copts"! Think of it, O Jubilee Radicals, intent upon filthy slander of British heroes buried in the far African plains!

Reader, reader, not utterly dead to mercy, ye who know what is meant by a long-suffering God, do you think a Carlyle Democritus an unnecessary thing for such a Jubilee England? Do you commence to realize the necessity for those slum prisons? And justice retributive? It was not by penny or by halfpenny charity-meals

---

* "Six miserably clad little children were placed in the dock at the Woolwich Police Court, and charged by the contractor of pig's-wash with stealing food from the Royal Artillery Barracks. A police sergeant had found the prisoners that morning picking refuse food out of the swill-tub; the food was what the soldiers could not eat. . . . The children had often been there before, and the sergeant said he could not keep them away [let us hope that thou *wouldst* not keep them away, O police sergeant]. Some of them took the food to their 'homes.' . . . The prisoners, in answer to the charge, said they were hungry, or they would not eat food from the pig-tub." . . . (221)

"Suffer little children to come unto Me." . . . O Christian England!

that Carlyle Democritus would see those starving children fed. . . . Oh, in those long dreary years of waiting and of preparation what were his sufferings—there, amongst them, sharing their trials, starving with them, loving every little helpless thing as if it were flesh of his flesh, heart of his heart. In later years he was heard to say that the sufferings of the children of the poor formed a living cross upon which he was transfixed. . . . And in the agony of his sympathy he had cried aloud: "Eli, Eli, lama sabachthani?" For "the moments of inspiration were short, and the hours of depression so long." But the dawn came at last—to him and to them.

Previous chapters have shown how the little and the larger children were fed, protected, made for ever the care of their country, had they votes or had they none.

No longer was it a necessity for womankind to seek their bread in the Hell-mud of Piccadilly pavements, or by roof-jumping into water tanks six feet deep, or by posturing in lion cages before wild beasts of the gaping ape and grinning jackass sort. Bow down thyself into the dust, O England, that there ever should have been such base necessity!

II.—*Woman after the Revolution.*

Great restrictions and precautions had been imposed upon the conditions of male employment in dangerous trades, but women were forbidden to be employed in them upon any condition whatsoever. The minimum age limit of employment for girls was the completion of their fifteenth year in all occupations. The wage laws for women were the surest means for preventing their engagement in callings unsuited to them. It was therefore enacted that the "minimum wage" prevailing for men should be extended to women in all industries of an arduous nature, or in which men were employed. The maximum hours for women employment in all trades and manufactures was eight hours a day, and overtime was absolutely forbidden. With regard to reasonably light occupations suited to women—such as shop assistants, clerks, medical nurses, etc.—the eight hours day was established, and the rate of wages adopted on a minimum basis of 20s. a week, permanency of contract being established throughout women's labour as with men's. It is impossible to go into all the humane details of the Revolutionary Code—such as the compulsory supply of seats in all shops or business places for female workers, the provision of female inspectors appointed by the respective women's labour guilds, etc. The conditions under which women and girls had to work at Jubilee times in laundries, dressmaking establishments, and generally, both as regards excessive work hours, inadequate sanitary provisions, and sweating wages, were all effectually reformed.

Technical training in all the schools formed as marked a feature of the girls' education as it did of the boys'. The system of apprenticeship was also as broadly introduced, and was superintended by the various women's guilds. Perhaps the most worthy, as it was amongst the most necessary, was the reform introduced into domestic service. The million and three-quarters of women and girls employed in in-door domestic service at the Jubilee period were without union, or adequate protection of any sort. Now and then a maid would fall from a window-sill and disclose by a cruel death some of the conditions of Jubilee domestic service. Want of due training on the servants' side, due to the defective school system, which conceived education to be mainly a matter of theoretical cram, turned out shoals of half useless girls, just sufficiently instructed, or *de*structed, to despise service, which narrowed the Jubilee conception of liberty, and sent them instead to seek an unhealthy and precarious living in poisonous lead works or other health-destroying factories. On the other hand, in the (220) absence of protection and inspection, the conditions of domestic service, in the vast majority of instances, were thoughtless and cruel to a rare degree. Overwork and underpay, too often accompanied by poor food—indeed, in numerous cases, scarcely removed from semi-starvation—was one of the main causes which accounted for the dearth of domestic servants throughout the Jubilee period, notwithstanding the fact that want and misery were so ubiquitous. Jubilee ladies intent upon Zenana Missions might have done better work nearer home in organising the neglected, slave-driven Jubilee maids-of-all-work. But Jubilee high-class women, like Jubilee high class other things, in the governing department, had a fatal way of overlooking mere duty, and adopting mere fads instead. We find in the year 1894 a noble lady, Captain General of a talking army, preparing to start on a quite gigantic fad mission to every part of the world with accessories of the most expensive sort, special steamer amongst such accessories—said Mission directed to the abolition of all liquor except water, all smoke except women vapours, and all vice except slum-purveying.

Meanwhile the noble lady, Captain-General-of-Teetotalers-all-over-the-World, was also Captain-General of one of the cruellest slum areas in the United Kingdom, and could have achieved more good by staying at home and doing her duty by her wretched tenants than all the water-missions and suppression of vice crusades in (221) creation could bring about. Indeed, it was a highly, or lowly, ominous sign of all those times the savage part which high-born dames played in the Jubilee world.

Amongst the most heartless evictors of Scotch peasants from their land, you will find none more ruthless than the female landowners, under whose administration women and children by the thousand were turned out wholesale to starvation and perennial (222) misery. Let those readers who cannot read Dante in the original, or for whom Milton is too magnificent, and who yet would know a little of hell's doings, read any of the many published accounts of the Highland clearances, or of the Irish, or even English clearances. This history has given but a small glimpse of them in an earlier chapter.* It is not productive of unlimited adoration, except of the lip sort, towards Jubilee femininity to see them so often emulative of the very worst and basest of their masters' examples.

Happily for the reforms which the Revolution brought about, they were first actual and practical, and only afterwards drawn up into definite law and code. It was not by edict that the cruel orgies of Piccadilly hell-scenes could be mitigated. Generations of putridity cannot be healed by Act of Parliament. Wise Acts of Parliament need never try *that* method. You will drain no marsh until you have first provided an outlet for the stagnant waters, and wisely constructed your canal or channel to draw off the marsh water into healthy river stream, or adequate lake basin. Piccadilly infernal occupations ceased to allure poor womankind when, on all hands, there was established—firstly, a healthy demand for healthy service under just and equitable conditions; and secondly (really higher than firstly), a need for the daughters'

---

* Pages 98, 99, 100-103.

services in the work at home: "Man for the field, and the woman for the hearth." There was no home in the Jubilee times for millions of workers—no home, nothing but incest dens—mother, father, and five or eight children "living" in one room, and 43,000 or 60,000, says Sir R. Temple, starving children a daily item of London Jubilee programme. (223)

The way that Carlyle Democritus cleared London and Great Britain generally of its unfortunate females was by not creating them; he did not clear Piccadilly streets; he simply by thunder-peal closed the sources of their manufacture—the awful slum dens, the casual employment, the sweating wages—*these* were the Jubilee social marshes which the brave reformer drained, until dry land appeared, and godly men and women could stand firm and work upon it, instead of being compelled to wallow in eternal mud-filth, dragging the country's manhood in unceasing mudstream, growing for ever fouler, even unto night blackness.

Let us get back to domestic service, and learn the conditions established by the Revolution. There was a minimum wage of one quarter which prevailed in factory or other service, independent of home and food. The engagements were annual. Unions were encouraged amongst all female workers; they had their Guilds and Councils as the men had. No case of injustice between mistress and maid could be passed over. Refusal of just character to a servant—"Go out to perpetual ruin for thy fault, O woman, because thou art poor"—could not get itself continued under any merciful system of government, as little for maids as for men. Women Councils—where Government Inspectors also attended—saw to the just application of all laws and regulations concerning women service. The sleeping-rooms of the servants were under their inspection (very much needed in Jubilee times indeed, but never applied); under-feeding was made impossible, overwork likewise. Female domestic slaves at Jubilee times had a sadly burdensome time, their hours commencing often at five in the morning and ending not before eleven at night, a ceaseless drudgery. As it was impossible to fix domestic work hours, the Code, instead, fixed the minimum of rest hours, and these were a minimum night or sleep period of eight and a half hours and a mininum day period of three hours. But the surest means by which reform was secured were the Unions. The State started them throughout the country, perfected their organisation on the same lines as workmen's Unions, and then delivered them over to the Women's Guilds, at the same time reserving a necessary Government Inspectorate as has been before indicated.

Courts of first instance were established in the Women's Guilds, for the hearing and arbitration of all women's cases; their organisation followed closely that of the Courts described under the Chapter on Law. In them, as in all Courts, the State bore the entire cost of administration.

We may now state a few of the laws which followed the reforms: Foreign dames of the unfortunate class were no longer permitted to land in British ports. The law which tolerated no idle man in the country tolerated also no (ostensibly) idle woman. The liberty of the subject was not interfered with, only the *licence* of the subject. Let it be quite clear that Carlyle Democritus was no child dreaming of universal purity Utopias. And also, on the other hand, that he was not prepared to tolerate universal mud-Utopias. You must remember that, with general work becoming the rule, and idleness the exception, the general tendency toward a higher order of things gradually slackened the demand for the old Jubilee "unfortunate" class. Not only that: the class itself was no longer manufactured. It was getting quite a lost art after the Revolution; so much so indeed that many of the foreign Ambassadors found it necessary to send private despatches to their Governments cautioning tourists against molesting English ladies, as so many cases were occurring, from mere ignorance on the part of foreigners to appreciate the fact that although Great Britain still remained a great commercial nation, it had stopped its traffic —or rather the traffic had stopped itself—of . . . . Happily, the traffic has no name.

Fashion, which in Jubilee times favoured bachelordom, looked rather askance at such an anomaly after the Revolution, and you did not find many men unmarried after their twenty-fourth year. There was no law upon the subject, but there was a healthy state of public opinion, which was more influential for good than any law.

A reference to the chapter on Education will help the reader to a better appreciation of this great social question. To have told a Jubilee young man of the fashionable sort that it was not a natural condition of things—that there should constantly prevail a floating population, relegated to what is only to be described as a living shambles—would have been at once to confess yourself outside the range of the human solar splendour—gone instead entirely moonward, or lunatic. Now it ought clearly to be grasped that an evil is remediable by solar methods as well as lunar methods. Has it not been shown that weeds and wildness will everywhere grow and spread if there is no cultivation, both in the moral world and in the material world? Do not let practical folk imagine that a Carlyle Democritus could ever descend to the unpractical. What could be more practical than the methods he adopted for ascertaining the actual origin of the most degrading form of the social evil? He employed no Royal Commission, and yet he arrived at a remarkable fund of information, which left the late Mr Acton a lame, halting, and impotent authority indeed. After the most earnest researches into the life-histories of 20,000 shambles cases, the 20,000 were found to have been supplied from the following classes of the community :—

1. From the peerage	None.
2. From the wealthy classes	None.
3. From the well-to-do middle classes	5
4. From the lower middle classes	107
5. From the poorer classes—	
6. (*a.*) Born in moderate poverty	2,709
(*b.*) Reduced to poverty from a superior station	3,073
7. (*c.*) Reared in extreme poverty	14,106
	20,000

Class 1, it will be perceived from the table, retained their lapses within their own ranks, and never went beyond occasional exhibitions in the divorce courts. With Class 2 it was similar; family wounds of the Dulcinea sort were always healable by gold ointment.

In the Classes 3 and 4, all the cases were attributable to the application of the principle of eternal punishment for sin. Not one of the 112 cases but who deplored the horrible necessity, or punishment, which had condemned her to such an existence and closed all other careers to her.

With regard to the three last classes, it is enough to record that poverty made temptation easy if not irresistible; poverty made regression next to impossible; and poverty for ever intensified the horrors and the degradation.

In the many cases where Jubilee remedial measures had been attempted, they had failed, for the reason that such work and service as could be got for the restored ones was invariably of a sort that, in nine cases out of ten, favoured a relapse.

After the Revolution it is not pretended that Eros dropped his wings, and was content to hold firmly to earth and the conventionalities, and stray no more. Let us remember that Cupid, according to Hesiod, was co-eval with Chaos and the earth, and, according to human experience, is likely to outlast the second institution, as he already has the first. Now, although the ancients gave Cupid many forms, it was left to the moderns to give him the hell-imp form. It was the hell-imp form which the Revolution abolished, no other.

Every one had to work. "If there is one man or woman begging in the streets for bread," said Democritus, "that is a reproach to the whole country."

No begging of any sort was allowed. If not for bread, certainly not for mud. There was an avenue open for every British worker under the sun, an avenue laid out by the Divine Creator of the world which it is compulsory for man to tread—the avenue of work. This history has shown sufficiently that there was no lack of work after the Revolution; there was, rather, lack of workmen. Any man found loitering was promptly and mercifully furnished with work.* That law applied to women also. There was never a lack of domestic work on the Colonial, Penal, or Labour Settlements. There is one thing in this world which God has given to mankind to be for ever unsaleable—his person. Carlyle Democritus and the Revolution upheld that law absolutely, both for men and women. With the giver he nor they interfered. But slavery, concupiscent or other, was abolished. If Eros—from his exuberant sweetness—gives away his feathers, happy they who receive them, but Eros shall not be let sell his dove-plumes in the market-place, or elsewhere. Poverty and starvation no longer compelled, or instigated, that awful sacrifice.

There is one other step that the Revolution took in the direction of raising the status of English women. But again, let it be well

---

* Pages 162, 250, 251.

understood, it was not the outcome of any law. In a preceding chapter * it was incidentally mentioned that female as well as male doctors were provided in all the labour palaces. That was not an isolated instance of a great reform in the customs and manners of a nation having grown from below upwards. Is it necessary to insist that the institution of female doctors for female patients was a step in a good direction? No, not necessary. The workers felt it to be a boon, and Carlyle Democritus left time to recommend it to the higher dames. And a wise historian will follow the example of the great legislator. Modesty needs not to be commended. Praise is detrimental to her. To a generation whose drawing-room women, while holding themselves to be the most refined of their species, delighted in exposing to the uttermost their arm and breast developments, and whose music-hall bacchantes —the least refined of their species—delighted in exposing to the uttermost their leg and thigh developments, gaping public supposed to be looking on applausive at both exhibitions—to such a generation let any wise historian speak of modesty only in the language which Christ adopted towards another generation which mocked at truth. Let the wise historian be content to record that there came a time when innocent-souled English women who had gone to the East to "convert" the "heathen"—the passionate beauty of India, the devoted woman of Cathay, and her flower-sister of Japan, sweet as a lotus bloom—returned themselves "converted." For they had seen a different but not a lower civilisation. Women less *talked* about as emancipated, but emancipated nevertheless. Those teeming millions would not have the "liberty" of a British woman. Liberty to expose her person without shame to every staring wight; liberty to shout upon the housetops their "equality" with man; liberty to compete with man in the platform jargon element, whilst they supplied slum dens for the poor, or turned them from their peasant farms on to the winter fields to starve. The tender *un*converted preferred a dearer empire — the supreme rule of home, the absolute queenship of the generation yet to be. Not talking on platforms to corrupted men is woman's mission in this or any world; but to train the undegenerate and uncorrupted man so that he never become corrupt. "The child is the father of the

---

* Page 263.

man," O British woman, when thou knowest purity and modesty in thine own soul, and exhibitest it a little in thine own body, thou canst then insinuate that infinite sweetness into his. Thy child will not listen to thy mere words, but he *will* imitate thy action. God has bereft the little child of knowledge whilst the mother feeds it at the fount of life. O woman, thou desecratest God's fairest law, thou outragest His greatest trust when thou teachest to thy son, by animal example, grossness bred of sensual vanity, the arch-origin of all corruption.

CHAPTER V.

EDUCATION.

"Plato rebukes the criminal folly of preoccupying the minds of children, when they are too young to protect themselves, with the traditions of the old mythologies.

"Woe to the unlucky man who as a child is taught, even as a portion of his creed, what his grown reason must forswear!"—*Froude*.

IN nothing was the Jubilee age more complex and chaotic than in its system or want of system, of national education. Its infinite varieties defy analysis, and would not repay the work when accomplished. The Jubilee people had very certain and scientific rules for rearing and training horses, pigs, sheep, and cattle, but for rearing and training human-kind the general rules (if any could be discovered) were uncertain and unscientific. There were the Board Schools for the poor, the governors whereof had wrangled for the best part of a year whether the teachers should or should not be compelled to tell helpless little children—60,000 of whom were half starved and not fit to learn anything—that God was not God, but a triple arrangement of Ghost, and Son, and Father. The teachers being sane men and women—practical, pious, and humane—revolted against such idiot-tyranny, and pointed out to the School Board governors (beset with Jubilee parsons) that tens of thousands of the poor children's stomachs were already fed with wind instead of food, and that to feed their sad little brains with wind also were quite the culmination of criminal folly. At any rate, the Board Schools possessed practically trained and duly certified teachers, hairbrained as many of the governors were. On the other hand, there were troops of teachers, outside Board Schools, uncertified, untrained, and incompetent. These were thought good enough for a large class of middle-conditioned people, whose children suffered in consequence. After the Revolution no person was allowed to follow the profession of teacher unless he or she had been duly certificated. The highest calling that a mortal could be put to was no longer permitted to remain a sort of refuge for the destitute. Happily there were merciful and sane provisions elsewhere for the destitute after the Revolution. Perhaps if we glance at the very highest Jubilee conception of "education," it will afford us a sufficiently vivid idea of what the medium or lowest must have been. "Very much of words and very little of things," applicable to all of them.

Here, then, is a small table of statistics of Jubilee education for boys of fourteen, collected and published in the year 1894 from twenty-two English public schools.

Five hundred and ninety-eight hours a week (for the 22 schools) were devoted to, and divided amongst, the following subjects :—

To English	32 hours.
„ Ancient and Modern History . .	39¾ „
„ Geography	18¾ „
„ Science	17¾ „
„ German	Nil.
„ French	71 „
„ Scripture and Religion . . .	43¼ „
„ Mathematics	119½ „
„ Greek	115¼ „
„ Latin	140¾ „

Total, 598 hours.

That is an instructive little table for many reasons :— (1) Greek and Latin absorbed not far short of one-half of the total instruction afforded to the British youth of high (or rich) degree. (2) Modern languages had one representative; all the others were entirely ignored, although the Government was offering high premiums to young men who could pass examinations in Chinese, Hindustani, Malay, and Russian, which would fit them for employment in State service throughout the wide and glorious empire where right understanding of those languages was so much required.

The grand colleges were turning out cartloads of useless brain-inflations, capable of doing Greek "verses," Latin rhymes, and such dead rubbish—mere windbags of education—blown out of any possibility of living usefulness, until they had voided their undigested classical *de*ducation.

The infinite and ceaseless professorial cant of appreciation and adulation for those ancient Greek and Latin literatures stood like a thistle abatis between the British youth and British usefulness. Dare any mortal man raise his voice against the lunatic squandering of the national brain forces, professorial prigs shrieked at him till the poor man fairly gave in from damaged tympanum. Not so Democritus. He dearly loved the wise and great, both Greek and Roman, and he proved his love by imitating what was good in them, not by mere lip-mockery of them. Cæsar and the Antonines were not unknown to him, nor the Gracchi. But he still dared to prefer Cromwell to Cæsar, Shakespeare to Sophocles, Froude to Fenestella, Ruskin to Rutilius, and Wren to Rhotus; or any of the glorious gods of British genius before all the dictionary-full of Lempriere-people—from which, by the way, the above names have been taken, more for purposes of alliteration than of particular appropriateness—much in the same way that British Jubilee youths were penning Greek "rhymes" at the expense of English reason. A Cromwell excelled a Cæsar to Carlyle Democritus as infinitely as a Jesus Christ a Cretan Jupiter; in spite of the fact that the Jupiter cant-priests, according to Varro, divided their Jupiter god into three hundred individualities, whilst the jubilee cant-priests only divided theirs into three. High-class British colleges turned out shoals of poor water-brains, crammed with the literature of two nations dead by their own corruption, while the living wisdom of Germany, the great God-fearing people of the world, was a close-sealed book to them. As for the literature of their own country, Heaven protect them—the mud-wash of idle women's sickly vapours, thrown off in three-volume novels, was their principal pabulum in the English-reading line. Choked at college with "classicalism," they afterwards craved for anything not classic — like an alcohol inebriate for soda-water.

Very much did the Revolution change the curriculum of the great educational establishments throughout the country. Those

598 hours of the high-class classical schools were turned upside down much in this fashion:—

Greek *and* Latin	25 hours.
English Literature and History, including Scripture reading	100 ,,
Modern History, other than English	30 ,,
Ancient History	15 ,,
Geography	50 ,,
Science	35 ,,
German, French, Italian, Spanish (a scholar to choose any two)	70 ,,
Science of Education and Human Physiology	50 ,,
Mathematics	120 ,,
Hindustani, or other Indian dialect	35 ,,
Chinese, Russian, Malay (one to be chosen by the scholar)	35 ,,
Military drill	33 ,,
Total,	**598 hours.**

No more details. We have only dilated upon the highest form of Jubilee education, because from the ludicrous unpracticalness of the highest, sane readers may be allowed to imagine what were the vagaries of the lowest. From the highest to the lowest all schools and colleges were made absolutely free. Wise and wholesome variety prevailed in different centres; but Parliament, through its Minister of Public Education, prevented any lapse from the practical reform introduced by the Revolution, which is best seen in the measures they adopted with the School Board. The post-revolutionary School Board curriculum was based upon the following four categories:—

    1. Technical training.
    2. Physical drill.
    3. The three R's.
    4. The science of education, including human physiology.

Dividing the school hours into 100 parts, the following will give a measure of the importance and value set to each subject:—

    1. Technical training, requiring proficiency in some one trade or calling before a child could pass to the secondary or Guild training schools . . 25 hrs.

2. Physical Drill, which included the art of self-defence, military drill, gymnastic exercise, and swimming. . . . . 15 hrs.
3. The three R's, pure and simple :—
   (*a.*) Reading, including Scripture, English history, and English literature . . 15 ,,
   (*b.*) Writing, including elementary shorthand . 10 ,,
   (*c.*) Arithmetic, theoretical and commercial . 15 ,,
4. The science of education, rearing and training of the young, and elementary human physiology . 20 ,,
                                                                                    ─────
                                                                                    100 hrs.

The fourth division—the science of education and human physiology—was the most valuable and vital of all the educational reforms of the Revolution. It is quite impossible to exaggerate the intense ignorance of the masses of the people, rich and poor, at Jubilee times, with reference to all matters concerning the care or training of the young, or the life duties which awaited a citizen beyond the region of his counting-house. A more deplorable piece of feminine futility than a young Jubilee mother is not to be conceived. Half the miseries of domestic disunion were directly caused by the launching of a raw, ignorant girl into the sacred temple of matrimony, without one fraction of previous domestic or physical training. As if the rearing of a man were of less regard than the rearing of a pig or a cow,—the care of neither of which would be intrusted to an untrained person, yet who was thought quite good enough to rear a British son of God. Whilst half the Jubilee world was running after political economy as usefully, though not as harmlessly, as a dog after its tail, domestic economy was an art scarcely introduced as a serious study even in the best of schools. The relation and duty of a child and man to the State was so little understood that, even amongst the clergy, it was a common rule to find the poorest of them dragging into misery and poverty a dozen children whom they could not properly feed, let alone train and educate. Such was the result of wise physiological training after the Revolution that it came justly to be looked upon as criminal wickedness for parents to increase their families beyond the number for whom they could honestly and worthily provide. If Carlyle Democritus had done no more than scotch the prurient cowardice which blinked those vital questions in Jubilee times, he had done well for his country. But more good followed from his brave instauration. The health of the people rose with the healthiness of their knowledge. Infant life ceased to pay its tribute to the Moloch of ignorance and fashion. Ah! Fashion! That ceased also to depend altogether upon foreign lunacies. Physiology taught the new generation of womankind the insane folly of pinching their vitals in two, and taught them to laugh less at Chinese crushed feet, and weep more at their own squeezed anatomies. A time came when in the room of horrors, at an exhibition which still flourished in Baker Street, were to be found certain specimens of whalebone and steel, cunningly covered with silk or cotton, and thus described in the Twentieth Century catalogue:—

"Models of implements of torture in use at the Jubilee period, called 'little-ease.' When first dug from an old grave at Hanwell it was supposed that they were relics of the Inquisition, but further research inclines authorities to the belief that they were constructions invented by the French for the destruction or prevention of population. Exact year of manufacture uncertain."

Briefly, it may be said that after the Revolution the national education set before everything the necessity of a high technical and physical training. Competitive examinations were entirely abolished. Degrees, certificates, and passes were granted to scholars who qualified themselves by passing the standards fixed by the governing bodies, but not upon any principle of competition. With reference to the freeing of all schools, it may be added that all voluntary schools that desired it were taken over by the State, and compensation given to them; but no capitation grants were made to any such schools which continued an independent existence. They gradually died away as the thoroughness and practicalness of the State schools commended themselves to the whole nation. Complete freedom was left to all such voluntary schools as continued to exist on all subjects, except that the State would tolerate no departure from truth in the study of history. In Jubilee times you would find histories, so called, which as absolutely refuted one another as did the old Jubilee Blackswhite and Whitesblack journals.* Upon that history question the

---

* Page 22.

Revolutionary Parliament permitted no quibbling. It is a sad business to inculcate in one part of your national children that King A was a saint, whilst another portion of your children are being taught that King A was a devil. The Educational Department of the Government decided the history text-books, and wherever opinion was irreconcilable with fact, history stated fact, and left opinion alone. Every student on leaving school had to pass a public examination, non-competitive. In history the examination was oral as well as written. Upon evidence appearing that the national history had been departed from, the school guilty of the misteaching was closed, or in the event of private tuition, the certificate of the teacher was forfeited, and the pupil required to attend a State boarding-school for three years.

"Woe to the unlucky man who as a child is taught, even as a portion of his creed, what his grown reason must forswear."

CHAPTER VI.

JUBILEE LAW—REVOLUTIONARY JUSTICE.

"Parliament will initiate no wise legislation. Until public opinion force it to the brink of the waters of reform it will but wallow in the mud-stream of Party. Compelled to the pure waters of reform, it will not drink, but turn away to appoint Royal Commissions, to analyse the constituent parts of its beloved mud-stream, and report—if pure water be preferable—Why? Royal Commission was the Jubilee name for Limbo, or Lethe, the black unutterable, which swallowed for ever and revealed nothing, never satisfied nor satisfying.

"Ancient Wisdom said: '*Doing*, not learning, is the thing.' Jubilee Parliament said: '*Learning*, not doing, is the thing,' so it set up its Royal Commissions filled with gangs of Party politicians, placed an unlimited quantity of soap-water before them, also clay or brass pipes, and bid them blow bubbles, and not be in any hurry to exhaust the soap-water."

Carlyle Democritus.

FIRST there was chaos, afterwards creation. Darkness preceded dawn. Was there ever a fouler darkness than that ever-increasing darkness which Jubilee law had made from what mankind called Justice?

The Jubilee Church had had its Trinity. Do not think that Jubilee Government was without a similar mystery:—

The Father was Party Government; the Son, Publicans and Public-houses; the Holy Ghost, Law.

It had also its three states in the regions above and beneath:—

Its Heaven was compounded of Office, Power, Company-mongering, and Peerages; its Purgatory was experienced in Opposition; its Hell lay in Poverty, Drunkenness, Misery, and Crime; its Styx or Hell-ferry might be entitled "Royal Commission."

The hundred and fifty millions a year which the publicans sucked from the Nation's wealth were slight, compared with the ubiquitous graspings and emasculations of the law. A Parliamentary return published in the year 1894 showed that in six years the "law" had sucked from "gas and water" companies, railway, canal, and tramway companies alone, over two millions sterling,

merely for the cost of obtaining Parliamentary "legislation." (225)
Could a return have been made of the cost of *litigation* produced
by that so-called *legislation*, it would probably have had to be
expressed in tens of millions. The dual legislature was choked
with publicans of one class or another, with lawyers of one sort or
another, and with company-mongers of all sorts. *They* made the
laws. It was as if it should be given to burglars to define the
weapons they were to be assaulted with, and the methods to be
adopted for their circumvention. Let us take first the question of
public companies.

The Inspector-General of Companies in Liquidation published
a report in the Jubilee year 1894. He put one year's "loss" (226)
(legalised thieving by promoters and company-mongers) at twenty-
five millions sterling. This loss was *not* ascribable to disasters
incidental to trading or bad times. On the contrary, he said:
"One looks in vain for any signs of failure caused by real
misfortune, or by any other of such causes." The real causes
he attributed "to a conspicuous *absence* of honesty of purpose,
intelligence of management, and telling the truth" (the last
phrase was written "accuracy of statement placed before the
public"). Yet, in spite of the fact that twenty-five millions
sterling had been robbed from the hard-working masses by mere
chartered thieves, such was the infamy of the Parliamentary (227)
"Acts" that, says a high authority, "all concerned [in those
public robberies] probably kept within the letter of the Companies'
Acts, and a prosecution under the Larceny Act, or under *any*
of the penal provisions of those Acts, would have almost certainly
failed. *Such is the perfection* of the art of the modern promoter,
that he can, and does, victimise the public with absolute immunity
from punishment. A large class of abuses goes on briskly *under
cover of the very statutes passed to prevent them.*" *

---

* "The gain to directors of Companies is so great," said the *Times*,
"and the chance of final escape so considerable, that rascals will always be
found to swindle shareholders . . . and evade justice ; . . . there are enough
of such refugees at large to found a small colony . . . there will be no real
reform and no real security for shareholders, mostly of the poorer classes,
until the law takes a very different view of the duty and responsibility
of directors from that now in vogue. It seems positively to be thought
a sufficient defence for a director to avow that he did not know anything
that went on at his Board. It is his business to know, and if he does not (227a)
know, he stands self-confessed as an impostor."

Hearken, hearken, reader; here is a contrast:—

(228) "Elizabeth Dash, aged thirty-nine, who was given a chair in the dock 'owing to the condition she was in,' was yesterday [Christmas-week 1893] charged with stealing a woollen petticoat, value one shilling and ninepence, from a pawnbroker's shop where she had gone to redeem something. The prisoner, weeping bitterly, said she had four little children, all of them ill, one dying, and whom she feared would be dead before she could return home [and one more yet to come]. Her little boy told her when he got home from the pawnbroker's shop that he had picked up the petticoat on the floor of the shop, and she put it round the child who was dying to keep it warm, and she went to the shop the next day and offered to pay for it, but the pawnbroker said 'I cannot compromise,' and was hard to her till the policeman came, then he was very civil, but would have her locked up. The prisoner's little son said he picked the article up in the shop, and his mother did not know it. The magistrate said, 'This is a very sad case.' And the bench of magistrates said, 'You are to be fined ten shillings, or in default seven days.' The police knew nothing against the poor woman. She had only six shillings in the world, four children ill, and a fifth coming."

The poor widow whose child stole the shilling petticoat did not know that the poor little pilferer had taken it—but they condemned her to prison nevertheless.*

Sentence ten shillings fine, or in default seven days! What do you think about it, Right Honourable Jubilee gentlemen M.P., Q.C., G.C.M.G., and many other grand letters of the alphabet, who paid ten per cent. dividend as directors of a company at a time when its realised losses exceeded a quarter of a million sterling, and which failed a few months later for some millions sterling, but who were *not* imprisoned for seven *days*, but made Cabinet Ministers for seven *years*, to rule a mad and degenerate Jubilee people in the name of "Party"?

Such was Jubilee justice. Ponder, ye who would know what CORRUPTION means!

Your right honourable Company-promoters, M.P., P.C., K.C.M.G., etc., could, with impunity, rob tens of thousands of widows and

---

* Page 367 (note).

humble toilers and go scot free? Reader, do you know how that was possible in Jubilee times? A fearless historian will tell you. Because the crew in Parliament who "made the laws" did not need to steal a little flannel to clothe their naked, starving children with, but they *did* require to invent phrases and clauses which would enable them to wriggle out of the devastating consequences of their directoral "mismanagement," and thus enable them with impunity to "lose" annually Twenty-five Millions of the national wealth. In what dictionary must we look for the actual meaning of that word "lose"? Had the money fallen to the bottom of the sea? Had it passed through those directors' hands and fallen nowhither? Had any of it stopped in their pockets, or in those of their friends? Verily, the historian knoweth not. He only knows that the Inspector-General of Companies in Liquidation assured the Jubilee world that those Twenty-five Millions sterling a year were "lost" owing to "a conspicuous absence of honesty of purpose." May not a truth-loving mortal humbly opine that where there is a conspicuous *absence* of honesty of any sort, there is a perspicuous *presence* of dishonesty of a sort? In the Radical Party Government of the year 1894, you would find at least half a score of Her Majesty's Ministers Company Directors. Some of them—peers and legislators—" directed" any number of companies from twenty down to ten, or less. One of those Companies, included in the Report of Her Majesty's Inspector-General, etc., had failed for a sum of Seven Millions sterling, and had brought ruin upon tens of thousands of the struggling masses throughout the Kingdom. It had for its President a peer, and for its arch-fiend (Director-in-Chief) one of the most pious of Radical administrators. A President of the Board of Trade was Director of another exploded Company. A First Lord of the Admiralty in a Tory administration had directed another exploded Company. Take this as a passing searchlight glance into Jubilee Company-mongering:— (229)

CHANCERY DIVISION OF THE HIGH COURT OF JUSTICE.

In *re* the New Fleeceland Loan Agency Limited.

This was an application on behalf of the Right Honourable Sir James Fergusson Bart., M.P., the Right Hon. A. J. Mundella, M.P. (President of the Board of Trade), Sir F. W Stafford,

G.C.M.G., Sir George Russell, Bart., M.P., Sir J. E. Gorst, Q.C., M.P. (a Financial Secretary to the Treasury), that an order made in the winding up of the above-named Company for the public examination of the above-named five honourable and right honourable gentlemen might be discharged.

Counsel Q.C., M.P., for the five honourable and right honourable gentlemen explained that his clients desired to be examined under some section of the Companies' Act which did not convey the impression that fraud had been committed by them.

The Judge:—"Fraud *has* been committed by some one."

Counsel, Q.C., M.P.:—"My clients object to any examination based on the notion that the slightest fraud has been committed by them, or any one with whom they had acted. I and my learned friend [brother counsel for the above worthies M.P.] will take upon ourselves to say [*i.e.* are duly paid for saying] that the stigma of fraud could not rest on any of those honourable and right honourable gentlemen M.P."

Could not rest! It would glide from the right honourable shoulders like water from a duck's back, or like the golden money which had glided, and become "lost," from the pockets of the unfortunate shareholders.

After floating through "learned" arguments in the usual manner, to prove that inasmuch as his honourable and right honourable clients had only "lost" a few millions, or hundreds of thousands, of the British public's money which had been entrusted to them, and had not at all stolen it like the wicked slum people, who stole pennies and flannel petticoats to feed and clothe their starving children with, therefore his honourable and right honourable clients ought only to be examined in a quiet and comfortable way, "and not by public examination." And the "learned" counsel further argued that, if fraud had been committed, "the Official Receiver was wanting in moral courage not to say so."

The Judge:—"Oh, I don't agree to *that*, Mr Counsel, Q.C., M.P."

Counsel, continuing, referred to the report of the Official Receiver and said that "the Company was a substantial one, and the applicants were gentlemen [Jubilee gentlemen], whose position was indisputable as regarded their integrity and business capacity."

Indisputable! Yet the wicked Judge disputed the "indisputable integrity and business capacity" of the honourable and right honourable gentlemen, Q.C., G.C.M.G., Cabinet Ministers, M.P.

And the Judge said: "The Company was 'wound up' in July 1893, and the hon. and right hon. gentlemen authorised a dividend of ten per cent. in 1892."

"Ah," said the learned Council, Q.C., on the other side, "grant the examination, your Lordship; a public investigation is necessary, and it is right and proper that the gentlemen *should* be examined, for it is evident that *some one* has committed fraud." And he referred the Court to various precedents from the days of the deluge down to Anno Jubili 1894, to try and prove that if a poor starving woman with five children could be arraigned and sentenced to seven days' imprisonment because her baby stole a piece of flannel, might not wealthy Right honourables be examined for etc. etc. ?

All the learned and unlearned arguments being completed, the learned Judge went home and studied the Companies' Acts, and spent much time and labour upon them. And after three days he re-appeared in the great Court of Justice, and pronounced a grave and careful decision—not of the concrete Salomaic sort—"divide the child in two;" but of the Jubilee diffusive sort, poor man—for let us love our dutiful brother man at all times—it was not the Judge that had made Jubilee law and Jubilee Acts of Parliament, it was they that had made, or unmade, him, and condemned him to wade in a never-ceasing tide of confused limbo-jargon. For hours the learned Judge poured forth his verdict, using more words than are employed in the recital of the entire history of the great King Solomon; more words than have sufficed for the average chapter of this history with its store of truth and wisdom. Be not dismayed, O reader; we will not set out that Jubilee judgment here for you, but only the kernel of it, and always with deep sympathy and pity for the brave Judge who, with a fear of God in his heart, and not the fear of men, thus "divided the babe in two :"—

The actual verdict was: "Fraud *has* been committed by someone, and there must be public examination; thus says the Act of Parliament, and thus say I, one of Her Majesty's Judges. The accused are all honourable men, innocent beyond doubt, anxious still more beyond doubt to prove their innocence; but the poor starving accused gets public trial and sentence of ten days for stealing three-penn'orth of flannel, and these honourable men must be similarly examined for 'losing' millions of the public's money."

Now, when the learned counsel of those honourable men heard the wise Judge's verdict, he gathered his counsellor's robes around him, pressed his horse-hair wig firmly upon his head, and made a wild rush to the Appeal Court next door, and he bowed low before the supreme lords of Jubilee Appeal-Justice, and he said, " O great and most learned Judges of Appeal, reverse the verdict of the less-learned Judge of the Queen's High Court of Justice. He has studied the Companies' Acts for three days, and thereafter has decided that the Ministers of the Queen and other great, mighty, and most honourable men are to be tried for 'losing' a few hundred thousands of the people's money, as if the amount were only sixpence stolen by a starving slum thief. Justice ! O most learned ones, Justice !—I mean of course Jubilee justice—*Jubilee justice !*" *

And he got it. For the most learned supreme Judges reversed the seven thousand words of their brother Judge. And . . . the poor widow doing her seven days in the prison cell, with the four little children starving outside, was praying to the Father of all to forgive her sin and watch over her hungry children. Dost thou begin to grasp what was Jubilee justice, O reader?

(229a) * Public examination of the honourable and right honourable gentlemen did eventually follow under a rule which did not contemplate fraud. The examination extended over a month or more, with the due array of learned counsel on both sides. The Judge made a further "statement," which occupied five hours in delivering, and involved 7000 more words. We find the brave Official Receiver—so grossly insulted by the Q.C., M.P., on behalf of the honourable and right honourable gentlemen—upheld by the Judge, and his report declared to be "admirably clear and accurate, and unimpugnable," and not by any means "cowardly," O learned counsel Q.C., M.P., but infinitely brave and true. The Judge heard evidence for a whole month, which involved more printed words than would furnish type for half a dozen Old and New Testaments combined. And the Judge said that fraud *had* been committed by the directors, "collectively," in a very cruel and wholesale fashion. " COLLECTIVELY ! " Sweet Jubilee euphemism : wholesale fraud by directors "collectively," but individually they were held as innocent as baa-lambs mumbling grass in the summer fields. " Collectively " fraudulent and eminently dishonourable men, but individually "honourable," ay, " RIGHT honourable " men. For Jubilee Justice wore seven-league boots to crush out the small criminalities, and quickly sentenced the hungry ones who stole bread or shillings, but by no means exercised itself

· But then, for what were the lawyers in Parliament, except to confound judgment? When hon. members complained that a clause of an important Bill was altogether incomprehensible, would not a right hon. gentleman rise and read a lengthy explanatory (230a) statement by the draftsmen of the Jubilee word-maze, called Bill," which left the hon. members probably more bewildered than before? "The difficulty of interpreting the thing is insuper-

over the "great thieves." Ten housebreakers, by Jubilee law, were both "collectively" and "individually" guilty, but pocket-breakers, so long as they put "Limited" after their names, and "Honourable" or other title, before them, would only be "collectively" and *not* "individually" responsible. Exquisite refinement of Jubilee wig-law and party corruption. Let us from our heart admire the sturdy outspokenness of the *Times* on this occasion: "It is idle cant to pretend anxiety for the better distribu- (229b) tion of wealth until we can devise means by which the preying upon people of small incomes can be put a stop to ['until we can devise means!' It is *so* difficult to catch big thieves, so easy to catch the poor little ones.] Men of business could not be hoodwinked with an illusory debenture which was good enough for the general public. . . . The holders of debentures were extensively deceived as to the nature and value of the security they held. The balance-sheets were systematically cooked to conceal the true state of affairs. The reserve had totally disappeared, but figures were manipulated to make it appear that the reserve existed. . . . Public and shareholders alike have been tricked and defrauded during a long term of years through the fault of a Board of Directors. . . . Yet, as we see every day, neither the law [the Jubilee law] nor public opinion [party opinion] offers any serious guarantee for care, attention, or honesty upon the part of directors. On the contrary, their punishment, even in bad cases, is difficult, and they boldly claim to be regarded as 'honourable' men after collectively doing the most dishonourable things."

Ay, even so, out of all those persons "collectively guilty of fraud," only one resigned, and his resignation did not take place till many weeks after the Official Receiver's denunciation, and after the Press—duly "inspired"—had assured the British public that the Cabinet Ministers "collectively" "saw no reason" why their right honourable colleague should resign; and he himself felt so supremely innocent that he declared his intention of visiting his constituents "to seek an expression of renewal of confidence." (229c) Whilst Jubilee justice was thus passing unpunished those honourable and right honourable "collective" defrauders of millions of the public money, she was sentencing, at that very moment, to three months' hard labour a poor (229d) wretch who had obtained, not one or two millions sterling by false pretences, but ten pounds sterling, by false pretence of charity from a right honourable gentleman M.P. It was fraud, justly punishable, to rob ten pounds from a right honourable M.P., but it was only "collective" fraud, or Jubilee innocence, for half-a-dozen right honourables to rob the poorer middle classe of millions sterling.

able," said hon. members. That was *inside* the "House;" let the reader imagine its insuperability when, in the form of an "Act," it got *outside* the "House,"—when not two hundred but *two thousand* lawyers would tear and rend at it as a bird of prey tears the carrion.

Perhaps the impartial reader would like to hear the opinion of the greatest newspaper in the world upon this matter. Upon a case that had suffered the usual battledore and shuttlecock business at the hands of the law courts, in the Jubilee year 1894, a case involving some £200,000, the *Times* said:—

"The Legislature escapes responsibility in a cloud of verbiage. One party attaches to a vague set of words one meaning, another party another meaning, and Parliament attaches to them no meaning in particular. No two tribunals were at one as to the purport of words on which depended thousands of pounds. All felt the difficulty of a sentence which began by saying one thing and ended only to unsay it. The arbitrator appointed under the Act thought it meant one thing, which was the opinion of the majority of the judges of the Court of Sessions in Scotland. The Divisional Court thought the arbitrator (and the majority of the Session judges) wrong. The Lords Justices (on the case being taken to another court) thought the Divisional judges wrong. Every court before which the question has come has complained of the 'great difficulty' in construing the section. Apart from the hardship to be inflicted, it is unsatisfactory to note the element of gambling in the whole litigation. There is something amiss when property of great value is inflated or depreciated according to the meaning which judges extract from, or give to, *words barely intelligible*. Counsel have given diverse opinions as to the purport of the thing; and the Court of Appeal do not conceal their perplexity in presence of the *statutory gibberish* on which the dispute turns. . . . The fault rests with Parliament, which does not say in plain terms what it means, does not make use of familiar and well-ascertained meanings."

Yes, "STATUTORY GIBBERISH," says the *Times* newspaper of the year 1894, and also: "*This is an example of a favourite mode of drafting Bills dealing with controversial matter.*" Lawyer-subterfuges and chicanery, mediæval mud-jargon, imbroglio of "learned asses," universal Pandemonium, parliamentary corruption—verily a Carlyle Democritus was required to sweep away such *canaille*.

At the time when the Divine Philosopher, Jesus of Galilee, was teaching in Jerusalem to a deaf and corrupt people, there was a philosopher in Rome saying to another corrupt people:—" One day may make all the difference between the greatest city in the world and no city at all." Thou shalt know later on what that "one day" means, O reader. Meanwhile, thou hast seen a little of Jubilee law, of Jubilee makers of law, and of Jubilee breakers of law.

And of such were the Kingdom of Mammon. With such ministers to make the laws, need an intelligent public wonder why company thieves might rob them wholesale of Twenty-five Millions sterling a year with impunity? Diplomatists, ambassadors, peers, members of Parliament, were amongst those Directors; those were the people whom Parliamentary laws practically privileged to "lose" the public's money wholesale. Twenty-five Millions in one year (and going on year after year in the same fashion). It is not a little thing, O English people. It meant ruin to untold numbers of silent, hopeless savers, who had no redress anywhere. Amongst the victims of one of those companies of whom the Inspector-General spoke, there were numbers of men and women, from the ages of fifty up to eighty, who were robbed to the last penny of their hard earnings and savings of a lifetime. Many in sheer despair committed suicide; the distress was so general that a charity subscription-list was organised, in order to modify to a small extent the worst sufferings of some of them.

If, amongst all those wrecked fortunes, any desperate mortal dared to try for justice, what befel him? Costs, contumely, star-chamber cross-examination, and this decision by one of Her Majesty's judges:—

"There is no doubt that the Directors of this Company are morally guilty of the ruin they have brought on thousands; there is no doubt they have wantonly squandered the millions of money that a confiding public has entrusted to their hands, misled by their high position, misled by high-sounding names. If I, as a Judge, had to mete out *justice*, there is not one of these men but upon whose head the heaviest sentence of the law should fall, but alas, it is not law that I have to dispense, but only Jubilee law, and therefore, after these wasted months of 'trial,' after all the frightful evidence of what is the most culpable misrepresentation of facts, and misappropriation of funds, I must declare, not

(230b)

that the prisoners are innocent, but that the wizard enchantments of the 'law' cannot touch them."

"The law," said Democritus, "dragged the poor gutter thief by an iron chain, whilst it was but as a gossamer thread to the practised Company scoundrel. God have mercy on a country (231) which compels its judges to dispense such law."

There was no hope for any mortal ruined by a Company who should venture to appeal for justice. Only costs, contumely, and an adverse verdict awaited him, further disaster added to already unbearable ruin. Legal sharks were let loose upon the unfortunate protesting mortal ruined by a Company, by the same power that had raised fraudulent directorship into an organised brigandage to prey upon society in all directions.

The liquor and legal traffic shared between them the principal power in the political arena. Just as the *liquor* interests diverted the nation's savings from health into drunkenness and waste, so the *legal* interests diverted the healthy English language into mere mediæval doggerel, which no man, not even the lawyers themselves, could understand. Just as the "Company Acts" of Parliament bred the very abuses they were pretended to be passed to "prevent," so was it with every conceivable statute made by Jubilee Parliaments; the newspapers teemed with accounts of the ruin and ravage brought upon trade through the hopelessness of ever getting justice out of them. What one judge in one court declared to be black, a judge in the next court decided was white, and the judges in the superior court determined was both black *and* white. Nothing was commoner than to find wigged idiocies voting both (232) ways. Here is a case that will illustrate a thousand :—

"Sixty miners were killed by an explosion in a colliery. Their wretched widows sued for compensation. One court interpreted the Act of Parliament, which dealt with such cases, and decided that the widows were to have justice and compensation. The next court of wig idiots reversed the first court's interpretation, and decided that the widows were *not* to be compensated. The poor widows tried the Supreme Court, and that third court reversed the second court wiggeries' decision, and determined that the Act *did* allow compensation. Meanwhile untold months had been wasted, enormous costs incurred, and by the time the poor widows got their 'judgment,' they might have died of starvation, had not charity, or the men's Labour Union, given them food."

Or take this: Again it is a widow, this time of a sailor (233)
drowned at sea, through the admitted carelessness of the
captain. Widow appeals for compensation against the shipowners. The first court interpreted the Act and gave the widow
£175 damages; the owners appealed, and the superior wiggeries
decided that the Act of Parliament did *not* allow the poor widow
compensation. She could appeal no more, so she got nothing.
Only the lawyers got anything.

On the same day which saw the poor widow's discomfiture we
find this other Jubilee law interpretation:— (234)

A member of a School Board became bankrupt. No. 1
court of wigs decided that he was disqualified to serve as a
member of the School Board according to the Act of Parliament.
He appealed. No. 2 court decided both ways, viz. two judges
held that the Act did *not* disqualify him, and one judge (the
Master of the Rolls) decided that the Act *did* disqualify him.
Two wigs counted more than one wig, so the unfortunate bankrupt remained a member of the School Board. Such was Jubilee
law, and such were Jubilee judges.

Do not let it be imagined that complex questions had anything
to do with the law's delay, uncertainty, expense, and general worthlessness.* The more simple the question, the more protracted
were the legal "arguments." The bewildered and stupefied
reader doubts it! Take these actual cases, boiled down and
extricated from more words than were employed in the Bible,
Homer, and Shakespeare taken together; and, if you include the
references to "leading cases" and mis-leading cases, involving
probably more books (of the sheepskin description) than would
fill a slum-room ten feet by ten.

"Are the London streets intended for traffic, or for trade?" (236)
The costermongers said: "For trade."

---

* "They (the merchants and traders) had over and over again advocated
practical measures which the United Chambers of Commerce *had ten times
approved*, but Bills for the consolidation and amendment of the most important branches of commercial and shipping law had been killed by
obstruction and by our Party and Parliamentary systems. *It was useless for
the President of the Board of Trade to point the injured trader to the remedy of
costly litigation for breaches of the law*. . . . The Board of Trade must vindi-
cate the law, and if it had not the power, the sooner it got and exercised it (235)
the better for the community and for trade."—THE PRESIDENT OF THE
ASSOCIATION OF CHAMBERS OF COMMERCE OF THE UNITED KINGDOM.

The Municipalities said: "For traffic."

The law courts—after multifarious trials, peals, and appeals, and costs interminable, and much wasted time, disagreed as follows:—The first court said that the Act of Parliament intended the streets for traffic and not for trade; the next court reversed the verdict, and decided that the Act of Parliament meant the streets for costermonger-trade and not for traffic; and the supreme court of horsehair wigs decided that the Act of Parliament meant— meant—that they didn't know what it did mean, and they must divide upon the matter. They did so with this result: Three wigs interpreted the Act in favour of the costermongers, and one wig in favour of the Municipalities; three wigs counting more than one wig, it was finally decided that the Act of Parliament meant that the London streets might be blocked by costermongers' carts, and, we suppose, the traffic must go over the roofs of houses.

(237) One more example, and we have finished:—

Smith, Brown, Robinson & Co., well-known Oxford Street tradesmen, delivered a cartload of tinsel and toys on loan to a wedding party, said tinsel and toys to be fetched back after three hours. Cart and horses put up during those three hours at the stable of a greengrocer of the name of Jones. The cart had upon it, writ large on all sides, Smith, Brown, Robinson & Co., Oxford Street. Jubilee landlord comes on the scene, and walks off with Smith, Brown, Robinson, & Co.'s cart and horses, in spite of vehement protest, in order to compensate himself for Greengrocer Jones's arrears of rent. After the due Jubilee legal delay of many months, after columns of vapid "argument," precedents, and messydents, horsehair-wig finally decided in this manner (we will leave his "argument" about the cart, and listen to him on the horses)—

"Upon the question of the horses," said the learned Judge (they called all judges in Jubilee time learned, in the same way that they called the £15,000-a-year archbishops "most reverend," or the swindling ministerial directors "right honourable." The actual signification of the titles was really this: "Learned"—stuffed idiocy; "most reverend"—inflated cant; "right honourable"— licensed to commit fraud, or to utter unending falsehoods with immunity and impunity). "Upon the question of the horses," said the learned Judge, "three points of 'law' arose: (1) Was a horse, temporarily resting for three hours, privileged from distress? (2) Was it so privileged because it was an implement of trade?

[You are not to smile, reader; those are the actual words of his wigship, as reported in the *Times* newspaper, under the heading "AN IMPORTANT POINT IN THE LAW OF DISTRESS."] (3) "Was the horse a privileged implement because etc., etc. On the first point the learned judge decided that the horse was *not* privileged because etc., etc. On the second point he entertained doubts, but on the authority of Read v. Burley, 2 Cro. Eliz. 596, and Muspratt v. Gregory, 1 M. and W. 596, and 3 M. and W. 677, he answered the second point in the *negative* and the third point in the *affirmative*. Thus," etc.

As all readers do not speak mediæval "English," twisted into downright idiocy by lawyer-jargon, we will translate the learned judge's decision into plain English:—

Point 1. Landlord *may* steal Smith, Brown & Robinson's horses because his tenant Jones owes him rent.

Point 2. Landlord *may*, and he *may not* steal Smith, Brown, Robinson, & Co.'s horses, *but*, as a learned ass in Queen Elizabeth's time said that a then landlord of Jones might not steal a then Robinson's horses, he (the present learned ass) would say also that the present landlord of Jones must not steal the present Robinson's horses.

Point 3. Landlord *may* steal Smith, Brown, Robinson, & Co.'s horses, and he may *not*, but as a learned ass in Queen Elizabeth's time decided that the emphasis was to be on the *not*, he (the present learned ass) would decide that way also.

Result—Two points in the negative, and one point in the affirmative; balance of points therefore in favour of the negative. Therefore the judgment of the court is that the landlord may *not* steal Smith, Brown, Robinson, & Co.'s horses. Time involved in that sapiency of judgment over five months; expenses several hundred pounds.

Would the reader like any *more* Jubilee "leading cases," or is he satisfied? We could give him some rare specimens, one involving upwards of £300,000; another involving several millions (238, of pounds, with Right Hon. Privy Councillors, Peers, Ministers, K.C.B.'s, K.C.M.G.'s, and all manner of magnificent Directors swindling the British public within two or three years of their Companies' floating, *all* let off because—because—as Luther says: "Thieving is the most common trade in the world, and great thieves go scot free like the Pope and his crew." Carlyle Democritus had only to alter the last four words to mirror perfectly the Jubilee period. The last four words will then read: "like the Party-Ministers and their crew."

(239) "Acts" passed by Jubilee Parliaments pretending to protect labour were, like all the other Acts, mere traps for litigation and costs. Hear a learned Judge incidentally say:— " In his experience he had found that actions under the Employers' Liability Act were subject to great uncertainties and to great costs, rarely recoverable." That, of an Act for the protection of poor working men. A rare fuss was made by a Jubilee Parliament of the year 1894 because of another such Act, which they had not quite managed to foist upon an innocent and ignorant public. The Chairman of a London Hospital for accidents to workmen
(240) spoke thus of it :—

"The conduct of employers of men who suffered from accidents was little short of a scandal, and the one thing that the men needed was the opportunity of getting a reasonable hearing of their case at a reasonable price. But the Government Bill was a downright farce, and the members of the Bar were the only people who would get money out of it. It is as useless to tell poor men when they are ill that they should take turtle soup and champagne as to tell them when injured to take proceedings at law. Both remedies are for the rich only. . . . "

As for the law of libel, it beat everything under the sun for sheer cruelty. Let no son of Adam in those times dare venture to protect himself. The courts teemed with wigged brigands, whose whole stock-in-trade consisted in verbal assegais, which they levelled at witnesses' heads and hearts. There was no Star-Chamber to tear a man's limbs to pieces in Jubilee times, but there was an infinitely crueller thing, which aimed at tearing the reputation and character of any victim who sought for justice.* If the witness

---

(340a) * In the Jubilee year 1892 a very "fashionable" case was before the courts, and here is a description published in the *Times* newspaper, by a "learned brother," of how the two highest right honourable titled counsel, Q.C., M.P., treated gentlemen in the witness-box :—"The Solicitor-General made himself the vehicle of imputing unnatural crimes to Mr Dash. This he did on a valueless suggestion, though he was aware there was no other evidence to support it. He also, on the same suggestion, exposed two doubtful or discreditable antecedents of the witness, neither of which had any relevance to

happened to be a woman, the cruel feast was all the more base.
In a famous case where the lady gained her verdict, she had previously " to submit, for four hours on the rack, to be tortured with
'questions and insinuations.'" That is a description by a Jubilee (341)
law minister himself. And by whom was such torture inflicted?
By another Government law minister, the highest of his kind
(subsequently promoted into "Supreme Judge" by his party!)
Let innocent souls conceive the fate of women at the hands of the
lowest, instead of the highest barrister-luminaries. Hundreds of
women submitted to any life-torment sooner than brave the infinite
degradation of a British Court of "Justice." When once they
dared venture there to get divorce or separation from some male
fiend, they had to submit to "examination" by barrister harpies,
beside which the foulest Zola-realism was fair.

We have glanced (p. 249) at some of the stepping-stones of the
duly prepared Jubilee law student (sufficiently stuffed with Coke,
Littleton & Co.'s horsehair), by which he mounted to Jubilee
judgeship :—" Political exigences;" "a troublesome barrister self-
seeker to be got out of the way;" "party services to be rewarded,"
&c. But the supreme stepping-stone which, according to the
greatest newspaper in the world, " with few exceptions, led to a
judgeship, was being made an Attorney-General's 'devil.'" (342)
Seldom has legal slang more adequately and forcibly defined itself.

---

the issue, and which could have been asked with the sole object of causing
pain. . . ."
That, of a Tory Solicitor-General. *This*, of a Radical Solicitor-General :—
" He makes himself the vehicle of imputing to Major Blank that his visit
to a French watering-place was necessitated by an infamous disease, of which
there was no evidence whatever, nor would it have affected the issue before
the court had the witness suffered from one or fifty diseases. . . . Such
conduct should have led to both these 'distinguished' men being seriously
admonished, if not disbarred by the benchers of their Inn. Instead of that,
they received fulsome, not to say sickening compliments from the weak
Judge, in whom gentlemen of this stamp [right honourable learned gentlemen,
Q.C., M.P. stamp] inspire a positive terror. . . . It is well known that the
[Radical] Solicitor-General insulted three judges in one court." (One of
them died in 1894, and was declared to be one of the best and most upright
judges England had ever had.) " These men have turned our law courts into
theatres, and before their rough tongues the judges stand in awe." That
worthy, right honourable, learned, titled " gentleman" Q.C., M.P., was not
disbarred for insulting the Jubilee judges, and terrorising and torturing witnesses, but was instead himself made, by a Radical party-" Government,"
a supreme of supreme judges—a Lord Judge of Appeal.

(243) It may afford a small insight into the abominations of the barrister-harpies who fed upon women's reputations in the divorce courts, when we find that great newspaper offering as a meed of the highest praise to a Jubilee judge, who died in the year 1894, "that he would not permit in *his* *Court* unseemly mirth, jocularity, or ribaldry, by even the boldest advocate." Is it not interesting to learn that there *was* such a judge in Jubilee times, O British reader? But is it not also a little tragic to learn that the scales of justice in those times were held by Attorney-General's devils, surrounded by grinning crews of ribald barrister-harpies, with much jocularity proclaiming to all suppliants for justice :—"All character abandon, ye who enter here. There is no sanctuary of sorrow which we will not desecrate and invade: we will tear open the holiest secrets of your heart and life, and lay them bare before a gaping, prurient multitude. Come to our courts of justice, ye fashionable ones, and witness the dissection of the foul. Zola's bestialities may not be translated into English, but we will out-Zola Zola,—ay, and the fairer and sweeter our women-victims, the coarser will we denude them. Walk up! walk up!"

And indeed it was a very common thing throughout Jubilee times to see those fashionable ones respond with zest to the barrister-harpies' invitation—even the Judge's dais being placed at the disposal of the fair.

Then as to costs,* it was ordinary business for even a successful litigant to be half ruined by a lawyer's bill. Costs were piled on by thousands. *Without* money there was no "law," and even *with* money there was rarely justice. What did Carlyle Democritus with such an Augean stable of abuse?

Now let it not be thought that the Revolution abolished lawyers by Act of Parliament. It was not by Act of Parliament that the Revolution had abolished unfortunate females, nor was it by such method that they attempted to abolish unfortunate males, of the wig species, or other. For it is indeed altogether unfortunate that any human male should have to depend for his livelihood upon the

---

(243a) * Not only was Jubilee law becoming impossible for the poor and the middle classes; it was fast becoming impossible even for the rich. We find a wealthy peer in the year 1894 writing to the *Times*, and urging that, in cases of dispute in the assessment of probate duties, appeal should be made to the County Council or some other local authority, on the ground that few taxpayers could afford to come before the Courts of Law.

strife, vice, or crime of his fellow-men. Even the lowest order of vermin do not feed upon one another—except when driven to it by actual starvation ; that awful supremacy of verminity has been left to perverted human-kind. Jubilee cant, which loved things in trinities, had its vampire-trinity in rare consummation—three orders which fed upon the vices of their fellow-men :—

1. The manufacturers, purveyors, and abettors of drunkenness, or publican class—the direct authors of two-thirds of the crime of the country.

2. The slum-owning; jerry-building, and rack-rent class, evicting and starving the people off the land—the direct cause of the poverty and misery of millions.

3. The lawyer-barrister class, confounding wisdom in mere wordiness, hiding the divine spirit of human language by ever-increasing agglomeration and obfustication of the mere letter of language, until one word required many Acts of Parliament to define it ; each "Act" many judges to interpret *it ;* and each judge other lord judges to interpret *him.*

Not by Act of Parliament were these beasts of prey abolished. But by action of combined wisdom and justice they disappeared, as fog-mist disappears before the north wind. In previous chapters * it has been made clear how practical men were selected by their fellow-men in all trades and callings to constitute courts of honour, conciliation, and arbitration, for the hearing and adjudication of all questions, differences, and disputes arising in their respective trades and professions, or in the course of domestic misunderstandings. Only those practical men who have had actual experience of such admirable arbitration courts can adequately appreciate their worth : the precision, simplicity, costlessness, and speed with which they discharge their duties. The cases were rare which required appeal beyond those courts of first instance. The courts of second instance were constituted in a similar manner, from members of the central bodies of the various trades and professions. All the arbitration and conciliation courts were free, it being the very essence of justice that the poorest and the richest should stand absolutely equal before the Judge. The State, therefore, bore the entire cost of all those courts. They were a part—the deep and worthy foundation of the entire post-Revolutionary judicial system. It has

---

* Pages 209, 249.

been explained how the members of the various arbitration courts were chosen, and what were their methods of procedure.* The following table will afford a clear view of the system which formed so admirable a judicial training-school, and from whence the new magistrates and judges were selected.

Constitution of the Courts of Honour.

Local branches of traders, workers, professors, literators, merchants, etc., each appointed its own court of honour, consisting of ten, or more members, according to the requirements of the locality. These courts arbitrated and adjudicated upon all causes and cases of a private or business nature which concerned the members of the respective callings. The hearings were absolutely private. Any breach of trust by a member of a court of honour was punishable by fine and dismissal, and incapacity for any future public office. The State paid all members of the court and of all courts. The members of a court of honour (M.C.H.) were elected for life, and were only removable by voluntary resignation, or any offence against the national laws, or failure of health; their election followed the principles which governed all elections† and was by ballot. No case could be taken before a higher court until it had first been adjudicated upon by a court of honour.

The Women's Courts of Honour and Arbitration‡ had to deal solely with domestic cases, and questions concerning the welfare and protection of their sex generally. Only single women were eligible as officers and officials of the courts, and only married women were eligible as dames of honour and arbitration; and in order to prevent the public service from unduly encroaching upon the home duties of the latter, their attendances were restricted by the statute to three alternate days a week, and a maximum of two hours on any one day. Members of the Women's Honour Court were entitled to the prefix "honourable" before their names, and of the Higher Arbitration Courts to the title for life of "Lady." In all other respects the rules and regulations which governed the men's courts governed theirs also, except that there was no further public magisterial service open to them. The age-limit (completion of the sixtieth year) at which all public officers were obliged to retire—members of Parliament, judges, magistrates, civil ser-

---

* Page 248.   † Pages 417, 426.   ‡ Page 353.

vants, and officials of every description *—included the women also. This wise law not only secured the healthy infusion of new life into all the State and public services; it kept open also a constant avenue for promotion. Breach of confidence by a member of the courts of either sex, in addition to the penalties already indicated,† forfeited also the right of title.

Throughout the country, in Jubilee times, charitable institutions of every conceivable sort bore witness to the exquisite sensibility and depth of heart (never mind the occasional shallowness of head) of the great British people. Noble as many of those institutions were, the management of many required considerable winnowing and wisdoming. A more painful sight to eye and heart than was afforded by the tasteless hideousness of too many of the poor uniformed creatures sheltered by the sad cold charity-hand in those times is not easily imaginable. The reforms, and bettered condition of the nation generally, inaugurated by the Revolution, gradually superseded nearly all Jubilee charities. Unprotected orphans became the care and charge of the State, as did unprotected children of any sort. They were not allowed to be accumulated in doleful charity-heaps, but were individually boarded in carefully selected homes at the expense of the State, and thus assured the warmth of family attention and affection. Over such cases the women's guilds and courts retained a watchful superintendence until the children reached the age when they could independently support themselves.

The improved condition of the nation, the prevailing justice of Government, was a practical security against the continuance of such helpless classes as saturated the country with misery in Jubilee times, and of which the "charities" only touched the outermost fringe.‡ "Charity" received another interpretation after the Revolution. "Charities" had scarcely an interpretation at all. Justice had eclipsed them so entirely that a later generation knew not the meaning of the word in its concrete plural form.

CONSTITUTION OF THE COURTS OF ARBITRATION.

Trade Unions, literary and professorial associations, chambers of commerce, and all guilds, appointed their own courts of arbitration, consisting of ten or more members, according to the requirements

---

* Page 258.   † Page 384.   ‡ Page 152.

of the particular centre. The primary object in all cases was to prevent any delay in the trial of causes. The Arbitration Courts, besides adjudicating upon causes arising in their own guilds and unions, were also Courts of Appeal (of first instance) to the Honour Courts. All causes were heard in private, and the same stern rules applied to the members of the arbitration courts (M.C.A.) as to those of the inferior and superior courts. Election was by ballot and for life, determinable only by resignation, or offence against the law.

Remember, that the Revolutionary Codex left no law open to ambiguity. An offence against the laws was not liable to any misinterpretation; it might be said required no interpretation, inasmuch as it bore its meaning on its face. Truth, honour, and honesty were the absolutely indispensable qualifications of the humblest or highest members of the judicial system. Any proved offence, whether of pecuniary, moral, political, or other sort, inevitably terminated the offender's tenure of office. There was no Jubilee "Justice" in the prisoner's dock one moment and on (109) the magisterial bench five seconds afterwards. *That* was the order of the day in Jubilee mud-period. All officers of the Courts, high and low, were appointed for life, upon conditions as to conduct similar to those of the justices. The pay of all concerned in the administration of the law was on the highest possible scale, far above the necessity of temptation. Personal merit was the only qualification for judicial appointments, and any attempt at nepotism, favouritism, or politicalism, most heavily penal. (In the case of mixed suits in either the Courts of Honour or of Arbitration, the said Courts were empowered to appoint joint-committees consisting of equal numbers from each section concerned.)

After five years' service in either of those Courts, members were eligible for selection as magistrates, and after ten years' service as judges. The magistrates were also eligible for selection as judges after three years' service. The magistrates and judges were nominated by the Minister of Public Justice, and appointed, after confirmation by a Joint Committee of the two Houses of Parliament. Thus was provided a class of men drawn from all the great practical avenues of the nation—military, naval, professional, literary, commercial, trade, and labour, trained in the brave, stern school of experience and fact, chosen first by their fellow-men to judge over them, and after a long trial-period available for the highest offices in the national administration of justice. Judges and magistrates were thus trained by living contact with fact, instead of dead contact with mediæval verbiage of Cokes upon Littletons, Littletons upon Biggletons, Chitty's Contracts, Croke's Reports, Addison's Torts, Oliphant's horses ("implements of trade" to be divided into three),* Leading Cases in Equity, meaning misleading cases in iniquity, etc. There was a thrice blessed end to all that. The whole mass of "learned" garbage got ended for ever. Post-Revolutionary reports of the Gaslight and Coke Company, and of the Patent Water-Gas Company, record the substitution of Jubilee law-books in lieu of their ordinary fuel, for a space of no less than six months and eight days, during all which time the furnaces were fed by superannuated law-books, with a result, said the reports, "that never in the history of the Companies had more gas been produced in proportion to the quantity of material consumed."

It was in that manner, and not by any Act abolishing lawyers and barristers, that the whole legal fraternity (59,652 strong, says the latest Jubilee Census, Vol. IV. page 85) melted into oblivion, gradually took to worthier work, and ceased to weary mankind any more.

To all Courts, officers of justice were attached, whose duties were to assist applicants in matters of procedure, etc. Everything was of the most straightforward, businesslike, and simple nature. The entire procedure in all cases was the business of the Courts, from the summoning of witnesses to the drawing up, or rather setting down, in plain, unvarnished, or unmudded English, of the plaintiff's and the defendant's case. Justice was as absolutely free as the air of Heaven, and as pure and unpolluted. Mere litigiousness was rendered almost impossible by the adjudication of the Courts of first instance, and, if attempted in the superior courts, was punished as one of the most serious misdemeanours before the law. Crimes such as were common in Jubilee times were scarcely known after the Revolution. This was the Jubilee order of things:—

1. Acknowledged and tolerated floating population of habitual criminals at large—about 30,000.

2. Annual, or rather perennial population of drunkards proceeded against for disorderly conduct—180,000.

---

* Page 378.

3. Anarchists, of the foreign sort, dynamitards,* etc.—all that liked to come to Great Britain—variously estimated at from 2000 to 5000.

4. Normal prison and reformatory population—over 55,000.

5. Number of cases of cruelty to children recorded by the Society for the Prevention of Cruelty to Children—100,000.

6. Juvenile criminals and offenders committed and sent to reformatories, etc., in one year—8000. (In England and Wales alone over 18,000 of such juvenile criminals are recorded in the last Jubilee census as so imprisoned.)

7. Total annual number of convictions of all sorts—about 600,000.

To all truly discerning men those cruel records show less the criminality of the criminals than that of the vile Jubilee system which not only was responsible for them, but which actually created them, and kept them floating upon society. Whilst human nature endures there will be human passions, and there will be errors bred of those passions—human vices, human crimes, —but never more such a hell-record of inhuman crimes as those of Jubilee times, in a country calling itself Christian. Let us inquire a little into some of that Jubilee criminality, and see if it was the result of human weakness in the individual criminal, or of positive and deliberate manufacture by the corrupt, cowardly, and degenerate party-Government system of fostering and abetting the vilest temptations, side by side with a cowardly fear to tie up acknowledged and blatant crime, and abolish the hideous monster.

---

* Of this class of people, welcomed by Jubilee Party-governors, here is a small record from an 1894 newspaper:—

"In London there are 2000 Anarchists; their headquarters are in the centre of one of the most crowded thoroughfares of the metropolis. It was from that centre, or Club, that the recent Spanish massacre was incepted [women and men blown to pieces in a theatre, by a dynamite bomb]. Amongst the members of the 'Club' is a fugitive Italian murderer, under sentence of twenty years' penal servitude. These 2000 foreign scoundrels are the scum of Continental gaols, including an enormous percentage of prostitutes' bullies. It is indisputably due to their presence in London that the streets of the West End, and whole districts, swarm with foreign women of the worst type. The sums of money stolen yearly in the Soho quarter are enormous, and the connection of the thieves with the Continent allows of the disposal of the property with the greatest ease."

Empty your pockets, and visit one of the gambling hells of those foreign scum at any time after midnight; see them and listen to them, and then

The Jubilee definition "habitual criminal," applied to thirty thousand human beings, is a confession of the brutal civilization which manufactured the criminal, and dared not, therefore, fearlessly do away with him, by compelling him to labour usefully, and preventing him for ever from further desecrating God's earth and God's people. Here are some specimens of the "habitual criminal" cut from the greatest newspaper in the world, within almost a few days of one another :—

"Two men waylaid a passer-by, assaulted him, dragged him into (246) a side street, and robbed him. The prisoners were old offenders, against whom a number of previous convictions were proved; the magistrate told them they were curses to the parish, and he committed them to prison for two months."

Habitual criminals, well known to be so, "the curses of their parish," found guilty of the cowardliest of crimes, hindered in their career for just two months, and then let loose again to hide in dark corners, and recommence their street brigandage. Almost at the same time two other such habituals were being tried before another magistrate; one of them had "served" forty years, and the other thirty years, at various times, for larcenies of one sort or another. (247) At another court a habitual criminal was convicted of larceny; he (248) was described by the police as "a terror to the locality," had been "up" at that court alone four times—but his longest sentence had

---

decide for a bewildered Englishman who were more utterly vile and contemptible, those murder-plotters, thieves, and anarchists, or the party mud-politicians, who welcomed them to pollute our brave island with their cowardly plots for the wholesale massacre of friendly foreign people, and even of our own men and women. The *Times* of those days described a visit to another of their haunts, and said :—"A collection of more dangerous-looking persons has rarely been collected in a criminal dock. They consisted almost exclusively of Frenchmen and Frenchwomen, the latter being the choicest specimens of *petroleuses*. They 'sang' choice songs, invoking every kind of destruction by dynamite upon respectable people and property. Such (245) 'Clubs' ought to be swept off the face of the earth."

Yet, in face of all those things, the Government Home Secretary (of the usual Jubilee barrister type, all words and windbaggery) and the British Party Government, did nothing. That would be "to interfere with the liberty of the subject." Jubilee Ministers, of party mud-slime sort, were utterly unable to distinguish between Godly liberty, and murder-licence! How could they ?—their own so-called Government was but Anarchy glossed over with smooth lies. They naturally had a real, though unconscious, sympathy with the other anarchists.

been fourteen days, and after each sentence he was "free" again to prey upon his helpless victims. At the same court, on the same day, a man was brought up, one of a fearful class known in Jubilee times, and described in the papers as "prostitutes' bullies," for bashing his wife and another woman, both unfortunates, with boots, fist, and knife, in a manner which need not be described here; he had been convicted of the same brutal offence on three previous occasions. In this case the verdict was tantamount to saying, "Lock him up again for a few months, then let him out,"
(248a) actually to murder his wife and other unfortunates. In another case (of robbery with violence) the prisoner had thirteen previous
(249) convictions proved against him. Sometimes whole batches of these ruffians would be caught and brought—six at a time—"well-known thieves," before the magistrate—and let off, because of some flaw
(250) in the prosecution.

"H. H. Collin, an old man, was waylaid by two men. One seized him by the throat, whilst the other robbed him of all he possessed; they then kicked and otherwise ill-treated him. The detectives caught these worthies; they turned out to be well known, and a number of previous convictions were proved against them for highway robbery with violence. One of them had undergone a sentence for manslaughter; both of them lived upon the prostitution of women." Their regular meeting-place was a well-known public-house, described by the police as "the resort of loose characters, and in a neighbourhood which it was dangerous for persons to frequent." Robberies were of nightly occurrence, but people were frightened to give evidence owing to the intimidation to which they
(251) were subjected by the friends of the accused. The judge said he could not understand why such public-houses should be licensed. Poor Jubilee judge, dost thou not know that the licensing
(252) magistrates, like their masters, are political slime-things, bred and made fat by the liquor-prostitution of the masses? And thus your Jubilee civilization kept a floating stock of thirty thousand of such and other criminals upon Jubilee society. Thirty thousand of *that* sort, and certain thousands of unconvicted criminals of the company-swindling-directorial-Cabinet-Minister-sort M.P.

"Five men attacked and brutally assaulted a Custom-House officer, knocked him down, kicked him, inflicted severe wounds, and left him for dying. One of the gang was caught, and twenty
(253) previous convictions proved against him—the others made off."

What did it matter?—six more or less out of a permanent floating population of habitual criminals thirty thousand strong. Thirty thousand habitual criminals! And that number did not include the "great thieves who go scot-free;" they were not so strong in numbers, but infinitely stronger in power and performance of mischief.

The 180,000 perennial Jubilee drunkards.

Reader, you may remember that report of a brave Jubilee School Board Inspector,* wherein it was recorded that in his district of starving children, overcrowded incest-dens, hell-desolation of misery, hopelessness, and wretchedness, to 429 bread shops there existed 912 public-houses. It should be written that the 429 bread shops *existed;* the 912 public-house hells *throve.* That was but a sample of the whole of London; in many districts the domination of the drink-hells was yet more pronounced. Even the courtly *Times* newspaper—a strong supporter of the "rights" of public-house land and public-house peers—had to confess, or did confess in a moment of unwonted candour, that "there are far too many public-houses. The temptations thrown in the way of weak humanity are too many and too strong. The brewers and the distillers are too powerful; and the system of 'tied houses' tends to all sorts of abuses." A wonderful admission that, and (254) not to be lightly passed over: "The brewers and the distillers and their system too powerful." Their work—180,000 perennial drunkards; their reward—peerages! And perennial, or hereditary power of Government in Great Britain. Perennial! Yes, perennial when it shall be a perennial law of the long-suffering God that vice and the abettors of vice shall perennially rule mankind. Otherwise *not* perennial, except in the sense of the Jubilee-party-slime-government.

You must be brought to realise a little, O British people, what that population of 180,000 perennial drunkards really meant:—

There was a Society in Jubilee times called the Society for the Prevention of Cruelty to Children. Try to realise what underlay the necessity for those charitable watchers over the helpless innocence whom the Almighty Father of us all—with divine supremacy of wisdom—entrusted to mankind in the form of perfect dependency, in order that the sweet mysteries of heavenly tenderness and

---

* Page 348.

infinite love should be for ever renewed in man. The strong man thus tutored in love-worship and protection of the weak and helpless,—*that*, the never-varying God-lesson to mankind. In it consists the mysterious, unconscious, and divinely perennial link between the Eternal Creator and His creation :—

"I send for ever into the world the little child—helpless, innocent, pure and undefiled, whom to neglect one day is to slay; whom to protect is the great privilege of man. It is My bond unto thee, O man. As thou shalt guard over the angel-weakness of thy son, so will I guard over thee; and as thou guardest over the little children I entrust to thee, so will I guard over thee. And verily I have set My Law of Laws upon the little child, and I will never depart from it. In the little child is My love and My trust to the sons of men. And in him shall all reward and punishment lie. For this say I ever unto man : For evermore, from the first day of the creation down unto the latest day when life shall move in the created world, the little child is My message, which as thou shalt hearken to, understand, and fulfil, so shall thy reward or punishment be. For it shall be that if thou guardest the purity and innocence of thy child, and shalt train him in manful ways, so shall he grow up manful to continue thy strength, thy love, thy worth, and all that is good in thee. But if thou neglectest My great trust, and neglectest thy son, and rearest him not in love, in reverence, in truth, and complete manfulness—which is virtue—verily I say unto thee, thy child shall work thy ruin. Thou rearest thyself the rod that shall break thine own back. If thou withdrawest from the child the needful protection, and rearest him in falsehood, in wickedness, and in corruption, thou art in him rearing the nation which shall effect thine own overthrow."

World of men, is that mighty God-lesson understood by you? Think you it was understood by Jubilee mankind? How were they rearing *their* children? Is it true that Jubilee mothers, in vile example of undress and worldliness, taught their sons impudicity from their earliest childhood?* That there existed in one city, supreme in Christian civilisation, 60,000 little children wanting food? That the place of the Jubilee mother, in 100,000 cases, had to be taken by the Jubilee Society for the Prevention of Cruelty to Children? So that down to the year 1894 such Society

---

* Pages 75, 261, 358.

had to record 23,000 cases of child-neglect and starvation, 10,000 cases of violence to little children, 5000 cases of child exposure by begging, and 2000 cases of child-immorality. Altogether 100,000 little child-lives involved in that sad work of a Society so worthy; (255) but of the need for such a Society how infinitely *un*worthy!

"Verily I say unto you: I have set My Law of Laws upon the little child, and will not ever depart from it. In the little child is My love and My trust to mankind, and in the care which man bestows upon the little child shall all reward and punishment lie."

. . . .

The brewers and the distillers and their "tied-houses" are too powerful and tend to all sorts of abuses; there are brewer-peers and brewer-legislators; *they* make the laws. There are brewer and publican justices of the peace and magistrates, and *they* carry on, in their own way, those laws. Let us see how. Has the reader forgotten the slum-manifesto of Carlyle Democritus, with its awful pastor-record of the Great Wild Street orgies? Look back at that,* and then ponder over these other beer and distiller-kings' orgies. All the quoted records which follow are derived from the most authentic of all the Jubilee archives, to wit, the *Times* newspaper of the Jubilee era. Wherever any record is from another source it shall be stated:—

"The attempt to clear the streets of persons in a state of simple intoxication was beyond the power of the police, and we have now reached such a point of affairs that unless drunkards are very disorderly, or absolutely incapable of motion, and without friends to take charge of them, arrests are never made." (256)

Lose not the significance of that, O reader; it meant that for every one of the 180,000 besotted wretches "taken up" before magistrates for *disorderly* drunkenness, there were ten or more, no less bestial, "taken up" by their friends, to make work, in their homes and slum-dens, for the Society for the Prevention of Cruelty to Women and Children.

In the Jubilee commemorative year 1887, three-quarters of a million women signed a memorial to the good Queen Victoria, praying her to close the public-houses on Sundays. "Let us have (257) one day in the seven free from the cruel drink-fiend, O British Queen, one day when we can see our children not beaten, and ourselves not kicked and bashed by besotten beast-men."

---

* Page 85.

The depth of meaning and the awful necessity of that prayer of the poor British women, perhaps their Jubilee Government (258) "Parliamentary Return" will make manifest:—

"During the past three years (including the period of the women's petition) there were 442,736 *convictions* for drunkenness in England and Wales alone, and nearly *ten per cent.* of them occurred on Sundays."

But the poor British Queen could do nothing. British Party men took care of *that;* British Party men made the laws, the powerful amongst them owned the breweries, distilleries, and public-houses. "So you must continue to be bashed and your children starved and kicked, even on Sundays, O three-quarters of a million British women, otherwise we of the brewer, distiller, and public-house sort will make less profits." Here is a light-flash into drink in the army:—"In one regiment of the Royal Scots Fusiliers there were seven hundred cases of drunkenness in six months; that fact came casually to light owing to one of the men, (259) in a drunken fit, having shot dead two of his comrades."

We hear of no withdrawal of the drink from that regiment, only withdrawal of the soldiers' ammunition. It would never suit a Parliament of beer and distillery legislators to stop drunkenness in the army. "Good heavens—rob us of two hundred thousand victims?" Not to be thought of. "So long as you have a Parliament made up of law and liquor traffickers, so long will you have destitution throughout the country, as the self-interest of those (260) few prevents their passing measures for the benefit of the many."

Let no mortal be misled into the fancy that the occasional party-braying of Jubilee politicians portended any serious effort to overthrow the villainous traffic, for it was quite true what the great "Thunderer" said on many an occasion : "The liquor traffic, with all its effects on morality and social liberty, was made a mere counter in a game played by cynical politicians in caucuses and division (261) lobbies."

There was a statesman in Jubilee times called Sir William Harcourt, and when he could get votes from the publican people he shrieked against "interfering" with the liquor traffic, and the three-quarters of a million Jubilee women praying for help were unheeded by him; he admired and quoted the bishop who said he would sooner see England drunk than controlled in its liquor bestiality, or, to put it in its due Episcopalian eloquentiality, "he

would sooner see England 'free' than sober"—free to murder, free (262)
to bash tender women, *free* to send hundreds of thousands of
besotted beasts to conviction year after year. But wait; look at
this other scene. Suddenly that great Jubilee statesman, named
Sir William Harcourt, discovered that he might get more votes
from the temperance than from the *in*temperance party; thereupon
he swallowed all his rant about "freedom" and "interference,"
and offered to close *all* the public-houses, if only the poor silly
people would give him their votes, and—O all Merciful, those were
the gods in Israel, in Jubilee times!

In the previous chapter it has been said that Want was the great
factor in the awful horrors of Jubilee prostitution; that was the
opinion of most workers amongst the poor—"sheer necessity" was
the cause. (263)

Some of the worthy pastors who worked amongst the poorest
said that "strong drink" was also a potent cause, and in any event
was the considerable stimulating cause. (264)

There was no limit in the Jubilee era to the number of times
that a hopeless drunkard might be brought before the magistrates.
At one court a woman had been charged with being drunk and
disorderly in the streets two hundred and thirty times. (265)

Another woman was "charged" before the magistrates forty
times, not including various attempts to commit suicide. Day (266)
after day, year after year, the police courts of London and Great
Britain were choked with such cases, and worse. As for the
coroner's courts, one illustration will serve for a thousand. (267)

A child of four years had died from neglect — one of the
hundred thousand cases brought to God's light by the brave
Society for the Protection of Children. They had watched the
woman—must it be written, the mother—of the child, because she
had already killed one of her children by neglect and cruelty a
year or two before, and had been imprisoned for the crime. The
mother was one of the habitual Jubilee drunkards. Her husband,
in evidence, said that whenever he reached home his wife was
intoxicated and abusive, and—the children were all insured in the
Prudential Office, and—the woman was "censured" by the Jubilee
coroner, and let go to starve and murder her other children, who
were all "insured." Of that other hell-refinement, *child-life
insurance*, let it only be known that it was no common thing for a
mother to have "*lost*"—not murdered, reader, not tortured by

neglect and slow starvation, only "*lost*"—(sweet, Jubilee euphemism for the hell-blackest cruelty ever tolerated by brewery and distillery legislators and peers)—"*lost*" six or seven children, all "insured."

Here is an "Insurance" case with the prices fixed for the (266) murder-temptation:—

A man and woman were summoned at North London for neglecting their four children—Charles, aged 10; William, aged 8; Emily, aged 6; and Thomas, aged 4. The boy Charles was insured for £9, William for £8, and Thomas for £3, 15s. The girl Emily was a cripple, and could not be insured. She was allowed to sleep on a box, though without clothes; the other little children were huddled on the bare boards, naked except for a few rags. They were in a shocking condition. The room was filthy and smelt offensively. The children were all emaciated, and covered with vermin and dirt. Two of the younger children were brought into Court in that year of Jubilee 1894—a little boy aged 4, and a little girl aged 6, and neither of them was bigger than a baby of eighteen months.

The Jubilee sentence on that "mother" was "three months;" after that period "free" to complete the insurance-murders.

One of the brave women of the Children's Protection Society, (267) "attracted by the frightful screams of a child—between ten and eleven at night—obtained entrance into the rooms of a man who was found beating a little four-year-old boy with the buckle-end of a strap, and, when remonstrated with, bid the woman 'Mind her own business, as the child was insured for £7, 10s., and was worth more dead than it was alive.' They examined the little child in the court, and found its back cruelly marked by the buckle, and one mass of bruises."

Yes, murder was positively attempted in *that* way—for £7, 10s. —although the Doctors, at a Royal Commission, or Lords' Commission, years before, had implored the British Government to stop that "insurance of children which was but a premium on murder." But had little Jubilee children votes, O Jubilee Government? Assuredly not, any more than right hon. swindlers M.P. had bowels of compassion.

Yes, Parliament knew all about it; had they not had their Royal Commission, or Lords' Commission, years before upon it, and as usual nothing achieved, nothing but unending talk, and unending expense of printer's ink.

The committee consisted of two bishops, the Lord Chancellor, five Earls, and seven sundry Lords. To them speaks a medical officer of health. Here is some evidence from that Lords' Commission or Committee :—

"I am quite convinced that in cases in which the children of poor parents in my district were insured, the chief anxiety of the parents was to see their children dead. I have no doubt that insurance operates as an inducement to neglect children, and let them waste away. A sum of thirty shillings, or a much less sum, would be a sufficient inducement for a parent to neglect a child. . . . I have known cases where a child of two and a-half years old only weighed seven pounds."

Another medical officer gave similar evidence. He said: "I have seen children with their tongues so parched that I have taken a knife and handed it to the mother, and said, ' Be merciful, and kill it that way.' . . . The Insurance Companies must be well aware that such cases occurred."

Many doctors from all parts of the country gave similar evidence. And Jubilee years passed on, and the Jubilee Bishops and Peers still sat mumbling in patent commission, in their Jubilee Juggernauth Car, which, with Mammon for driver, crunched on and on over the bodies of men and women, and over the bodies of little children. And the silent stars were above, and the Eternal God over them. And the Jubilee Lords, and the other slime things, talked on unceasingly.

You have heard the merciful doctors and their evidence before the Jubilee Peers. Now enter the Police Court and listen again. Here is one of the cases on trial :—

John Gee, and Sarah his wife, were charged with having caused the death of their son by starving and neglecting him. All the children of the prisoners were "insured."

The Magistrate :—" What were they insured for?"

Counsel for the Prisoners :—" I do not know the amount."

The Magistrate :—" What is the usual amount?"

Counsel :—" Thirty shillings to two pounds. And for that amount they pay a penny or more per week."

Magistrate :—" Then, for a penny a week, a child just born can be insured, and the parents get the sum of two pounds, or so, when it dies?"

Counsel :—" Yes."

Magistrate:—" And how much does it cost to bury a child?"

Counsel:—" I do not know exactly; about eight shillings."

Magistrate:—" And the parents get a profit of about twenty-two to thirty-two shillings."

The Magistrate's Clerk:—" It is a premium on manslaughter and murder!"

Magistrate:—" It is scandalous, and have you many Insurance Companies like that?"

Clerk:—"Oh, plenty."

O reader, those cases were going on all over Jubilee England. Yet people railed at the brutalised poor, not at the brutalised Parliaments who had crunched out humanity from their victims, until the love which God placed in every heart had dried up before starvation, filth, misery, and despair.

(272) At the end of the world the Final Judge will see this case also when he tries those child-murderers:—

An inquest was held on the body of Charles Wootten, who had died from exhaustion by falling from his van whilst asleep. The evidence of his widow proved that for years he had had to work from half-past four in the morning until ten at night; those were his continual hours, and "he was wore out," . . . and the van crushed over him and released him from further Jubilee toil.

And a Duke was being "pensioned" at that time by Parliament with £600,000, because his great-great-grandfather was an Ass-in-Ordinary to Charles the Second.* And another Duke later on was getting a quarter of a million or so from Parliament for a piece of land which the Lord God had made, and which the British (273) people by their industry had enriched. They, the people, were to get the acre of land, and the Duke (descendant of him who shot himself because he already possessed £500,000 which he did not know how to invest) was to get the quarter of a million sterling. By what enchantment the Duke "owned" that land, this Jubilee history hath already recorded.

And now to revert to the Jubilee Insurance Companies and the little children. This is an inquest on Henry Frederick, a little (274) child (*not* insured, this little one):—

(Witness a widow with four children, and the little starved one—dead).

---

* Page 309.

Coroner:—"Were you at home much?"

Widow:—"No, the children used to look after themselves. I had all my work to find bread for them."

The Jury:—"What could you earn?"

Widow:—"When there was work at the laundry, I would get three shillings and ninepence for a day and a half. At other times I would work at covering tennis-balls."

Jury:—"What was the pay for that?"

Widow:—"Fourpence a gross; I could earn altogether about four shillings and ninepence a week."

She had to keep herself and five children, and the rent was three shillings out of it. She had a son at work, a long distance away, who used to send her a shilling, or a shilling and sixpence a week, sometimes.

The Jury:—"Do you mean to say that your family had never more than three shillings a week left for food and clothing?"

Widow:—"Yes; I am compelled to make it do, we only eat dry bread for days together; when I can spare the money, I give them a little butter. I have often worked until eleven at night—twelve hours a day."

Let the curtain fall, O reader, and marvel no more that the heart and breast of a woman can be dried up. When thou shalt have seen starvation and misery, and twelve hours a day work, and three shillings a week balance of pay, then shalt thou condemn the poor. Meanwhile there is the Eternal Judge, and He will condemn, perhaps, other than the poor.

But get back to the drink, and hear these last words of a London magistrate: "It was impossible to sit for a month, or a week, or (275) even a day, in any one of the London police courts without seeing how homes were devastated, domestic happiness ruined, and lives wrecked by the abuse of strong drink."

And the abettors of that villainous traffic were Jubilee England's "greatest." It was one vile ubiquitous mud-stream of "law" and "liquor." Enough! Enough!

You who would understand Jubilee England, look not to the laws and lawyers, nor to the courts and judges, nor to the peers and politicians. Look to the silent and patient multitude; look to the societies who tried to undo the wide-spreading evils of the governing pollutions; look to the heroic men pursuing England's greatness far away from the corruption of place and party. It was a nation too brave and beautiful to be lost.

"O mighty British Oak, sore beset with vermin, send from thy knotty heart's strength new flood of potent sap to swell out thy giant limbs, and shake the foul creeping things clear from thy branches. O mighty and invisible Power of good, permit not this glorious people to decline: send from all corners of the earth and heaven thy storm-winds and thy purging winter-blast to shake off the poison-growths from the British Tree of Life. For the people are in their heart a God-fearing, earnest nation; it is only the governors who are vile."

Thus had answered Carlyle Democritus those who, in the early days of the Revolution, still mad with the sufferings they had endured, had wanted to carry fire and sword among all the children of Mammon. In that prayer he had answered them, and they let him pursue his way.

We can but dimly record the immensity of the reforms which the Revolution established in the judicial system of the country. Closely analysed, we see in them no particular innovation anywhere, but rather a universal burning up of unutterable abuses; a wiping away of vermin and verminous excrescences everywhere. The British Oak tree was left unharmed, but cleansed of the legal and political slime of ages which had been allowed to gather there.

For instance, in all the old various millions of legal, mediæval, verbose twaddle-volumes, it was nowhere an offence for a man's dog to bite and tear a child or adult, provided it was the dog's first human feast. Now, although the whole codex of the Revolution consisted of only one moderately sized volume, that dog-matter, and a thousand kindred matters, were settled in a very few lines. Under "Injury" was the following:—"Whoso by himself, his servant, his animal, his machinery, or by whomsoever or whatsoever is his, or employed by him, or to him responsible in any manner directly or indirectly, accidentally or wilfully, by neglect or otherwise, causeth harm to another,—to that other shall he be responsible, and shall make reparation."

Jubilee Parliament would have required fifty "Acts" of some thousands of clauses to have conveyed one-tenth of that law, and other fifty "Acts" of more thousands of clauses to amend the first fifty "Acts," and *then* would not have achieved the simple and just result of the one Revolutionary law.

Under the word "Reparation" the codex set forth:—"The jury, assisted and directed by the judge, shall determine in every case, upon the evidence before them, the nature of the reparation, whether it shall be by restitution, fine, compensation, imprisonment, or one, or any, or all of them."

It must be remembered that after the Revolution all cases were tried by practical men, not by mere windbags and horsehair wigs. The training of the Revolutionary magistrates and judges has been already explained. Plaintiff and defendant came before the courts equal; no pleaders, or paid liars, were tolerated any more. Pure, simple justice existed, unchoked by Coke or Littleton. Poverty on one side, and wealth on the other, made no difference. Before the august majesty of the pure Revolutionary courts of justice the poorest stood level with the king. Money could avail neither party. The poorest suitor, or the richest peer, enjoyed common privileges. It went ill with the court official who should slight a poor suitor. The Balance which the Revolutionary courts set up swerved not for mortal man. The age of Mammon was dead; right alone could turn the divine scales. *That* was the only weight in British courts thenceforth.

We have said that the entire laws of Great Britain were comprehended in one volume of simple, unadulterated plainness of statement. It is impossible to do more than indicate some of the contents of the great codex. Life-insurance of children was forbidden. Labour insurance was permitted—that is to say, a child might be insured even at its birth against accident and dependency, but no payment resulted in the event of its death before the age of adult work-years—twenty-one for males, and eighteen for females. Nor could any money payment whatsoever be made to any person on behalf of an insured, other than to those dependent on the deceased for support—unless by the written order, or testament, of the insured after the completion of his or her majority. The Company Laws have been mentioned in an earlier chapter.* Briefly

---

* Pages 264-266.

a public company was treated precisely as a private trader. Every director and managing person concerned and interested in a company was made absolutely responsible for all acts and deeds of the whole body of directors and managers, just the same as in the case of a partner in a private business. He was also made responsible for every statement made in prospectus or report, and not only responsible in the amount of his immediate interest in the company, but responsible to any and every shareholder to the extent of his private fortune also. The Revolution did not trifle with fraud, nor with defrauders. It held that the greater the man who robbed, the more "noble" the thief, the greater was the scoundrel. £25,000,000 sterling a year were no longer sucked from the earnings of a confiding people into the endless maw of company thieves. The Revolutionary net might now and then perhaps let a minnow escape, but *not* a whale. It was not a Jubilee net by any means. Quackery of all sorts was so effectually suppressed— mainly by making an advertiser absolutely responsible for every word he advertised—quite irrespective of one or one thousand fools who might come forward to "prove" that the quack or his quackery had cured them of all evils under the sun, that early in the twentieth century a Jubilite would have imagined, from the dearth of soap, pill, and patent-medicine advertisements, that all diseases had disappeared, and twentieth century folk required no washing. Distilled water could not be sold by plausible Italian thieves, even of the titled sort, as a cure for cancer at half-a-guinea a bottle; idiot British editor vowing that the water

(131) was a true gift of the gods, notwithstanding. The medical guild courts exercised a check on such conduct, and the like of it. Advertisers altogether were compelled to accommodate themselves to truth and fact. The Revolutionary era traded neither in lies, subterfuges, nor ubiquitous cant, the prevailing characteristics of the entire Jubilee period. Jubilee statesmen, perhaps rightly enough, had been considered fit objects for vulgar display on advertisement boards, or at the back of useful papers; no one objected in those times, and it must be confessed with very abundant reason. But the Revolutionary statesmen were England's best and noblest, most truthful, not most lying; most honest, not most fraudulent; and woe betide him who dared to pollute the name of the man of honour and worth. It was not left to public men to protect themselves against such degrading

offensiveness. England's great men were England's pride; their names and their glory her keen solicitude. The Board of Public Prosecutors were responsible for all duties in connection with the protection of their honour, so far as abuse, slander, or libel by public journals, advertisements, or otherwise, was concerned. Half the gin-hells in Jubilee times would be called by the name of Jubilee statesmen or British heroes. That was possible then; but it was not possible afterwards. England treasured her hero-titles, and jealously guarded them against pollution; no name of a national hero or statesman could be used as a trade-mark or designation of goods without permission of the individual if he were living, or of the Council of Public Prosecutors were he dead. Owners of wax-nonsenses had to obtain a man's written permission before they could imitate the god-image of him. Criminals and Jubilee statesmen they were free to appropriate unasked, but no others. The law of libel was altogether simplified. Freedom of the Press was not allowed to mean filthy licence of the Press. There was an end of mud-gutter Jubilee, so called — perhaps very properly called — "Society papers," bespattering every decent name with scandal and base insinuation, their whole business to sniff out the unsavoury in human character; the swine and jackals of the Press, to whom all wholesome food was repugnant, and whose instincts led them only to the dung heap. The dishing of such ragouts for society curs as base as themselves ceased with all other Jubilee barbarisms. The libel and slander trade was no longer a business in which a man could defend himself only with the certainty of ruinous expense to his pocket, whether he won or lost his case. The licensed Jubilee libeller had to cease his trade after the Revolution. If any journal insulted the king because he was a king, or a peer because he was a peer, or any public man because he was a public man, or a hero because he was a hero,—and because the mud-journal was infinitely vile; not the king or the peer, the public man or the hero, had to ruin himself to punish foul libel. That had become the duty of the State. A healthy generation could not, and would not, tolerate an atmosphere of perennial mud and stench, and "Society Papers," being unable to live in any other than that vitiated atmosphere, died.

The laws of marriage, divorce, and breach of promise, were considerably changed. Insanity, criminal conviction, and drunkenness were made grounds of divorce. Insanity, because it condemned the sane partner to needless misery, to an unnatural and unhealthy life, and the progeny to infamous danger. Only the sad cant of a Jubilee era could have so long tolerated the horrible burden of being bound by such a foul custom. If the insane recovered, there was no security against a relapse. Moreover, should a cure be effected, the divorced was free; and for one such case there were a hundred which did *not* recover. Drunkenness as a ground for divorce was a law after the Revolution, but happily had not often to be called upon, because the vice had practically disappeared; still, it remained in the codex. Whatever might be the grounds of divorce, no man was permitted to retain any money that the wife brought to settlement. If there were children, a portion had to be settled upon them; if none, it reverted entirely to the woman or to her family, never mind how guilty she may have been. The Revolutionary laws were on too noble a basis to permit a man to profit by a wife's error, crime, or misfortune. On the other hand, reasonable provision for the divorced wife had to be made in every case by the man in cases where she had not her own provision, according to his position and to the circumstances occasioning the divorce; but always provision—never mind how guilty the wife; otherwise there could be no divorce. Wise laws must regard all sides, and not only one side. Let the evidence be what it will, there is no mortal to be so damned for the errors of passion by his or her fellow-men that hope shall be entirely and for ever cut off. A woman left without provision is worse than killed. No true system of justice shall punish mercilessly; else it is not justice, but mere revenge. Leave the door open to reform; where that is barred, it is not a porch of heaven or of earth, but of hell. Even when the "habitual criminal" was removed for ever from the society of his fellows by a wise penal code, he was only removed to prevent him from harming others—removed to the penal settlements, where work and duty (*i.e.* a useful life) were compulsory to him, and for which reason he was free who had once been a slave, since habitual criminality is not freedom, but is an awful and unutterable slavery to the Infernal One. In order to prevent any temptation to unnecessary litigation, there were clear limits set to the provisions required in cases of divorce. They were severe where the offender was the husband, and proportionately light if the offence was on, or provoked by, the other side. Furthermore, the sexes were made equal before the law, and the grounds which enabled the man to sue for divorce could be invoked by the woman also. The mischief and scandal of the Jubilee breach of promise laws were effectively remedied. In Jubilee times the weak woman bore the heaviest blame and the sorest burden; on the other hand, the strong or the brazen woman levied a system of blackmail which did not compensate for the other evil, but made only *two* evils. The Revolutionary codex remedied both of them. The laws were simple and clear, and their application no less so. Breach of promise, with no ulterior harm than the change of mind of the parties, or party, was amenable to no punishment at all; why should it be? But if a suitor induced a woman to forego her employment, he was responsible to the full amount of the income or wages he had caused her to lose. Nothing was considered beyond that. A just law refused to grant money allotments for "feelings." An engagement entered into with an ignoble intent and act, or ignoble act irrespective of intent, was treated as serious crime, and was punishable not only by heavy pecuniary levies, but by imprisonment to boot. All money fines were laid down in the code, and were not left open as speculative temptations to blackmail. They were calculated upon clear proportion of the income of the offender. Towards the support of a child the Jubilee sum was doubled—that was a minimum. But justice must take all things into consideration; and, according to the position of an offender, that weekly allowance increased. On the other hand, an end was put to mere blackmail cases by the Courts of Honour and Arbitration. All those courts were private, and they dealt with all cases between the sexes. Appeal to the High Courts was open to the parties *afterwards*. But if, after the adjudication of the courts of first instance, a case was continued merely for worthless motives, the penalty upon the offender was severe, and carried with it abrogation of all monetary claim, and, in extreme cases, imprisonment. As a fact, however, such cases could scarcely occur; in Jubilee times they had been the direct produce of shark-lawyers, and they disappeared together with the producing cause. Perhaps the most difficult of all problems between the sexes are those arising out of what is conveniently called "incompatibility of temper." Carlyle Democritus was too wise a legislator to slacken the laws of divorce in any undue manner. Therefore, beyond the equalising of the husband and wife before the law, the Revolution made no change beyond what has already been indicated, except in the simplicity of the procedure. But separation was granted upon easier conditions. The courts were rarely able to effect conciliation in matrimonial cases; any hopes in that direction could never occur to practical legislators. Where family influence has failed, the necessarily cold and inflexible hand of the law is not likely to avail. But a decided and simple code could, and did, mitigate many evils. Either party could obtain judicial separation, instead of divorce, in cases where the heavier penalty might have been obtainable, as in Jubilee time. Judicial separation, however, not being irrevocable, and often conducing to reconciliation at a later period, was open to husband and wife, the courts laying down very clear and definite rules in the matter of ample provision for wife and children. If the evidence before the court showed the wife to have been the aggressive or offending party, the penalties and restriction bore more upon her; if, on the other hand, the husband was the prime offender, the pecuniary provision and other penalties exacted from him were more severe. Unless for good cause to the contrary, the mother retained charge of all the children up to the age of fourteen, after that age the children were allowed to choose with which parent they would dwell. The frequency and the conditions of visiting the children by the separated spouse depended upon the cause which had engendered the separation. The law set no limit to the number of times parties might separate and reconcile. But, after one reconciliation, the penalties upon the provoking or offending party were materially increased.

There was one other species of sexual relation known in Jubilee times, and productive of wholesale misery and mischief, for want of definite legislation: that of "free" unions. After the Revolution such cases were considerably diminished owing to the healthy marriage laws, and the stigma which rested upon bachelordom.[*] A sane society saw nothing but the reprehensible in mud-existences of any sort; whether they were commercial, political, connubial, or free-connubial. There *were* such cases, and there probably always will be such cases. And the parties, being human, will be prone to suffer the usual incompatibilities. Now, it behoves wise law-makers to face evils, to stare them in the face, and make

---

[*] Page 354.

them (the evils) disappear; not let themselves be cowed, like ineffable cowards, by any evil, or accumulation of evils. Men must not deal with dangers and difficulties in ostrich-fashion—the tail feathers turned skyward, and the eyes buried in desert sand. " Free" incompatibilities having cause of quarrel could not try universal blackmail *à la* Jubilee breach-of-promise futility. The courts and the codex had very definite rules for such cases; the only portion needing here to be touched upon being the provision, or pecuniary one. Tired Lotharios were required to settle proper provision upon a discarded mistress. Freedom of the licence sort was not tolerable upon other conditions. Seldom were the public ears offended by such cases after the Revolution; not one case in a hundred needed to appeal beyond the Honour or Arbitration Courts. The "free" laws were just; they did not assume unmitigated scamphood for all Romeos, or unmitigated Magdelinity for all Juliets. A practical Carlyle Democritus said (with, and beyond, the poet Schiller):—"A fox knows much, but a woman in love knows more ; and a woman *not* in love, but pretending to be in love, knows most."

The cruellest scourge of society in Jubilee times was cunning self-seeking, hidden behind the mask of simplicity. The Revolutionary Courts distinguished clearly between the alluring playfulness of kittenhood and the matured (and by no means alluring) scratchfulness of full-blown cathood. Wise laws overlook nothing; they look *into* everything calmly, dispassionately, and absolutely without cant.

The Revolution left the railways in the hands of the Companies.[*]
With few exceptions they were worked infinitely better than any Continental railways under the direction of the State. Some of the great English companies were indeed models of able management. What the Revolution did was to compel all Companies to "level up" to the working of the best. Those which could not, for want of capital, were purchased by the State. The following, amongst other laws, were then made applicable to all the railways:
—All Companies were held responsible for the due carrying out of the time-services printed in their time-tables. Any departure from

---

[*] Page 223.

the contract time, except in cases of accident, rendered the defaulting company liable to a fine, summarily recoverable by the aggrieved passengers. A railway company could no more be permitted to deceive its customers in the matter of the work for which it was paid than any other public or private caterer. The days of fraud of any sort were past. If a company found it difficult to arrive within the period notified in its time-tables, that company had to alter its time-tables, and not continue to deceive the public. One minute in every hour's journey was allowed, after that the statutory fine was one penny on every ticket for every minute later than the arrival-time notified in the tables. Every company had to adopt the safest and best system of brakes and signals, and in lighting and warming their carriages. The labour conditions of all were already safeguarded by the Labour Laws. All Companies had to mark the names of their stations in a sufficiently conspicuous manner, at minimum distances of thirty feet, along all divisions and walls of platforms, and no advertisement was permitted to appear within six feet of any portion of the name-boards. All the station lamps had also to bear the name of the station upon them. Failure to light a carriage under a tunnel subjected a company to a summary fine which the aggrieved passengers could levy at the end of their journey, by lodging a complaint at the justice-room of the station post-office.* With regard to the rates for carriage of goods, a very simple but stringent law was made. No preferential rates were permitted on the carriage of British goods, nor any evasion of that law by means of discounts or otherwise; the mileage rate, for rich or poor, of the same class of goods, was identical, whether the quantity were large or small. Also the scandalous Jubilee preferential rates for foreign carriage were abolished, and in their stead all companies were compelled to reverse their old unpatriotic Jubilee policy, by charging one-tenth less upon British goods than upon foreign wares of the same description. The State laws discouraged competition between companies, and by every means induced co-operation instead. There was no longer any cost to the companies in obtaining Parliamentary legislation. The days of the barrister-harpies were over. No millions of capital were wasted † in mere senseless legal jabber —a fact of great advantage to railway and all other companies.

---

* Page 413. † Page 366.

Finally, there was the Railway Guild, with its masters and men all represented—a kind of railway parliament in fact, where reforms and improvements were considered and discussed, and whose general meetings were attended by an official representing the Government, as a central authority in all railway matters. By means of this assembly necessary changes and improvements were made general throughout the whole railway service.

Throughout all the agricultural districts of the Kingdom, the Government built light railways and connected them with the great Trunk lines. As these light railways were erected on land owned by the State, and without ruinous fees having to be paid to landlords, land-agents, lawyers, or any of the old Jubilee bloodsuckers, their construction rarely exceeded a cost of from £3000 to £4000 a mile. They proved a rich source of direct revenue to the nation, and the facilities they afforded to the farmers added a yet more valuable, though indirect, revenue to the country—a revenue of widespread prosperity. Not the Jubilee prosperity of a few, at the expense and degradation of the many; but a prosperity which, like the equal sun, cast its radiance in the lowest as in the highest places, and lit the humblest village with a rosy glow of that healthy life which regained for this fair Isle her old poetic title of "Merry England." On all freights brought by the agricultural light railways to the main lines, special rates were made; and thus, and by other kinds of State help, Great Britain, in the twentieth century, grew to be once more a vast agricultural producing country. Its peasants were the bravest and sturdiest in all the world. "Sons of God" was written on the simple honest features of them all. Their children were once again the wonder of the world,—as in those old Roman times when the Roman mothers who saw them cried: "*Non Angli sed angeli.*"

The adulteration laws have been touched upon elsewhere.* That old Jubilee trick of advertising sawdust as gold-dust was as dead as cant; Carlyle Democritus was in no way tolerant of it. To advertise a ware of supreme quality, and then sell ten inferior articles under the same title, was Jubilee dodge-business but was not permitted after the Revolution. The reader will remember that healthy law† which required every article to bear marked upon its face, in unmistakable plainness, what it actually was. Imagine this Jubilee article under Revolutionary law :—

---

* Pages 208-209. † Page 208.

"Divine Arabian Revelation! A certain cure for asthma, cancer, croup, measles, obesity, chilblains, and childbirth."

Imagine further, under such an advertisement, in plain honest English: "This preparation, price 3s. 6d. a packet of 8 ozs., is plain and unadulterated ground lentils; obtainable in plain wrapper, under its proper title, and without the above named lies, for ten-pence, or less, a pound."

In Jubilee times the British Government directly "patented" that fraud, and others like it, and absolutely robbed the public out of £200,000 a year over the bargain. Let the dubious reader invest sixpence and read a little book called "Quack Medicines," which he will find to contain over 160 closely printed pages of such devil-swindles, of which the above is but a very humble example. Post-Revolutionary British Government happily derived nothing from infamous fraud of the quack species, whereof indeed Jubilee Government was the supreme head. Was there not the "Sorrypebble Jubilee Mixture," guaranteed to make a lie look like truth? and "The Sorrypebble Gin-Hell," guaranteed to fire a man's brains and render him fit for any bestiality or crime in ten minutes? With a Sorrypebble for supreme quack, an infinity of transcendent quackeries are inevitable. *Perimus licitis.*

With regard to "*advertisements in public thoroughfares,*" rural scenery was protected against desecration by advertisements. However much the land and the houses were the property of the owner and worker, yet was no man permitted to carry on offensive or obnoxious trades to the detriment or annoyance of his neighbour. And as vulgar advertisements, amid peaceful valleys and beautiful scenery, are amongst the most outrageous forms of nuisance, they were severely forbidden. Similarly, with regard to houses, the owner was limited to the exhibition of his own trade notices, and not permitted to rent his walls, or in any way disfigure them with extraneous advertisements. The beauty of the streets is the common property of every citizen. To vehicles the same law applied; every trade vehicle had to bear its owner's name and distinctive number clearly upon it. The trade and calling of the owner might appear, but mere advertisement waggons were rigidly forbidden. All public vehicles came under the same law, and were restricted absolutely to notices concerning their own business or route. The unsightly Jubilee omnibus placards, the peripatetic advertisements (called sandwich men) disappeared altogether. The

streets were laid out and preserved for traffic, and not permitted
to be invaded by exhibitions of any description. The various
county and district councils jealously preserved them against
disfigurement by soulless advertisers.

The drink laws have been dealt with in many parts of this
history. In a word, the Revolution regarded drink (drunkenness)
as the most heinous of all crimes; the worst, because it was the
father of so many others. Murder committed murder and ceased.
But drink instigated a thousand crimes, and was not satisfied.
Three times convicted for drunkenness, and your beast-man came
forth from the penal colony no more. That was the end of him,
and, as far as this history is concerned, the end of further reference
to him.

With regard to the observance of Sunday, a word should be said,
for the Revolution dealt with that matter in a brave and characteristic way. In Jubilee times, as has already been shown,* drunkenness was at its height on Sundays, liquor Parliaments having quite
cunningly arranged *that* matter. Every conceivable means of human
recreation was carefully cut away from the people, except the recreation of getting drunk, and of that, as we have seen, they duly
availed themselves. Now, let Carlyle Democritus be praised, that
supreme consummation of cant was made to go the way of all other
Jubilee cant. The public-houses existed no longer, so laws had
not to be made for them. For all beside, the law was conclusive.
No *work* on Sunday! That was emphatic and clear. It was to
be a day of rest and recreation. "No work," says the pure, beautiful
Book of the world; but it nowhere says, "No play." Consequently,
with the exception of refreshment-houses (and only those whose
assistants or owners—no exception was made—received an alternative rest-day), every shop in the kingdom had to close. But,
owing to the healthier state of public life, the shutter-horrors were
almost entirely done away with, as no longer necessary; and the
streets, though without the bustle of business, were not without
the refreshing brightness which tasteful shop-window decorations
afforded. All museums were open, and the parks were free for
play in their respective fields. All the chief walks and avenues,
and the grass plots near them, were preserved for those who
preferred perfect quiet; but the ponds and the streams and the

---

* Page 394.

playing fields were, under wise regulations, free for the young to play in and rejoice. "Ye shall rejoice," the Scriptures say everywhere; nowhere do the lovely pages say, "Ye shall be glum." And where is rejoicing more pure and righteous than under the fair canopy of heaven? Rejoice then, O young ones of England, no more cooped up in filthy murder-slums, where little children starved and pined! God's light and justice is everywhere; there is no more poisonous gloom. Play, little children, and rejoice greatly; for herein lies the truest worship of God. Let us, however, be just to the Jubilee times; they did permit one source of recreation in the parks, since boats were at all times for hire on the ornamental waters. That permission to play upon the water, but not upon the land, is perhaps not altogether inscrutable; had the Jubilee governing folk an unconscious sympathy for a pastime of a liquid nature?

There was one period of sublime quiet, a beautiful contrast to the lively day. At eleven o'clock bells were sounded in all the parks, and play ceased until two in the afternoon. During the same interval all public buildings and all refreshment-houses were closed; only the churches remained open. In them, at half-past eleven, were held simple, godly services. Few were they who did not attend to hear the honest, truthful voices of the people's pastors. There was no cant-whine, no more of the soul-curdling throat-monotone, as of mud-water gurgling through a half-choked pipe. The voices of MEN (not of Jubilee cant-prigs) allured true men to worship by their piety, sympathy, and manful counsel. The English Sunday had become noble and true, like the national life. Few were they who did not visit the pastors' services after the great purification, or Revolution. Nonconformity had become a lost word. The nearest approach to it was a much more fatal word, used to designate those who cut themselves from union with their God. *Deformity* that was called—an old word with an added meaning, half-contempt, half-pity. The English were ever a deep, earnest, and religious people. Even Jubilee cant could not kill the divine link in them. It had cruelly cloaked it, and suppressed it; but killed it could not be, and it burst out in all its soulful splendour with the reversion to the pure and pious worship which the Church reforms had established.

Here is, perhaps, the most beautiful of all the extensions of the Revolution: the ubiquitous assistance furnished by the State in connection with its administration of justice. There was a principle which dominated or underlay all Carlyle Democritus's legislation. The principle, viz., that it is better to support a man in danger of falling into the stream, than to grapple and fish him out of the mud-ooze *after* he has fallen. Justice, legal help, was placed at every man's door literally, in this manner :—

It has already been said that the Government erected permanent post-offices wherever there had been temporary ones or agencies. In every post-office was a division set apart for judicial officers. Here a citizen could apply for any needful help under the sun of British law. The official directed the applicant as to the relief he required, as to the court he should apply to. The making, recording, and registering of wills, and any occasions of transfer, were undertaken in them for the great central authorities. Wills, like all other post-Revolutionary documents, were no longer expressed in terms of almost idiotic verbosity, but were recorded in honest, simple English. And, if the citizen desired it, the State provided official trustees. There were no fees for any of this work. The State taxes on wealth and the revenue from land* amply provided all revenues, as has been effectually set forth in earlier chapters. Very small matters often cause very large distress ; for instance, one objectionable man in Jubilee times could disturb the peace, convenience, and comfort of a whole neighbourhood. He could not continue to perpetuate a nuisance, even for a few hours, after the establishment of the Revolutionary judicial system. Converting a back garden in a crowded neighbourhood into a cock and hen yard ; opening a fried-fish shop in a street thenceforward rendered uninhabitable, and almost impassable by human kind, was not possible to an offensive Briton after the Revolution. Such and kindred luxuries could only be indulged in with the written sanction of the majority of the neighbours of the would-be-frier-of-fish or cock-keeper. In one day, often in an hour, at no cost to the parties, a Court of First Instance heard and adjudicated upon a matter that required six months at Jubilee times, and ruinous expense. And now may the Law Chapter end. The great codex was the triumph of the Revolution. There remained only to preserve it against desecration by future asinine commentators. The new Parliament, therefore, made it contempt of court,

---

* Pages 136, 137, 143, 144.

and an act of treason against the laws, for any man to start any commentary business upon the great codex. All the laws contained in it were as honestly clear and simple as human righteousness and truth could make them. If any doubt existed on any law, the Revising Council at once took the matter in hand, and set the doubt at rest. The Revising Council was a permanent institution. It consisted of five judges selected by the Bench of Judges, five lay members elected by the Central Chamber of Commerce, and five members elected by the professional associations. As all officers and officials had to retire after their sixtieth year, there was no stagnation possible anywhere nor amongst this body; and there was no possibility of the codex suffering from the decay which has overtaken less wise institutions. The Revolutionary Council not only guarded over the purity and simplicity of the Code, but from time to time (with the sanction of Parliament) amended laws which had grown obsolete, and recommended new ones to Parliament when new were required. Mere bibliolatry was bravely guarded against. Coke, Littleton & Company were not wanted here.

And now let the Law Chapter fitly close with the wise words which stood at the great Codex's opening:—

"NEMO PRUDENS PUNIT QUIA PECCATUM EST, SED NE PECCETUR."

PART III.
APOTHEOSIS.

Book I.
PARLIAMENT AGAIN.

"DEMOCRACY is always the willing subject of the autocracy, either of true or of false and plausible individuals. At this hour it is the bond-slave of the tongue. The Empire has become a rhetorical 'phantasm,' and its councils are flitting *ignes fatui*. The rule and power of the people is thought to be advancing with great strides during these years; but is the people more powerful for their power? Unless this is the case, the word Democracy —signifying the strength of the nation, and the embodiment of the national will in active force—is an assumption and a mistake. Democracy without this condition is compatible with increased feebleness, with greater ductility to designing men, with having its own honest will turned out of doors, and the place of it supplanted by tyrannical agitators and self-seekers. Democracy may be like a large ant-hill of most commercial and industrial ants, each intent upon his one grain of stuff, and carrying it home on his back to his proper young, and to his typically respectable community. Democracy in this case may have a neighbour which watches its prosperous trading, and wants it, soul and body. There may be a Great Ant-Eater in the neighbourhood—a Grand Old Ant-Eater. If Democracy is not something more than a community of trading pismires, the Great Ant-Eater has only to protrude his long tongue in the path of the stream of ants—a tongue attractive with glistening trail of promises—and to keep his tongue well out in talk, immovable, vocal motion so incessant in vibration as to simulate rest and preach peace. The ants climb the sweet tongue, and are raised by the promises; and, when the tongue is well covered by the creatures, the Great Ant-Eater draws them in, and has them in his belly, nourishing his shagginess. And as swallowed-up ants tell no tales, he lays out his tongue again and again, and draws in well nigh the whole nation of them. . . . Of course, the swallowing process may be avoided, but only by keeping sedulously out of the way of the tongue, by discerning the selfhood in the tongue, detecting what it wants, and giving its cajoleries a wide berth and a religious inattention. But it may be feared that Democracy will have to find itself many times in the belly of the Grand Old Ant-Eater and his successors before it learns to distrust and righteously to detest him and the likes of him."

GARTH WILKINSON.

CHAPTER I.

THE NEW ELECTORATE.

HAS not this history many times declared, what all wise men have always known, what all unwise men do not know, and will with difficulty believe—which yet is true—that an Act of Parliament (that is to say, of a Parliament made on the Jubilee principle) will reform very little, least of all itself. And yet mankind—British mankind—long looked to it to reform the makers of Parliament—the Electorate. In all throes and troubles, *that* has been the one never-ceasing hope: Extend your electorate, make it "cheaper," bring in every grade of mortal, criminals included, and when you have exhausted them, bring in the women. No wisdom to be had from four millions of electors?—try *six* millions, and that will hurry on the millennium. That not enough?—try what we can do with *eight* millions of electors, or for supreme effort try the women, and let us have twelve millions of electors!

Poor innocent English people. Have you, or any one of you, ever yet "elected" a hero, except of the talking sort? And yet there *is* a means of heroic selection. For it is abundantly true what a keen master of men has said : "The people have judgment ;" but he added—"when not misled by orators." That was one of the most pregnant sayings of the First Napoleon. Dwell upon it, reader, for Carlyle Democritus *acted* upon it.

"Trust the people"—a Jubilee phrase of Sorrypebble—a vastly different matter, a mere oratorical wind-phrase, ear-tickling flattery, deliberate Jubilee lie. That, and nothing other. The people "elected" Jabez Balfour to swindle them out of seven millions sterling of their savings. They passed over a fearless man of action who had added a wide world to Britain's empire, and they preferred a chattering brown baboo of barrister sort. Their entire Parliament was scarcely other than an agglomeration of men of the liquor, land, and legal sort—plus money. And from such as they wisdom of Government was awaited. Awaited! The people are *not* to be trusted; the people are far too simple and honest. The mass of them—of the working sort—are incapable of telling lies as a trade, still less capable of *acting* lies—therefore unable to believe that Soft Sawder and Company are liars by nature, more intent upon party and personal aggrandisement than true devotion to the service of their country. The people are no more to be "trusted," unprotected by wise laws, than children are to be trusted in the neighbourhood of dangerous traffic, or more dangerous criminals.

There are "rights of man," but they are far other than the political party sort. "The rights of man," it has been truly said, "are that he be governed by unswerving justice!" Those are "the rights of man," which until man achieve he will suffer. Will you submit to the rule of knaves, fools, and word-babblers? Or will you put those under your feet, and have true *men* over you, never mind though their pockets are not furnished with golden guineas for your charity bun-feasts, charity bazaars, or hundred-fold kindred blackmail vanities?

Of all the Jubilee Parliament people, how many, think ye, had a desire which went beyond the "next election"? "Party" was a Jubilee shibboleth before which the vilest Barabbas, with glib tongue, would have been preferred to the divinest Jesus, minus the glib tongue and sufficiency of guineas. The simple electorate, "trusted" by Sorrypebble and Company, had been so dinned with inanities of party, that they believed the thing was a real god, and that there was no other. The "trust" which the Jubilee politicians preached was of that sort which meant: "Trust *me*, my somnolent friend, with thy purse (or thy vote), and see what I will do with it." See! it was a very considerable thing to see—

A million paupers in and out of workhouses;

Four millions of others worse off than paupers—people on the verge of pauperism, too noble to beg, infinite in patience, endurance, and suffering;

One hundred thousand children cruelly and barbarously suffering, "insured," and given up to endless misery—but for a little brave help now and then of a Charity Society;

Sixty thousand starving Board School children in London alone, and some forty thousand other starving children in London, not in Board Schools;

Scotch, Irish, Welsh, and English evictions;
Free Trade for foreigners, and hampered trade for Britons;
Liquor Peerages, rack-renters, political Judges and Magistrates.
If men are to be judged by their works, then, since the world began, there has been no fouler Beelzebub than that of Jubilee "Party." And realise at once, reader, with such shock as the occasion may require, that Carlyle Democritus as effectually did away with party as he had done away with the whole Jubilee vermin species. And you shall discover how:—Every British man who could read and mark a voting-paper, and who was not a criminal, floating or otherwise, enjoyed the Franchise—no other. So much educational qualification was necessary to keep your cant priest and mammon agent out from between the citizen and his liberty. Women did not share the Franchise, except in so much as their good influence ennobled and purified the men's choice. Remember, that debasing occupations for women had ceased, that a freedom which they *imagined* they enjoyed in Jubilee times, after the Revolution they *actually* enjoyed—not a few favoured ones amongst them, but *all*. Their voices could therefore be heard "like linnets in the pausings of the wind;" well heard, for was not the wind abated—the political wind—and wisdom become possible in place of it.

The age qualification for exercising the Franchise and for members of the Commons was twenty-five (in spite of, perhaps because of, the fact that unhappy Britain had once upon a time possessed a Prime Minister aged twenty-four—prime author of England's mad indebtedness and general anarchy, all of it well traceable from that time downward). In the Upper House the age qualification was thirty-five. There were nine millions of men in Great Britain of the age of twenty-five and upwards entitled to the Franchise, and as the number of representatives was, by the Constitution, limited to six hundred, this gave one representative for every fifteen thousand voters. Future increase of population would not increase the number of representatives, but only the number of voters whom each Member of Parliament represented. In the meanwhile nine millions of post-Revolutionary male Britons had, each man, one vote—no more. One *man* to represent every 15,000 electors—*i.e.* 600 men to represent the Nation in its Parliament, and not to be chosen *by* money, or *for* money considerations. A strange problem for a generation mostly inured to

Jubilee guinea-pig landowners, lawyer word-mongers, and liquor-lords. The money considerations were overcome by a series of reforms. The State undertook every matter concerning the elections, and it was made a misdemeanour for any candidate to expend any coin in connection with his candidature. Any breach of that law disfranchised a candidate for ten years, and rendered him incapable of ever coming forward again. Next, a candidate was debarred from charity or other subscription lists altogether, that being but a Jubilee system of blackmail in disguise. As far as money was concerned, all candidates were thus rendered equal. The Revolution then established Parliamentary districts of 15,000 electors, and sub-divided them again into 150 electoral wards, each consisting of 100 members. Two months * before the time of a general election each Hundred was required to meet, and within twenty days select one or more candidates from amongst the residents or workers within their *district* (not necessarily ward), and to appoint also a chairman and deputy-chairman to represent them on the combined Electoral Hundreds of the district. At the first meeting of the Ward Hundreds the senior member present of a Court of Arbitration or Honour—or failing such an one, the senior elector present—presided, until the meeting could elect its own chairman. The names of the Hundred of the electoral ward were then read out to the meeting, and the members invited to elect a permanent chairman. After discussion, the meeting proceeded to elect its chairman and deputy chairman by ballot, with the ordinary formality and procedure. The candidate or candidates of each Hundred were then selected, and the chairmen duly deputed to consult the chairmen of the other ward divisions. There would thus be one hundred and fifty chairmen and deputy-chairmen forming the central electoral committees of three hundred —representing the full 15,000 of the electoral division.

With that notable common-sense and business capacity—the prominent feature of the true Briton—the various Electoral Hundreds quickly fell into a perfect system of friendly human interaction. Within ten days of the great revolutionary political instauration the Hundreds had met, appointed their chairmen and hon. secretaries, and deputed their respective chairmen to hold

---

* This period could be shortened by Parliament if urgency or emergency required.

counsel, and discuss the preliminary list of candidates which each Hundred had nominated. After the second week these had met and winnowed their lists to a few mutually-agreed-upon candidates, and the lists, as reduced, were referred back to the various Ward Hundreds. Within a few weeks each electoral division (of 15,000) had definitely selected its candidate or candidates. In numerous instances the lists were reduced to two candidates, often to only one—and in no case were more than three names left in any single constituency.

After the final adoption of the candidates, they were invited to attend meetings of the electors throughout the division, for which purpose the large halls of the School Board, or the justice-rooms attached to the Post-offices, were placed at their disposal. The meetings were used not for purposes of speech-making; they were more in the nature of interviews and discussions between the candidate and his constituents. The candidates were no longer mere representatives of money, land, law, liquor, or talk. They had not been selected for their speech-proclivity. They were perforce men well known to the communities who chose them, were selected because of the work they had *done*, and the way they did it, there, amongst the men who were to select or elect them. No longer to be chosen upon *promise* of work. Let that change between the Revolutionary, practical representative, selected by the calm judgment of the people among whom he worked and was known, and the old Jubilee windbag, often drawn indiscriminately from limbo because he had money in his pocket, or a voluble tongue in his head, never mind how void of brain, justice, or wisdom.

There were thus created throughout Great Britain electoral committees from all portions of the people, no longer self-constituted blatancies of the Jubilee caucus-type, but practical everyday business and working men, of all shades of opinion, and mostly acquainted with one another (the Ward Hundreds being necessarily close neighbours). If a member of the Electoral Hundred failed to serve at one-third of its meetings, such a member (unless good cause obtained for his absence) was disfranchised for ten years, besides having to submit to a fine before the Arbitration Courts. If the final choice of the electors fell upon a candidate whose pecuniary position did not enable him to bear the loss of partial dissociation from his calling, the State paid him £200 a year, if representing a London constituency; or £300 a year if a provincial, during his period of service.

Thus left to themselves and to their own calm judgment, not "misled by orators," the electors—from the men whom they saw day by day striving, working, and doing—at least *knew* whom they were selecting, and did not have to rely upon words, promises, party-lying, or trickery of any sort. Canvassing was strictly forbidden, disqualified any candidate who directly or indirectly partook of it, and subjected the canvasser to heavy penalty.

Wise administration, more than word-legislation, was the business of Parliament after the Revolution. Endless and senseless piling up of Acts no longer necessary as in mad Jubilee times. A Bill, after the Revolution, was discussed in Parliament often in a few days, and drawn up by practical men in less words than many Jubilee Bills had had clauses. A Jubilee Bill was often discussed for years, and then put into the Jubilee waste mud-basket—a mere heap of clotted lawyer-jargon—damnable alike to gods and men.

At one sweep of the gigantic Revolutionary broom the Jubilee accumulation of political corruptions disappeared. Not a light disappearance at all:—

 Subscription tolls without end.
 Paid canvassers, male.
 Paid canvassers, female.
 Voluntary canvassers, male.
 Voluntary canvassers, female.
 Paid agents, pretending not to be paid.
 Unpaid agents.
 Speakers: party, demagogic, secretly paid, and other.
 Wire-pullers, caucus-mongers.
 Party clubs—mostly disguised drink-hells.
 Liberal hundreds, or caucus gangs.
 Radical ditto, ditto.
 Tory ditto, ditto.
 Unionist ditto, ditto.
 Variorum ditto, ditto; and

Universal associations of fad-mongeries beyond the enumerating power of mortal man—the whole forming a complex and widespread political-jesuit-party-brotherhood, demoniacal, bewildering to all honest men.

Contrast the simple establishment of Carlyle Democritus: Those universal local committees of one hundred men; the chairmen of those Hundreds, and beyond that nothing more. After the electoral divisions had selected their candidates, they set about drawing up in brief, concise, plain English a list of such local, general, or national matters as they deemed required attention. A copy of that list, or local programme, was given to each candidate of the division, but he was not pledged to adopt such programme. Its object was to afford him a guide of the wishes and wants of his constituents. The judgment of the electors had been freed from the mass of Jubilee corruption which had formerly enthralled them; it would have been most unwise to send a representative to the great Assembly of his nation a tied and hampered thing. If you have elected a *man*, to his wisdom and judgment leave the expression of your wants; you have laid before him your wishes and desires as you have seen them *locally;* he will have to judge from the imperial point of view, as well as the local one, what is the truest and best for *all*, and not only for one. Therefore no election pledges were allowed to be exacted from any candidate, only the pledge of the electors' own hearts, understandings, and judgment, that they had selected the man in sympathy with them. It was for them to choose a God-fearing, sincere, practical British man; having so chosen, and having given to him the record of their wants, leave him free to act wisely. If experience should prove that they had mistaken their man, that their judgment had erred, they must be wiser and warier next time. The candidate once become the elected representative, was debarred from Company Directorates of any sort, beyond such as he had filled before his selection as candidate. He was forbidden to make political speeches outside his own constituency, except in the Parliament where he had been elected to serve.

In early days of the Revolution printed explanations of the great reform, and of the methods to be observed at future elections, had been circulated to every elector in the land, and printed lists of the various "Hundreds" were duly delivered to every member of the electoral wards. These lists were revised every six months by the secretaries of the respective Hundreds, and amendments, or, where necessary, new lists, regularly notified to all concerned. After the meeting of the "Hundreds," and the appointment by them of their chairmen, who formed the central electoral "Three Hundreds," printed lists of these also were distributed in the same manner. For all purposes of delivery within the "Hundred" Wards the services of the street-keepers (p. 185) of the immediate locality were requisitioned, this being a part of their duties. No expenses were allowed to be incurred by any of the electoral bodies, either in their individual or corporate capacity. Printed circular-forms for calling the members together at any time were supplied, and all printing in connection with the list of members, and other necessary printing work, was undertaken by the Election Department of the post-office nearest to the particular Ward Hundred. The Electoral Department could also undertake any other outlay in connection with the elections which circumstances or the locality rendered necessary. The "Hundreds" and "Three Hundreds" were permanent establishments, and could be called together by their respective chairmen, or at the written request, delivered to the chairmen, of not less than ten electors, upon the minimum notice of seven days.

And now observe the great election day—one and the same day throughout the kingdom—and its mode of operation. On that day all the law offices in the kingdom were closed for law, and converted for that day—both the law offices, officers, and officials—into polling stations and election officials, the latter aided also by the clerks of the local authorities, with their registers and other necessary paraphernalia. The day was not made a holiday; far better otherwise; election is not a matter for play, but for earnest and serious—ay, solemnest consideration. The polling stations were open from seven in the morning until seven at night. Enumerators were then drawn from all parts of the Civil Service, and other services if necessary, for the occasion; and early on the next morning, posted underneath the clock of every post-office throughout the kingdom, appeared the results of the poll. And seven days later, there, at Westminster, appeared also the result of the poll.

Pause, O British reader, and draw into your heart of hearts, into your inmost thought of thoughts, the deep result of a people's choice, untrammelled by the rhodomontade of Party, not misled by the twaddle of orators. But to enable you to appreciate the great

Revolutionary Parliament, first look at a Jubilee Party-Parliament. We will take six hundred of each.

These are six hundred of a Jubilee Parliament, classified by a Jubilee authority :—

1. MAMMON CLASS :—
   Landlords and mine-owners . . . 155
   Liquor and lawyer people 124
   Peerage people 96
   Government ex-official Party people . . 12
   Bankers 17
   No occupation 20
                                           424

2. WORKING CLASS :—
   Labour members 10
   Manufacturers, shipowners, railway people, literary and professional men, and merchants . . . 55
   Army and Navy men . . . 26
   Colonial and Civil Service . . 7
                                         98

3. Journalists—mostly of the "Blackswhite" or "Whitesblack" class 28
4. Unclassed and nondescript, including the moonlight sort 50
                           Total   600

Briefly, as that table shows, Mammon had 424 representatives. The workers of all sorts only 98 ,,
Mere Party scribblers and indescribables 78 ,,

Need thoughtful men wonder whither such a Parliament could "lead" a nation? Now contrast the six hundred of the reformed Parliament, as elected by nine millions of free and untrammelled British men :—

1. WORKING CLASS :—
   Master-artisans, independent of State salaries 90
   Artisans in receipt of State salary . . 25

Master workmen — manufacturers, ship-owners, merchants, traders	210
Professional and literary men	75
Ditto in receipt of State salaries	10
Railway directors, bankers, and Company Managers	45
Journalists *not* of the Blackswhite sort	5
Army and Navy men	30
2. RETIRED WORKERS :—	
Labour	70
Professional	25
General	15
Total	600

The mere word-class—the lawyers—had entirely disappeared, so had the no-work class—the landlords—and also the peer-, beer-, and moonlight-class.

There remained, instead, 470 trained practical workers, and 130 literary and professional men.

Those are six hundred men who are not likely to waste time in mere verbosity.

Exactly the same methods of selection and election were established for all public bodies. In commemoration of the Revolution, the 14th of February was the date fixed for all municipal elections, one such election taking place on that date every year, viz. the County Council, School Board, and District or Parish Councils. (There were no other bodies municipal; all others which had been were merged in the four described.) Elections for those bodies took place in successive years, and as each one of them served for three years, there was thus an election on the 14th of February in every year. The Parliamentary election, taking place at every septennial year, gave two elections for that year, but the law required that a minimum period of three months should elapse between a parliamentary and any municipal election—a matter easily arranged, as Parliament fixed its own time, but the municipal date could not be interfered with.

Before closing this chapter let it be repeated what has been before set down, that Parliament could not alter any article of the Constitution without a reference, or referendum, to the entire Nation, which required for its adoption a two-thirds majority.

CHAPTER II.

THE SIX HUNDRED REPRESENTATIVES OF GREAT BRITAIN.

"Shape your heart to front the hour, but dream not that the hour will last. . .
Babble, babble ; our old England may go down in babble at last. . . .
You that woo the voices—tell them 'old experience is a fool,'
Teach your flatter'd kings that only those who cannot read can rule.
Charm us, Orator, till the lion look no larger than the cat. . . .
FREEDOM, free to slay herself, and dying while they shout her name. . . .
When was age so cramm'd with menace ? madness ? written, spoken lies ? . . .
Step by step we rose to greatness,—thro' the tonguesters we may fall.
     . . . Take the suffrage of the plough ? . .
Nay, but these would feel and follow TRUTH if only you and you,—
Rivals of realm-ruining party,—when you speak were wholly true.
Ploughmen, shepherds, have I found, and more than once, and still could find,
Sons of God and kings of men in utter nobleness of mind,
Truthful, trustful, looking upward to the practised hustings-liar ;
So the higher wields the lower, while the lower is the higher.
Here and there a cotter's babe is royal-born by right divine ;
Here and there my lord is lower than his oxen, or his swine.
Bring the old dark ages back without the faith, without the hope,
Break the State, the Church, the Throne, and roll their ruins down the slope."
                TENNYSON.

"It is a strange world, and in nothing stranger than in its loves and its hates:

"It is recorded that in Jubilee times a grand old orator dearly loved the Poet Homer, yet has Ben Jonson recorded that ' Homer says he hates him worse than hell-mouth that utters one thing with his tongue and keeps another in his breast.' Most strange perverseness of human affection."
            CARLYLE DEMOCRITUS.

CARLYLE DEMOCRITUS to the new Electorate: "By platform tests will you discover your true man ? By virtue of the facility of his soft talk—commonly called eloquence? You shall discover your lawyer-hero that way, your 'learned friend'—easy of speech for easy pay—' the practised hustings-liar.' Not by that method is a son of God discoverable. Examine a little the sort of men who by that method have been raised up. We shall find a Barabbas mob-worshipped and a Jesus slain; a Charles II., with his whores and minions, national saviour—and a Cromwell hung in gallows' chains; a Gladstone—people's William—and a Gordon blanching in the desert sand. Was it by popular election that the Jesus, Cromwell, Gordon, Mahomet, Confucius, and other strong and noble men rose amidst the crumbling vanities of their nation's effeteness—to bring a new halo of the Eternal Heaven Fire or Glory upon their people? Or was it not rather by the irresistible power and work and freedom from cant and insincerity—the God-reliance—of the men themselves, lifting their souls beyond and above the universal pettiness of sordid self-seeking and selfishness into the divine arena which all great souls attain,—the Eden of self-sacrifice, devotion, sincerity, duty done for duty's sake, unmindful of all except the universal creation law: 'Justice, and only Justice, shall prevail.' *Not* by platform tests or caucus crawlings are such men discoverable. Close those much-beflattered ears of yours, O voters, overfilled by claptrap spouters, eager to grasp at power,—by treacly, lying tongues, pandering to your ignorance and gullibility. You hard-working men in factory and field, far other duty is this of mine than to be lying to you, or seeking by delusive vapourings and flatterings to attribute to you other power than honourably to perform the labour which has been set you in the world to do. Is it by your WORK or by your WORD that your masters have distinguished you? Not by his words shalt thou, O workman, or any other, distinguish in all time the merit of any man; his *works* may prove a better guide,—ay, the *only* guide. Can you see beyond the frothy turmoil of election jargonings and party recriminations, sufficiently to understand, if only a little, whither your caucus-imposed mud-gods have been hurrying the nation? Millions of your starving brethren crowding workhouse and no-workhouse; workless men driven to self-murder for relief; women and children 'rotting in heaps;' stone pavements lined at nights with hungry men, and women, and little children; sack-clad women and naked children frozen to death by winter sleet,—all that, whilst wealth on all hands was increasing and accumulating! Or will you rely upon the 'Upper House' of brewer-peers and mammon-kings, of ancestor-selling, turf-swindling, divorce-court peers, cant-bishops, fraudulent ministerial directors, and the like?

Are *no* purer Parliaments a possibility ? Can no higher house be constituted—the assembly of the nation's best and wisest,—God's nobility, instead of Mammon's?"

To a Jubilite entering the stately Assembly-room of the Palace of Westminster after the Revolution its changed appearance first attracted his attention. It was double its old dimensions, and its form octagonal, with a slightly raised dais at one end for the ministers, who faced the representatives. Each seat bore a small metal slide-plate with the name of the constituency engraved upon it. The members sat according to the alphabetical order of the constituencies. In Jubilee times the disorder which had reigned outside the House was fitly symbolised inside the House. Most of the members had fought and struggled through corruption— party-, or money-anarchies—into the Parliament, and, when there, had to struggle again before they could get even decent seat accommodation—there being about 400 seats provided for some 670 representatives—emblematic indeed of the millions of the nation outside, who were struggling violently, and more fatally, for work-places where none were provided. Can it be possible that the Government of Great Britain had become a concern of patriotism, of justice, and of sincerity, and no longer a club for land and peer appendages, moneyed wind-bags, and legal tongue-fencers ? Can a generation inured to such things believe?—believe that Party could yield before patriotism? believe that men ceased to be selected by blinded Party slaves, because they had money in their pockets, and could pay registration fees, agents' blackmailings, charity subscriptions, etc., and rob them afterwards as Company promoters ? Believe that CHARACTER and not MONEY had become the gauge of a representative's merit? Heavens, the Jubilee brain must whirl at such a revolution in its mode of thought ! PARTY no longer the supreme mundane god, or devil? Who is this little David that with his history-sling bodes death to the Goliath Party? Goliath with eight heads ! For the Jubilee Party Goliath had many heads, or blocks. Let them be recorded for a future age. Here are they all:—

1. Radical Party.
2. Gladstonian Party.
3. Liberal Party.

4. Labour Party.
5. Unionist Party.
6. Conservative Party.
7. Parnellite Party.
8. Anti-Parnellite Party.

Besides these, there were smaller Parties, such as—

9. Gallant-little-Wales Party, and
10. Scotch-home-rule Party.

Those ten Party-regiments coalesced now and then into two mutually opposing Parties, and carried on the "Government" of Great Britain much in the way that the following illustration will typify. GOVERN means "to steer;" remember that, reader. Now picture to yourselves a brave ship. On the upper deck, and in the state-cabins, are the fairest and whitest of people, playful, not particularly aware of other object in life than to agreeably pass the time in shooting gulls, of one sort or another, eating prolonged dinners, dancing, piping, and love-making. On the lower deck is another set of people of various sort, but all busy, intent upon working the ship well, and doing manful duty, if they can. Below them is another deck, whose rotten boards let the bilge-water in. Enquire not too narrowly of what is going on *there*. Human life in all its saddest, lowest, foulest form. Occasional moans ascend, penetrate for a moment even to the uppermost deck; then there is quiet again—for a time. By the rudder are two helmsmen; in the captain's cabin are two commanders. When one helmsman will turn the helm to north, the other spits at and fights with him, and will try to pull the helm to south; they call the sailors who, bewildered by the lies and fatuities of either helmsmen, join the fight, and—according to the preponderance of numbers on either side—for a little time, they drag and incline the rudder chain. So also when one of the captains proclaims an order, the other captain shrieks a counter order. Over all is only turmoil, vacuity, and idiocy; the bewildered crew—in the name of Party—at one time backing one commander, at another time the other. In this precarious way the poor ship braves storms and rocks, groaning heavier day by day, dangers for ever increasing—the upper deck ever playful, the middle deck ever toiling, the third deck ever suffering. Some of the toilers from the middle deck, after violent struggle, or insidious robbing of their fellow-workers, scramble on to the upper deck, but oftener, from overwork, numbers continually fall, but no one notices them, the occurrences are so familiar—a hatch is opened, and—crunch—fall the wounded into the bilge-hell below. That was the Jubilee ship "Britannia" down to the year 1894.

．　　　．　　　．　　　．　　　．　　　．

The Revolution set more store upon DOING than upon Talking. And it took certain measures to promote the former, and discourage the latter. A time-limit was fixed for all speakers in Parliament. Ministers introducing a measure were allowed half-an-hour; at other times, in common with all other members, the maximum for any individual speaker was twenty minutes. The cant-nonsense of addressing members as "Honourables" and "Right Honourables" was abolished, and in its place "the Member," or "the Representative for ——," or in the case of ministers, "the Minister of ——," or the title of his office substituted.

Mediæval garbage was also sent into oblivion, and plain English substituted for it. Ridiculous iteration of "humble," "loyal," "gracious," "faithful," and all that cant-jargon, used in Jubilee addresses to the Throne, was altogether done away with.

As Parliament was no longer made up of mere money people, the expensive Jubilee political dinner-craze was put an end to. In fact, that insensate habit died out in private as well as in political circles. Honourable poverty, or moderateness of income, was a power after the Revolution. Height of character had supplanted depth of pocket. There were no longer two sets of governors; there was only one. There was abundant opportunity for able men to range themselves in the fore-front of the nation. The age-limit of sixty years, which required all public men to retire, opened the way to reasonably speedy promotion in the political world as in all other State employments.

The grand solidity and strength which her unity of purpose and Government gave Great Britain released her giant energies from war scares, and enabled them to be concentrated upon the perfecting of the country's commercial interests throughout the world. Her Consuls and Ambassadors were no longer ornamental gentry, "lying abroad," but practical, truthful men, more honoured and appreciated by their countrymen if they secured a new trade avenue for Britain than if they overreached a hundred foreign diplomatists "lying abroad." The Parliament had become more an administrative than a legislative machine, after the Revolution, and more work was done in Committees than had ever been the case before. Talking for talking's sake having ceased, sessions were short and the meetings of Parliament rarely exceeded four days a week. The House did not meet till five in the afternoon, and no Committees were allowed to be held whilst the House was sitting. The Committee hours might be fixed for any time in the morning, and until five o'clock in the afternoon, but not later, except on those days when the House did not meet. All Colonies and Dependencies, or groups of the smaller ones, had their particular Committees, and no snatch "resolution" could be passed by the House which concerned any Colony or Dependency until it had been referred for report to the Committee concerned.

(277a) Red-tape was a forbidden article in the new Parliament. Promoters of Bills could consult the proper authorities at any time, and get them drawn up in proper, simple form. The old Jubilee system was an ineffable scandal. Corporations and business men might spend months of labour in preparing their Bills, or appeals to Parliament, or Parliamentary Committees, only to find at the last moment that the red tape-worm officialities rejected their papers, plans, or Bills, as "not complying with the red-tape standing orders." Thousands upon thousands of pounds were thus wasted every year, not to speak of the wasted time and opportunity.

All ministers enjoyed the privilege—when introducing measures into Parliament—of attending and addressing both Houses, but their voting power was restricted to the House in which they habitually sat.

(278) As for the reforms which the new Parliament introduced into the Civil Service, they may be described in a phrase :—Parliament ordered the public service on the same wise system as private service. State clerks were no longer appointed because they were relations of peers, or place-hunters. There were many hundreds of such in receipt of State pay in Jubilee time—not so many afterwards. Here is one Jubilee branch of the public service—and very much like that one were they all: "The War Office occupied 19 houses of 289 rooms, and for staff employed 805 clerk-personages." The public service was permeated with political abuse, and was a refuge for empty-headed peer—and politician—sons. By righteous administration and wise dis-

cipline—as of the merchants' order—by true selection, by merit only—that one department was reduced by the Revolution, and better served than it ever had been, to one building of less than a hundred rooms, with a total staff of 350 clerks—all engaged upon the eight hours' system—from the highest official to the lowest messenger boy. And so it went throughout the service of the State.

The age of babble and Babel was dead.

CHAPTER III.

THE FIVE HUNDRED OF GREATER BRITAIN.

THE pre-Revolutionary hereditary peerages (except those which have been referred to in a preceding chapter) were not abolished by the Revolution; they formed a valuable feature of a remarkable nation. They were the orchids of the national garden, and amongst their other advantages attracted much American wealth to the country. The great American people cultivated great fortunes, but no nobility, and much as the sons of the Western Republic despised titles, their daughters did not, and many a golden queen-bee from the Western hive would settle upon a British mulberry-, strawberry-, or other leaf, and spread considerable money there. Titles are the glittering jewels of humanity, precious in poor humanity's eyes as the night flame to the insect world, and not always so fatal. The dangerous features of Jubilee nobility—its wanton luxury, partridge-shooting futility, and general vampirity of constitution *—had disappeared

---

* Here is the history of how a Jubilee beer-peer extracted from the public a million of golden sovereigns more than his brewery was worth, most of the money extracted from widows and small investors: Years passed, and no return was made to the said widows and small investors, who had thriftily saved their earnings, and entrusted them to the beer-lord and his brewery. And the women wept when they saw their money gone, and themselves driven to part with the paper shares of the beer-lord's brewery, not at the £100 which they had paid for them, but for thirteen to twenty pounds or so. Now when those £100 shares were originally foisted on the poor, confiding, silly people, great promises were made, a dividend was paid, and just for a little time the £100 shares were dangled before the people's eyes at the enhanced value of from £120 to £125, giving the innocent public, who did not think that peers were pickpockets, visions of tiny El Dorados. Then, when the swindle was apparent, and distress compelled them to take a few pounds for their wasted hundreds, the peer did a wonderful thing. He came into "the market," and "bought up" all the silly people's shares

with the Revolution. Nobility had to work. Mere existence upon the toil of the masses was its privilege no more. As the British people enriched the land, the British land enriched the people, and no longer were the few noble or other Jubilee landlords allowed to stand, like a living Danaid-sieve, between the nation and its prosperity. They remained highly ornamental, and the title-plumage continued an ever-harmless decoy-bird to the Western cousinry. That was their allotted task after the Revolution, for a time. Most of the beer-, fitz-, and other froth-creations entirely disappeared. The fair ones over the Atlantic, practical business damsels, being a little particular as to the true quality of their purchases, though quite willing to "hold the diamond necklace dearer than the golden ring"—yet required diamonds of a sort, and not mere paste. But much as Carlyle Democritus scoffed at the partridge-lords and the titled liquor-Jubilites; much as the thought of them made his very soul heave at the desecration which pretended that such things were a nation's—*his* nation's—"best"; unutterably vile as they were, and the yet fouler things who had "made" them, yet he knew there *was* a "best," a *real* Aristocracy, gaugeable by heart and work and merit, not by pocket, beer, or tongue-prostitution. And it was his crown of work to seek out that "best," and hold it up imperishable, divine, fit for the love and worship of British human-kind. Let wise readers decide how he succeeded.

---

at the worthless price of the day, due to no dividend having been paid for years. Now when the pickpocket peer had got back all the shares for which he had been paid £100, for the smaller sum of £20 or £30, he went to many publicans and said: "O seller of beer to the working man, lo! I bring you a little bit of paper, being £100 share of my patent brewery, limited; now, if you will buy my beer, I will give you this nice little £100 share (which I have bought from the ruined widows for £20). True, it is not worth £100 to-day, but if you buy beer of me it *will* be." And so, of a surety, it came to pass. The publicans bought their beer of the pickpocket-peer, and enabled him to pay a dividend, and so the shares "went up." And so your Mammon-peer, by lying prospectus, and other limited company dodgeries, extracted one million sterling from the pockets of the confiding British public, and made another quarter of a million by quietly buying back their shares at the rate of a dollar for every pound. And his brother peers and Mammonites thought that quite a clever transaction. No seven or seven hundred days' imprisonment with hard labour for such wholesale fraud, but perennial (Jubilee perennial) peerage! And of such were the kingdom of Mammon.

The peerage had its Courts of Honour and of arbitration, with final appeal to the House of Lords. "Noblesse oblige" was made a living force once more—the ideal atmosphere of a true aristocracy. Accordingly any offence against the laws, social or imperial, brought the offender before the courts, and rendered him liable even to the forfeiture of the title altogether.

The Second Chamber, after the Revolution, was constituted of those only who, by service to the State or to the people, rose by their own merit to a place among the nation's best and highest,—*Aristos*, indeed, *Panaristos*.

The Five Hundred were not of the British Isles only, but were gathered from the best and greatest of the whole Empire. The following formed the order of life-peerages, with the number of each respective order, and the method of their appointment :—

1. Members of the House of Commons, elected by ballot by three-fifths' majority of the House,[*] 1, . . 20
2. Judges (constituting also the Lords of Appeal) selected by the Bench of Judges by ballot,[*] 3, . 50
3. Voyagers and Discoverers who had added to the dominion, strength, or development of the Empire, elected by the Upper House by ballot,[*] 3, . . 10
4. The eminent in literature (40), science (40), and art (20), elected by ballot of their respective Guilds,[*] 2, ... 100
5. Governors, or Heads of Colonies, Dependencies, and Settlements, after five years' service, by ballot of the Upper House,[*] 3, ... 60
6. Colonial representative Peers, one elected by ballot of the joint Houses of every Colony, Dependency, or Settlement,[*] 2 and 1, ... 40
7. Ambassadors and Consuls, after five years' service, eligible for election by ballot of the Upper House,[*] 3, ... 20
8. Presidents of Chambers of Commerce (50), and Trade Guilds (50), by ballot of the House of Commons, and confirmation by the Lords,[*] 3, . 100

[*] 1. Requiring confirmation by the House of Lords. 2. Three-fifths majority. 3. Bare majority.

9. Admirals, elected from amongst themselves by ballot, ... 50
10. Field-Marshals and Generals, by ballot amongst themselves, ... 50

Total, 500

Any life-peer desirous of serving or seeking election in the House of Commons, could resign his privilege of a seat in the Lords, whilst retaining his title, but he could not, on any future occasion, reclaim a seat in the Upper House. With reference to the sixth order (Colonial Representative Peers) as the number of British Colonies and Dependencies was liable to change by extension, consolidation, or otherwise, the numbers were preserved by grouping together the smaller Colonies or Dependencies, as occasion might require. All members of the Upper House serving as life-peers were granted the following titles according to the various orders :—

1. Members of Parliament—according to the selection and decision of the Commons.
2. Judges—" Lords Justices."
3. Discoverers and Voyagers—according to the greatness of their service—Dukes, Marquises, or Earls, of the Dominions of their exploits.
4. Literature, science, and art—Viscounts, Baronets, or Knights, under their family name.
5. and 6. Colonial Governors, and Colonial Representative Peers—Dukes, Marquises, or Earls of their respective states, settlements, etc.
7. Ambassadors and Consuls—Earls, Viscounts, or Barons.
8. Presidents of Chambers of Commerce and Trade Guilds—" Lords President."
9. Admirals—" Admiral Lord——"
10. Field Marshals and Generals—" Field Marshal Lord," or " General Lord ——"

In the event of especial merit a title could be made hereditary—but not bearing any privilege beyond the honour—by a three-fifths majority of the House of Lords voting in ballot, or by recommendation of the Commons and approval by bare majority of the Upper

House, voting by ballot. Such hereditary titles descended to direct male issue only, and carried no collateral titles with them. In order that absence of wealth should not defeat presence of merit, and honourable poverty be no bar to advancement, any member elected to the peerage was entitled (if his means required it) to a life annuity of £500. All Colonial peers, and peers employed abroad, enjoyed free transit to and from their colonies or stations, and the mother country. Members of the Upper House were subject to the same laws which governed the members of the Commons. They were restricted from giving public dinners or public banquets of any kind, and were prohibited from subscription lists, and all such old forms of Jubilee blackmailing.

In that manner were five hundred of a nation's best and worthiest gathered together; by no means an idly ornamental peerage, but the very flower of a nation's manhood, and, as such, the proudest actual ornament of a God-fearing people. No mere toy-glitter of the jewel sort those, but the rich flower and fruit of a glorious nation.

It may be remarked in passing that the old tinsel-order of nobility enjoyed all the privileges of an ordinary British citizen, but as they were without the old Jubilee adventitious powers which landlordism, unearned wealth, and consequent undue influence over the electorate had engendered, they were not much in requisition as representatives in the Revolutionary Parliament.

Only five were chosen amongst the first lists of candidates, of whom only three received the final vote of the people.

As the average age at which a member entered the Upper House was necessarily a somewhat advanced one, the age of compulsory retirement was somewhat relaxed, and a member who held his seat in the Upper House for a less period than ten years was permitted to serve until the completion of his sixty-fifth year.

If any measure—after its rejection by the Lords, and re-introduction in the House of Commons—failed a second time to pass the House of Lords, the measure was submitted to a joint assembly of both Houses. If that failed to secure a majority in its favour, such a measure could not be re-introduced during the existing session.

Book II.

CONCLUSION.

CHAPTER L.

THE REVOLUTIONISTS DISARM.

ON the 14th of August 19—, ten years and six months after the outbreak of the Revolution, those of the troops still remaining under the command of Carlyle Democritus laid down their arms. The day was made the occasion of a national holiday, at once solemn and magnificent. Throughout the entire country similar ceremonies were to take place, and the regiments quartered in the various towns and cities, 300,000 men in all—whereof in London were 100,000 of the troops—laid down their arms. The rest of the Revolutionists had been gradually disbanded and absorbed into the working populations of the Empire, and these, the last battalions, had, to a man, pensions and places secured for them. The London through which the last Revolutionary troops were to make their final march was a different city to that in which the same troops had assembled ten years before, then clad in rags, now in brilliant uniform. One looked in vain for the slums, for the endless dreary streets, for the miles of mere brick walls with square holes for windows; the dead, cold lines, without a curve, for mile upon mile, of roofs and eaves. The streets were alive with trees and flowers,* every ground-floor room had its window-box of growing plants.† Graceful pillars of stone or brick relieved the old monotonies of flat dead walls.‡

Curves, lattices, and gables gave variety and grace to the house-tops as they merged from earth into the ether-curve, called sky-line. Has not the architect's work been described as "frozen

---

* Page 184.

† The Land Court had induced the universal adoption of the simple and beautiful custom by allowing an appreciable reduction on the rents of all houses so adorned.

‡ For an account of the architectural care of London buildings, see pages 179, 183-4.

music"? There is melody in every beauty—even as there is dissonance in ugliness and neglect. Cleanliness and purity were everywhere. The old death-pall, called London dirt, had disappeared—no thread of it was visible.* Even the slum prisons had at last disappeared; the surviving prisoners had been amnestied three months before the great disarmament. The foul slum sites had been razed, and each of them laid out as memorial gardens. The troops commenced their march from the same barracks at Knightsbridge from whence they had emerged ten years before, armed to deliver their countrymen. But how different the masses who welcomed them! No longer the starving, clad in rags and misery, but everywhere bright, free men and women. The roar of despair had given way to the warm acclamation of the heart, and the bright grateful people who remembered what had been, and what now was, received the men—whose task was done—with a fervour of enthusiasm which shook the valiant heroes as they marched. As they passed what had been the slum purlieus of Jubilee degradation, but where magnificent labour palaces had usurped their place, huge banners and decorations marked the sites, and everywhere along the route such records as these appeared:—
"The land whereon these buildings stand, now the homes of 2000 men, women, and children, in Jubilee times belonged to the Marquis of ——, who, into a room-space less than one-third of that which we now enjoy, crowded 3200 human beings in filth and rottenness, and extracted from them three times the rent we pay."

[The Marquis there referred to fell a victim to the fury of the people, and the rest of his belongings perished in the slum prisons.]

In a wide district in the northern regions of the great Metropolis the troops marched through broad avenues of alternate poplar and plane trees, their bases alive with summer flowers, the roadways flanked by stately labour dwellings, whose verandahs shone bright, like the flowers under the tree-branches, with merry children, the love and glory of the Revolution. And from above and all sides there burst forth, as the devoted troops advanced, one never-ceasing heaven-artillery of enthusiasm. Never waved the proud banners of a Revolutionary soldiery in glory more sublime, the

---

* For abolition of the smoke-fiend, see pages 221, 222.

red now changed to white, the black letters into gold—"For God and for the People." On, the heroes of the Nation marched, under a love-rain of flowers and blessings. Arrived in the centre of the great district of Winters-Town, they halted. This enormous district had been in Jubilee times one of the typical slum-areas of Great Britain, the property of a titled family, with a woman for chief. It had been condemned over and over again by the Municipalities, ordered by the Government to be razed, and the scandalous owners to be "compensated." "Never!" had the brave Municipalities declared; "we will not waste the ratepayers' millions on these soulless land-thieves; we demand justice!" But no justice came. The wretched slum-people died at the rate of sixty in the thousand, whilst their owners lived ambrosially in palaces and castles—until the people at last arose and cast the vile owners in the slum-prisons, confiscated their land, and reversed the brutal mandate of plutocracy and Mammon. In Winters-Town, ten years after the Revolution, the death-rate was only seventeen in the thousand, and in the slum-prison where the old owners lived the life to which they had formerly condemned their thousands of wretched tenants—*there* the death-rate had been sixty—and the Jubilee nobility there learnt, in all its horrible reality, the meaning of slum-land. Through such scenes and such remembrances the soldiers passed—fifty divisions of the last hundred-thousand Revolutionary troops—through the London of the Revolutionary year 19—, until, at four o'clock in the afternoon, the various divisions converged in the park which faced the Palace of Westminster.* Company by company the men crossed the Palace-yard, and laid their burdens down, and as, unarmed, they emerged from the golden gates, the women seized them, and armed them yet again, not in steel this time, but with an enthusiasm of gratitude and human love. The emancipated people, fired by the all-pervading ecstasy, hailed their deliverers with salvoes of the Revolutionary watchword that they had so well redeemed, "For

---

* For two thousand yards on all the land sides of the Parliament the houses had been cleared, and approaches worthy of the site made to the glorious Senate of a now free people. The formation of this park, and the extension of the gardens and open spaces of the Metropolis, had been facilitated by the reflux of vast numbers of the people from the towns to the land. In the Revolutionary decade the population of London had decreased by nearly three-quarters of a million.

God and for the People." Six chimes sounded from the great Westminster bells as the last company left the Palace-yard.

And slowly, with an emotion such as rarely has stirred the heart of a nation, the crowds melted back into their homes; ay, into their HOMES. Brave English word, pure emblem of God's peace on earth!

. . . . . .

And Carlyle Democritus was once more at the Bar of the House of Commons.

CHAPTER II.

CARLYLE DEMOCRITUS LAYS ASIDE THE THORN-CROWN.

"The wicked have no power, their works are as nothing in the sight of God. The great Chaos is Hell—the sempeternal churn for the annihilation of evil, the recrudescence of good. The wicked think themselves powerful, and the good deem themselves not powerful. Yet is good the only power, and evil no power at all. Good everlasting. Evil but transitory, and not to prevail.

"The wicked attribute everything to self-derived prudence. The good attribute everything to God Omnipotent. Evil has no spiritual life, and hence cannot endure. Good is all spiritual life, and hence cannot die.

"Love, purified by wisdom, is the highest spiritual life. Reason and liberty are the divine prerogatives of man. From their abuse originates evil, the hell attribute which is pre-destined to self-annihilation."—SWEDENBORG.

AND the great wave of popular enthusiasm receded homeward, leaving here and there little groups thinking over the deep meaning of the day that was passing, like sea-drops left by the receding tide to reflect the glory of the setting sun.

Unable to bear the emotion of such a scene, Democritus had proceeded by the river to Parliament. A calm and noble peace now enveloped the place; the soul-stirring scenes whose far-off echoes were still faintly audible, like distant music, flushed the attendants and caused a glistening in their eyes, as, with every mark of reverence and loving respect, they saluted the General as he passed.

The beautiful approaches and staircases to the National Chamber had been cleared of their legions of statues of past talkers. Only the best and greatest of them remained—a most small company. But others were added who had not previously been there, England's greatest, *not* of the talking sort.

He has read this History to small purpose who has not discovered the source of Carlyle Democritus's power.

He understands naught of the greatness of the brave English people who knows not the deep soul of religion burning in them.

Over the dais of the National Chamber, like the ægis of a guardian spirit, spread the wide wings of an organ, through whose grand diapason a hymn of glory thrilled as the General entered the Chamber. Involuntarily the House rose to its feet, as with bent head and wasted form Carlyle Democritus stood before them. There was one moment of silence as the last sound hushed from the reeds, and then the pastor spoke :—

"Mysterious Power, under Whom man uses the marvellous gifts Thou hast bestowed in him, sees or ignores the origin and condition of all good, succeeds as he perceives, and fails as he disregards. Success as *Thou* adjudgest, Almighty Father; failure as Thou pitiest, All-merciful Judge. The success of a Christ, in torture on the cross; the failure of a Charles, acclaimed as divine saviour by poor England. To Thee, O Eternal Spirit of Good, incline us in obedience. As the Sun, which Thou hast set to guard and reproduce the life with which Thou hast filled this planet, with its light and warmth ripeneth the fruit of the husbandman, whether he knoweth it or regardeth it not, so we perceive is it with the spiritual warmth of Thy perennial Love and Wisdom, which continueth though man may ignore it, disregard it, or deny it. It continueth for ever. A nation rises and a nation falls. But that nation cannot fall whose spirit of justice has not fallen first. It is that spirit of justice which Thou hast caused to be re-awakened in this Nation, O Divine and Omnipotent God, and we lay our hearts open before Thee, and in this solemn moment of national re-birth resolve that Truth, Simplicity, and Justice shall be our guide."

. . . . .

The stillness was scarcely broken as the representatives resumed their seats, Carlyle Democritus still standing at the bar. Then the first minister rose: "Not at the bar of the House, General, but here; you, who are higher than the first; it is the unanimous desire of the House, your place is here." And the Members rose again as one man. But Carlyle Democritus remained at the bar, thanked them for their courtesy, but he would not be the first to break their rules, which he had helped to re-establish. Had he not broken enough in the former House?

"I implore you, be seated, colleagues; friends, I had not hoped so much from public sympathy and gratitude as to see here to-day all those elected by a free people who have for ten weary years worked with me to make them free. Let those who are new to the great task which lies before them, lose not the beautiful significance of that tribute of a free nation, whose judgment has not been trammelled by orators. Do not ever aim at oratory, my brothers; train yourselves in wisdom, work, and to gain knowledge. Leave for ever your Demosthenes, your Ciceros, and their horrible Jubilee imitators. We have torn the wretched models from the schools, stopped the vain debate-societies, and substituted technical-, work-, and thought-societies, in order that earnest men can be trained, instead of mere tongue men. . . . To those who have worked with me need I say aught? We have been a small company of men, given more to action than to speech; will not our ten years' labour bear that out?

"To those who are new to me and to the task of government, I would say: O my countrymen, regard the trust of your constituencies as the dearest treasure under heaven. Be not eager to justify their choice, only be determined never to sully it. Be not anxious that they shall hear that you have spoken. Be only anxious that they shall not hear that you have spoken foolishly or selfishly. Look not to your constituents for praise, only to your consciences for approval. Our laws protect you for three years from addressing your constituents. The framers of that wise law have hoped that after that time the debased appetite for mere talk, bred by insensate men in Jubilee times, will have died. Whilst anxious to preserve good laws, be not dismayed at new growths and new desires. Pin no faith to the silly example of Lycurgus, lauded in the schools. He who makes a law, or constitution (which is but a great aggregation of laws), not tolerant of change, does like one who would plant a goodly tree and tether it with inflexible chains instead of a reasonable guiding stake. Such a tree, in time, could only grow distorted, earthward, its free inclination upward, heavenward, prevented. Who has seen finality in the work of man? Finality is the attribute of the work of Divinity, and not of man. Durability, not finality, is the best of man's power in all directions. Be sure that a State need not die; it is not a man, but an infinitude of men; but be sure that a State cannot live unless Justice be the atmosphere of its life, for so has God made the world. As you free Justice, so will she free your people, and as you cloak and disguise her, or hide her from the people, so will the people be enslaved. Watch the growth and expansion of your nation, not hurrying and not hasting it, also not retarding it; but protecting it bravely; silently encouraging it; ever ready to widen and extend your laws. Hasten no change, but also retard no healthy growth. . . . You, who have been so patient with me, and who desire that I say yet a little upon the order of things which our Revolution has established, hear me then. After your own consciences is the Court of Honour of your Parliament; true, its laws are stern, but your Assembly is the guiding-light of the nation, a lamp that must not be fouled, not even by rumour's breath; let the laws of the Court for ever remain inflexible, and its justice immaculate. Dwell upon the true words of your pastor: 'The passing opinion of the world must not be your measure of failure or success.' Duty done for duty's sake, let that be the only measure. Be not like the Jubilee ministers who scoffed at justice and let the people starve because one of their most contemptible of 'Parties' was not satisfied with the Radical sweetening of the Party-Cerberus-sop.

"Do not think we have tried to abolish poverty; we *have* abolished pauperism. Poverty—the calm antithesis of wealth—is not an evil but a good. But the degradation of the poor? *That* for ever contend against: For every free man let there be work; for every enslaved man (the idle man is the only slave) let there be compulsory or penal work.

"Do not listen to the scoffer who shall endeavour to persuade you that all this is a counsel of perfection; it is not that; perfection is for God, the path which leads to it is for man, a path endless, but sublime; a path over which justice and wisdom forever guide; there are few gold deposits along its borders, but there is no lack of wealth. The wealth of a contented and happy people, a wealth that increases the more with every honest endeavour that is made to protect it. Be unmindful of mere riches. Come not here, you who are anxious to fill your pockets with gold. But come here all you who are anxious to fill your souls with God. . . .

"The land! That is God's wealth, which He has entrusted to you to watch over and preserve; O look to it that never again in this noble empire the greedy be let absorb it. To-day is my last with you; I go to see with my eyes the trees and the flowers of this England, the innocent children brighter than the corn-flowers, the workmen sturdier than the oak, and the women pure and confiding, like the sweet climbing plants uniting the earth, and the flowers, and the trees. Like them, let your religion be, for that is the true binding—not, as the old Jubilee priests pretended, of futile dogmas, lies, and cant, which is the *un*binding, the *ir*religion. The care of religion which concerns a nation is the heart and core of the thing—this dear land has selected the purest of all the world's teachings; maintain that purity, and it can never die; it is the 'worship of sorrow,' the adoration of the highest, its example—renunciation of self, *of all*, in the cause of Love, Charity, and Mercy. Religion is not to be bound, religion is to bind you, me, us all, to our Divine Creator. Permit no 'Articles,' but that undying One and Eternal Article: the beautiful Book record. . . .

"When you come to ponder upon all these things, you will perceive that it is not so much new laws that will become necessary, as ever new, brave, and untiring application of them. Therefore let your minds be more intent upon wise, just, and fearless administration than mere feverish desire for never-ending legislation. . . .

"With regard to the Second Chamber, do not think that we have left the appointment of its future members unduly in the hands of the Upper House. That would be to overlook the fact that the original appointment of all those who are not elected by the great independent bodies of the State (the Judges, the Literati, the Guilds) is entirely the work of this house, namely, the governors of Colonies, the ambassadors, and the heads of the Army and the Navy. But even in that, as in all the laws of the Revolution, there is no Lycurgunism; if there be weakness anywhere, that is but proof that their authors have been human; to amend as well as to preserve have you been called into power, a power which it is for you to exert with all the wisdom and sincerity that you can command. . . . It was an evil of the old guilds that they degenerated and bred monopoly. Again I bid you remember that to establish justice in the land have you been placed here, and to guard against corruption. We have laid down the Guild laws in no narrow spirit, and even though there be many spots in the sun, the wise astronomers fear not that the light will be extinguished. We have not legislated for to-day only, but for all time. Will you not emulate us in that, and remember that posterity is in your loins; your children are the seeds of the great future; for them prepare the soil, that soil whereon your fathers sleep, and your sons will work. It is for you to be the husbandmen of the laws, and if you see the weeds growing, to bravely clear them from the field. . . . Think of what has been and what will be, see what now is—and ignore only, each one man, himself. . . . Beware, when you shall see the germ of 'party' uprearing again its serpent head. It is the first sign of discontent, of incipient agitation; touch not the party, but eradicate the evil which gives rise to it. Be like wise captains, and treat such manifestations as surf-signs on the waves of time, bodeful of hidden rocks, or bars beneath. Decry not the agitator; that is the province of the coward or the fool—but bravely face the cause of agitation, and remedy it. It is only the fool who believes that the agitator breeds discontent. When they can persuade you that the forest agitates the storm, and not the storm the forest, then shall you believe that man agitates injustice, instead of by injustice being agitated.

"Be not dismayed before words. 'State interference' will always be the cry of rogues who fear disturbance of their villainy. Fear only State *indifference*. Be the guardians of your people, and not their oppressors; and, before all things, say the thing you mean, fearlessly, bravely. Speak not to the people that you trust them, but give them good cause to love and trust *you*. The words which have guided you, my colleagues, through ten years of toil, let continue to be the guide of this free Assembly. So may it be that when each man yields up his power into the hands of those who have trusted him, he shall be able to say as man to man, as man before the Eternal Maker of man: 'To the best of my sincerity and strength I have worked, intent only upon the public good, unmindful of self-interest—FOR GOD AND FOR THE PEOPLE.'"

CHAPTER III.

EUTHANASIA.

"I made no haste in my work; my house was framed and ready for raising."—THOREAU.

"I am neither author nor fautor of any sect. I will have no man addict himself to me, but if I have anything right, defend it as TRUTH's, not mine. It profits not me to have any man fence or fight for me, to nourish, or take my side. Stand for TRUTH, and 'tis enough."—BEN JONSON.

"The frailty of a man, the equanimity of a god."

CARLYLE DEMOCRITUS entered upon his last journey. He went not into the large towns and cities to wonder at the noble buildings of brick or stone. Whatever their grandeur, he knew they could never even distantly approach the awful magnificence of the vast mysterious palaces and temples of Assyria, Babylon, Tyre, or Egypt. He had stood in the King's chamber of Ghizeh, a soul in a labyrinth of stone, pyramidic toy of the Pharaohs twenty hundred years before Christ, and he said: "Even the purpose of your buildings is unknown, poor vanished kings; to-day they are but playthings for men's wonderment. THY purpose, O Sufferer on the Cross—there upon the Golgotha-waste? Do men ask THY purpose, after two thousand years? Hast Thou not designed the palace which is growing in my soul, O Divine Teacher of renunciation, the palace of spirit and not of matter, the alone imperishable?"

Between Tyre and Palmyra he had come upon the ghostly ruins of Phœnician Heliopolis, "a wonder of the world" to John of Antioch. Will Europe equal its marble doors, its Titan pillars, gigantic yet fairy-like in beauty — "frozen music"? or the Karnack Palace of Thebes, which great Homer declared to be unrivalled? And, beneath the forests of a thousand years, he had stood amidst the ruined temples of Yucatan, Mexico, and Peru also sublime in their awful grandeur, in their more awful warning to mankind. " Build not thy greatness upon stone, O son of man, not upon accumulation of any matter. I, TIME, will wash away thy landmarks as the sea the rock. I am a spirit, and as such have power over matter. But, O son of man, build up thy palaces upon Justice, and thou buildest upon the everlasting corner-stone of God's creation, which not all Time can destroy, for JUSTICE is of Heaven, and shall outlast all time."

Then, away from the sublime, he had seen the hollow skull-apery of the black Haytian, King Christophe, with his many palaces—palace of "Glory," of "Conquest," of "Victory," of "King's Beautiful View," and "Sans Souci"—that last a strange black mockery of the white "Sans Souci." Thirty thousand black workmen were killed by "accident," over-work, or under-feeding during its construction; and from the majestic height of the palace-citadel the black "Sans Souci" King hurled thousands of his subjects into chaos and death, until finally—with modern pistol and gunpowder—he hurled his beast-brains into endless night.

It is told of the highest of all palaces—Babel Tower—that there was much weeping and gnashing of teeth if a stone fell from the battlements, but when a worker fell no man cared. "Like Jubilee Babylon State," said Carlyle Democritus, as he stood upon the fabled spot where that old "Heaven-defying" fabric is said to have been erected.

He looked not, then, to piles of brick and mortar, or stone or marble, to discover the veins of his nation's wealth and greatness, but down into the humblest homes of the masses. Those would tell him of the healthfulness of the Nation's blood and life. And down into the sunny fields and the peasants' cottages he went, to see the merry children and the contented women, the free, toiling men, and their godly homes. And he remembered what had been before, and what the great Master had permitted him to teach to His people and to achieve. Silent and alone, unknown to them, he continued his journey through the land, the glorious promise of peace rising daily in him as he saw that his task was done.

His last visit was to the field of Purbeck.* There the pilgrim arrived late one summer evening. Some little children, who had

---

* Page 232.

been playing in the field, told how they had seen him at the shrine which marked the historic site there; and had seen him, later, enter the memorial church, whither one of them—induced, he could not tell why—followed him. It was a little golden-haired lad, whom they found, after anxious search, asleep, like an angel of peace, on the tomb of Terence Grey, warmly wrapped in the cloak which Carlyle Democritus had worn. The vault of the tomb was open. . . . They asked the child what had happened? who had wrapped him on that strange couch? He told them that after he had entered the church the strange man saw him, and beckoned to him, and he went up to him and kissed him, . . . and soon he heard beautiful music—but could remember nothing more. . . . And no one to this day knows more than that of the end of the Great Commander of the Revolution of the Twentieth Century.

PENDENTE LITE.

" When God was about to create man, the angels gathered around him, and some of them said, 'Wilt Thou create a being, O God, to bring glory to Thee on earth as we attest it in heaven?'

"And others of the angel host said, 'O King, create no more, lest the glorious harmony which Thou hast established be destroyed.'

"And silence fell upon the host, and the Angel of Mercy spoke, and sweet was the voice which said entreatingly, 'O Father, create Thou man after Thine own image. With heavenly pity will I fill his heart, and with sympathy towards every living thing.'

"'O create him not, All Merciful,' spake sorrowfully the Angel of Peace, 'lest he sow dissension upon the fair earth which Thou hast made.'

"'Then I will be there,' said the Angel of Justice, 'and before the Divine Footstool shall man answer for his works.'

"And the Angel of Truth spoke and said, 'Create him not, O God, lest with man Thou sendest falsehood to the earth.'

"Then all were silent, and out of the deep stillness came the Divine command, 'I will create man, and thou, O Truth, shalt go to earth with him, and yet remain an angel of the Eternal Host— the connecting-link between heaven and earth.'"

INDEX.

'Acts." *See* Parliament.
Adulteration. *See* Law.
Advertisements, 185, 208, 313, 402, 403, 409, 410, 411.
Afghanistan, 293, 300, 312, 323, 349.
Africa (*see* also Colonies), 109, 154, 292, 293, 328 (*note*).
Age, old age, etc., 201, 205, 258, 322, 340, 343, 344, 384-85, 419, 431, 438.
Agitation, Agitators, 101, 314, 450.
Agriculture. *See* Land.
Alien Immigration. *See* I.
America. *See* United States.
Amherst, Earl of, 309.
Anarchists, Anarchy, 329, 330, 344, 388, 389.
Apprentices, Apprenticeship, 193, 200-201, 227, 262-63, 274, 279-80, 351.
Arbitration. *See* Courts of Justice.
Arbitrators, 209, 249, 383-84.
Archbishops. *See* Church.
Aristocracy, 211, 435, 436-38.
Army, 33, 44, 46, 148, 258, 291, 300, 304-13, 319, 394.
—— Military Lands, 250, 253, 308.
—— of Revolution. *See* R.
Artisans' Dwellings. *See* Labour.
Assessment. *See* Land.
—— to Income Tax. *See* Finance.
Australia (*see* also Colonies), 109, 110, 288, 289, 312.

BAKERIES, horrible condition of, in Jubilee Period, 120-21.
Baker-shops, requisitioned by the Revolution, 53, 62.
Banks, 60, 64.
Banquets, 194, 431, 438.
Barristers. *See* Law.
Battle of Purbeck. *See* P.
Deer, 118, 162, 189, 274.
Beggars, begging, 153, 356.
Bishops. *See* Church.

Black, Colonel Andrew, 157.
Blackswhite (Jubilee party-newspaper), 22, 66.
Bloodletting. *See* Medical.
Board of Trade, 215, 264, 267, 271, 280, 283, 342, 344, 377 (*note*).
Board Schools. *See* School Board.
Booth, General, 28, 29, 31, 43.
—— Secundus, 29, 32, 33.
Borrioboolah-Gha, 336.
Bournemouth, 228.
British Museum, 70.
British People, The, 96, 113, 134, 283, 287, 296, 318, 399, 400, 418, 420, 446.
Buildings, Street Improvements, Architecture, etc., 175, 178-79, 183-84.
Burial, 259, 336-37.
—— Boards, 147.
Burmah, 311.

Cabmen, Carmen, etc., 242-43.
Canada (*see* also Colonies), 109, 110, 111, 215, 289, 307, 312.
Candidates. *See* Electorate.
Cant, 17-18, 24, 115, 331, 335, 336, 361, 402, 407, 419.
Capital and Labour, 281-82.
Carlyle, Thomas, 22, 27, 28, 43, 104, 113, 234, 236, 320, 336.
Carlyle Democritus, member of Parliament, 30; Colonel in the Army, 33; world-wanderings, 30, 451-52; resigns his Marquisate, and consecrates his inheritance to the public service, 30-31; visits Slumland, 33, 42, 80; his trials and sufferings, there and elsewhere, 80, 239, 277, 350; his vow, 277; his connection with the Salvation Army, 29, 31, 32, 44; becomes its General-in-Chief, 33, 43; his advent a necessity of the time, 314; he introduces new organisation and discipline, 33,

34, 44, 43, 81, 95-96; visits the shelters, 35; his personal appearance, 42, 43, 80-81; meets Terence Grey, 36; his influence over his followers, 34, 35, 42, 44, 81; Fourteenth of February, 35, 49-50; re-enters Parliament, 67; has interview with the King, 69-76; —— with his Revolutionary Councils, 156-60, 165-71; notable utterances:—to those in despair, 34; his prayer, 35, 400; address to his troops, 50; to the Royal Guards, 52; *to* the Jubilee Parliament, 67; *of* the Jubilee Parliament, 366; to the evicted, 104; on the State's duty to labour, 183, 234-35, 261; on the duty of labour to the State, 192; upon the victory of Purbeck, 233; on poverty, 236; on children, 247, 261; on Jubilee law, 253, 376; on mistresses, 407; on justice being better than charity, 272-73; his disregard of praise, 278, 296; on a great orator, 427; to the reformed electorate, 426-29; grief at the death of Terence Grey, 233; at the bar of the reformed Parliament, 444, 445, 446-50; his vow redeemed, 451-52; casts his mantle, 453.

Caucus, 421.
Caveat emptor, 208, 263, 266.
Cecil Richard. *See* Peerage.
Chambers of Commerce, 215, 267, 283, 377, 383, 385, 414.
Charities, 73, 235, 263, 272, 304, 349, 385, 418, 420.
Cheap and——, 340, 341 (*note*).
Cheatem, Sir Hardy, 119-23.
Children, God's trust to mankind, 391, 392.
—— Sufferings of, and cruelty to Jubilee children, 10, 85, 152, 185, 255, 259, 270, 323, 331, 340, 341, 342, 343, 344, 345, 346-50, 388, 392, 393, 395, 396, 401, 418.
—— The care and protection of the Revolution, 246-47, 255, 273, 278, 385, 442, 449, 452.
Church, The, 24, 59, 86, 89, 91, 97, 100, 105-6, 177, 226, 236, 247, 258, 323-37, 347, 348 (*note*), 394, 412.

Civil Service, 147, 148, 200, 258, 259, 432.
Civilisation, 125, 180, 357.
Clergy. *See* Church.
Coal. *See* Mines.
Coaling Stations, 146, 148, 220, 291, 292, 321.
Codex of the Revolution, 400, 401, 405, 407, 413, 414.
Coke, Littleton & Company, unlimited, 249, 346, 387, 401, 414.
Colonies, The, 106, 110, 149, 154, 224, 283, 287-89, 290-91, 292, 298, 312, 336, 432, 436, 437.
Commander-in-Chief of the British Army, The, 258-59, 307.
"Commissions." *See* Royal Commission.
Companies, Limited Liability, in Jubilee period, 253, 263, 264-65, 266, 291, 367, 368, 369-73.
—— "Acts," 367, 369, 372, 376.
—— Twenty-five millions sterling annually "lost," strayed, or stolen, 367, 369, 402, 434-35.
—— After the Revolution, 264, 265, 402, 423.
Competition, 204-7, 220-21, 274.
Conciliation Courts. *See* Courts.
Constitution. *See* Parliament.
Co-operation, 193, 274, 281, 282.
Copts, higher education of the, etc., 324.
Councils, 156, 166, 208, 283, 296, 321, 414.
Courts of Justice (Arbitration, Honour, Guild, Commerce, etc.), 201, 209, 210, 249, 275, 311, 339, 354, 383, 384, 385, 402, 405, 407, 413, 420, 421, 436, 448.
—— all costs borne by the State, 209, 354, 383.
—— Procedure, 210, 248-49, 384, 385, 387, 401, 413, 414.
—— Qualification, appointment of Judges, Justices, Arbitrators, 383, 385, 386.
Cradley iron-workers, 343.
Crime, Criminals (*see* also Companies, Limited), 96, 240, 251, 252, 387-88, 389, 404 417, 419.
—— Small thieves punished and big thieves let go scot free, 264, 369-73.
Crimps. *See* Navy.

INDEX. 457

Cruisers. *See* Navy.
Customs (Excise), 150, 208, 280, 292.
Cyprus (*see* also Colonies), 291, 321.

"DAILY GUIDE to the Gin-Shop."
  See Newspapers.
Dangerous trades, 203-204, 205, 207, 225-26, 260-62.
Davidxhume, the Right Hon., M.P., 58, 89, 302.
Democracy, 416.
Democritus of Abdera, 29, 236.
Dickson, Sergeant, 58, 59.
Dinner-parties, ancient and modern, 12, 18, 194, 431, 438.
Directors. *See* Companies.
"Disestablishment," Radical Universal panacea, 207, 326, 327, 328, 329, 330, 339, 344 (*note*), 349.
Divorce. *See* Marriage.
Dog-bite, 400.
Drink Traffic, 106, 109, 189, 376, 383, 391, 393.
Drunkenness, 85, 189, 190, 251, 343, 387, 391, 393, 394, 395, 399, 404, 411.
Dudley slavery, 343.
Dynamitards. *See* Anarchists.

EDUCATION, 73, 296-97, 298, 337, 354, 359-65.
Egypt, 17, 55, 216, 291, 302-303, 324.
Eight hours' day. *See* Labour.
Electorate, Elections, etc., 30, 71, 97, 106, 284, 417-26.
Electric Lighting, 146, 196, 222.
Emigration, 106, 109, 110, 154-55, 188, 291-92.
Employees. *See* Labour.
Employers, 201, 233.
England, 111. *See further*, Great Britain.
English language. *See* "Plain English."
"Enquiry," "will enquire," Jubilee Government lie-phrase, 306.
Entail. *See* Land.
Established Church. *See* C.
"Everywhere," Jubilee Utopia, 83-87.
Evictions, 98-99, 100-103, 112, 115, 117, 329, 352, 419.
"Exceptional," "Not exceptional." *See* Jubilee cant-phrases.
Excise. *See* Customs.
Expenditure. *See* Finance.
Exports. *See* Trade.

FACTORIES, State, 312.
Fetish. *See* Jubilee Free Trade.
Finance—
  Expenditure, 145-50.
  Guild, 266.
  Income-tax, 122, 293, 299.
  National debt, 133, 134, 147, 150.
  —— extinguished by the Revolution, 133, 146, 148, 150.
  National Reserve, 136, 150.
  Revenue, 132-44, 147.
  Revolutionary Funds, 45, 60, 62, 64, 105, 109.
  Sequestrations, 89, 91-92.
  Sinking Funds, 145, 146, 150.
  Stock and Loans, 145, 146 (Foreign), 265.
  Taxes and Taxation, 119, 123, 132, 133, 139, 140, 141, 144, 147, 148, 150, 414.
Fishing industry. *See* Merchant Navy.
Fleet. *See* Navy.
Flowers in public thoroughfares, 184, 441, 442.
Foreign loans. *See* Finance.
Foreigners, 152-53, 201, 204, 205 (*note*), 238, 241, 270, 276, 278-79, 282, 314, 354, 388 (*note*).
France, 215-16, 293-94, 315-16, 317, 339.
Franchise. *See* Electorate.
Free-trade, 153, 181, 204, 205, 206, 207, 208, 212, 213-18, 292.
Freedom, 101, 207.
Froude, 10, 323, 350, 359, 365.

GAS, Gas Companies, 146, 196, 221-23, 387.
German bands. *See* Nuisances.
Germany, 154, 216, 218, 361.
Gibraltar (*see also* Colonies), 291, 315, 321.
Gin-hells. *See* Public-houses.
Gladstone, the Right Hon. W. E. M.P., 428.
Glenbeigh, Joan of, 100-101.
Gornal iron slaves, 343.
Graduated taxation. *See* Finance.
Grafton, Duke of. 309-10.
Great Britain, 22, 98, 110, 111, 313-14, 316-17, 320, 330, 332, 400, 409, 431.
"Great Commander," H.M.S., 55.

Great thieves, etc. *See* T.
Great Wild Street slum, 84, 393.
Grey, Terence, artist, philanthropist, and sinner, 12, 36; his expeditions into Slumland, 37; meets Delilah Callida, 37-38; his success at the Royal Academy, 38; Delilah's law-scissors, 38-39; he raises 10,000 followers, 39; at the battle of Purbeck, 231; is slain, 232; memorial of him at Purbeck, 232-33, 260, 453.
Guilds, 127, 193-94, 224, 238, 333, 351, 409, 449, 200.

HARCOURT, Sir Wm. V., 394-95.
Hawks and Jubilee Lawyers, 309.
History, 12, 17, 18, 19, 364-65.
Holidays, 245, 266, 280.
Holland, Canon Scott, 178, 325-27.
Home Rule, 329, 344.
Homer, 377, 427.
Homes of the People, 104, 105, 130, 149, 166, 178-79, 181-84, 194, 263, 275, 357, 444, 452.
Homestead Law. *See* Land.
Hospitals, 263, 380.
House-property. *See* Land.
Houses, Statistics of, etc., 64, 182, 183, 197.
Housing of the Working Classes. *See* Homes.
"Hundreds" Electoral. *See* Electorate.
Huxley, Professor, 31.

IDLE, Idleness, 162, 167, 180, 243, 250-51, 354, 356.
Immigration. *See* Pauper.
Imports. *See* Trade.
Income Tax. *See* Finance.
India, 213, 293-302, 311, 312, 315, 432.
Insurance, National, 149-50, 164, 192, 195-97, 200, 202, 203, 254-59, 263, 275, 278, 299, 310, 401.
—— of Children in Jubilee Time, 185, 395-98.
Ireland, 41, 100-103, 111, 125, 163, 183, 240-41, 272, 292, 345.

JERRY-BUILDERS, 175, 184, 238.
Jewelry (*see also* Requisition), 64, 71-72, 75.
Joan of Glenbeigh, 100, 101.
Jonson, Ben, 427, 451.

Jubilee Year 1887, 22, 28, 307.
—— French, 23.
Judges, 209, 249, 258, 346, 376, 381-82, 383-84, 386-87, 401, 414.
Justice, 101-102, 181, 189, 209, 239, 253, 267-68, 279, 368, 387, 401, 447-48, 452.

KASHGARIA, 301.
Keepers. *See* Street Keepers.
Khokand, 300.
King (The), and Carlyle Democritus, 69-76.
Kilkeel, 272.
Knightsbridge Barracks, 49, 442.

LABOUR, 117, 125, 212, 234.
    Army, Regimental System, etc., 126, 162, 166, 169-70, 194-95, 212, 245, 257, 275.
    Casual, abolished, 106, 191, 237.
    Compulsory on all, 125, 162, 250-51.
    Contract, permanency of, 179, 191, 192, 194, 243, 244, 273, 278.
    Dwellings. *See* Homes of the People.
    —— in Jubilee Period. *See* Slums.
    Increased demand for, after the Revolution, 65, 197-200, 241, 242, 243, 281.
    in Government Factories, etc., 165, 219, 221, 224, 225, 241.
    Jubilee, baneful conditions of, 115, 236, 237-38, 342-44.
    Laws, 192-96, 203-204, 380.
    Unions, 149, 201, 249-50, 247, 274, 281, 353-54, 385.
    Wages, 152, 239, 245, 278, 279, 282, 313, 344.
    Work Hours, 106, 169-70, 192, 196, 245, 251.
Land (The), 99, 108-123, 124-31, 146, 149, 211, 298.
—— absorbed by a few in Jubilee Era, 12, 97, 115-16, 281, 289.

INDEX. 459

Land, The, agglomeration forbidden, 128, 129.
—— Agricultural, or Settlements, 106, 126, 162, 163, 250-53.
—— —— Factories, 126-27.
—— —— Guilds, 127.
—— —— labourers in Jubilee period, 240.
—— —— labourers and others resettle on the land, 163, 221, 224, 240-41, 409, 443.
—— Agriculturalists, State help to, 127, 129, 409.
—— Appropriated by private persons in Jubilee period, 97, 115, 133, 281.
—— Assessment, 117, 127, 146, 181-82, 211, 239-40.
—— Cereal, destroyed by Jubilee Landlords, 98-99, 111-12.
—— Cultivable area in Great Britain, 113, 240.
—— Cultivated area, 113.
—— Cultivation after the Revolution, 127-28, 131.
—— Entail abolished, 104.
—— Fixity of tenure, 297.
—— God's wealth entrusted to Nations, 448, 450.
—— Holdings, Conditions of, etc., 104, 115, 126, 129, 130, 131, 241, 275.
—— —— for Factory workers, 261.
—— Homestead Laws, 106, 128, 296.
—— House Property, 118, 130, 131.
—— Landlordism, Landlords of the Jubilee era, their exactions, etc., 83, 97, 98-100, 104, 111, 113-23, 128, 152, 211, 228, 229, 232, 239-40, 281, 293, 294-95, 297-98, 329, 393.
—— Landlordism Killed, 104, 108, 237, 240, 290.
—— -Mortgage forbidden, 128.
—— Ownership and Occupation indispensable, 116, 117, 128, 130, 131, 184.
—— Peasant Proprietors, 108, 128, 130, 163, 250.
—— Penal Settlements, 149, 155, 162, 180, 243, 250-52, 404.
—— Produce-rents, 117, 128.
—— Reclamation of Waste, 106-49, 150, 161, 162, 163, 167-68.

Land, Rent, Rates, and Taxes on, in Jubilee Period, 103 (note), 104, 119-23.
—— Rent, Rates, and Taxes on, after the Revolution, 117, 128, 413.
—— Revenue, 136, 137, 143, 144.
—— Rome, Analogy of, and Jubilee Britain, 11.
—— Sequestrations by British Kings, 98-100, 104, 108, 116, 118.
—— Sequestrations by the Revolution, 145, 176.
—— State, The, sole landlord, 109, 118, 119, 298.
—— State help, 127, 129, 298.
—— Sub-division forbidden, 128 (ibid., note), 129, 163.
—— thrown out of cultivation in Jubilee Period, 98, 237, 281.
Law, 366-416.
 Adulteration, 208, 209, 409.
 Barristers, 312, 380, 381-82 (note), 383.
 —— abolished, 241, 401.
 Costs in Jubilee Period, 30, 229, 366, 382, and note.
 —— abolished by the Revolution, 209.
 Criminal Law, 252.
 Fines, 209, 405.
 Jubilee Law, 26, 98, 99, 100, 101, 345 (note), 346, 369, 389-90, 395, 396, 397-98, 400.
 —— defined by Carlyle Democritus, 253, 269.
 —— Futility of, 209, 269, 271, 309, 369.
 —— Verbiage, 387, 400.
 —— "Leading Cases," 376, 377, 378, 379, 389, 390, 391.
 Libel, 30, 380, 403.
 Litigiousness, how discouraged, 209, 210, 404.
 Nuisance, 185, 197, 413.
 Plaintiff and Defendant, 209, 248, 387, 401.
 Reforms, Provision for, 129, 414, 447.
Lawyers of the Jubilee Era, 117, 269, 297, 309, 312, 367, 383, 405.
—— abolished by the Revolution, 210, 241, 382, 387.

Lambeth, 176.
Leather Manufacture, 312.
Liberty of the Subject, 166, 238, 251, 354.
—— to work, 251.
—— and Licence not to be confounded, 162, 190.
Lichfield, Bishop of, 323-24.
Lies, lying, subterfuges, circumlocution—Jubilee fine arts, 23, 103, 276, 304, 305, 306, 314, 318, 327, 367, 416, 417, 418, 427.
Life, Human, a Sacred Trust to Righteous Governments, 260-61.
Literary Associations and Guilds, 385.
Literature, English, at British Seminaries, 361.
Living Wage. *See* Labour Wages.
Luther, 79, 109, 334, 335, 379.
Loafers. *See* Idleness.
Local Taxation. *See* Finance.
London, Bishop of, 324.
Lords, House of, 265, 434.
Lycurgus, 447, 449.

MACDONALD, Father, 102-103.
"Made in Germany," 239.
Magistrates, 210, 248-49, 252, 253, 315, 384, 386-87, 389-90, 393.
Malta (*see also* Colonies), 291.
Mammon, Mammonites, Mammonism, 153, 212, 220, 229, 231, 236, 270, 342, 397, 419, 420, 429, 413.
Manufacturers. *See* Trade, *also* Employers.
Markets, Free, 274.
Marriage, Laws, etc., 162, 170, 201, 351, 401, 405-407.
Martins, Daniel, 2, 3, 5, 6, 7, 9, 12, 14.
Masters and Men, 281-82.
Medical: Aid in Labour Dwellings, 263, 357.
—— Ancient Practice of Blood-letting, 134-35.
Mediterranean, 315.
Merry England in Jubilee Period, 98.
Merry England after the Revolution, 409.
Mines, 130, 195, 212, 215, 218, 219-25, 282, 291.
Ministers. *See* Parliament.

Missions and Missionaries. *See* Church.
Mob, The, 23, 66.
Model Work-shops and Factories, 193, 273-74.
Money, Jubilee-god, 19, 26, 211.
Money-lenders, 89, 129, 297.
Monuments, 336-37, 443.
Morocco, 291.
Mortgages on Land forbidden, 128.
Mundella, The Right Honourable A. J., M.P., etc., 369.
Municipal Councils, 149, 150, 192, 195-98, 411, 426.
Murder. *See* Insurance of Jubilee Children.
Museums, 411
Music Halls, 190.

NATIONAL DEBT. *See* Finance.
Navy, Merchant, and Fishing Fleets, etc., 146, 148, 149, 152, 216, 218, 267-84, 314, 315, 319, 320, 321.
—— Royal, 54, 55, 146, 147, 148, 160, 165, 220, 230, 253, 258-59, 313-22.
New Fleeceland Loan Company, 369-73.
New Zealand. *See also* Colonies, 288.
Newspapers of the Jubilee Era—
 Blackswhite, 22, 66.
 Church Bazaar and Exchange Gazette, 327.
 Daily Guide to the Gin-Shop, 66.
 Whitesblack, 22, 66.
Nuisances. *See* Law.

OLD AGE. *See* Insurance.
"Opposition." *See* Party.
Orators. *See* Verbosity.

PALACES AND THE REVOLUTION, 64, 147, 176-77.
Pamirs, 300.
Pan-Anglican Union, 283, 287-303.
Parks and Gardens, 185, 192, 196, 199, 246, 247, 248, 411-12.
Parliament, Parliamentary Government, etc., 18, 23, 26, 30, 42, 45, 66, 68, 100, 106, 115, 116, 193, 208, 265, 303, 307, 315, 344, 349, 389, 394, 398, 427, 430-31, 432.

INDEX. 461

Parliament, Acts of, mediæval twaddle, incentives to litigation :— 268-69, 367, 369, 372, 373, 374, 380, 383, 401, 417, 432.
—— Acts of, Drafting after the Revolution, 117, 422.
—— Constitution, in Jubilee period, 376, 394, 417, 425.
—— Constitution after the Revolution, 419, 420, 422, 425, 426, 436, 448.
—— Houses of, 429, 443, 446.
—— Ministers of the Jubilee Period, 44, 45, 97, 162, 222, 276, 279, 282, 304, 305, 309, 344, 346-47, 368, 369, 380, 389, 390.
' Party," "Parties," 10, 12, 18, 23, 26, 27, 42, 45, 66-68, 79, 86-87, 89, 134, 162, 206, 208, 265, 276, 288, 296, 298, 299, 301, 304, 305, 313, 315, 316, 317, 318-19, 324, 329, 344, 347, 368, 369, 389, 394, 400, 418, 419, 429, 430, 448, 450.
Pauper Immigration, 106, 151, 152-53, 155, 240, 241, 276.
Pauperism, Paupers. *See* Poverty.
Peasant Proprietors. *See* Land.
Peers, Peerage, etc., of the Jubilee Period, 60, 73, 89, 98, 100, 106, 114, 133, 227.
—— R. Cecil's, 97.
—— W. Paget's, 97.
—— The Sutherland, 98-99.
—— Pensions, 106, 309.
—— Money-Peerages, Party-, and Beer-titles abolished by the Revolution, 210, 211, 337, 434, 435.
Penal Settlements. *See* Land.
Pendjeh, 300.
Pensions in Jubilee Era, 59, 106, 309, 310, 346, 398.
People, The. *See* British.
Perim. *See also* Colonies, 291.
Persia, 301.
Petersborough, Bishop of, 331.
Piccadilly, 339, 342, 346, 350, 352, 353.
Plain English, 117, 269, 273, 387, 414, 450.
Police, 47, 66, 79, 268.
Poor Law, 150.
Post Offices, extension after the Revolution, 142.
—— Electoral Department, 424.
—— Judicial Division, 413.

Port Yarrock, The, Wreck of, 269-70, 272.
Portugal, 217.
Poverty, Pauperism, Jubilee Misery, etc., 19, 26, 27, 28, 34, 101, 151, 152, 161, 236, 237, 239, 255, 324, 325, 339, 342, 343, 353, 355-56, 398, 399, 418, 448.
Prisons, 251, 252.
Professional Associations or Guilds, 385.
Profit-sharing, 243-44, 274.
Prosecutors, Public, Board of, 208, 403.
Public-Houses, Publicans (*see also* Drink Traffic), 53, 54, 118, 129, 189, 246, 308, 325, 326, 348, 367, 376, 411.
Punch, 317.
Purbeck, ancient Quarry District, 227-30, 260, 452-53.
—— Battle of, 231-32, 233.

QUACKS, Quackery, 203, 208, 238, 262, 263, 264, 402, 409-10.
Quarries, 225-33.

RADICALISM, 66, 95-96, 114, 116, 292, 296, 298, 302, 316, 327, 328, 369, 448.
Ragged Schools, 348.
Railways, 150, 209, 223, 242, 247, 407-409.
Recreation, 129, 170, 246, 274, 411.
Reclamation of Waste Lands. *See* Land.
Referendum, 106, 129, 426.
Regimental System applied to Labour. *See* Labour Army.
Religion, Religiousness, 11, 12, 17, 28, 35, 327, 330, 337, 446, 449.
Rent. *See* Land.
Requisition, The Great, 62-65, 71, 151-55, 164.
Reserve Fund. *See* Finance.
Retirement from Public Service. *See* Age.
Revolution, 18, 19, 231, 233, 281, 290.
Richmond, Duke of, 309, 310, 398.
Rights of Man, 418.
Road-cleaning, etc., 198.
Rome, 10-12, 112-13.
Royal Commissions, 152-53, 271-72, 345, 366, 396-97.

Royal Household, 73-74, 147, 149.
Ruskin, 94.
Russell, Sir George, Baronet, M.P., etc., 370.
Russia, 154, 216-17, 293, 294, 299-302, 312, 315, 316, 317, 360.

SAILORS. *See* Navy.
Saint Albans, Duke of, 309.
Saint-Hilaire, Barthélemy, 293.
Saint Paul's. *See* Church.
Saltaire, 215.
Schiller, 407.
School Board, 346, 359.
—— Inspector's Report, 347-49.
Schools. *See* Education.
Scotland, 40, 111, 114, 183, 241, 281, 352.
Sedgley, 343.
Senilities in High Places, 226, 258.
Shops, Shop-assistants, etc., 235-243.
Shropshire, 100.
Shuttlecock, The Right Hon., M.P., Secretary to the Admiralty, 316.
Sinecures, 26, 73, 90, 147, 167.
Skobeleff, 299-300.
Slavery, Slaves, 11, 99, 152, 160, 238, 343, 344, 353, 356.
Slumland, Slums, 11, 12, 24, 80, 85-87, 104, 152, 161, 176, 186, 325, 339, 342, 343, 347, 348 (*note*), 441, 442, 443.
Slum-prisons, 83, 90, 124, 184, 186-87, 236, 325, 349, 442, 443.
Smoke-abatement, 221-22, 442.
Society Papers, 403.
Society for the Protection of Children, 391, 393, 395, 396.
Socotra (*see also* Colonies), 291.
Sorrypebble, The Right Hon., M.P., 23, 45, 96, 114, 152, 153, 181, 203, 230, 302, 325, 410, 416, 417, 418.
Spain, 217.
Spirits (*see also* Drink), 150, 189.
Stafford, Sir E. W., G.C.M.G., etc., 369-70.
Staffordshire, 100.

Starvation, 18, 19, 26, 27, 34, 72, 99, 102, 109, 110, 112, 115, 188, 318.
Statistics and Statisticians, 27, 109, 110, 115, 188, 318.
State Service, 192.
Stocks. *See* Finance, Loans, etc.
Strathglass, 227.
Street improvements, 97, 184-85, 196, 197, 198, 199.
Street-keepers, 149, 165, 185, 196-98, 242, 257, 424.
Submerged, The, 160-61, 277.
Suez Canal, 315.
Suffrage. *See* Electorate.
Sunday Observance, 274, 411, 412.
Sutherland County, 98.
—— Dukes, etc., of, 98-99, 227.
Sutton, Charles Manners, Archbishop, 105.
Swanage, 228.
"Sweating," 152, 315, 343.
Swedenborg, 445.

TALK, Talkers. *See* Verbosity.
Talmudic Fable of Truth, 453.
Taxation, Taxes. *See* Land-rent, Rates, etc., and Finance.
Teachers. *See* Education.
Technical Training. *See* Labour and Education.
Temple, Sir R., 348.
Tennyson, 103, 317, 319, 338, 353, 419, 427.
Tent Harley, 157.
Thieves, Thieving, etc., 115, 116, 367-69, 402.
Thoreau, 451.
Tiflis, 300.
*Times on "Acts" of Parliament, 374; African Conquest, 328.
Anarchy, 389; Arran, 101-103; Church Reform, 323, 331.
Company Frauds, 373; Drink Traffic, 391, 394.
Emigration, 110-11, 188; False Sentimentality, 181.

---

* The Historian of the Revolution of the Twentieth Century has almost invariably drawn his references to occurrences of the Jubilee Period (1880-1894) from the magnificent emporium of this justly world-famous journal, and his Editor has adopted a similar course, not only because *The Times* is incontestibly the highest authority upon current events, but because it reflects the best and highest thought in all the avenues of public and private life of those times—and also the errors and prejudices which abounded there—perhaps "*si non crasset, fecerat ille minus.*"

Times on Huxley, Professor, 31 ; Irish Evictions, 100. "Living Wage," 188 ; Loth Tenancies, 99. Millionaire quoted, 123 ; Ministerial Corruption, 305-306. Ministerial Lying, 305, 318 ; Navy, 230, 318. Peers and Pensions, 309 ; Purbeck, 227-30. Starvation of Little Children, 348-49. Trade Returns, 214 ; Variorum, 382, 389, 393. Women and Children Employment, 342-44.
Titles, 210, 211, 248, 385.
Toilers of the Deep, 267-84.
"Tools and the Man," 234-53.
Toryism. *See also* Radicalism, 305, 306, 369.
Town-holdings. *See* Land.
Trade, 193, 204-207, 208, 211, 212-18, 223-24, 240, 260, 280, 312, 318, 377.
Trade Councils. *See* Courts of Justice.
—— Unions. *See* Labour.
Trafalgar Square, 45, 49.
Trees in Public Thoroughfares, 184.
Trieditt, David, farmer, 126, 158.
Trinities : Ecclesiastical. *See* Church.
Jubilee Government, 366.
Law, 383.
Pagan, 361.
Truslove, Pastor, 157-60, 277.
Truth and the Jubilee Period, 276, 326-27.
Tucker, A. R., Bishop of Kiushiu, 324.
Tugwell, H., Bishop of Equatorial Africa, 324.
Turkestan, 301.

"UNFORTUNATES." *See* Women.

Uniforms, 268, 273, 313.
Unions. *See* Labour.
United States of America, 71, 73, 214, 216, 217-18, 292-93, 435, 436.
Utopia, 83-87, 354.

VAMBERY, 299.
Verbosity of the Jubilee Era, 22, 241, 268-69, 276, 297, 298, 312, 416, 417, 423, 431, 432, 433, 447.
Victoria, Australia (*see also* Colonies), 289.
Volunteers, 310-11.
Votes (being the Jubilee Government Votive or Motive Power), 276, 344, 346, 349, 396, 418.

WAGES. *See* Labour.
Wales, 111, 214.
War Office, 432-33.
Waste Hands are Wedded to Waste Lands, 165-71.
Water Companies, 146.
Waxworks, 403.
West Indies, 215.
Westminster, 281, 429.
Weymouth, 228.
Wigs, Wiggeries, etc., 211, 226.
Wilkinson, John Garth, 416.
Winans, Jubilee Landowner, 281.
Winterstown, 443.
Women, 50, 75-76, 85, 98-99, 100, 103, 104, 152, 153, 162, 169, 190, 204, 256, 260, 261, 263, 273, 278, 338-58, 363-64, 381, 382, 388, 392, 393, 404-405, 417, 419.
Word-deluge. *See* Verbosity.
Work, 162, 237, 356.
Work for the Weakest and the Worst, 156-60.
Workhouses, 60, 113, 164, 310.
Workhours. *See* Labour.

York, Archbishop of, 324.

Zola, Zolaism, 381-82.

Crown 8vo, cloth. Price One Shilling net.

LANDLORDISM

AN ILLUSTRATION OF THE RISE AND SPREAD OF SLUMLAND AS EVINCED ON THE GREAT ESTATES OF THE GREAT GROUND LANDLORDS OF LONDON.

By HENRY LAZARUS.

The Daily Chronicle says:—" Mr Lazarus lays on the lash and spares not. . . . He distinguishes sharply between real and merely apparent improvements. . . . He speaks with the authority of one who deals with things at first hand. . . . He maintains that 'the origin of the degradation is neglect by the landlord to provide for even the barest necessities of decency.' He makes suggestions for reform, and quotes examples of successful attempts to introduce a more wholesome order of things. The pamphlet deserves attention."

The Citizen says:—" *The book calls attention to what is admittedly one of the great questions of the age;* the object of the writer is to prove that the great ground landlords are utterly callous to the wants and requirements of the miserable tenants of the slums whence they (the landlords) draw an exorbitant revenue. The author says:—'The English are verily a long-suffering people, but I foresee an end to this patience, this heavy paying of premiums upon the vilest system of dishonesty—vilest, because not prompted by starvation, misery, or want, which urge the wretched pauper into crime, but deliberately and systematically planned to swell an already lordly revenue, not for noble or for worthy purposes, but too often only to minister to worthless and soulless extravagancies. Toil on, good people, and let your hard-earned wage be filched from you to give, and ever to give, to him that hath and who deserveth not even that which he hath.'"

RATS'-RENTS, THE RENTERS AND THE RENTED.

[In which GINGER JIMMY gives his views of Lazarus, Dives, Dirt, Mother Church, Slum Freeholders, and " Freedom of Contract."]

"THE Golgotha of Slumland!" That's a phrase as I am told
Is made use of by a party,—wich that party must be bold,—
In the name of Mister LAZARUS, a good Saint Pancrage gent,
Wot has writ a book on Slumland, and its Landlords, and its Rent.
He's a Member of the "Westry 'Ealth Committee," so it seems,
And the story wot he tells will sound, *to some*, like 'orrid dreams.
But, lor bless yer! *we* knows better, and if sech 'cute coves as 'im
Want to ferret hout the *facks*, they might apply to GINGER JIM.—*Punch,* Feb. 1892.

The Journal of Sanitary Engineering says:—" The devil that broods in diabolical glee over the pestering horrors of the lower classes in our towns and cities is the slum landlord. In London among the chief of his helpers are Bishops, Cabinet Ministers, noble Lords, etc. What are we to think of the reverend and noble owners of such districts? These people draw hundreds of thousands a year out of the rents of London hovels and fever dens, and seem to care nought for those who dwell in the slums they own, and who drag out sin-blasted and diseased lives in horrible courts and alleys. Mr Henry Lazarus has issued an admirable brochure on the matter."

[" Do the poor make the slums, or the slums make the poor?"—*Henry Lazarus, in "Landlordism."*]

Is it the poor wot makes the Slums, or the Slums wot makes the poor?
Well, that's the question, Guv'nor, and I've 'eard it arsked afore,
And the arnser ain't so easy, if you wants to be O.K.
Don't suppose as *I* can settle it, but I'll have my little say.
My old friend Mister LAZARUS, now, he ups and sez, sez he,
The great Ground Landlord is the great *prime* cause.—*Punch,* Nov. 1892.

The Weekly Times and Echo says:—" GET AND READ THAT ADMIRABLE LITTLE SHILLING BROCHURE BY MR HENRY LAZARUS . . . Go with Mr Lazarus into the slums which still defy the Sanitary Inspector, visit with him some of the estates of that pious youth, the Marquis of Camden, who, far away from the foul breeding-places of his wealth, enjoys himself with it at Brecknock Priory or Bayham Abbey; go and see what sort of accommodation this English peer, and the Lady Somerset, the great Church lords, and other great landowners, provide for their poor tenants. Go to any of the endless list of slums with Mr Lazarus: the whole origin of the horrible degradation is to be directly traced to the neglect of the landlords to provide even the barest necessities of cleanliness and decency. IF SOME SUCH REMEDY AS MR LAZARUS INDICATES IS NOT DONE SOON, WHO WILL WONDER, IF, DRIVEN TO DESPERATION, THE SLUM DWELLERS SOME DAY TRY THE LAST WEAPON OF DESPAIR? We look round day by day on the wretched rows of hovels in which the noblest race of workers on God's earth are compelled to herd, and wonder sometimes if another great Fire of London would not be an unmixed blessing."

The Newcastle Chronicle says:—" THIS IS A POWERFUL PAMPHLET, in which ground-landlordism is indicted as the creator of slums. The facts about Slumland are horrible."

The Metropolitan says:—" Landlordism is the title of a book which has been written by Mr Henry Lazarus. Most of our readers are familiar with his name. The book depicts the rise and spread of the slums on land which is owned by some of the greatest ground landlords of London. . . . THE PAMPHLET IS ONE WHICH DESERVES TO BE READ BY EVERY PUBLIC MAN IN LONDON."

www.ingramcontent.com/pod-product-compliance
Lightning Source LLC
Chambersburg PA
CBHW051235300426
44114CB00011B/752